AF600686

RIGHTEOUS ANGER IN CONTEMPORARY ITALIAN LITERARY AND CINEMATIC NARRATIVES

RIGHTEOUS ANGER in Contemporary Italian Literary and Cinematic Narratives

Stefania Lucamante

UNIVERSITY OF TORONTO PRESS
Toronto Buffalo London

Toronto Buffalo London
utorontopress.com

ISBN 978-1-4875-0688-9 (cloth)
ISBN 978-1-4875-3509-4 (EPUB)
ISBN 978-1-4875-3508-7 (PDF)

Toronto Italian Studies

Library and Archives Canada Cataloguing in Publication

Title: Righteous anger in contemporary Italian literary and cinematic narratives / Stefania Lucamante.
Names: Lucamante, Stefania, author.
Series: Toronto Italian studies.
Description: Series statement: Toronto Italian studies | Includes bibliographical references and index.
Identifiers: Canadiana (print) 20190240768 | Canadiana (ebook) 20190240776 | ISBN 9781487506889 (cloth) | ISBN 9781487535094 (EPUB) | ISBN 9781487535087 (PDF)
Subjects: LCSH: Italian fiction – 21st century – History and criticism. | LCSH: Motion pictures – Italy – History – 21st century. | LCSH: Anger in literature.
Classification: LCC PQ4090.L83 2020 | DDC 853/.9209353–dc23

This book has been published with the assistance of The Catholic University of America.

University of Toronto Press acknowledges the financial assistance to its publishing program of the Canada Council for the Arts and the Ontario Arts Council, an agency of the Government of Ontario.

Canada Council for the Arts
Conseil des Arts du Canada

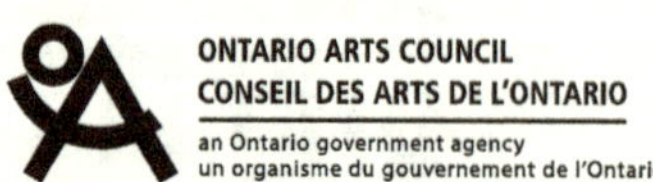

Funded by the Government of Canada
Financé par le gouvernement du Canada
Canada

Contents

Acknowledgments

I would like to thank the Catholic University of America for the generous support that it granted toward the publication of *Righteous Anger.* My deepest gratitude goes also to the members of the Department of Italian Studies at the University of Toronto for my Emilio Goggio Visiting Professorship in 2014–15, when this project on the constructive side of anger first took shape and form in a course devoted to this topic. Earlier versions of "The Making and Unmaking of the Eternal City: A History of Violence on an Everyday, Perfect Day" appeared in *Annali d'Italianistica* 28 (2010): 373–405 and "Road Movies and Gas Stations: Monica Stambrini's *Benzina* as Creation of Alternative Spaces" in *Quaderni d'Italianistica* xxiv.2 (2008): 111–34.

I am very grateful to Mark Thompson, acquisitions editor at the University of Toronto Press, and Christine Robertson, managing editor at the University of Toronto Press, for their excellent work and advice during the production of the book. My copyeditor, Margaret Allen, has my gratitude for her precise and kind comments and for bringing clarity to parts of the manuscript that could have remained opaque otherwise. My gratitude goes also to the anonymous readers who provided perceptive comments and useful suggestions on the first draft of my manuscript. To my friends, who have read earlier drafts of some parts of this book, my warmest thanks.

Finally, I thank Laurana publisher for kindly allowing the publication of excerpts from Veronica Tomassini's *Sangue di cane.* Excerpts from Simona Vinci's *Stanza 411* are here published by arrangement with Agenzia Santachiara © 2006 and © 2018 Giulio Einaudi publisher s.p.a., Turin. All Italian excerpts of Tiziano Scarpa's works have been reprinted by permission of the author. *Il cipiglio del gufo* © 2018 Giulio Einaudi publisher s.p.a., Turin, is published by arrangement with The Italian Literary Agency. Excerpts from Melania Mazzucco's *Un giorno perfetto* are published by arrangement with Rosaria Carpinelli Consulenze editoriali © Melania Mazzucco and © 2017 Giulio Einaudi publisher s.p.a. Turin.

On behalf of Ed Ruscha, Gagosian gallery and the Hood Museum of Art, Dartmouth granted the University of Toronto Press their permission to reproduce the image of his work, *Standard Station, Amarillo, Texas,* (1963).

I dedicate this book to Anne Lloyd Lang, my precious and dearest mother-in-law, whose righteous anger furthered the cause of American feminism in the seventies.

Abbreviations

BE	*Benzina*
BF	*Batticuore fuorilegge*
BG	*Il brevetto del geco*
CA	*Le conseguenze dell'amore*
CF	*Le cose fondamentali*
CQF	*Cos'è questo fracasso*
GP	*Un giorno perfetto*
GS	*Groppi d'amore nella scuraglia*
KO	*Kamikaze d'Occidente*
OG	*Occhi sulla graticola*
S411	*Stanza 411*
SC	*Sangue di cane*

RIGHTEOUS ANGER IN CONTEMPORARY ITALIAN LITERARY AND CINEMATIC NARRATIVES

Introduction

The wise man will never cease to be angry once he begins.

– Seneca

To create is to resist. To resist is to create.

– Stéphane Hessel

Reason is, and ought only to be the slave of the passions.

– David Hume

Righteous Anger in Contemporary Italian Literary and Cinematic Narratives examines the role of the passions as functional in the composition of aesthetic acts and the ways in which constructive indignation shapes the authorial intentions of contemporary Italian artists. Considered to be one of the so-called social passions, indignation is a catalyst for authorial intentions and can shape an artist's individual response to events through an aesthetic act of reflection on events that have wronged those who compose the very fabric of his or her community. Righteous anger, if understood not merely as the result of restitutive demand but as the culmination of indignation towards injustice, produces reflective impressions from which stem the will to denounce things and the manner in which we live. Reflective impressions, in turn, engender emotions that demand action. The artist's act produces narratives whose structure and composition provide useful insight into how things are, by presenting unique knowledge of the world. Art itself does not necessarily remedy anything, as Theodor W. Adorno famously noted, but it can protest against the ills of reality. As Jacques Rancière states, "literature itself was constituted as a kind of symptomatology of society, and it set this symptomatology in contrast with the clamour and imagination of the public stage."[1] Symptomatology can be understood, then, in terms of a sense of awareness of and commitment to denounce inequity, inequality, and injustice, strengthening its ethical function as a viable tool of sociopolitical protest. Fighting the idea that political and social events leave us powerless, artists wield their anger as a weapon of resistance against negative and oppressive forces, thereby validating the axiom that ethics and aesthetics can still collaborate in the creation of meaning, even if the years marked by a conventional notion of *impegno* (commitment) are behind us. Anger is a constructive propellant for the investigation of our constantly negotiable relationship with politics, society, and a fluctuating system of ethics. In contemporary society, space for intellectuals has become increasingly limited, but there always exists the possibility, as Stéphane Hessel writes, "to resist the monopoly of the media owned by the powerful"[2] by using the tools of perception and the formal devices of verbal and visual language to express such resistance.

This book presents case studies of works in which realism affirms its ever-changing mode in shaping narratives. As reality is constantly in flux, the realist mode acts accordingly and devises fictional narratives of reality in such flux. Committed artists constantly tease out new strategies for conceiving images that shape an ethical vision of the community in which they live. While many works influenced by the legacy of postmodernism seem to divorce the formal aesthetic from the ideologically engaged idea of making art in order to narrate the world, the works analysed here unite the elements of ethics and aesthetics into a single act. The responsibility of acting politically is delegated to the responsibility of performing a culturally correct, and true, language act that generates a form of entrustment. Language regulates the boundaries between the visible and the audible in a given aesthetic-political setting through what Jacques Rancière calls "the distribution of the sensible,"[3] the forms of inclusion and exclusion that are capable of being apprehended by the senses. The fictional narratives studied here propose a symptomatology of society through aesthetic commentaries about specific events and interweave the threads of society, art, and the individual to promote what Rancière conceives as the core of aesthetics as *inclusive* of ethical responsibility. The impact of emotions in such acts, while apparent, has not been systematized until recently. My observation of the ethical impact of emotions on literary and cinematic narratives draws on the work of Jacques Rancière as an apt theoretical support for the analysis of indignation in the works presented here. My own framework connects David Hume's study of social passions with Rancière's aesthetics, and takes into consideration Sianne Ngai's[4] and Sara Ahmed's theories of ugly feelings and affects[5] as an inestimable asset (or as capital, in Marx's sense of the word) in the study of how emotions mould literary and cinematic narratives and their reception.

As Aleksondra Hultquist notes in her "New Directions in History of Emotion and Affect Theory in Eighteenth-Century Studies,"[6] the history of emotion and affect theory has recently offered two different perspectives on a renewed attention to feelings, or the "emotional turn" of the study of the humanities. Whereas today by "history of emotion" we tend to understand its wide impact on cultural and political practices, by "affect theory" we refer to the positioning of affects that lie in the spaces in-between that are triggered by the text. Affect and emotion were actually "hiding in plain sight,"[7] Hultquist relates, but were not quite systematized in their epistemological concern, whose goal tends often to collapse the two perspectives.[8] Hultquist draws attention however to the mutability of practices of emotion, as they can "differ in time, space, and place."[9] "Emotion words" differ as well. Her consideration stresses how "the passions" – discussed by both René Descartes and David Hume – constitute the catalyst for, and a component of, the artistic act. My book grounds the impact of feelings in twenty-first-century Italian works that disclose thought-provoking discourses and practices in hopes of generating new directions in literary criticism and finding a place for Italian cinematic and literary narratives within the international current debate on the theory of emotion and affect.

Righteous indignation needs to be presented in order to prove its own validity as a feeling that can be intimately connected to action. Just as Hultquist writes that in the eighteenth century "feeling was *not separate* from action, movement, cognition, or rationality ... and none were understood to be distinct from rationality or reason,"[10] my research considers also the possibility that aesthetic actions may not necessarily produce pro-social behaviour in readers and spectators because not all members of a community share the same feelings with respect to a given event. The point is that passions are never equally distributed in society: we cannot be indignant unless we are involved in an issue we feel compelled to engage with. The actors of such commitment are often our artists, individuals for whom the aesthetic act represents always a tool for social protest that in our time does not specifically reside in the realm of politics but involves it in civic and ethical actions. Emotional regimes, as theorized by Barbara H. Rosenwein, do not present an "overarching nature"[11] in any period, but social expectations can shape feelings both in the production of a text and also in its reception. In short, Hultquist's recognition of emotion and affect theory endorses the "affective turn"[12] and the "affective economies"[13] for a study of the humanities as a healthy repository of feelings, each endowed with a specific aesthetic value.

Vehement feelings like indignation motivate humans to respond to certain states of mind that otherwise would remain isolated emotional reactions with no discernible outcome. If guided by what the Scottish philosopher David Hume calls "a good passion," such as reason, vehement passions often compel us to respond to what we consider unjust acts. While anger as rage is linked to both negative and positive behavioural consequences, positive responses express moral indignation from which equity concerns can arise. Such a reaction promotes counter-narratives to the current ones enforced by media and political agents, as Stéphane Hessel argues, in hopes of prompting a moral response in readers and spectators alike. *Righteous Anger* reflects on how some Italian artists who have been the focus of my scholarship for quite some time – specifically Tiziano Scarpa, Melania Mazzucco, Simona Vinci, Paolo Sorrentino, Monica Stambrini, and Veronica Tomassini – understand their presence in the world and develop an aesthetic form shaped by a progressive disillusionment with the moral system that, in turn, advances the need for new narratives regarding their epoch as the political vulnerability of denizens. The notion of *impegno* (commitment) should be considered equally as a variable and an ever-present possibility in aesthetic pursuits from which emotions are never far removed. Conventionally intended as the ethical stance supported by a specific political and ideological belief in an artist's work, *impegno* also indicates the artist's desire to generate a reaction in readers and spectators that does not necessarily align with a specific political creed but still participates in the aesthetic act. But this commitment remains persuasive, constructing narratives of reality that it is hoped will promote pro-social behaviour in line with the artist's moral stance. Constructive indignation that manifests itself in aesthetic works, rather than reflecting a mere desire for retribution or showcasing outrage or hostility, illustrates the artist's desire to implement an interpersonal and positive strategy that can promote the readers' and spectators' ethical response.[14]

Literary and cinematic narratives offer a wide array of readings on how environmental provocations affect an emotional and moral response. In *Upheavals of Thought*, Martha Nussbaum uses Marcel Proust's descriptions of the Baron's mind in *Remembrance of Things Past* as a starting point for her investigation into the role of emotions whose importance has been overlooked by moral philosophy and how its cognitive structure (derived also by cultural sources) shapes narratives: "To talk well about [emotions] we will need to turn to texts that contain a narrative dimension."[15] Proust's narrative (he calls emotions "geological upheavals of thought")[16] is an appropriate site for Nussbaum's enquiry, as it is through the essayistic parts of his novel that we discover how emotions – a system of beliefs themselves – determine the characters' judgments and their evaluative dimensions together with the narrator's, who himself firmly defines his own ethical space alongside that of the author, demonstrating how emotions are bodily feelings that project, as William James understood, an outward-directed sense of reality. Conversion experiences bring to the fore the interconnection between feelings of reality and another distinct kind of emotion – transformational emotion. Without emotions, we could not see reality the way we do,[17] as emotions depend on and are generated by our own set of expectations with regard to the world around us. Emotions are also determined by a set code of values that society establishes for its individuals, and that the individual confronts guided by his or her own values. In order to look at the way we live now, we must use all of our emotions as well as our judgment for some truths to be revealed. The literary form, in the shape of Proust's masterpiece, has much to offer in this regard, because it subjects us to a "painful self-examination "[18] that is more subjective than "conventional philosophical texts."[19] "Emotions," Nussbaum relates, "are not just the fuel that powers the psychological mechanism of a reasoning creature, they are parts, highly complex and messy parts, of this creature reasoning itself."[20]

The leading concern of *Righteous Anger* reflects on the passion of constructive indignation and how the artist uses it in the textual and visual composition of works that deal with our own vulnerability in the face of social injustice. One wonders what kind of response the artist expects to elicit from imagined and actual readers. There are two answers. The short answer is that the sense of life embodied by aesthetic works might support the sharing of ideas in a constructive communal (emotive) structure that compels us to design and implement actions in opposition to what we consider wrong. The long answer suggests that literary imagination produces real works that investigate expressions of societal roles, living conditions, identity, and subjectivity to which readers and spectators can relate. The empirical author is embedded in a society that constantly compels him or her to conceive projects that will function/serve as aesthetic commentaries (or counter-narratives) about reality. Our moral position as readers/spectators derives from our ability to respond to such counter-narratives and depends on whether we belong to what Rosenwein calls the author's emotional communities. This can be illustrated through a straightforward simile: we have a primary text – society – that requires secondary sources by intellectuals to expose societal unrest and distress through the power of ethically charged refigurations of reality. Imagination constructs possible readings of society and allows for an artist's response to locate a suitable space in which subjective takes and collective issues cooperate in the discovery of alternative (counter) ways of thinking about such reality, while placing that reality under scrutiny. A moral and compassionate stance shapes imagination that expresses what artists deem indispensable to their aesthetic object, ultimately positing alternative readings of injustice and social issues. While Nussbaum's statement concerning literary form as the only place where "certain truths about the human being can be told" might be an arguable point, what is not arguable is that literary and cinematic narratives by committed artists labour to extract new meaning and new readings of the human being.

The notion of indignation brings with it also that of empathy, a more other-directed emotion than sympathy for others.[21] Empathy involves the notion of compassion that not only indicates our feeling sorry for others (sympathy) but also means that others' suffering moves us to action. Compassion is the moral companion of indignation, and its etymon indicates the ability to share with others their pain, and not merely sympathize with them. Compassion, as Nussbaum states, is indeed an emotion that "has often been relied on to hook our imaginations to the good of others and to make them the object of our intense care."[22] An active reader or spectator can hardly remain impassive before injustice, as emotions are culturally bound and establish our own sense of belonging to a given community. Emotions promote our collaborative responsiveness in reading narratives about our imperfect control over reality and raise awareness of pernicious issues that affect the artist's community. Righteous indignation, no longer just an emotion but rather a complex construct of which emotions are a part, connects the individual to the community, since by definition, indignation, as Descartes describes, cannot be directed at oneself.[23] If this is true, one can reasonably assert that much of the content of and reaction to aesthetic works stems from how emotions work as a complex system of beliefs shaped by the expressive force of their narratives. *The Way We Live Now*,[24] the title of Anthony Trollope's 1875 novel about the scandalous world of industrialists that marked British society of the period, epitomizes the question raised in the act of receiving aesthetic works. What is *the way we live now*? The poetics of anger and disillusionment, ever present in the arts, is intensified in twenty-first-century works. Indignation prompts a reaction to current events through narrative commentaries on a wide variety of symptoms of social malaise and political disavowal. The artist's aesthetic project interprets and narrates reality in ways that a constructive and "not unvirtuous"[25] anger prompts and defines.

Artists shape their endeavours by rationalizing and questioning the moral chaos around them. As the community of which we are members often determines the relationship between corporeal actions and their reactions, the artist's act connects subjective passions to the community and highlights the necessity of intersubjectivity. As sensory activity lies at the core of aesthetic intervention, we must examine the effect of anger on authorial intentions, how it even determines the construction of plots or the use of the fragment for their narratives. My overall argument stresses how indignation is a passion that propels strategies to awaken readers' reactions, as the authorial intentions underlying them clearly use emotions to structure knowledge of the world. Working against the idea that political and social events render us powerless, *Righteous Anger* examines works published or released approximately around 2001, a year marked by the attack on New York's Twin Towers as a historic event defining the epoch in which we live. The selected narratives show the salience of vehement passions in fuelling the thoughtful development of resistance to such events and tie the artist's individual indignant response to the individual's sense of belonging to his/her community. Narratives work within the very boundaries of their genres, literature and cinema in the case of my study, but their scope expresses a desired freedom to alter – at least fictionally – the world we live in.

The Moral Stance of Anger

Considered a negative indirect passion, anger, or *rabbia* in Italian, has however always prompted civic and aesthetic commitment. In Italian there exists a term, *angheria,* that appears deceptively close to "anger." However, its meaning suggests a substantial difference with regard to who is the object of such furious passion. *Angheria* is understood as an unjust or unfair action that we feel we have personally been subjected to by another individual or external cause. Basically a tort, it entails an offensive or negative use of verbal force, a lack of etiquette, and a vexation at someone else's damage. Anger, which is distinct from rage, distinguishes itself by its inherent possibility to do good to others *because* of the offence received by the individual. The Devoto-Oli *Dictionary* defines *rabbia* as a feeling that is "violent, often irate and generally not justifiable on a rational and human level."[26] Rage derives from the Latin *rabies* and includes the notion of loss of physical and mental control and, like vindictive passion, demands retribution. The present study does not consider this state of anger, since, if understood in this way, it does not necessarily come equipped with a full control of emotions. Rage is ire; it is the Furies; it is an unleashing of emotions untempered by reflection, while *rabbia* can be a positive anger characterized by righteous indignation.[27] This type of anger is prompted by an instinctive aversion to an action we have witnessed or experienced. As holding beliefs is intrinsic to human nature, such beliefs cannot be extinguished by the simple understanding that we do not like what we see. When we are not forced into a position of passiveness by external forces, our reflections and our beliefs spur us to action – to protest against injustice and to create vivid images that incorporate our anger while prompting others to act. Emotions imply moral judgment that is dynamic rather than static. This judgment compels us to incite our community to loftier things, moving us to administer an intellectual remedy for a social ill and expose, through literature, the scandal of our everyday alienated existence – one that, if mended, could hold deeper meaning and even become a *good life.* Indeed, "the passions," Roger Giner-Sorolla relates, "give important input to our moral judgment, providing fuel and direction for moral action. Morality is rooted in concern about living with other people, in relationships, but also in larger groups."[28]

Anger and indignation abound. Aware of our rights, we constantly apprehend major injustice festering in a society that has lost its internal compass. The more we attempt to resist injustice and the more we see the social contract lose its effectiveness, the more we feel powerless. The reflective emotion that leads us to condemn violent acts arises from anger. Anger against social injustice stirs indignation in ways that Nussbaum condemns, unless they can be employed at certain specific moments to further political action:

> Anger is not only not necessary for the pursuit of justice, but also a large impediment to the generosity and empathy that help to construct a future of justice. Anger might still have limited utility in the three instrumental ways ... (as signal, as motivation, and as deterrent), but it is crucial that the leader of a revolutionary movement, and many of the followers, be strange sorts of people, part Stoic and part creatures of love.[29]

While Nussbaum hopes for a proper management of anger, the weakening of theory ironically mirrors our personal sense of vulnerability and impotence in the face of evidence that our body is marked by historical conjuncture and that we are seemingly powerless to act. As Pankaj Mishra states, when resentment takes over without the generosity and empathy Nussbaum calls for (forgiveness proper), a kind of "pervasive panic" ensues.[30] This sentiment induces people to feel that "anything can happen anywhere to anybody at any time."[31] For Mishra, "the sense of a world spinning out of control is aggravated by the reality of climate change, which makes the planet itself seem under siege from ourselves."[32] The existential resentment Mishra reflects on can have the power to poison society if not controlled by a constructive exercise of indignation generated by compassion for others. As such, the interrogation of alterity demonstrates that the relationship between politics and culture – however weakened – is always alive and never of a conclusive nature. The object of what we perceive as unjust acts is connected to the relationship between the artist and a society that is increasingly driven by many negative elements. Daily, we face external forces such as the economic warfare which has supplanted that of nation-states, the rise of terrorism, a general sense that in the age of globalization we lack distinct and positive outlooks for our community, the tendency to dismiss culture as a fundamental asset to combat resentment and anger, open and reinforced misogyny, the growing complexities of affective relationships, and the denial of gender perturbation. Artists constantly scrutinize the way we live amid such evident unrest.

The Italian community defies any *imagined* one, calling for new community narratives in this age of anger. The understanding of the possibility of aesthetically representing this passion demands dealing empathically with the problems that everyone faces. Contemporary narratives of righteous indignation deal with the variation and innovation of themes that are eternal and yet constantly presented with new images. As Werner Sollors puts it, "thematics may be interesting to the scholar concerned with constants as well as to the reader interested in variations."[33] One might infer that the constants and the variations of a theme do not represent an alternative but are synonymic; they both refer to a possibility to investigate the emotional and historical conditions that "make its [the theme's] use plausible."[34] While not always investigated in a frontal manner, passions construct the intentions, become thematic in many works, and often suggest narrative techniques – even the naming of a character, as Suzanne Keen states[35] – for analysing subjectivity as well as the community at large. Thematic criticism offers an opportunity to examine diachronically how themes are used and to assess the contingencies that have determined changes in thematic treatment and the construction of narrative.

In the case of anger, then, one wonders if Achilles's feeling, the one that prompted Homer's narrative of the Trojan war, was indeed anger, rather than ire – or *ira,* as the Italian translation reads.[36] Achilles was no fool. He was a prince whose feelings were shaped by a profound sense of justice and love for his people, and his anger was of a collective kind and entailed the good of many other people aside from his own. The gods were asked to narrate his anger as a collective account borne by an individual's feelings. Though prompted by feelings that tied him to his community, Achilles's ire was nevertheless *deadly,* allowing the possibility of myth construction. What we learn from his ire is that anger is endowed with collective properties. One cannot be angry solely at oneself, for lack of the external object from which anger arises. Anger nests almost invariably in a kind of zeal and a sacred idea of what justice should be. Anger at oneself, what Heinz Kohut calls "narcissistic anger,"[37] brings about another feeling, almost a choleric mode, a sense of helplessness in the individual who realizes his/her own impotence in relation to other individuals and society in general. But this choleric mode does not provide a productive form of agency. Also, narcissistic rage should not be confused with mature aggressive behaviour. The first dominates the ego and makes it function as its own instrument, while mature aggressiveness is controlled by the ego.[38] To even exist, indignation requires interaction between the subject and society. In Peter Fisher's words:

> It is in the details of anger that these features of the will can be grasped most easily. Anger has been subjected historically to the most detailed scrutiny because of the acts of violence to which anger leads. Anger is the necessary bridge between a purely *internal account of the passions and an interest in action,* because it is with anger that the aroused state in the soul or spirit has the most immediate links to the physical acts of our fists or our body in the outer world. And it is with anger that we find, not just arguments against the passions, *but explicit social intervention,* through the legal system's response to violence.[39]

For a better understanding of the moral stance of anger, Peter Fisher suggests a reconsideration of "our therapeutic, post-Freudian culture"[40] that leads to the control over such passion and the subsequent need for therapy. For Fisher, anger "lies at the root of an intuitive and manageable sense of daily justice and is not to be confined to such primitive forms of justice designed for major crimes and offences as the revenge or honour systems, which we pride ourselves on having replaced by our idea of a civilized life under an objective system of explicit laws and impersonal justice."[41] Fisher's statements challenge the concept of anger as a "primitive form of justice" with retribution as its consequence, but he also problematizes the impersonality of justice. Passions are never quite that simple to direct and define. As David Hume states,

> A man who, from any motives, has entertained a resolution of performing an action, naturally runs into every other view or motive which may fortify that resolution, and give it authority and influence on the mind. To confirm us in any design, we search for motives drawn from interest, from honour, from duty. What wonder, then, that pity and benevolence, malice

> and anger, being the same desires arising from different principles, should so totally mix together as to be indistinguishable? As to the connection betwixt benevolence and love, anger and hatred, being *original* and primary, it admits of no difficulty. [42]

Fisher expands on his analysis of anger and diminution by setting forth several examples in which our own will remains powerless, such as with the death of a friend from a simple fever or a storm threatening our boat:

> The irritation to the will arises over the indefinites of the will's boundaries. The passions arise from, marking for our notice and the notice of others, a *militant state of the will,* patrolling its own borders, or what it imagines those borders to be. The intensity of fear and anger, along with the tendency of formal descriptions of the passions to begin with either fear or anger, makes clear *this negotiation of the radius of the will in which the self remains in a state of alert to any injury to the claims that the will makes on the surrounding world.*[43]

What Fisher calls "negotiation" defines that delicate tool by which we measure our need to intervene because of our outrage and make a difference with our word, work, and art at the risk of turning into impossible narcissists. In other words, one can build a claim about the surrounding world without having irrational thoughts, and thus generate a useful reaction that is at once *personal* (even narcissistic) and *collective.* Fisher suggests that a reconsideration of the passion of anger not be read through stereotypical terms and literary allusions. But once we unburden anger from the historical subjections of the most detailed scrutiny, can we entertain the idea that anger is a powerful and useful tool in aesthetics today? This book argues that constructive indignation leads to concrete social intervention that is not tied to a specific domain but is often allocated a narrative space by artistic endeavours. Being indignant signifies being an active member of a society and capable of using the power of words to resist the pressures to remain passive. For some, that's all we have.

The passion of anger wields great power, and the only way to use such power effectively is to analyse its source and act upon it with the energy of images that result in narratives. As Edward Said observes, "real intellectuals are never more themselves than when, moved by metaphysical passion and disinterested principles of justice and truth, they denounce corruption, defend the weak, defy imperfect or oppressive authority."[44] Static mimesis is filtered through wilful appropriation of sensible forms by artists who produce aesthetic works that, although deriving their matter from reality, have a unique and dissonant perspective and "denounce [any type of] corruption" with their counter-narratives. The ethical rage that some Italian artists share when beholding a world that does not function in the way they would like serves as a prompt to constructive anger.[45] There is no longer an apt expression to allude to the general sense of powerlessness. What matters most remains the critical productivity arising from the awareness that something needs to change. Anger is useful. Anger is constructive.

Of Anger and Corporeality

Passions are clearly linked to our senses and bodies. By definition, passions are corporeal in nature. Elizabeth Grosz comments on this interrelation between our body and the world:

> Pleasure and pain are the corporeal registrations of the forces of the world, the visceral impact of forces, what we use to struggle with and against, in order to become more and other. They are the most powerful aids to learning and the most direct and effective stimuli for action, and thus for the expansion of force. Pleasure and pain are not the object or goal of forces but rather their by-products, the epiphenomena that result from the drive to exertion and self-expansion of the will to power.[46]

In fact, for all this rage and anger, for all this corruption and confusion, everyone seeks and demands happiness. Zygmunt Bauman calls the forced pursuit of happiness of today's society the "*coercion to seek happiness*"[47] imposed upon all citizens of the global world. Citizens are

> hard pressed to turn into workers ready to sacrifice the rest of their lives for the sake of competitive enterprise or enterprising competition, into consumers moved by infinitely expandable desires and wants, into citizens embracing fully and unreservedly the "there is no alternative" to the "political correctness" of the day, which prods them, among other things, to be closed and blind to disinterested generosity and indifferent to the common weal in case it can't be deployed to enhance their egos ...[48]

The oppressive lack of a viable alternative to the way economics forces citizens to think and live so as *not* to be prompted towards acts of generosity and *not* to be moved by lofty feelings seems to reinforce the idea of the presumed futility of good deeds in our society. In turn, that "milk of human kindness" Lady Macbeth so despised in her spouse triggers and enhances what Sianne Ngai calls the "ugly feelings" that define negative aesthetics. Emotions are no longer regulated by ideals, and disenchantment plays an undisputed role. The milk has definitely turned sour. Elements constitutive of bourgeois life are routinely scrutinized, from the nobility of a job well done and work, traditionally considered a noble Western ideal and locus for ethics as Primo Levi argues in his *Survival in Auschwitz*, to family and politics, other famous bulwarks of European post-industrialist society.

Through such scrutiny, artists demonstrate dissatisfaction on multiple levels that reveal forms of obsoleteness: the personal, political, and even literary. They tend to *look back in anger* for all the right reasons. A disillusion with the notion of the past, which Guy Debord identified in the society of spectacle, appears to work on a par with the perpetual and verifiable ignorance of our contemporaries as to its cause and effect. Such disillusion shapes the causes of abandonment of such forms of evaluation. Italian contemporary writers and filmmakers are often reluctant to create narratives about events that are not temporally framed by their own existence. Emotions and feelings modify their time's arrow. As Bauman states,

> in the event of a genuine 'upheaval' past evaluations are reversed only because they were voiced in the now disapproved of and deprecated "past." *Virtues are rewritten as vices, achievements as misdeeds, loyalties as treachery* – and vice versa. The devaluation of the valuations and practices of the past must be all the more decisive and uncompromising because the future, just taking off, is wrapped in mist.[49]

If there is little that artists and critics can do to reinvigorate kindness and not turn the Macbethian milk sour, they can improve understanding of how emotions and feelings – however reshaped and revisited as passions – constitute the object and the medium of artistic self-reflection. Art can not only represent the subversive but can also wield lofty feelings to create constructive reflections on reality.

It should not be a surprise that, in this book, an analysis of the weakness and nastiness of affects[50] comes coupled with an analysis of the *rewriting* of the original good affects, namely love and dedication to love. Extrapolating from Bauman's claims, the holistic negative situation also determines the aesthetic outcome of *traditional feelings*. Ugly feelings pollute and pervade those high and noble sentiments that would otherwise propel readers towards a higher and nobler ideal, namely love. The devaluation of such feelings, in turn, promotes the acceleration of generational changes. Indeed, Bauman seems to say that the more quickly each generation is devalued, the more quickly the next change can take place. Fleeting products make a case for lasting aesthetic products that *incarnate* the meaning of writing.

At present, neither writers nor critics can advance aesthetic remedies for any type of unrest, for the intolerance and lack of values from which we all suffer. Social efficacy resides in authors' ability to renew forms and modes that have constructed earlier narratives. In order to be declared "healthy" while simultaneously "interpreting human events,"[51] art cannot mimetically mirror society in its obvious and concrete terms, for it is often through the use of rhetorical figures, syncopated prose, and neologisms that readers come to learn the matter behind – or within – the renewal of the aesthetic figuration of such society. It is important to assess these writers' reflections on their (our) world. We live in Debord's integrated spectacle. In this spectacle, objects as individuals become devoid of their traditional meanings/essences; the spectacle turns them into symptoms of societal malaise. In J.M. Coetzee's novel *Elizabeth Costello,* a renowned writer representing the author's fictional alter ego while busy globetrotting for her lectures, states in one of her public speeches, "There used to be a time, we believe, when we could say who we were. Now we are just performers speaking our parts."[52] Could we agree with the notion that writers "are just *performers* speaking [their] parts"? Performance plays a role in shaping aesthetics; however, as we are all in this spectacle, artists make us realize how our own culture consists of anachronisms, of ridicule that we breathe, and alert us, even in a parodic manner, to think otherwise. Counter-narratives are an ever-present tool to denounce unrest.

This book is divided into three parts. Part 1, "Anger and Commitment in the Narratives of Tiziano Scarpa," examines the work of Venetian writer-performer-critic-poet Tiziano Scarpa. Perhaps one of the most idiosyncratic and compelling contemporary Italian writers, Scarpa deploys a ludic notion of corporeality with such an urge *de la chair* that pierces through the pages of his works. We deal here with matter as materiality of which the artist's body constitutes an essential component. The kamikaze character that Scarpa utilizes to demonstrate his body-to-body struggle with representing his own culture to members of a distant and foreign society is emblematic of his artistic project as a whole. The artist's body is necessary to develop a bond, or a degree of relation as opposed to one of separation, with the members of his own society. In his 2010 novel, *Le cose fondamentali,*[53] Scarpa places his protagonist, Leo, within a narrative in which paternity and authorship trace an ethical approach to existence. Throughout Scarpa's works, however, futurity reveals its importance, as the next generation needs committed fathers who are not wrapped up in their own frustrations. Despite the evident critique, these are positive counter-narratives about the fundamental things it is important to keep in mind when Mario comes to inhabit the world of his father in *Le cose fondamentali.*[54] Adorno's reflections on art as a form of human expression that must sustain itself with the necessary elements to "dissolve the subject-matter and reorganize it in a way which does create a perspective [that] determine[s] the aesthetic content of modern art"[55] are reconfirmed by the artist's gesture of *dissolving* the subject-matter with his passion and recuperating another constructive dimension in which reality can be imagined.

Part 2, "Anger and Spaces of Vulnerability in the Narratives of Melania Mazzucco and Monica Stambrini," examines the moral stance underlying *Un giorno perfetto* (A Perfect Day) and *Benzina* (Gasoline) respectively, as a form of commitment that quickly dismisses labels of escapism or essentialism. Critical analyses of the traditional binary opposition of vulnerability and resistance reveal an ethical sense that pushes these artists to deal with the disavowal of and failure to revisit a social contract. Everyday lives are scrutinized in the face of neoliberal and austerity conditions that define the idea of *precariato* (precarious work), sexual orientation, and age discrimination as stable elements in Italian society. These works see women as a significant component of the disenfranchised population and reject the notion of a stabilizing gender division while rethinking modes of resistance to imposed notions of vulnerability. "Power has long established the disenfranchised as 'vulnerable populations,'" as Judith Butler, Zeynep Gambetti, and Leticia Sabsay state.[56] The disenfranchised characters' lives as designed by Mazzucco and Stambrini reveal striking similarities with everyday women's lives. But it is the form of estrangement within the narrative that highlights how everyday banal lives are replete with the same cruelty and violence that permeate Roman myths just as much as contemporary narratives. Melania Mazzucco and Monica Stambrini expose the neo-patriarchal Italian society, still considered the site of agency, and expose its inability to cope with women's resistance. As anger can be constructive and propose counter-narratives of real events, both narratives reflect how Mazzucco and Stambrini posit the vulnerability of their characters as something to be understood not simply in terms of victimization and passivity, as so frequently happens in the narratives of newspapers and police reports. They challenge us to rethink vulnerability as a viable conduit to the subject's own agency and resistance. The terms must change by which women of every sexual orientation are made vulnerable within or around a city whose forces make of Rome itself an exceedingly vulnerable epicentre for social unrest.

Part 3, "Anger and Love in Spaces of Otherness in the Narratives of Paolo Sorrentino, Simona Vinci, and Veronica Tomassini," examines narratives in which righteous anger deals with the irrationality of feelings caused by love. As the character of writer Matilda Carbury ponders in Trollope's *The Way We Live Now,* "how few women there are who can raise themselves above the quagmires of what we call love, and make themselves anything but playthings for men?"[57] Not only women but also men can either be ruined, as in the famous *Blaue Engel*, or graced forever. Neapolitan director and writer Paolo Sorrentino's *Le conseguenze dell'amore* (*The Consequences of Love*) and *L'amico di famiglia* (*The Family Friend*)[58] depict the fear or attraction individuals feel when falling in love as they come undone because of it. One of the trickier subjects in fiction – both literary and cinematic – is that of the hapless suitor, smitten with love, locked in a lifelong obsession with a woman he cannot have. Yet, for all the perils of that soupy scenario, great works of literature and films have come out of it. Adding to those triumphant chronicles of the lovelorn come Neapolitan director Paolo Sorrentino and his auteur films. Sorrentino probes his own dictum in them: as it is for a writer, a lover's best hope is patience. And nothing comes of it anyway. As familiar as the subject of love might seem, Sorrentino investigates new ways of reading erotic passion. He links the condition of social confinement and entrapment that often comes with unrequited love to modern societal illness, from the Mafia to corrupted contemporary Italy. His stories are all too human, spellbindingly shot in mesmerizing surroundings that resemble De Chirico still lifes where the old issue of ugliness and beauty, of beauty and the beast, finds new settings and circumstances.

The space in which Simona Vinci situates her short novel *Stanza 411*[59] is a testimony to Paolo Sorrentino's idea of Rome as a gigantic simulacrum – a Rome that appears to be "a faded shroud with no God inside" ("Una Sindone. Sbiadita. E dentro non c'è nessun dio").[60] Vinci twists the notion of Rome as a simulacrum of itself and takes it on a tangential trajectory. *Stanza 411* is the narrative of a brief but intense love that partly stems from an autobiographical love affair and partly from Vinci's observation of Italian current reality. Her relationship elicits reflections on love and the way women yield to its power. Vinci acknowledges the power that love has over her protagonist but also the ability of such passion to shape new images for narratives about the exploitation and mistreatment of women that are at least as old as Rome's Pantheon. Her ideas about men and women – about their relationships, whether or not based on monetary considerations, love, sex as merchandise, and the power of logos presiding over love – develop reflections that are in an almost essayistic vein in the second part of this work that appears to play with the notion of auto and non-fiction.

Finally, *Sangue di cane*[61] by Veronica Tomassini propounds an arresting reading of love and anger. Her story represents a vexing love: an all-consuming, all-encompassing, disinterested love set against the background of a provincial and remote town. Romantic in its conceptualization, Tomassini's novel reveals, instead, how the author possesses a unique ability to eliminate all traces of the sentimentality that often encumbers romantic work. It reminds us of how these two passions, in combination, can result in great accomplishments rather than simply testifying to the impressive force of love and anger – a twinning that, despite the burden that the loved one brings to his Sicilian fiancée and then wife with his complex life, renews the daring force of love. *Sangue di cane* elicits many questions regarding the different degrees of ascribed humanity to which citizens and immigrant subjects belong. The dynamics of the diversity and anatomy of love underlie *Sangue di cane* and frame its material and symbolic space. The author, however, proposes the trope of the wronged stranger and the indignation that arises from such a spectacle to communicate her dissatisfaction with the practices established by her community. Indignation paves the way for a re-evaluation of the way we live now. Filtered through the media of mimesis and rhetorical strategies, current social concerns create a dissonant space of meaning in the construction of the novel.

The rationale for selecting the narratives from Sorrentino, Vinci, and Tomassini lies in the fact that each of these stories deals with falling in love, love, and the effects of love by revisiting both traditional themes and modes of narration and inserting into each of them new elements: the Mafia, the abuse of women, new migrants, and failed assimilation. Needless to say, none of them provides a happy ending for its reader. The unusual settings – hotel rooms, Foucault's heterotopias, or a city remote from the rest of the country (as in Tomassini's daunting love story) – all hint at the ghost of feelings. Something we tend to overlook in contemporary society reveals its extreme power and manages to uncover the most recondite caves of human feeling.

Passion affects both the writing and the reading of all these works. Poets' anger is never destructive: it is a necessary tool. Poets' anger refrains from doctrinal and trite erotic images, drawing back from past images of idyllic and selfish love that cannot perhaps represent an option, for the past amounts to an obsolete set of values and manners. Yet passions and emotions constitute an appropriate field for studying the aesthetic implicit in human behaviour in specific situations. As I consider constructive indignation to be a productive way to put emotions to work, upholding cooperative and moral behaviour and suggesting a possible role for equity concerns, I hope this book explains the role indignation plays as an empathetic means to convey and also shape the ethical stance of the artist.

PART ONE

Anger and Commitment in the Narratives of Tiziano Scarpa: *Impegno* in a Liquid Age

Amid the lack of a renewal of politics and ideology and of tangible alternatives to the politics of Silvio Berlusconi, whose vestiges appear stronger than ever with his return to the political stage in the 2018 elections, Italian filmmakers and writers continue to produce works of social denunciation. In the twenty-first century, straightforward and conventional narrative forms have long since been displaced by hybrid narrative forms of denunciation, thus demonstrating the possibility of conveying passions through permeable genres and through media to allow discussion and denounce unrest. As Pier Paolo Pasolini noted, "every work of art, as such, even small, is a work of dispute – as difference of opinion – not of revolution."[1] If nothing else, art instils doubt that systems have proven to be adequate, and aesthetics permits a constant search for ways to modify the spaces and predicaments artists uncover in their respective communities.

In her *After La Dolce Vita,* Alessia Ricciardi speaks of Italy's cultural history and the period preceding the rise of Berlusconismo by focusing on "the key tropes of belonging and self-identification"[2] of Italians: sweetness, lightness, weakness, softness. A fundamental question arises: why have intellectuals allowed Berlusconismo to taint many postmodern narrative innovations and helped unwittingly to produce a pattern of progressive disillusionment in Italian mass culture? Ricciardi explores the compelling theoretical implications of diverse cultural and aesthetic theories promoted by intellectuals in various fields that often result from their relative misunderstanding of the intrinsic threats associated with this Milanese industrialist's rise to power and its long-lasting effects on Italian society, the same effects Zygmunt Bauman denounces in his works on the liquid age. Essentially, Italian intellectuals, though well aware of the advancing threat of culture as a mass-market object, did not devote adequate attention to the Berlusconi phenomenon of appropriation of the media. Italian postmodernism appears to be one of the elements produced by intellectuals of the left, who, seemingly indifferent to Pier Paolo Pasolini's warnings, appear oblivious, for instance, to the significance of the advent of television, which pauperized youth through its proliferation in Italian homes as a parental substitute. During an era in which ambiguous historic political compromises represent the dawn of a dangerous banalization of cultural politics, the Italian leftist politics of culture enacted its own failure.

Rather than speaking of the Berlusconi phenomenon as a progressive disillusionment in Italian culture generated by his ascent to power as Ricciardi does, philosopher Mario Perniola considers his ascent as the result of a process of delegitimization of intellectuals that started in the 1960s throughout the industrialized countries of the West. Berlusconi – for Perniola only *one* of its epiphenomena – represents the "concretization"[3] of the program elaborated by the members of one of the leading groups of the *Sessantotto* movement. The content of this program concerned the "idea that everybody can do politics and politics does not require a specific education or a political party school."[4] Not in the footsteps of Lenin, then, but in the wake of Polish philosopher Jan Wacław Machajski, did this particular group of the *Sessantotto* perceive intellectuals to be, along with capitalism, enemies of the working class. Perniola is fully aware that his contention of locating in Berlusconi's "will to power" and his "triumphalist ravings" the very same "extreme determination to destabilize society" that pervades the *Sessantotto* might surprise readers. Yet, he maintains that with Berlusconi we see the closing of a historical period, starting in the 1960s, that determined the demise of the idea of work and family and accelerated the process of de-schooling, the deregulation of sexuality, the turning of the university system into a pernicious melting pot of the worst elements taken from American and Italian education, hostility towards the judicial branch, obliviousness to history, and the triumph of the mass media in replacing many values until then considered the pillars of a democratic society.[5] Though a tireless worker himself, Perniola continues, Berlusconi has forever modified the very notion of work in our society. The essence of his financial capitalism is not based on *actual* work but on a game, in the sense Hans-Georg Gadamer gives to the word: "a game is an impersonal entity that imposes its own reasons on the participants."[6] Perniola considers the gradual loss of Italians' sense of dignity as partly due to this sinister "concretization." In the concluding pages of his pamphlet, Perniola emphatically asks,

> Can we be indignant if we ourselves have no dignity? If we are completely incoherent with ourselves as we are immersed in the world of communication,

> one in which everything is turned upside down ... We Italians ... are too weak to allow ourselves to be indignant.[7]

Although Perniola's considerations do not warrant the real possibility of intervention, they nevertheless solicit answers. Artists' commitment to their communities reveals that explicit social intervention is always possible, even if it leads to unintended results. As Zygmunt Bauman declares,

> the proposition "life is a work of art" is not a postulate or an admonition (of the 'try to make your life beautiful, harmonious, sensible and full of meaning – just as painters try to make their paintings, or musicians their compositions' kind), but a statement of fact. Life can *not be* a work if this is a *human* life – the life of a being endowed with will and freedom of choice.[8]

Moreover,

> human life consists of a perpetual confrontation between "external conditions" (perceived as "reality," by definition a matter always resistant to, and all too often defying, the agent's will) and the design of its "auctors" (authors/actors): their aim to overcome the active or passive resistance, defiance and/or inertia of matter and to remould reality in accordance with their chosen vision of the "good life."[9]

Whether making art as a form of instruction, activism, or inspiration, artists consider their work essential to challenging established thought and realizing a more equitable culture. They make apparent the acknowledgment that art is endowed with what Rancière calls "a new modesty, in regards to its capacity to transform the world."[10] Art's new modesty also weans it from its "claims about the singularity of its objects,"[11] while still adhering to Pasolini's statement that every work of art is a work of dispute. At this temporal conjuncture, artists reveal "a systematic distrust of historically grounded power, combined with a de-naturalizing critique of ideology."[12] Though Pierpaolo Antonello and Florian Mussnug recognize that fictional works invariably propose social commentaries about specific events, they see the distrust of historically grounded power as postmodernism's *pars destruens.* The Italian tradition of ideological and political commitment was *so* lifeless/bloodless during the post-Calvino era that *impegno* was considered "an outdated, monological illustration of ideology."[13] Just as the realist mode can rework different narratives of reality, so *impegno* as a form of commitment can resume its activity in the different narratives analysed in *Righteous Anger.*

Impegno today manifests a different approach to the content of the text. Rather than focusing on one particular socio-political theme, a recognized attention to the body and the passions as an epistemological concern underlying the text, as well as to the text's corporeality (a text is a body), diffuses the theme of commitment by encompassing a considerable part of the narrative and visual construction in literature and cinema. These narratives investigate a negotiable relationship with politics and society, accounting for a fluctuating and vulnerable system of ethics. They have significance for their contemporaries and extend their authors' perspectives to other living spaces as visible and audible forms of their participation.[14] Commitment as such has not disappeared, but its forms have been transformed into critical reconsiderations of how to read ourselves without claiming a monopolizing power for our *Weltanschauung* and our *Umwelt.* Therefore, as Pierpaolo Antonello and Florian Mussnug state, "what postmodernism challenges ... is not *impegno* as such, but its essentialist, rationalistic and humanistic underpinnings. To describe postmodernism as an expression of nihilism means to understand this specific challenge to established totalities."[15] All the while, the position of artists with respect to society always considers their empathetic participation in what takes place in their immediate surroundings.

Artists build relations to public life with no impulse towards prevarication (usually). When we discuss artists, politics, and literature, the terms in which we establish comparisons between the literary act and the political act feed at least three types of relations, all stimulated and guided by the same question: What is the role of the artist in public life? The three possible types of relations are determined based on the political content of the artists' works and/or their political activities in a concrete sense – pragmatic ("organic"), that is – such as the relationships between writers and organs of power and/or classes. Corollary to the second point is the relationship that the artist entertains with the nation-state (a state that respects the rights of authors and the rights of the word). Some artists move with apparent ease between these possible relations: they take complete charge of their subjectivity and of their words/images. They *fit* into their own societal context. This approach allows for a more transparent reading of their commitment as expressed in their works. Others extricate their work from a mimetic logic that, in some relations, approaches social realism. They prefer isolation, and, both politically and in their understanding of aesthetics, turn away from narratives whose linguistic referent, in its literariness, runs the risk of appearing comparable to its concrete object of narration. For some, there is a need for isolation and distance from any form or possession of power, the most corruptive tool for the free use of reason.[16] If, among its various functions, art conceived of as an ethical tool suggests the impossibility of action in self-constructed seclusion, I implicitly question the artist's ability to express his or her sense of helplessness in such a void. Action cannot take place in a vacuum; it must reimagine the borders of our being-with-others in the world as fluid, as in our times of liquid modernity.

In *Liquid Life,* Zygmunt Bauman declares, in fact, that, in the transition from the solid to the liquid state of modernity, it is the liquidity of the character that dissolves the sense of contemporary society.[17] To Bauman, liquidity cannot ensure that the process of perfectibility can see an end. In other words, everything is in a perpetual (liquid) state of flux. Liquidity does not negate the idea of perfectibility, but it turns it into an infinite process with no end. Aesthetic expression liquefies on the surface of things as change is the only stable entity of our time. The expectation of finding individual solutions to our problems is something already present in an artist's attitude towards society and his or her own task. No one believes at this point that reason applied to social organization can make a difference towards the attainment of the ideal of the just society. Yet, media power makes it possible for the artist to nourish the possession of an illusory freedom or, at the very least, one that does not belong to the artist in a conventional sense. Consciously constrained by the media system and the industry of consumer-consent in a Debordian sense of the concept, the artist cautiously proceeds through blogs and tweets – a product of the horizontal proliferation of networks that is paradoxically proportional to our desire to know the Other(s) – looking at the foundation of things to distil their ideological essence. The artist arrives at this task armed with words, dealing with issues as a sexed and thinking individual, as the work of Tiziano Scarpa emblematically suggests. Subjectivity becomes a formidable weapon when dealing with emotions that operate also to comprehend the implications of externality.[18] But liquidity also indicates the abuse of the political thinking space. We are tempted to agree with David Bromwich that "we can make everything end in politics."[19] What *Righteous Anger* tries to show is that, even in the age of liquidity, there exists an ethical bond between artists and what they say about their community. Even if not always explicitly stated, their narrative conveys a civic concern and an ethical bond that define a sense of responsibility towards community that is independent of market logic and publishers' mass marketing.[20] Such responsibility constitutes the artists' *munus* (gift) to their respective communities and determines their sense of compassion. A rising form of commitment or *impegno* as knowledge cannot look nostalgically to the old form of activism that sustained the intersubjective relationship between the political realm and the organic intellectual of yesteryear. Rather, *impegno* can result from a healthy form of the virtuous indignation Descartes writes about, produced by the awareness of being a witness during times of unrest that have shaped one's aesthetic sense.

The initial transformative emotional state constitutes the essence of moral indignation in artists. Anger and indignation are powerful, politically charged passions that prompt creation as artists engage with the world through their own corporeal existences. As the epigraph of my study reads, "to create is to resist. To resist is to create."[21] For many artists, passivity is not a viable option. On the contrary, they often do not accept defeat and, provoked by inaction, they get angry. As anger is a dynamic state of the individual, artists set anger in motion. Confident in the pacts established with their readers and spectators, artists deploy their so-called negative passions in what can be considered creative, positive action. As Sianne Ngai holds,

> the very effort of thinking the aesthetic and political together – a task whose urgency seems to increase in proportion to its difficulty in an increasingly anti-utopian and functionally differentiated society – is a prime occasion for ugly feelings.[22]

Vehement passions are often referred to as ugly feelings, and I use them interchangeably throughout this book when my understanding mirrors Ngai's reflections. *Rabbia,* or anger, despite being considered a negative feeling, has always prompted civic and aesthetic commitment. It is an emotion, as William James would write, that makes us see reality in a *certain* way because our passions *do change* reality. "Not so long ago," as Zygmunt Bauman states,

> the arts strove to prove their right to survive by trying to document their usefulness to the world and its inhabitants. They needed to leave behind solid and durable traces of their accomplishments, hard proof of the valuable services they render – tangible and possibly irremovable traces and indestructible proof, promising to last forever; now, however, they not only manage well without solid traces of their presence, but all too often seem to be careful not to threaten to outstay their welcome and so avoid any traces that are too deep for a speedy and expedient effacement.[23]

The idea of a "speedy and expedient effacement" of the arts, of their quick consumption, puts at risk the notion of an art capable of incarnating the meaning of writing as the practical tool for disruption of "dominant forms of representation for something about the precariousness of life to be apprehended."[24]

Perhaps Bauman is right in his observation: quick consumption might diminish the very essence of art. But art is not essential *per se*, nor can it provide more than explanations of symptoms of societal malaise, as we know from Adorno. "For art to exist," Jacques Rancière claims, "what is required is a *specific gaze and form of thought* to identify with it."[25] We may be running the risk of losing both tools that permit art to exist, as suggested by Rancière. We can no longer understand the specificity of art because we have lost the gaze and the thought that, in turn, *could* transform society. By inference, politics and its hegemonic narrative would hold an undisputed sway and leave us hapless. But I believe that some artists can still see in William James's "certain way" something that already bears the process of differentiation and determines the ability to locate what Judith Butler calls the dominant forms of expression. When Pier Paolo Pasolini composed his cinematic poem *La rabbia*, he foreshadowed deleterious developments in Italian contemporary society, chiefly its dangerous fascination with the power of television, a tool that, in the artist's view, enlists "candidates to the death of the soul."[26] He establishes a moral paradigm that cannot be overlooked. This spiritual death is preconized by the seductive charm of Hollywood icon Marilyn Monroe, immortalized by Pasolini's poetic visual obituary dedicated to the actress. Many years have passed since Pasolini's narratives expressed the author's ethical stances. Can we still analyse the work of Italian writers and filmmakers in the same terms of commitment to political and social issues as Pasolini? When Kristin Thompson affirms that "the political effectiveness of realism depends on contingent aesthetic coordinates,"[27] one must rethink realism as a descriptive mode that is not necessarily prescriptive and consider how such a mode works in the process of the defamiliarization and reappropriation of reflexive objects. At such an unstable and fluid juncture, it is anachronistic to ask a writer or a filmmaker to commit to politics in a conventional, but inadequate, understanding of the term. One wonders, in fact, whether it is perhaps a kind of outdated neorealist need, such that we *need* to see at any cost in the writing of our intellectuals a *positive* message of visible commitment and concrete practice confined to narratives tackling traditional forms in the political sphere. Taking a cue from Bauman, if the sense of what constitutes the "political" today spreads and liquefies without clear trajectories, commitment is just as liquefied and rhizomatic. We need to recognize this shift and come to terms with how artists engage today.

Tiziano Scarpa constantly reflects on the ethical regime of images. To this intellectual enquiry, Scarpa adds the more practical enquiry concerning the meaning and role of the artist who resists the effacement of the arts. What then is the political meaning of constructing counter-narratives today? What are the stylistic strategies that allow critics to sift through the authority and honesty of current events representation in the scribal practices? According to what Judith Butler postulates, our age has upset both the terms in which we conceive of political practice and a possible theory. Butler asserts that "politics has entered the catachresis":[28] it no longer has its own name; it is outside our borders; it is, in every sense, "beside itself."[29] It is not by chance that Butler employs the image of Antigone to illustrate the desire for individual legitimacy of this offence in space. The political desire, innate in the individual, moves politics beyond its designed borders, "points the finger elsewhere,"[30] and is thought to flow into another place where politics is still possible, but only by *abusing* a space (from Latin *abūtere*) that does not pertain to it.

If, as Judith Butler claims, politics has entered a stage of catachresis, if the practice of politics is beside itself and modifying itself in a very tangible expressive way, why should we continue thinking, without flexibility, that an artist's reply should repeat obsolete strategies of meaning with respect to politics and commitment? This hardly constitutes a viable option. Spaces of unrest are so de-territorialized that we need new options to understand how we can (still) feel that we are political beings. Authors conceive the *word* as a rather complex means to testify to their presence as a political force in society. Artists become *actual* characters in their novels, empowered by their own words. The politics of poetics has turned political and civic poetry into an almost invisible genre because it has hybridized the novel, which, in turn, has lost some conventional borders but also acquired others. The political today amounts to, and permeates more than ever, the awareness of the role of corporeality in the aesthetic act, the matter and physical substance of the narrative artists incorporate in their images. The allegory of a possible ideology that defines the rights of subjectivity with respect to the community in terms of body politics *is* a political act in itself.

1
Pasolini's *La rabbia* and the Spectacularization of Scarpa's Posthuman Aesthetics

I poeti, questi eterni indignati, questi campioni della rabbia intellettuale, della furia filosofica.[1]

– Pier Paolo Pasolini

This part of *Righteous Anger* focuses on the role of the artist in Tiziano Scarpa's narratives, on his presumed narcissistic writing, on the importance of words that Scarpa attributes to the process of developing verbal images, and on his constant attempt to engage his readers in the discussion of the elements we should consider as fundamental in life. Scarpa[2] avoids setting his literary narratives in more frequently treated geographic spaces, such as Rome and its suburbs. Scarpa's narratives are usually set in northern Italy, framed on the one hand by Milan, the industrial centre in which the artist has lived for an extended period, and on the other by Venice, his hometown. Whether situated in Lombardy or in the delicate ecosystem of the *Serenissima*, Scarpa's narrators speculate over the subjective, sensuous experience of living and what makes life worth living. Milan is an industrial city that reflects the mechanism of a modern Italy and seems to be not only geographically but also intellectually closer to the rest of Europe than Rome. Partially set against the historical backdrop of Berlusconi's tenure and post-Berlusconi society,[3] Scarpa's writings investigate the Italian community through its everyday events. This imagined community (one that has several understandings described by Benedict Anderson)[4] includes quotidian elements from the real community in which his fictional protagonists live. A surreal, parodic atmosphere develops from the friction of the fictional with the actual community. Scarpa's narratives usually centre on a character, often an artist, who discusses the necessity of art and his own presence in the community as a medium for exploring new meanings and re-evaluating societal norms and values. These discussions emerge from narrative fragments alternating between the settings of Milan and Venice.

Scarpa's extraordinary appetite for literary locution produces fragmented plots that outline his specific model of counter-discourse. He constantly questions preconceived notions of Italian contemporary society to speak up for his own community, to which he assigns ethical responsibility. While Milan emerges as a main (but not exclusive) background element in novels such as *Kamikaze d'Occidente* (Western Kamikaze) and *Il brevetto del geco*[5] (The Gecko Patent), Scarpa has been recently devoting his attention to the image of Venice and its delicate geopolitics. One of his most important themes, already present in *Occhi sulla graticola* (Eyes on the Grill) and continuing in the more recent novels *Le cose fondamentali* (The Fundamental Things) and *Il cipiglio del gufo* (The Frown of the Owl),[6] concerns Venetians' complex relationship with their city – a city that is constantly on the verge of physical extinction. Venice is more often analysed and depicted by foreign writers than by Italian writers (leaving aside some notable exceptions, such as Andrea Zanzotto and Goffredo Parise). However, Scarpa's narratives about everyday Venetians recast the image of the city by avoiding the trappings of a restrictive approach. His gaze is neither nostalgic nor melancholic, and mirrors the complex web of characteristics that define the city, not for exotic individuals engaged in soul-searching journeys into the lagoon but for Italians who actually conduct their everyday lives on those waters. Venice's beauty takes the form of elements that acquire their aesthetic value through a braiding of grotesque and sophisticated narrative content pulled from both an *everyday* Venice and a Venice of mystery. Only by acknowledging a combination of material and sensory elements can reality claim beauty as inherent to everyday life. Scarpa's material is the living community of Venice (with himself as a vocal member) and its relationship to a unique natural environment marked by the presence of water as a determining factor in the city's physical survival. His novels transform Venetian settings into an ideal space for a linguistic experimentalism that reveals – in a subtle play of references – the relationship between the literary fabric and that of the place he writes about.

The literary past linked to Venice produces a culture suspended between various identities that Scarpa knows and parodies. Evoking the petrified trunks of trees – the pillars of Venetian buildings – as metaphors for the sacred texts that tie the city to its past, Scarpa creates a personal Venice whose inhabitants participate in Italy's general unrest. Scarpa's intentionally and parodically intertextual narratives appropriate themes present in canonical works set in the *Serenissima*: Casanovism and libertinism, tourism, the motif of the *vaporetto*, and the still waters of the lagoon. His own sense of irony subsumes all references into an image of Venice that refrains from romanticizing it. Scarpa exhibits an outstanding control of language based on the careful evaluation of elements that still today constitute an aesthetic *verum.* This life philosophy is available to Scarpa's individual who wants Venice to thrive in the third millennium (despite the cruise liners obstructing the view of Piazza San Marco) but witnesses its decline. Such a revisiting of the geographics of Venice, and the way in which especially foreign literature has transmitted recurring themes, suggests Scarpa's own posture as a committed artist who can connect multiple material elements simultaneously in his writing. Drawing from Serenella Iovino's analysis of the theme of death in Venice in the work of Thomas Mann and Andrea Zanzotto, one might also argue that Scarpa's novels read the city as a text assembled from its embodied stories and the voices of its reality *fighting* for its salvation. The city, suspended on a lagoon, appears as "an exercise in hybridity not only because it mixes water and land into a new elemental combination, but most of all because it is an act of *hybris*, a violation of ontological pacts"[7] that can produce creative acts such as the city itself. In his narratives on Venice Scarpa assembles a plurality of voices that problematize the basic immobility to which the city is confined by the lack of a communal agreement on the course of its destiny. The callous character of the dilettante thriller writer Enzo Stagnaro in *Il cipiglio del gufo* utters a statement dangerously close to what many Venetians might believe to be a fact:

> Il Mediterraneo si è ridotto a un laghetto secondario. E Venezia che poteva fare? È diventata un gingillo per richiamare la gente da fuori a spendere, fare feste, andare a teatro, pagare le prostitute, giocare d'azzardo, lasciare qui più soldi possibile. È almeno da tre secoli che è così, inutile cianciare; è questa la nostra vera tradizione, il nostro destino: Svuotare le tasche a chi viene qui. Venezia, se vuol restare in piedi, deve gettare sul lastrico più turisti che può.[8]
>
> (The Mediterranean has been reduced to a marginal pond. And what could Venice do? She has become a trinket to attract foreigners to spend, party, go to the theatre, pay prostitutes, gamble, leave here as much money as possible. It has been like this for at least for three centuries, so it is useless to babble; this is our true tradition, our destiny: Emptying the pockets of those who come here. Venice, if she wants to remain standing, must leave as many tourists broke on the pavement as she can.)

It is no coincidence that Stagnaro, a high-school teacher, is also a thriller writer. He banks – like many – on genres that Scarpa regards as the antithesis of commitment. Scarpa is witness to an era that hardly permits clear lines of political conduct, as conventional methods of political speech seem not to provide effective remedies. He demonstrates, however, how artists can present and describe symptoms of malaise on a micro-geopolitical level. The narrator of *Kamikaze d'Occidente* epitomizes Scarpa's attitude. The relationship between the artist and his community illustrates how Scarpa's understanding of culture resembles and amplifies Raymond Williams's definition of culture:

> Culture is ordinary: that is the first fact. Every human society has its own shape, its own purposes, its own meanings. Every human society expresses these, in institutions, and in arts and learning. The making of a society is the finding of common meanings and directions, and its growth is an active debate and amendment under the pressures of experience, contact, and discovery, writing themselves into the land. The growing society is there, yet it is also *made and remade in every individual mind* ... A culture has two aspects: the known meanings and directions, which its members are trained to; the new observations and meanings, which are offered and tested. These are the ordinary processes of human societies and human minds, and we see through them the *nature of a culture: that it is always both traditional and creative*; that it is both the most ordinary common meanings and the finest individual meanings.[9]

Williams underscores the interaction that results from the "remaking" of a growing society in each individual's mind. In a similar vein, Scarpa maps out an intellectual project that is deeply political. Also visible in his theatrical performances, Scarpa's culturally subversive political project is based on a firm understanding of techniques and rhetorical strategies, framing his entire work with Menippean satire and filtering it through an expert reading of Bakhtin's notion of the carnivalesque.[10] The satirical mode articulates the discursive practices of sexuo-cynicism as theorized by Peter Sloterdijk: activated by the visceral disgust that idealistic philosophies have segregated from sentiments, emotions reclaim their importance in Scarpa's writings.[11] The sexuo-cynical approach to content alongside Menippean satire elicits a general sense of malaise towards everything imposed by, and within, the institutions that crystallize knowledge, such as libraries, schools, and the publishing industry. It should come as no surprise that the idea of enforcing, rather than enjoying, knowledge is extraneous to Scarpa's characters. For the writer, one must always *play* with knowledge to understand and establish a healthy relationship with it. A healthy relationship with a non-institutionalized knowledge signifies an interactive and critical approach to the learning experience and reinforces the idea that the politics of art should always struggle against its own crystallization. Sloterdijk's reflections are also mindful of Hume's views of the indissoluble ties between body, mind, and reason as connected elements in the production of experience. Knowledge, always an experience, appears to be based on our bodily impressions. The conflation of the erotic-sexual sphere, the corporeal aspect of Scarpa's writings, with his intellectualization of everyday cultural and political events offers engaging and daring narratives about how an artist lives and creates in twenty-first-century Italy. The corporeal is an intrinsic component of Scarpa's logorrheic characters' monologues, eliciting what Nussbaum calls reflective impressions and triggering a counter-discourse that regulates the discussion of themes. If unaccompanied by the idea of bodily experience as itself an act of creation, the long tirades of Scarpa's characters would amount to a tiresome, endless rumination. Art and commitment must grab our attention with joy and irony. And the effect must be subtle and sophisticated.

By extolling the grotesque and paradoxical quality of everyday acts, Scarpa analyses the effectiveness of language at revealing what is visible or not in a common space, endowed with a common language, and the forms of visibility that disclose artistic practices. His ethical stance on the interpretation of reality supports Rancière's idea that "art consists in constructing spaces and relations to reconfigure materially and symbolically the territory of the common."[12] As witness to Berlusconi's Second Republic and the resulting disconnect between many Italian intellectuals and the political class, as well as to the social unrest sparked by twenty years of "disgusting" government, Scarpa demonstrates his talent in expressing with humour and sagacity the artist's frustration at the failures of Italian society to defeat hegemonic forms of expression proposed by Berlusconi's media and other forms of cultural monopoly. Though it has distinct features that belong to postmodernism and beyond, Scarpa's work often echoes Pasolini's manifold attempt at challenging dominant social structures and hegemonic narratives by denouncing reality as a scandal. In *Cos'è questo fracasso? Alfabeto e intemperanze,*[13] Scarpa acknowledges the artistic influence on his work of three writers, Pier Paolo Pasolini, Pier Vittorio Tondelli, and Aldo Busi. He defines as actual "capolavori della letteratura civile" (CQF 37; civic literary masterpieces) Pasolini's *Scritti corsari,* Tondelli's *Un week-end postmoderno,* and Busi's *Seminario sulla gioventú* (CQF 37). He illustrates his clear predilection for what he calls their "dimensione notturna" (CQF 37; nocturnal dimension). For Scarpa, this "volto notturno" (CQF 37; nocturnal face) of the three homosexual authors represents a way of looking at their commitment in society other than their "dimensione diurna" (CQF 37; daily dimension). The nocturnal dimension is not merely suggestive of the three artists' sexual orientation. Rather, it offers another possibility of taking a lesson from them and the issues they present in their works. Scarpa focuses on the committed dimension of their passion; he focuses on the "passion" that moved these authors' "knowledge and commitment" (CQF 37) – nocturnal passion that presents discrepancies and "sembra spuria e inconfessabile rispetto all'ideale politico puro" (CQF 37; seems spurious and unsayable with respect to the pure political ideal). But it is a sensuous and sensual passion that moves him nevertheless to knowledge and *impegno.* As Scarpa asserts, "senza passione non c'è conoscenza, senza passione non c'è esperienza e nemmeno Storia" (CQF 37; without passion there is no knowledge, without passion there is no experience and not even History).

Scarpa favours a fragmented narrative structure and utilizes parody and the grotesque as narrative modes, and his voice differs from the one deployed by the previously mentioned three authors, as his own way to produce a "scandalo espressivo" (expressive scandal)[14] consistently picks upon grotesque aspects of life to unmask the monsters of unreality with a skilful use of the carnivalesque. While an anti-essentialist form of commitment coupled with a great sense of irony and a Bakhtinian delight in presenting the reverse of every situation delineates Scarpa's work, his approach to literature, and to the arts in general, has nevertheless suggested that his form of commitment can be traced back, *mutatis mutandis,* to these authors, and to Pasolini's relentless *j'accuse* in particular. Scarpa's constant overlapping of genres, ranging from the novelistic and the poetic to the theatrical, reveals his desire to identify the pieces of a puzzling society in which he situates almost invariably the artist (or a student, as in the case of *Occhi sulla graticola*) as his alter-ego and spokesperson for the denunciation of societal ills and the promotion of diagnoses. His anger is personal but demonstrates an indignation that concerns the society in which he lives and works. Though graced by a relentless wit, Tiziano Scarpa makes his own Pasolini's *gesto del poeta* (poet's gesture). The corporeal dimension of the aesthetic is essential to his work because the artist's body is constitutive of, and integral to, the artistic project, as in the work of Sophie Calle, one of Scarpa's favourite visual artists. Regarding the poet's gesture, we no longer suggest the concept of an oracle (*il poeta-vate*) who investigates the world *for* us:[15] Scarpa's poet implies *us.*

The poem "Il capitalismo straniero" (BF 151–3; Foreign Capitalism) begins with verses taken from Pier Paolo Pasolini's poem "Il pianto della scavatrice." The parodic use of intertextuality suggests an understanding of Pasolini's anguish while transferring some of his themes on capitalism into Scarpa's age. Pasolini's allusion to the importance of love and knowledge is skilfully reversed in "Il capitalismo straniero." Scarpa ties

Berlusconi's deadly power (television killed the narrator's uncle of this poem!) with the Italians' lack of prospects:

> Capisco gli elettori del padrone / di mezza Italia, perché nella vita / l'unica cosa che conta è incappare / in qualcuno che voglia la tua vita. / Silvio Berlusconi mi vuole, mi ama , /mi fa sentire che anch'io ho qualche cosa / da dargli, che a lui risulta gradito! /
>
> La mafia, il Papa, la televisione, / la Ferrari, gli industriali del Nord, / la pubblicità, il campionato, il festival, / Miss Italia si accaparrano me. / Il potere mi vuole! Vuole me! / Solo la vita spesso non mi vuole. / Non si vive se nessuno ti vuole. / Mi volete forse voi comunisti? / Mi volete forse voi democratici / di sinistra? Mi bramate con tutte / le vostre forze come mi dimostra (con mille prove fedele) / di bramarmi il mio dolce Berlusconi? Io / sono la Romania dopo la fine / dell'impero sovietico. È bellissimo / che arrivino finanziamenti esteri, / è commovente sentirsi contesi. / È luminoso, è nuovissimo questo / supermercato aperto nel mio cuore. (BF 152–3)
>
> (I understand the voters of the master / of half Italy, because in life / the only thing that matters is to run / into someone who wants your life. / Silvio Berlusconi wants me, loves me, / makes me feel that I too have something / to give him, which is pleasing to him! /
>
> The Mafia, the Pope, the television, / Ferrari, the industrialists of the North, / the publicity, the championship, the festival, / Miss Italia, they all get hold of me. / Power wants me! It wants me! / Only life often does not want me. / You do not live if nobody wants you. / Do you want me, you Communists? / Do you want me, perhaps, Democrats / of the left? Do you crave me with all / your strength as shows (with a thousand proofs of faithful love) / my sweet Berlusconi to crave me? I am / Romania after the fall of the Soviet empire. It is wonderful / that foreign funding arrives, / it is moving to feel disputed. / It's bright, it is brand new this / supermarket open in my heart.)

This poem constitutes one of several examples of how Scarpa engages in an intellectual dialogue with Pasolini's body of work (my chosen influence but by no means Scarpa's only one). What Bauman calls "the liquid age" has partly contributed to a social failure in constructing "projects," but artists maintain the potential to act as catalysts for protests about what disgusts them, as Scarpa's invective clearly reveals. But "what does it mean," Sara Ahmed wonders, "to designate something as disgusting?"[16] Ahmed argues that, by finding *something* disgusting, we establish material relationships among bodies, objects, and other means. We understand how our actions are fuelled by emotion, prompted by sensuous, hence material and pragmatic, activities. Ambivalent feelings (attraction and repulsion) activate disgust towards something that captures our attention precisely because it is distasteful in our eyes. Our attention is never raw, for it is generated by something other than us after being mediated by our senses. Our attention is a response to something from which we dissociate ourselves once our senses have mediated it and which needs an explanation.

My reading of Scarpa's passionate narratives and aesthetic practices begins by examining his artistic ethical position as a rereading of Pier Paolo Pasolini's own indignation, the poet's anger (*la rabbia del poeta).* In past years, several critical approaches have been undertaken concerning the breadth of Pasolini's influence. In *Dimenticare Pasolini,* Pierpaolo Antonello speaks of the difficulty of describing Pasolini's intellectual trajectory (unlike those traced by Italo Calvino and Elio Vittorini, among others), as his Christological model displays an "assoluta *impraticabilità*" (absolute unworkability) due to its "biographical dimension."[17] In Antonello's view, such impossibility results from the relationship of Pasolini's works to his biography, which is marked by volatile public opinion and media harassment that eventually resulted in his intellectual martyrdom.[18] The concept of sacrifice is for Antonello neither useful nor realistic in our society, at least in terms of commitment. Antonio Tricomi points instead to Pasolini's "socially useful writings because always literary, never divested of aesthetic value."[19] An ever-present ethics of narrative remains for Tricomi integral to Pasolini's legacy, "una trentennale orazione pubblica"[20] (a thirty-year old public oration), alongside his uncanny ability to "be a factious witness of his own epoch, or better, of those socio-cultural phenomena that put into question his way of being an individual and an author."[21]

While Antonello advances valid points about Pasolini's "impractical model" (though followed by many artists over the years, such as Marco Tullio Giordana, Marco Paolini, and others), Tricomi reflects on the artist's tireless intellectual agency and proposes a positive dimension to his legacy. Tiziano Scarpa's ludic and contentious prose and poetry as well as his ode to life and his healthy indignation at various forms of absurd behaviour by politicians activate a particular form of commitment that relentlessly questions dominant narratives of power and the conventions embedded in the word *aesthetics.* Scarpa's socio-political meditations on the performative power of counter-narratives of reality, his polemical vein, and the corporeal dimension of his writing owe much to Pasolini's "impractical" example as illustrated in Scarpa's love for the nocturnal dimension (CQF 37; "il volto notturno") of his art and personality. Scarpa's protagonists are critical members of the Italian community, and his narrators oppose any populistic idea of governmentality, challenging dominant social norms, often rather overtly. His "aesthetic regime asserts the absolute singularity of art, and, at the same time, destroys any pragmatic criterion for isolating this singularity."[22] What he makes apparent in his work and critical writing is the possibility of a concrete action of the performative word. Bearing witness to his understanding that "aesthetics has its own politics, or its own meta-politics,"[23] Scarpa's form of commitment approaches that proposed by Pierpaolo Antonello and Florian Mussnug. "Progressive art," Antonello and Mussnug note, "is not defined as a struggle for a new hegemonic affirmation – the transformation of plurality into a new *habitus* – but as a challenge to any form of hegemony. The alternative to rigid ideological definitions, in other words, is an 'emancipatory' or 'reformistic' *impegno*, a shift from politics to micropolitics."[24] If Pasolini deemed the intellectual courage to speak truth and political practice "two irreconcilable realities in Italy,"[25] postmodernist Scarpa confronts hegemonic narratives and shapes narrative possibilities into a reformatory project in which art still holds ethical value. Scarpa looks at himself in the mirror of Pasolini's poet in "Io so" (I Know).[26] His poet "tries to keep track," to find "coordinates," to piece "together the disorganized and fragmentary bits of a whole, coherent political scene," and "re-establishes logic"[27] within his own society. Especially, he tries to "re-establish logic where chance, folly, and mystery seem to reign."[28] As in any mirror, its space reflects our reversed image. In reflecting himself in the mirror of Pasolini's statement, Scarpa's poet sees, then, something more than and different from what Pasolini's *j'accuse* presents. Rather than following in his footsteps, he adds to his vision the element of the grotesque. By deploying the grotesque mode inherent in the analysis of every society, evoked by "a clashing between form and content, the unstable mixture of heterogeneous elements, [and] the explosive force of the paradoxical,"[29] as suggested by Wolfgang Kayser, Scarpa often refers to an intellectual and ideological emergency that is just as dangerous as the one Pasolini sensed in his own epoch. At the same time, he recognizes his freedom to establish his own form of "correspondence between aesthetic virtue and political virtue."[30]

Scarpa's moral indignation stems from his assessment of and commitment to his society, just as that of Pasolini led him to compose the 1963 cinematic poem *La rabbia*. Scarpa's characters are dissenting agents who expose the degree of the country's decadence. Post-hegemonic intellectual labour resides in the ability to construct an aesthetic that considers cultural production as a valid counterpart of the *disgusting* system. Disgusted from within, we can always react. In promoting agency, disgust functions alongside indignation to trigger a process of defamiliarization with the *way* in which *we live now.* As post-Berlusconi culture continues to advocate renewable forms of populism, Scarpa's characters voice indignation about what they must face. They act upon their disgust[31] and show its usefulness because "disgust is performative."[32] When "we name something as disgusting,"[33] we perform with our words an act that results from our reaction to what we dislike. Scarpa's characters do not sit still: they react in disgust and inhabit narratives that hybridize genres with freedom and delectation.

Within such narratives, Scarpa's narrators are powerful orators in the narrative *polis* they inhabit, and their posture speaks volumes about their author's ability to show his civic commitment through the meta-politics of aesthetics. Though divested of the tragic undertones that fill Pasolini's prose and poetry, Scarpa's role is that of the *parrhesiastes*[34] who bluntly relates a truth that cannot be divorced from commitment, as Michel Foucault clearly elaborated.[35] Both his fiction and his poems could be read as a prolonged essay bearing his philosophy, as could Pasolini's body of work ("reasonings in verse"), in the view of Giovanni Raboni.[36] Scarpa purposely develops narratives without concrete plots: their emplotment rests in the hands of his characters, who are either writers forced to figuratively prostitute themselves to survive, as in the case of *Kamikaze d'Occidente,* or failed artists like Federico Morpio in *Il brevetto del geco,* who literally carves the feet of deceased human beings. Embracing the only remaining tactic for artists in the posthuman society, Morpio writes with, and on, the body by using actual human feet as the material for his sculptures. The material aspect of Morpio's action of carving actual bodies is comparable to what Scarpa does with the physical material of the world to develop an alternative to disgust. He fights disgust with disgust, but the grotesque reveals its importance in such a duel, as, as Bakhtin observes, "the grotesque body is not separated from the rest of the world. It is not a closed, complete unit; it is unfinished, outgrows itself, transgresses its own limits"[37] as the "apertures" of the body, "the open mouth, the genital organs, the breast, the phallus"[38] all emit fluids that flow in and out, to and from our bodies.

Morpio considers the pedicure he gives to his father, Ivano (whose skinny body reminds him of a "statua di Giacometti coricata su un letto" [a Giacometti statue lying in bed]),[39] as a possible technique for sculpting a material that could not be more natural than his own father's body (BG 116–19) and that reminds him of his own body. Also, as technology creates more physical separations than connections, there is a cultural longing to experience something tangible and related to nature. We *are* nature. We need to be aware of our body and how we connect to the other material texts that compose the world, from its early stages to death. Ron Mueck's hyperrealistic sculptures are cited in Scarpa's *Il brevetto del geco* as an evocative point of reference for what he wants to do with his words (BG 112). His work feels more real than reality. As Bauman postulates, the pursuit of happiness cannot be concerned with virtuosity, and this is apparent in Scarpa's grotesque universe, one in which the grotesque is characterized not by transgression *per se* but by conscious acts that are both transgressive to the point of perversion and utter fetishism and yet restrained in their refined prose. Rousseau's "coercion to happiness" is an impractical admonition, for humans can hardly be *happy* when their entire life is spent being coerced into doing something productive and "turn[ing] their back on what they have held dear and what they thought had been making them happy, and ... becom[ing] different from what they are."[40] Scarpa's citizens appear coerced into "infinitely expandable desires and wants, into ... embracing fully and unreservedly the 'there is no alternative edition' of the 'political correctness' of the day."[41] Federico Morpio, in this case, aims to instil in his readers indignation at and an active disgust for current politics, making them understand the power that the freedom of aesthetics gives to words (*le parole*) along with the body and touch with which we play in our everyday life. If the world of the internet deprives us of the sense of touch and smell, Scarpa's artist can still define the political in art while showing political awareness of "our liquid modern society of consumers"[42] by designing a place and a time that engage his readers in retrieving their bodily sensations as the sole tool we possess to fight the monopoly of media. In a formal sense, Scarpa's artist elects the novel as "una delle principali vie d'accesso alla partecipazione democratica. Insieme alla rete, è una delle poche armi civiche a disposizione dei cittadini privi di altre forme di potere, sia esso politico, mediatico, economico" (BG 5; one of the main access routes to democratic participation. Together with the internet, it is one of the few civic weapons available to citizens without other forms of power, be it political, mediatic, [or] economic).

Pasolini and Scarpa share an attention to a materialism that is sensory, aware of the performativity of emotions as a physical reaction to the external and the political. Emotions attach us to the world around us, to reality. Forms of visibility disclose aesthetic practices. Corporeality, ever-present in Pasolini's work, explodes quite literally in Scarpa's hyperbolic narratives of bodily fluids, which function to transform indignation and disgust into performative tools. Bodily fluids construct a metaphorical paradigm that is also material because they connect reason with the power to think critically about what results from a connection to our body and flesh. We sense experience, as Rancière writes, through our body. Civic attention to politics can also, as we have seen, be manifested through the corporeal that Scarpa derives also from the "nocturnal dimension" of Pasolini's life. The intellectual influence of Pasolini rests also in his posture before power and the world. A self-proclaimed "inventor of stories,"[43] Pasolini reveals, as Scarpa does, his "repugnance of entering into such a political world."[44] Yet, precisely in the stories he "invents," he reclaims facts distorted by the media to demystify their readings as ordered by the power. To these readings, he opposes his own redistribution of meaning.

La normalité, ou notre catastrophe insue:[45] The *rabbia* of the Poet

Pasolini's cinematic poem *La rabbia,*[46] produced in 1962 at roughly the same time as the philosophical tale of *La Ricotta,* exhibits an artistic stance that embraces a personal and unceasing engagement with reality and politics. *La rabbia* functions as a model for those artists who want to expose the mechanisms of what Pasolini called "unreality," the monopoly of the media by the few. Often considered a marginal text in Pasolini's opus,[47] *La rabbia* reads instead like a testament to Pasolini's artistic practice of converting the travesty of tragedy into news for the crowd. In Roberto Chiesi's recounting of the genesis of Pasolini's cinematic poem, "a unique and anomalous case in the history of Italian cinema,"[48] *La rabbia* was originally a project by producer Gastone Ferranti, and only later did Pasolini convince this producer of *Mondo libero* to create a montage film, exclusively based on previous footage, that in Pasolini's intentions was to become "an essay of cinematic journalism."[49] Advertised as an "apocryphal variation of the Don Camillo and Peppone saga,"[50] the film had a limited release and was immediately withdrawn from theatres. There are several reasons for this failure, but Chiesi attributes the film's withdrawal chiefly to Giovannino Guareschi's virulent anti-American attacks in the part he conceived and directed upon Ferranti's request.[51] Perhaps the Italian public was not ready to see its own inchoate state during reconstruction: Italians wanted to believe in the economic boom.[52] It seems that the Italian public was not ready to be implicated in its own ruin. In 1963, Italians were searching for hope, and were being encouraged to embrace consumerism. As with *Rome Open City* and other neorealist works, authorial intentions and public reception clashed. Rising from the ashes of the Second World War, and now projected into the economic boom, Italians were deaf to Pasolini's prophetic words.[53]

In *La rabbia,* Pasolini frames the space and time of his personal postwar history by repurposing archival footage of events framed by the Cold

War and the economic boom[54] and positing political arguments about the edited sequences of archival material. The intervention of the artist, who repurposes a pre-existing lexicon and linguistic codes, is of an ethical and aesthetic order in the "reworking of the meaning of the sign."[55] In *La rabbia* we can isolate significant elements that inform Scarpa's conceptualization of his role as artist, his work, and his poetic action. My theoretical link ties Pasolini's stance in *La rabbia* to Scarpa's position through Rancière's idea of the distribution of the sensible as, through verbal and visual images, their work reassigns a different order to space and time, to the visible and the invisible. The artist makes this redistribution available to his community of readers by assigning value to images and words through his own ethical criteria, which, in turn, create new meaning for those ideas and words. The idea of the artist's immersion in culture and politics can be understood as generating an aesthetics that Rancière explains as "the system of *a priori* forms determining what presents itself to sense experience."[56]

As Georges Didi-Huberman writes in his essay on *La rabbia*, by diverting (*detourning*) the images presented by the newsreels and offering distinct commentaries that force us to reread the images, Pasolini demands that spectators shoulder an active role. He focuses their attention on what he would call "the unreality" that spectators had overlooked the first time they experienced the images in newsreels about wars, racism, and worker exploitation. In Pasolini's prophetic opinion, passive viewing of media's manipulations of domestic and global societal ills results in the consequential danger of becoming incapable of an emotional reaction. Indirect passions produced by a double relation of impressions and ideas trigger the conceptualizing behind *La rabbia* and construct the fresco of a universal exploitation of the lower classes. Pasolini strongly empathizes with the Hungarian victims, with the colonized Congolese, with the families of the twenty-three casualties of the deadly firedamp gas incident on 22 March 1955 in Morgnano (near Spoleto). The intervention of his own emotions in the making of this cinematic collage should have resulted (in the artist's intentions) in a transformation of the spectators' point of view. When looking at those images that now present a world rather different from the one emerging in the original showings of the 1950s, willing spectators perceive how the role of vehement passions can virtually transform the image and can propose a reading that is a far cry from the pretended obiectivity of newsreels. Regarding emotions, Pasolini himself realized that, while aware that the poet's anger pervaded his work, he could not quite pinpoint the reasons behind such an unconventional project. In "Una visione del mondo epico-religiosa,"[57] Pasolini responds as follows to Giuseppe Francone's questions about his authorial intentions regarding *La rabbia*:

> What I meant to say in *La rabbia* is something confusing I have in me, still an irrational idea, not well defined, undetermined, which is present throughout my work in these years and which will be the leading motif of the poetry book that is about to come out: it is the idea of a *new prehistory*. My sub-proletarians still live in the *ancient prehistory*, in the real prehistory, while the bourgeois world, the world of technology, the neo-capitalist one is moving toward a new prehistory and the similarity between the two prehistories is purely accidental. Evidently, these are two entirely distinct facts.[58]

For Pasolini, *La rabbia* represents an "act of indignation against the unreality of the bourgeois world and its consequent historical irresponsibility."[59] *La rabbia* manifests his "growing discomfort with the conformism of the Italians"[60] by exposing the passive acceptance of consumerism by his contemporaries. Pasolini's self-declared "confused" attempt to capture the rising *new prehistory* originated in his didactic use of archival footage, illustrating a non-linear period of incongruity and cruelty. The result is a tragic retelling of current events.[61]

The original intended meaning of the footage can be deconstructed into three distinct elements: editing, commentary, and musical score. The cinematic poem presents a collage of genocides and wars interspersed with footage of Queen Elizabeth's coronation and speeches by heads of state. The most important public events marking those years are tied to footage of the humble working-class people who suffer the consequences of the immorality of regimes. The atomic bomb, whose images are interpolated with those of skulls designed by Renato Guttuso throughout the entire cinematic poem, symbolizes the annihilation of humanity, "the bombing of the 'ideological' diffusion" Pasolini criticizes.[62] Collage, a technique frequently used in Italian pop art (Mimmo Rotella's works are an apt example), displays Pasolini's assimilation of pop art techniques into the production of a politically committed montage. The intellectual project behind the montage is symptomatic of Pasolini's understanding, similar to Walter Benjamin's, of progress as a failure, as modern Western society (Italian primarily, but the panorama is international) quickly plunges into what the artist defines as a new form of prehistory. His treatment of the normality of "la vita che passa" (life going by) is the starting point in *La rabbia* for a succession of images of a postwar society in which people are preoccupied with living after having witnessed so much death and grief during the war. Thinking about the way people passively accept impositions on how to live does not accommodate their concept of progress, hence their negative reaction. Pasolini asserts that people preferred to focus on the normalcy of their everyday life without realizing that behind this novel postwar "normalcy" lurked the ghost of a new and different kind of prehistory. This form of prehistory shares little with that of Pasolini's *Lumpenproletariat.* Social and bodily spaces expose such scandal and offer a poignant counterpoint to images of bourgeois Italian ladies wearing the classic symbol of Western bourgeoisie, a pearl necklace, at social events. *La rabbia* also exposes the Western world's discrimination against the Third World, highlighting the widespread oppression that results in endemic misery and suffering in globalized and conflict-ridden times.

Didi-Huberman claims that the original footage of *La rabbia* is often *immonde* (lurid), ideologically repulsive for its pretence of neutrality.[63] The media largely shape modern prehistory, and *La rabbia* exposes the role of cinema newsreels and television as tools of a pernicious fascination. The only exceptions to the use of newsreel footage exist in the sequence devoted to the actress Marilyn Monroe. Pasolini chose photo stills to construct his personal eulogy to the American icon as she embodies the vulnerability of every act of beauty. Monroe's images (photos like those in Andy Warhol's 1962 silkscreen printing *Marilyn Diptych* based on a still from the 1953 *Niagara* at the Tate Gallery in London) form a sequence that functions as a threshold between the beauty of a world that could have been and the unsettling imminent future. Endowed with such special importance, Monroe's sequence achieves *gravitas* by slowing down. Velocity is eliminated: the narrative yields to description. Everything comes to a halt in front of Monroe's unbearable beauty – time is suspended. Forever framed by the stills, her vulnerability and frailty embody the greater vulnerability of our entire society. In this sequence, we are moved by grief instead of repulsive emotion as we are in other sequences. Monroe's stills allude to how easily human life can become a collective future suicide[64] as the images of atomic explosions interspersed with this sequence illustrate. The warning is, in fact, quite evident throughout the film: Pasolini's *memento mori* obsessively intersperses images of skulls throughout the collage of newsreels to remind us that, as in Counter-Reformation painting, the soul's death is imminent. The cult of the dead evoked by the presence of the skulls activates a poetics of exhumation that sustains Pasolini's commentary on Monroe's stills: "Tu sorella minore" (You, little sister).[65] It also envisages his friend Elsa Morante's "anger of atomic suicide."[66]

Pasolini's anger is a civic response to the spectators' passiveness and their neutralization of any reaction to an insidious understanding of cosmopolitics.[67] His anger uncovers evidence of a state of emergency that cannot be explained with conventional definitions, and a finite time to handle such an emergency hides within the current state of normalcy. Pasolini's poem is a civic ode in which intellectual anger and indignation generate an aesthetic act of great force, or, in Didi-Huberman's words, "a gesture of his body and his heart"[68] that his poem "La rabbia" already foresaw:

> A quasi quarant'anni, / io mi trovo alla rabbia, come un giovane / che di sé non sa altro che è nuovo, / e si accanisce contro il vecchio mondo. / E, come un giovane, senza pietà / o pudore, io non nascondo / questo mio stato: non avrò pace, mai.[69]

> (At almost forty, / I find myself in front of anger, as a young man / Who knows nothing else but that he is new, / And rages against the old world. / And, as a young man, with no pity / Or modesty, I do not hide / This state of mine: I will never have peace.)

The passion that led Pasolini to the subsequent visual composition of *La rabbia*, albeit in his self-pronounced "confused manner,"[70] concerns an indignation that impelled the poet to civic commitment. His *Weltanschauung* is reflected in his urge to "document the presence of a world that, against the bourgeois world, deeply owns reality. Reality, a true love for tradition, that is, that only revolution can give."[71] As Descartes states, the poet's anger "contains everything Indignation does, and this in addition: it is founded on an action which affects us and of which we have the Desire to avenge ourselves."[72] Private and public indignation are two sides of one coin: "La mia esistenza privata / non è più racchiusa tra i petali d'una rosa, / una casa, una madre, una passione affannosa. / È pubblica" (My private existence / is no longer enclosed within the petals of a rose, / a house, a mother, a frantic passion. / It is public),[73] Pasolini declares in the poem "La rabbia."

Didi-Huberman reflects on the ways in which Pasolini's anger is expressed in his eponymous film.[74] How can a poet avenge himself for himself, and for the ills of society simultaneously? And why did Pasolini extend his creation from his poem to his visual *pastiche* to illustrate his growing discomfort? In *La rabbia*, solitary anger and collective indignation coexist, reinstating that beneficial "knot" of confusion Jacques Rancière discusses in his study on aesthetics and its discontents.[75] Thoughts, theories, and practice construct the knot of what is perceived as an unresolved film. It is our understanding of this tangle of intentions, reactions, and suggestions that defines our reception of Pasolini's *La rabbia*. Pasolini empathizes with Elsa Morante's notion of the unhappy masses (*infelici molti*) of the world. His close examination of media and language production outside of verbal language via newsreel footage enriches our understanding of Morante's tenets. Such an examination illustrates how manipulation of public opinion was most successfully achieved not through literature but through widely available and broadly disseminated visual information, with deleterious consequences. Morante limits her denunciation to poetic acts that favour *the things* that belong to art instead of focusing on the world (as society) and that turn *scrittori* into *scriventi*, the former assigned the role of exposing the cheating.[76] Pasolini understood and appropriated the "aesthetic regime" in which the difference between "those things that belong to art and those that belong to ordinary life is blurred"[77] by constructing a prophetic exposition of the ills of the contemporary world. In this, Pasolini appears even more visionary than his friend Morante.

Pasolini's statements reveal that anger – *la rabbia* – is a passion that moves him to act against the fear inspired in everyday people by those who pull the strings of a conservative trend *disguised* as progress to restore the *status quo*. It is the dualism Walter Benjamin mentions, in his tenth thesis, between the notion of progress as a linear concept and modernity.[78] *La rabbia*, then, must act against the impending neo-fascist ideology by which the middle classes identify themselves with the power of the state. *La rabbia* acts against insensitivity, against what Rancière calls "the delegitimation of positions of speech":[79] a distinct form of capitulation to the allure of mass media products (inclusive of that aberration of reading for Pasolini, the invention of *The Reader's Digest* and *similia*). Pasolini wielded his work as a weapon against television, a medium he condemned in many writings. His impetus produced a cinematic poem that functions as an instrument to awaken crowds and alert them to the current state of unreality through the same "monsters" that capitalist society was generating. The commercial flop of *La rabbia* signalled the response of Italians. The effect produced by Pasolini's aesthetic operation through the material rearrangement of signs and images clashed with spectators' expectations. As Rancière puts it, "the channels for political subjectivization are not those of imaginary identification but those of 'literary' disincorporation."[80] Pasolini does not enter a world that disgusts him, as he states in "I Know," but produces an act of political aesthetics through his literary and cinematic locutions (the stories he "invents").

Three Elements: Editing, Commentary, and Music

In an interview and press book accompanying the edition of Pasolini's complete film *La rabbia*, Giuseppe Bertolucci claims that the film does not have a historic linear trajectory, and that Pasolini isolates the "momento fondativo" (foundational moment) of television with newsreels from 1954 onward. Sequences of the newsreels and the two voice-overs of painter Renato Guttuso and writer Giorgio Bassani organize the synchrony of Pasolini's work. "There is a different temperature between the newsreels and Pasolini's work, that fever animating his work in the Sixties," Bertolucci adds. "One of the strongest things is that Pasolini takes up a genre very distant from him – that of the newsreels – appropriates it, empties it all out, and brings it to a new life."[81] Pasolini appropriated material through editing, music, and commentary; he did not shoot a single still. The commentary focused on three aspects: the Italian socio-political situation, international socio-political affairs, and the artist's interior thoughts. Pasolini spoke about contamination, which leads by necessity ("naturalmente" he claims) to the *pastiche*,[82] his particular application of editing, commentary, and music. We can think of this film constructed of sequences of events as an autobiographical compilation of what caught Pasolini's attention during his life prior to 1962, rather than as a *pastiche*.

Through montage and a composite operation of *détournement*, for which Chiesi and Didi-Huberman do not hesitate to refer to situationist Guy Debord,[83] Pasolini exposes the perils of the manipulation of public opinion, which, though not as obvious as in totalitarian times (Italians were used to Fascist LUCE newsreels), was just as dangerous. The mourning of the miners of Morgnano and the strikes at Fiat in Turin are parts of a modern history moving towards alienation. He repurposes images and comments through a montage of those images and the superimposition of two voices, the one poetic and the other in prose. Pasolini's authorial vision directs spectators away from the meaning of the narratives previously constructed for those images. His visual *collage* demonstrates what his civil indignation leads him to believe is the true aspect of unreality. By reversing (*détournement*) the established logic of elements of past newsreels and repurposing them in his cinematic text, Pasolini divests the parts of their original significance and gives them new meaning through their position in the diegesis. What Sergei Eisenstein calls "intellectual editing"[84] reveals its intrinsic importance in the tactic used by Pasolini for his film. He takes possession of images generated by a previous visual discourse as presented in Ferranti's newsreels of *Mondo Libero* to construct a new text through edited images and succession in the diegesis, in the same way in which recycled material forms a new artwork, as in a Dadaist collage. As Laura Rascaroli writes, "two primary markers of the form – reflectivity and subjectivity" determine the outcome of the *essai* film.[85] In his interview for the DVD *La rabbia di Pasolini*, director Giuseppe Bertolucci addresses the issue of contamination achieved through the process of misappropriation that lends new meaning to the footage:

> Contamination today is chance's daughter, like a tsunami that destroys and tears down. Back then, contamination meant taking a hated object, making it your own, turning it into a noble object, and making an object of poetry. It is also very important to find the dramaturgy by editing repertoire materials that are very different. Combinations by contrast, by affinity, always create strange dramaturgies. The great presence of verses constructs the compass of the entire creative operation. Each time [you watch *La rabbia*] you discover meanings you did not see, ambiguous ones. It is not a culturally correct film.[86]

According to Bertolucci, the most powerful tools of *La rabbia* are misappropriation and contamination. Like Didi-Huberman, Roberto Chiesi lists examples of Pasolini's *détournement*, including Ava Gardner's arrival at Ciampino or Sophia Loren's witnessing of the cleaning of eels in Polesine. The two sequences are both framed by a skull, an emblem of the transitory nature of life.[87] Inevitably, in these two sequences, the transitoriness of life is linked to the world of cinema and of *dive* who, like Monroe, are accidental participants in the mystification of rites and growing consumerism of the contemporary world.

Vulnerability is expressed in various ways throughout the film. The 90,000 metres of Ferranti's archival footage Pasolini envisioned as forming his cinematic poem were the *matter* that he needed to form a response to the conditions of vulnerability that accompanied the events in the footage. Pasolini's edits exposed not only the fallacy of an *official* narrative, but also, as Eisenstein theorized, demanded that viewers create other possible meanings. In *Precarious Life*, Judith Butler reflects on society's unbearable vulnerability – a cause for fear and mourning after the attacks on the Twin Towers. Pasolini seems to wonder whether vulnerability and loss inevitably lead to military violence and retribution. Along with Butler, he seems to ask what humans can politically make of grief, besides a cry for war. Butler argues that "no violent act of sovereignty will rid the world of fundamental dependency on anonymous others,"[88] and that, "if national sovereignty is challenged, that does not mean it must be shored up at all costs, if that results in suspending civil liberties and suppressing political dissent."[89] Pasolini, many years before Butler, proves that sustainable community and interdependence should be examined and acknowledged as the foundation of a healthy global political community. No distribution of the sensible can otherwise be possible.

The second step towards the reworking of previous images consists of the commentary. Pasolini works with three different elements that provide his non-linear reading of recent history: first, the characters' direct speech; second, indirect free speech, the openly subjective narrative part which he sees as his most original contribution ("la parte narrativa o didascalica che è quella mia").[90] The third element is the score: the *Adagio in G minor* by Tomaso Albinoni. What Pasolini calls the horizontal and vertical application of music drives "lo scandalo espressivo per cercare la poesia" (that expressive scandal to search for poetry).[91] He states that,

> Music in film can also be thought out before shooting the film ... but it is only when it is materially applied to the film that [it] is created as music of the film. Why? Because the encounter and eventual amalgam between music and image holds poetic, empirical traits, that is ... what music adds to the images, or better put, the way in which music transforms images, remains a mysterious and hardly explainable fact.[92]

For Pasolini, music adds indefinable value to montage because it simultaneously transcends cinema and presents a reality which is not illusory like that on the screen, where sounds locate their real depth. Vulnerability is addressed on all fronts, as each sequence, sustained by Albinoni's music and also popular songs from Cuba and other exploited countries, articulates the ways in which we prepare ourselves for the soul's death. The final shot consists of a hand that pushes the button of the atomic bomb and hits on high voltage poles to formally decree by means of abhorred progress the death of the soul of millions of candidates ("milioni di candidati alla morte dell'anima").[93]

His *cinema di poesia*, the lyrical and oneiric aspect of cinema, conceptualizes the passage of poetry from a purely linguistic form to an effective discursive, rather than monolithic, form of language. The *cinema di poesia*, by adding the "author's individual experience," offers fresh linguistic possibilities.[94] Cinema is a form of expression, not of mere communication, with different goals from a documentary. It establishes a narrative language consisting of images, whether new or appropriated, that are contaminated by meanings other than the original ones, and construct new concepts while still belonging to "a common patrimony."[95]

La rabbia begins with the voice of painter Renato Guttuso speaking for Pasolini. In a sombre tone, highly reminiscent of Alain Resnais's voice-over in his 1956 32-minute *Nuit et brouillard*, the voice addresses viewers with universal questions: "Why is our existence ruled by discontent, by anguish, by the fear of war, by war? To answer this question, I wrote this film without any chronological, and perhaps not even logical, thread. I merely followed my political reasoning and my poetic feelings."[96] Pasolini takes on the role of a "poetic" chronicler of a recent past. The voice-over in his visual poem is structural rather than occasional and expresses the author's views.[97] By selecting images that capture recent events, Pasolini, in his own unique way, disrupts things that are subsumed by the same regime of meaning and truth.[98] Once again, the question is, "Cos'è che rende scontento il poeta?" (What is it that makes the poet unhappy?). In Pasolini's words, delivered by Renato Guttuso's voice-over, the unhappiness of the poet stems from "un'infinità di problemi che esistono e nessuno è capace di risolvere: e senza la cui soluzione la pace, la pace vera, la pace del poeta, è irrealizzabile" (an infinity of problems which exist and no one is capable of solving. Without this solution, peace, true peace, the peace of the poet, is unachievable).[99] Countless insoluble problems exist: colonialism is "questa anacronistica violenza di una nazione su un'altra nazione, col suo strascico di martiri, di morti" (this anachronistic violence of a nation over another nation, with its theory of martyrs, of casualties);[100] hunger persists "per milioni e milioni di sottoproletari" (for millions and millions of sub-proletarians).[101] Racism is the sum of a multitude of problems: it is perceived as "come cancro morale dell'uomo moderno, e che, appunto come il cancro, ha infinite forme" (the moral cancer of the modern man, and, just like cancer, has infinite shapes).[102] Racism is "l'odio che nasce dal conformismo, dal culto della istruzione, dalla prepotenza della maggioranza" (hatred stemming from conformism, from the cult of institution, from the arrogance of the majority).[103] Racism is "l'odio per tutto ciò che è diverso, per tutto ciò che non rientra nella norma, e quindi turba l'ordine borghese" (hatred for everything different, for everything that does not fit the norm, and, as such, troubles the bourgeois order).[104]

La rabbia, with all its carefully studied misappropriations, renders concepts visually to expose unreality. Pasolini's narration deconstructs the categories of conformism only reinstated by the racist images in Guareschi's first part. While the director didn't see Guareschi's part before the release of the film, Pasolini's work sets his own polemical *détournement* of images against Guareschi's world of a right-wing ideology. *La rabbia* is moulded by Pasolini's moral indignation towards a conformist society. This society discriminates, orders, and subjugates all who deviate from *their* norm, while attempting to apply petit-bourgeois common sense to the growing ills of modern society.[105] Referring to Jean-Luc Godard's 1963 *Le mépris*, Pasolini states that anger might also signify "the will to break free from the patterns of classicism."[106] Perhaps Pasolini alludes to classicism as an aesthetic regime for common sense to be displayed *also* in and by cinema. An anti-classical, non-conformist application of film techniques illuminates the horror of the poet as images unfurl. Pasolini's passionate statements disrupt media tendencies. His editing, his score, and his poetic and civic commentaries disturb and problematize the way the *cinegiornali* impose news of this new prehistory onto passive spectators. His composition highlights how indignation at this postwar pretended "normalcy" moulds *La rabbia* – especially, if, as Chiesi states, *La rabbia* was a response, a sort of poetic justice, to the public attacks made against Pasolini himself in television programs,[107] particularly those that were blatantly homophobic.

The two motives for his anger, a personal attack on his declared homosexuality[108] and an attack on members of the collectivity, are channelled into a single, unified passionate intention: the production of an aesthetic act that uses the same material against which it has been created to offer evidence of the attacker's own unreality as bourgeois and conformist. Pasolini engages spectators in a discussion about a new world that is already contaminated by television and media. Pasolini contaminates the very concrete[109] footage of newsreels to promote the active participation of spectators in unmasking the unreality of the society (as spectacle). The *essai* film promotes an active spectatorship, its full commitment to the images and the triple narratives proposed by the author – the visual, the commentary by Renato Guttuso, and the poetic text read by Giorgio Bassani. By posing his questions to the audience, the author alerts us to and unmasks an unreality that deserves a critique. He challenges the status quo of images that are already stable in the collective imaginary and repurposes them to create alternative readings and interpretations of things already present but that demand new presentations in order to be challenged. Thirty-some years later, Tiziano Scarpa's moral indignation emerges in the wake of Pasolini's declaration of mystification to which we are all complicit witnesses. In his "postmodern *impegno*,"[110] and echoing Pasolini's *Corsaro*, Scarpa's polemical reflections on the state of Italian society stand against conformism and deeply reflect on Pasolini's public "diversity" that led him to his constructive anger.

Scarpa and the *Giovani Cannibali*'s Anger

In 1996, the same year as the publication of the *Gioventú cannibale* anthology, which also inaugurated the now famous Einaudi series *Stile Libero*,[111] Einaudi released Tiziano Scarpa's first novel, *Occhi sulla graticola*. Though he did not participate in the anthology, Scarpa has often been associated with the so-called *Giovani Cannibali*, as their work epitomized the quest for experimentation and renewal with respect to the

Nuovi narratori. Original experimental forms introduced the possibility of leaving behind the literary narrative impasse of the 1970s and 1980s. Artists like Scarpa were not concerned with a presumed postmodernist emptiness and ideological confusion after the *anni di piombo* (years of lead). Italian critics (*militanti* and not) overlooked what he shared with the *Cannibali* and their denunciation of "the political unawareness of the masses who deny or repress their alienated condition."[112] Like many groups with avant-gardist ambitions, the *Giovani Cannibali* deflected conventional forms of social denunciation, and theirs is a bleak world with no escape, as Scarpa does not fail to note (BF 142–6). Their aesthetic enquiry concerned the intersection of political commitment and ideological commitment with defamiliarizing modes of expression, raising many suspicions about their iconoclastic vision in readers and critics alike. In fact, some saw their works as relying on an unnecessary expansion of *cattivismo*,[113] through an intentional display of gory details and sexual situations. Nevertheless, their texts share the collective lament of a new generation about the lack of political and ideological values distinct to previous narrative groups, alerting us to the fact that everyone, writer and reader alike, lived their everyday existence inside Debord's integrated spectacle.[114] With Pier Vittorio Tondelli and Nanni Balestrini as their mentors,[115] the *Cannibali* writers challenged both an arcane literary mannerism and a postmodernist rarefaction of meaning and produced a vigilant manifestation of a generational awareness of collective alienation fuelled by consumerism and merchandise.

Ever since *Occhi sulla graticola*,[116] Scarpa's subject matter has derived from his observation of the everyday lives of Italians. Commentaries about a quotidian conflation of banal actions and conversations contrast sharply with earlier avant-gardist utopias based on the power of art as transformative of society.[117] Scarpa is keenly aware that, even if socio-political aims and aspirations are funnelled into an aesthetic conduit, they alone cannot mend society's ills. Leaving behind any binary oppositions, the system dislocates elements of power and disseminates observations about the value of everyday actions performed by members of the artist's community. Scarpa expounds on a notion of the figurative that partly developed after, or is concurrent with, the 1990s American literary phenomenon of hyperrealism. A term central to Hal Foster's *The Return of the Real*, "hyperrealism" (or "superrealism," as Foster calls it) is concerned with a hyperbolic quest for appearances,[118] a quest that aims to conceal a repressed reality. Imaginary reality does not have to be mimetic and cannot be translated into a mere illustration of real objects and real facts. Scarpa's ruling axiom is that, as reality changes, realism must find new forms – in particular, a hyper one that implodes *below* the surface of things rather than expanding its shapes. Hal Foster states that superrealism "lays down its layers of signs and surfaces drawn from the commodity world not only against representational depth but also against the traumatic real,"[119] which returns and "disrupts the superrealist surface of signs."[120]

Scarpa's narrative practice of fiction and poetry deflects from a by-now-classic Lukácsian notion of the need for realism[121] to be an artistic *mirror image* of the social privileging content. His aesthetic practice opts, instead, for a mode that challenges readers to revisit notions of consciousness and to consider the essence of the verbal image. Adorno's famous detraction from Lukács's work does not imply the absence of ideology, just as Scarpa's ideological *rabbia* points in a different direction from Pasolini's. Scarpa and Pasolini share a concern for the conduct of their community, of Italian society. Scarpa does not hesitate to parody Pasolini's verses, but the authority of this *father* in terms of ideological legacy remains intact.[122] In Scarpa's works, the defamiliarization of the practices of everyday life and radical disorientation are organized around the illustration of societal malaise. Against the escapism and cooptation by genres that inundate the market, like the *giallo* (the investigative novel) or any form of thriller, Scarpa challenges his readers' status quo and shakes them out of their aphasia. He puts the reader to trial and task by constructing imaginary situations created by the appropriation of elements from the everyday world, working against the vestiges of a typical Italian left *impegno* tenet, the "Adornian mistrust of the culture industry."[123] Likewise, he exercises his polemical vein to expose the ills of everyday life.

A thread in all of Scarpa's works is the repeated announcement of the performativity of words. In his books, words (*le parole*) are characters themselves. Words *generate* what they name. They affirm their own role in everyone's life and also the "power of discourse to produce effects through reiteration."[124] Words explain their own role in constructing elements of the main (and human) character's quotidian life. Hyperrealism has borrowed the iconography of daily life from pop art but has problematized the predictability of images and turned their banality into compelling cultural images. In turn, words reinterpret what is considered everyday material and transform it into an original aesthetic moment. The artist creates images through words, displaying an optimistic attitude towards the referentiality of his own words, and hence a belief in the existence of the good life. Words instil in their author an ability to construct images that move towards the good life. His aesthetic act fits in with Henri Lefebvre's definition of the fictional space as the "space of speech," noting that "words are in space, yet not in space."[125] He adds, "[words] speak of space, and enclose it. A discourse on space implies a truth of space, and this must derive not from a location within space, but rather from a place imaginary and real – and hence 'surreal,' yet concrete. And yes – conceptual also."[126]

In his essay "Reconciliation under Duress," Theodor W. Adorno scrutinizes the dogmatic statements on the responsibility of art postulated by Georg Lukács during his later period. For Adorno, "under the mantle of an ostensibly radical critique of society" Lukács had "surreptitiously reintroduced the most threadbare clichés of the very conformism which social criticism had once attacked."[127] By criticizing a formalist approach to modern art, Lukács fails to recognize "the objective function of formal elements in determining the aesthetic content of modern art ... He willfully misinterprets them as arbitrary ingredients added by an over-inflated subjectivism."[128] In Adorno's view, "the procedures and techniques" that Lukács dismisses are elements necessary to "dissolve the subject-matter and reorganize it in a way which does create a perspective [that] determine[s] the aesthetic content of modern art."[129] We endanger the very essence of the work's aesthetic function if we allow content to prevail over form, or over attempts to renew aesthetic form.

> The truth of the matter is that except where art goes against its own nature and simply duplicates existence, its task vis-à-vis that which *merely exists is to be its essence and image.* This alone constitutes the aesthetic; art does not become knowledge with reference to immediate reality, i.e. by doing justice to a reality which veils its own essence and suppresses its truth in favour of a merely classificatory order. Art and reality can only converge if art crystallizes out its own formal laws, not by passively accepting objects as they come. In art knowledge is mediated through and through.[130]

The ideological fear of decadence so pervasive in Lukács's theories represents for Adorno a category that "belongs to the vocabulary of conservatism."[131] In fact, "the idea of decadence can scarcely be entertained in the absence of its positive counterpart: the image of nature in all its vigour and abundance."[132] When this counterpart is absent, "responsibility is shifted away from conditions for which men are responsible and back on to nature, or alternatively, on to a decadence which is conceived as its opposite."[133] In contrast to how Lukács employs the concept of social health as the "foundation of great art," Adorno defines "the dichotomy of healthy/sick"[134] as non-dialectical, comparing it to the dichotomous rise and fall of the bourgeoisie. These binary oppositions derive from a "bourgeois consciousness that has failed to keep pace with its own development."[135] With Adorno's tenets, we must consider the ability of art to renew its forms and shun facile mannerisms while addressing social issues. Their analysis manifests in the aesthetic act only when this act develops and materializes innovative ways to present them *within* itself – in particular, when an ethical imperative propelled by indignation sustains the aesthetic act and declares the desire to resist and react against the state of things. An aesthetic work utilizes expressive forms and language as tools to interpret reality through images. It operates choices that denounce the artist's willingness to expose nonsensical propositions and protest injustice.[136]

Eric Auerbach describes realism as "the interpretation of reality through literary representation or 'imitation.'"[137] It resides neither in the mirroring content of representations of social well-being in distinctive classes nor in the reluctance to respond to those rhetorical figures of style and discourse, those procedures and techniques that, as Adorno states, shape a work of art. Rather, realism exists in the synergy activated by the complex relationship between form and content. Adorno's comments on the "new" in poetry, as conceptualized by Charles Baudelaire,[138] underscore that the "'essence' itself in this poetry is no abstract thing in itself; it is a *social phenomenon ... the new, the products of historical progress, are what has to be conjured up in his verse.*"[139] In other words, the *sub/*versive is not merely a theme but a constitution of the actual form in which the theme resides. Art's function in the real world is found not in its subject matter but in the art itself: "art remains the antithesis of that which is the case."[140] If interpreted through Lukács's tenets, limited and crystallized categories should govern how we perceive aesthetic works.[141] Instead, realism can also afford – and create an aesthetic singularity for – the aesthetic acknowledgment of "the doubleness of everyday life."[142] For Felski, this expression signifies two "distinct constellations of issues; a mundane social world and a phenomenological relationship to that world."[143] The knowledge of the "doubleness of everyday life" implies that if we try to untangle Rancière's knot of objects, modes of experience, and forms of thought that make up aesthetics, we might declare the fate of missing out on that ever-existing possibility of *sub*version in art itself.[144]

Despite how strange the real might look, the real of realism is a "continuous tendency of the imagination"[145] we cannot do without. Postmodern culture is visual, as the "frenzy of the visible"[146] is alarmingly present. We become parts of an ongoing show in which a critical gaze is absent, as the virtual supplants the visual and further asserts its dazzling possibilities. Defamiliarization with events and the formation of a narrative with the elements we have untangled from the previous narratives constitute an essential device for the final effect of *sub*version of the real.

This process, often attempted by Scarpa, recalls Pasolini's repurposing of archival footage in *La rabbia.* To construct an aesthetic and committed counter-narrative, Scarpa presents images in a reversed and subjective order that makes explicit his take on society. We simply can't understand the threat of the spectacle of everyday life unless it confronts us in a defamiliarizing manner. We not only need to receive defamiliarized objects but also to *imagine* an image in order to construct its authentic face in a fictional account of its reality. More than offering a remedy, Scarpa contaminates and "*detourns*" what is already thinkable or "sayable" within the prevailing social discourse and constructs new meaning. Literary discourse can reveal, through grotesque or deformed realism, the anachronisms, the ridicule, and the carnivalesque components of contemporary Italian society's modes of communication.

Ideally, we could find solace in our conviction that great narratives and canonical texts still provide answers. For artists like Pasolini and Morante, the idea of *denuncia* was tied to the presence of the execrated *Power.* In their times, it was relatively uncomplicated for an idealistic intellectual to conceive of a clear distinction between the role of the artist and that of the corrupted world of politics. Power today is displayed liquidly in the technological, be it television as in the case of Aldo Nove's characters, or the images received through our smartphones. Power lies in every cybernetic machine through its potential to transform us into such images. If my body is a machine, I am still capable of connecting it to my brain. We are under constant threat of enslavement to technology because of our temporary loss of sensations (technology turns us into machines), and this is perhaps why Scarpa rebels against this notion by firmly placing his own body at the centre of his (already corporeal) writing:

> La mia testa è una lampadina opaca. Sembra spenta, ma se chiudo gli occhi posso immaginare la luce ... La mia testa è una boccia di vetro, il mondo ci nuota dentro facendo vibrare le sue pinne iridescenti ... La mia testa è una conchiglia. Se accosto le orecchie alla mia testa, si sente il rumore del mare. Assomiglia a una calma risacca, un ritmico sfiato, un ruggito afono, un respiro.[147]

> (My head is a dull light bulb. It seems off, but if I close my eyes I can imagine the light ... My head is a glass bowl, the world swims in it vibrating its iridescent fins ... My head is a shell. If I put my ears to my head, I can hear the sound of the sea. It resembles a calm undertow, a rhythmic vent, an aphonous roar, a breath.)

Tactile experience, Scarpa seems to tell his readers, reminds us that our body is the epicentre of all our emotions. The advent of the virtual pushes the defamiliarization of daily events even further. In some of Scarpa's works, they return as syncopated *sub*verses. There exists the need to find a remedy, or what Morante simply called "*altro*" (other). As the fiasco of Pasolini's *La rabbia* illustrates, even an informed and sensitive readership needs time to absorb and figure out the significance of even the most engaging authorial intentions. In this, we might keep in mind, once again, Adorno's idea that, "by articulating the otherwise ineffable contradictions of society, figuration takes on the features of a praxis which is the opposite of escapism, transforming art into a mode of behaviour. Art is a type of praxis and there is no need to make apologies for its failure to act directly ... If art works have any social influence at all, it is not by haranguing, but by changing consciousness in ways that are ever so difficult to pin down."[148] The act of rearranging real events within a narrative, however, always implies an ethical selection of the signs and images that we need to relate in order to provide a frame for said contradictions. Rancière's knot cannot be tied without the ethical selection that the artist decides to use for his art.

2

An Apocalyptic Kamikaze: Tiziano Scarpa or How to Invade the Reader

Italia, paese di figure e batticuori, dov'è il poeta della tua legge?[1]

– Tiziano Scarpa

In an article entitled "Se lo scrittore morde," Roberto Saviano offered a passionate defence of the literary word. Bringing into the discussion Mayakovsky's phrase "literature is an athlete," Saviano goes on to write that "the specific weight of the literary word is determined by the presence of writing in the flesh of the world, or of the absence of flesh, instead, for some."[2] While Saviano wields a metaphor to prove his point about writing and literature, it is the corporeality of the body in Scarpa's writing that gives body to his words. Scarpa's *impegno* shines through his awareness of how the material element that makes up the word is directly related to the author's own flesh. The kamikaze's clinching fight with his own culture explores his relationship and possible kinship with the members of his community. What represents the "sameness" that he finds among other members of the Italian community? And what are the events that bind him to the rest of the community? Is our collective memory only one and the same with public memory? Who holds the power of memory? Can the capacity to take another's perspective be strong enough to take such role in the construction of the aesthetic work? Many answers to these interrogatives can be read in Scarpa's *Batticuore fuorilegge*, a text that defies generic borders in which he thoughtfully combines his poetic compositions with pages of literary criticism. His reflections on the power of poetry and the ethics of aesthetics are thoughtfully interspersed with his own poems as a way to demonstrate what sustained his production at the time. The chain of meanings in the essayistic montage *Batticuore fuorilegge* results in a dazzling display of reflections on the power of writing and the word and revisits the authorial conceptualization that led to *Kamikaze d'Occidente* while publishing a poem-rap with the same title (BF, 50–3; 85–7). This text combines short essays in a single composition – each aptly titled to avoid confusion – as in film editing, and locates its philosophical preamble in the collection of essays *Cos'è questo fracasso? Alfabeto e intemperanze* (What Is This Mess? Alphabet and Intemperances).[3] *Batticuore fuorilegge* lends further coherence to *Cos'è questo fracasso?* and helps us better understand Scarpa's more conventional works of fiction. These two theoretical works problematize how words narrate and how the author narrates with words. Scarpa could not be more explicit in "Due o tre cose che voglio riuscire a fare con i libri che scriverò" (CQF, 89–99; Two or three things I want to accomplish with the books I will write). *Batticuore e fuorilegge* speaks of an author emphatically reflecting on discursive and bodily practices that connect him to the literary work, and on his right to act in such spaces on behalf of his community, problematizing the ways in which we consume stories today, as we see in "Fiction geneticamente modificata (FGM)" (BF 218–24; genetically modified fiction).

Scarpa's critique of Pasolinian appropriations in the films *Io non ho paura* and *Respiro* reveals, for instance, both his deep appreciation of Pasolini's legacy and the ways in which he perceives his legacy to be misunderstood. He stresses the deceitful and uncommitted use of Pasolini's "autenticità italica premoderna" (BF 102; pre-modern italic authenticity) and offers an apt example of such deceitfulness in cinematic contexts. Drawing on Gabriele Salvatores's and Emanuele Crialese's movies he observes how, for temporal and historical reasons, their exercise in the retrieving of themes dear to Pasolini cannot translate into an active commitment to today's society because too many elements are missing from such unproblematic intertextual references:

> Da questi mondi di contadini e pescatori, da questi bambini del Sud, dalla loro spontaneità, sono del tutto esclusi gli spettatori urbanizzati, adulti, autoriflessivi, velleitariamente illuministi. Non c'è meraviglia e senso della vita, non c'è pratica del bene e del male se non a queste condizioni: un'Italia ancora neo-realista, pretelevisiva, in piccole comunità rurali o costiere, in una condizione di spirito ancora infantile, dove non si è separato il concetto di dovere da quello della pulsione irriflessa. (BF 103)

> (Urbanized, adult, self-reflexive, idealistic illuminati are completely excluded from these worlds of peasants and fishermen, from these children of the South, from their spontaneity. There is no wonder and sense of life, there is no practice of good and evil if not under these conditions: a still neo-realist, pre-television Italy, in small rural or coastal communities, in a state of a still childish spirit, where the concept of duty has not been divorced from that of an irrational drive.)

What Scarpa seems to fear here is the danger of crystallizing Pasolini's powerful aesthetic voice into nostalgic depictions of worlds that have not been subject to "una mediazione intellettuale" (BF 103; an intellectual mediation). The presence of pop culture in both movies (comic strips, music, television) reinstates the "allenza fortissima" (BF 105; very strong allegiance) between "innocenza and mass media" (BF 105; innocence and mass media) that Pasolini denounced. Drawing on facile and momentary emotions in the process of identification with the characters, spectators relinquish any eventual quest for an abstract ideal of justice. Against the very premise of a committed cinema in the wake of Pasolini, the works do not promote any form of reaction that should solicit an adequate response.

In *Batticuore fuorilegge*, Scarpa also launches his attack against the manipulative and coercive power of literary genres and elaborates on what prevents him, for instance, from appreciating the genetic code of the Italian psychological thriller, a recurring target of his body of work.[4] In what follows, I discuss the allegations of solipsism often levelled at Scarpa by drawing on the writings of *Batticuore fuorilegge*. I argue that even his more "conventional" works, like his novels, illustrate his theories about the power of words to combat the tyranny of literary genres as symbolic of detrimental conformism.[5] In essence, Scarpa rails against the mass culture clichés established by the left's hegemony; further, he also rails against the "generalized intellectualism" of the last forty years.[6] Scarpa's narrator successfully sells today's Italian spectacle to the Chinese republic, to the "grande popolo del Drago" (the great people of the dragon),[7] in *Kamikaze d'Occidente* precisely because elements composing the spectacle are at once familiar (by now they belong to the world of the internet) and intrinsic to what outsiders think of as the Italian community. But the material he needed to represent Italy and its inhabitants is constituted by a heap of experiential occurrences that find their space in a plot devoid of a conventional linear trajectory. Occurrences in the life of a writer define the content of the book: three months of incursions into the artist's own life along with other episodes in which the protagonist has the precise yet ephemeral task of producing a diary for the Chinese government, to be published as the testimony of a Western author to the degeneracy of the culture and lifestyle of the West. And the protagonist writes, knowing that he is an archetype of decay, abjection, and capitalist perversion, while trying to find a spark of passion to save Western ideals. This task is set at a precise moment of history, in the wake of the attack on the Twin Towers. In turn, personal memories and bodily experiences compose the thematic categories by which the artist systematizes a fictional account of an artist's true life and of public events occurring during a very specific time, the year 2001. In other words, the artist's imagination repurposes dialogues, encounters, and events in a transgressive and provocative collage of words and images. To project the assemblage of records and material for such a vast project, the artist must rely on his memory and ability to record data, dates, and events belonging to the real world that he will shuffle in his mediated re-composition of Italian contemporary life. But how can a writer present his community and his country if he does not even keep accurate records of events in his life? Can he really say "I know" (Io so) with the same firmness as did Pasolini in his famous *j'accuse*?

> Io non ricordo quasi niente di quello che faccio. Quando penso al mio passato, non so bene cosa dire. Le cose mi vengono in mente per categorie, per somiglianze, non per sequenze temporali. Le connessioni del mio cervello non sono narrative. (BF 37)
>
> (I don't quite remember much of what I do. When I think of my past, I don't quite know what to say. Things come to my mind in categories, by resemblance, not by temporal sequences. My brain's connections are not narrative.)

The connections his emotions and bodily senses make of what he experiences day by day do not afford such a thing as linear memory or linear history, he seems to tell us. The unshakeable belief in his power to remember Pasolini lies in the past. Uncertainty is not just limited to reality, but also to the imagining of it. The occasion for Scarpa's reflection on the use of memory arises from an interview by journalist Concita De Gregorio with renowned mason and *faccendiere* (fixer) Licio Gelli. Scarpa ironically states that the differences between mason Licio Gelli and himself (BF 38; le affinità e divergenze) is the former's formidable memory, which helps Gelli keep accurate, and constantly updated, diaries of his existence. In the trials centred on his fraudulent business dealings, Gelli is remarkable for the precision with which he provides evidence of his unbreakable alibi. As De Gregorio states, Gelli has recorded "84 anni di vita, attualmente archiviata in 33 faldoni al primo piano di villa Wanda" (BF 38; 84 years of life currently archived in 33 folders on the first floor of villa Wanda). Those who hold power, such as Gelli, are able to do so because they are endowed with impressive recall; but there are countless reasons why such individuals cultivate memory and the memory of events directly related to their lives. Awareness of one's own role "per la nostra piccola repubblica" (BF 39; for our little republic), in turn, has enabled Gelli to "impostare la sua vita storicamente, ovvero di fare la Storia" (BF 39; to set up his life historically, to make History, that is). This is one of the possibilities Scarpa advances for the mason's prodigious memory, one that directly links statesman Giulio Andreotti with Licio Gelli.[8] In between these two problematic figures in contemporary Italian history lies the writer with his presumed inability to remember. He has six hypotheses, all of which are rather appropriate to the persona of the writer Scarpa creates in nearly all his texts. As hypothesis number two states,

> Io non penso che il momento presente mi tornerà utile in futuro, nemmeno in forma di ricordo. Questo deve voler dire che sono completamente disperato. Ho deposto ogni speranza che il tempo in cui mi è dato di vivere (la filza di istanti che io attraverso con il mio corpo e la mia coscienza) possa essere speso in un modo o nell'altro nel futuro. (BF 41)
>
> (I don't think that this current moment will be useful to me in the future, not even in the shape of a memory. This must mean I am completely desperate. I have relinquished every hope that the time I have been given to live (the string of instants that I traverse with my body and my conscience) can be spent in one way or another in the future.)

Apparently, keeping track of time is useless. In the *hic et nunc* of Scarpa, the allusion to Dante's verses (Scarpa's "ho deposto ogni speranza" recalls "lasciate ogni speranza o voi ch'entrate" *Inferno* III, 9) evokes the infernal city before which the artist should give up hope. He is damned, just like the society that appears to him and of which he is a member. Remembering would signify finding a tie between himself and a community about which he has contrasting feelings. In hypothesis five, Scarpa states that all he cares about is the present – that he devotes all of himself to the present moment and there is no room for anything else beyond that moment (BF 41). There is nothing before and nothing after today. The artist connects constellations of meaning that do not follow a specific chronotope. Hence, even the conventional novelistic structure no longer suffices for an artist who sees his work *through* the physicality of his body ("la filza di istanti che io attraverso con il mio corpo e con la mia coscienza" [BF 41]; the string of moments I traverse with my body and my conscience). It is the body of his words that, in turn, makes up the world of which Saviano speaks. His narratives create connections more in terms of semantic fields endowed with a non-linear sequence than in a linear trajectory of the characters' lived actions. Characters are acted upon by the minutiae of society, of everyday living. Impatience with current society fuels critical reasoning about the possibility that his writing and his performance might stretch beyond the limits of representation and representativeness.

Scarpa's writing does not depend on the easy apolitical drifts offered by deconstructionism, nor can it be reduced to an inelegant mimicry detached from reality. *Batticuore fuorilegge* exemplifies his all-encompassing vision of narrating/writing. Working against publishers' preferred genre divisions, Scarpa promotes the continued integration of art with the politics of being, of poetry with prose, of fictional with non-fictional texts. Any writable material can be fictional; anything that is writable can be autobiographical. Finally, everything can be political in that it captures and indicates the author's stand against the social imperatives that produce generic and evaluative categories. Everything is devoured cannibalistically to create "catene di significati" (BF 13; strings of meanings) towards the fulfilment of dreams – towards the realization of the *dream of a thing* (or rather, of what Marx dreamed), as in the epigraph to Pasolini's novel *Il sogno di una cosa* (The Dream of a Thing): "Our motto must therefore be: reform of consciousness not through dogmas, but by analysing *the consciousness unclear to itself*, whether present in the form of religion or politics. Then it will appear that the world has long had *the dream of a thing*."[9] Scarpa's epigraph to *Batticuore fuorilegge* is a passage from Antonio Moresco's "Piccola nota" that comments upon Pasolini's dream –the hopeful dream of the ever-extant possibility of finding in another the signs of protest marked by "un'eguale ferita e uno stesso fuoco" (BF 7; the same wound and the same fire).

One is tempted to draw a critical trajectory from Marx to Pasolini via Moresco to Scarpa by way of epigraphs. Though Genette holds that an epigraph is a "silent gesture"[10] because it does not yet state the sense of the text, an epigraph is not randomly chosen. Its selection from an extensive body of texts that are meaningful to the author illustrates and potentially explains the reasons for the text as well as pointing to its referents. Moresco's brief essay records his reflections on Gramsci's concept of the organic intellectual: "One can be non-organic ... outdated, if the 'society' in which we are immersed horrifies us."[11] One can hope that "even within the same society ... in some remote point, lives a person who has on his body 'the *same* wound and the *same* fire' that we cannot hope to achieve unless we show helplessly our wound and our dream" (BF 7; emphasis added). [12] Scarpa, *equal to and the same as* Moresco, connects to his stance by choosing these words as the epigraph to *Batticuore fuorilegge*. To dismantle any criticism of narcissism, he refers to a mirror-image of the writer projected *towards* the reader. Intellectual kinship is established through these words on the mirror-image. Moresco's "fire" and "dream" declare the incendiary power of the artist, a political act of insubordination that only the word can accomplish. Intellectual isolation for Moresco rests as a sole possibility against the exasperated organicity of hegemonic thought. In this instance, the "non-organic" artist's isolation is not a sterile and solipsistic centripetal force. He aspires to an association with others who feel his fire and share his wound. The writer might meet his goals by exposing political fictions amid the sea of "fake news."[13] Like the angry poet Pasolini, and more actively than Moresco, Scarpa reworks displays of images and literary references to solicit in his readers disgust and establish kinship with them through shared disgust. The abject lives dangerously near us. Pasolini's legacy reminds us to be relentless with the scandal of reality.[14]

Batticuore fuorilegge also presents some of the political themes at the core of *Groppi d'amore nella scuraglia* (Lumps of Love in the Darkness), Scarpa's civic poem with at its core the request/blackmail to allow the creation of a landfill in a Campanian town in exchange for the installation of a telecommunications tower.[15] This is a comic verse narrative about a small village in central-southern Italy that is about to be transformed by an enormous waste collection site. *Groppi d'amore nella scuraglia* evokes in its lines the language of the fairy tales in Giambattista Basile's *Lu cunti de li cunti* and accommodates the pyrotechnic mixture of political poetry – "Oggi la manifestanza ne la piazza" (GS 19; Today demonstration in the square) – alternating with short pieces constituting a bestiary, a collection that incorporates the village animals into the larger narrative of the community. Accomplished by a skilled articulation of themes, the *scuraglia* (darkness) of feelings agitates the narrator Scatorchio, his lover Sirocchia, and his rival Cicerchio and defines the passions of thwarted love, rivalry, and jealousy. This piece, also performed in various theatres, fully embraces Scarpa's commitment to an innovative form of storytelling[16] that brings together the decline of Italian society through its compositional elements of which the landfill is a metaphor. Scarpa refuses to pathologize his chararacters' misdeeds, but he nevertheless deploys all shades of the grotesque to expose the scandal of today's society.

In literature, single authors "pronunciano parole differenti o completamente opposte a quelle della comunità" (BF 11; pronounce different or completely opposite words from those of the community). Scarpa is aware that he is one of the many "cittadini disarmati" (BF 11; unarmed citizens),but also recognizes that literature offers him his only means for discussing the ills of society, "un'eredità inestimabile" (BF 11; a priceless inheritance). The artist knows that he possesses a powerful instrument through which he can exercise his intellectual responsibility towards himself *as a* writing individual (*scrivente*). In other words, the artist acknowledges the power of the word's potential for performativity. The name, the individual, and his corporeal matter go hand in hand with the word, for

> literature never leaves the body to itself, it never nourishes the disembodied intellect. Writers are not intellectuals, are *corpal, corpual, corporal, corpoverbal*

beings, they are *logosomatic* individuals where language and body empathize (*si patiscono*) with each other. (CQF 91; emphasis added)

The ethical tools of protest and opposition are integral to Scarpa's aesthetic arguments against the "discorsi abbandonati" (abandoned speeches) of authors who prefer pseudonyms and do not assume responsibility for what they write (BF 12). The author's name is necessary for words to perform, to hold a political weight, and to be heard (BF 12; "In actuality, no credit can be given to the words of those who are not willing to defend what they say with their full name"). This suggests that the name alone, like the solitary word, is not enough. If the citizen is to be "armed with words," he must brandish them. Body and soul must have a name: that of the author who protests with his words, for himself and for his community. For Scarpa, every artistic gesture means something within the social consortium. His quest for meaning is not narcissistic but is concerned with his own subjectivity and role within his society.[17] The intellectual Scarpa, essentially an optimist, seeks a dialogue with Moresco and others who share the same appetite for intellectual truth; he invites responses from those he believes in, lest they feel compelled to respond to accusations of narcissism (BF 20–1).

Art cannot be simply a mirror of reality because we require its fruition, not merely its contemplation. Scarpa decries the imposition of this role onto art's own significance. The distortion of this role afflicts artists as recipients: "Accusing artists of narcissism is a political move: it assumes that the unarmed individual, without power, without institutional recognition, rich only in his talent and his will power, cannot give any contribution to the community" (CQF 20). Scarpa perceives community through adjectives that indicate the other apart from the Self, but still on the authorial Self's side – in short, those who are both *equal* and the *same,* as Moresco mentions in his note: "Tu che mi leggi sai che sto parlando anche con / per te" (You who read me, you know that I'm also talking with / for you). The main points of criticism against which the author, narrator, and character of some of *Batticuore fuorilegge*'s essays vigorously rebels are as follows:

1. *The artist's possibility of identifying with* a "bestiolina da allegoria" (a beast for allegory). "What you write has to be emblematic of something else, a part for the whole, the symptom of the condition of humanity today, a mirror of the times ... Such a conception of literature could also be exciting, if not for the fact that it is confined to inertia and purely ceremonial." (BF 42)
2. *The fixity of the character of the writer.* Scarpa proposes three possible non-exclusive postures (actually interactive in their use) to take

towards words and the Thing. The first posture is (a) when the writer invents a story. He assumes a frontal position with respect to both the words and the Thing, mastering both fantasy and literary awareness. In this posture, one of the possible "duties of a writer ... is to produce a Thing, to project it, not to receive its projection and to enjoy it" (BF 45).The second posture is (b) when the writer turns his *shoulders to the words* and projects the Thing before the Self through the story of others, not told to him, but which, nevertheless, catches the writer's ear and imagination. In turn, the artist's ear imagines "also things not necessarily part of what is said" (BF 46). Finally, with regard to the third posture, (c) standing with his back to the Thing implies that the writer does not see the Thing, but produces "words that take the Thing into account and constantly refer to it" (BF 46). The writing of the diary, a genre that uses all three possible postures, but in particular the third, places the author in front of the word without seeing the Thing. In this third instance, the word is comparable to "*una bomba nucleare fatta in casa*" (BF 42; a homemade nuclear bomb; emphasis in the original).

Scarpa implies that it is essential for the writer to accept the idea that what is narrated can never exhaust the subject of the narration (the Thing): the author must be democratic, leaving part of the task to the readers, while challenging their commitment and testing their ability to complete the meaning and construct their image of the verbal act. Of all the postures he describes and uses, Scarpa's author privileges the second for two important reasons. The invention of the story is not up to him, as it is in the first posture. The pressure of having to align his own experience with his own words does not exist as it does in the diary or the third posture. By assuming this posture, the writer can flee from the dreaded threat or possible flaws related to the *vraisemblable.* By acknowledging in his own words the arbitrariness that is symptomatic of any individual choice, Scarpa's author finds refuge in the factuality of a Thing narrated by others. The boundary of authorial narcissism lies in the author's ability to hear the Thing as narrated also by others.

While authorial narcissism takes the author's word as an exclusive tool to govern meaning, the narration of a Thing is a collaborative project. With the neologism of *narrification,* Scarpa indicates the process by which writers "reduce everything to a narrative ... and do not let into their work anything that is not convertible into a story" (BF 225–6). *Representation,* in Scarpa's understanding, cannot illustrate the scope of writing. Writers are not a "beast for allegory" (*bestiolina da allegoria*).[18] "Writing is always a devastating event, whether it is written for no one or for a billion and a half people who have to decide, depending on your pages, if it is worth destroying or saving you" (BF 53). Because writing is "devastating," writing "goes beyond" (*travalica*) the person of the writer, "but at the same time it comprises and engages him" (BF 53).

3. *The aestheticization of culture.* "A progressive aestheticization has weakened literature. The worst enemy of the art of the word is aestheticization." The "officials of aestheticization ... are the caretakers of literature. They monitor literature as a *morte-vivante* (*sepolta viva*) in the cemetery of aestheticization, from which [it] is forbidden to leave" (BF 43). It is apparent by now that Scarpa – along with Rancière – shows contempt for those who crystallize culture and understands aesthetics as a means to sense and form experience rather than encase words in a history of literature (BF 43).

Scarpa's points constitute a personal manifesto against a cohort of cultural mediators (critics, academics, etc.) whose sole task is that of belittling the writer's skills and for whom "the writer doesn't know what he is writing" (BF 43; "lo scrittore non sa quello che scrive"). For Scarpa, writers "do not represent at all a majority, or a minority, but infinitely more and infinitely less: they represent the single individual who has nothing else to express and to offer the community but his/her point of view, or rather, his/her point of word" (BF 65). The authorial task of projecting and experiencing sense through the word indicates how Scarpa assigns to the word the active task of producing the message. This message establishes in the writing subject, an individual producer of the meaning ascribed to the word, the conduit between the self as word and the agent who confirms the sense of the word. It is the writer who authorizes the sense of the word by, as Roberto Saviano writes, *invading* the reader.

In Scarpa's world, everyone lives a paradoxically spectacular everyday existence. We are all on stage, whether through the vicarious experience of reality TV shows, or through the fragmentary narratives we post on Facebook from our cell phones. We all perform. Debord, a contemporary of Pasolini, explained the essence of the modern spectacle.[19] Twenty years after *The Society of Spectacle*, the theorist still defended his previous stance in *Comments on the Society of the Spectacle*, insisting on the transformation of people enveloped by the sovereign tentacles of spectacularized society. The society was a product of "the autocratic reign of the market economy which had acceded to an irresponsible sovereignty and the totality of new techniques of government which accompanied this reign."[20] Sovereignty, itself a political term, is, as Butler states, "a tactic that produces its own effectivity as its aim: becomes the instrument of power by which the law is used tactically or suspended."[21] Unlike governmentality, sovereignty is then its own instrument and effect. If viewed through Butler's reading of Foucault, the sovereignty of the market economy relies (like its autocratic reign, Debord's "sovereign tentacles of spectacularized society") on an effective network established through the sagacious use and manipulation of media. Media are never irresponsible. The bond between the market economy and spectacle is strengthened by the diversification of the media's extravagances, which contribute to, and are responsible for, the expansion of the spectacle's claims, once the spectacle has clearly succeeded in "raising a whole generation moulded to its laws."[22] Scarpa exposes the claim for sovereignty of current forms of political power that abuse the word.

According to Guy Debord, there are three forms of spectacularization; the *concentrated* one, played around one "dictatorial person"; the *diffused* one, representing the highly seductive Americanization of the world; and, finally, the *integrated spectacle*, a combination of the first two.[23] The integrated spectacle is by far the most dangerous as "it has integrated itself into reality to the same extent as it was describing it, and ... was reconstructing it as it was describing it."[24] Its corollary is that "reality no longer confronts the integrated spectacle as something alien ... the spectacle has spread itself to the point where it now permeates all reality."[25] One of its accomplishments has been the "globalization of the false," which Debord equates to "the falsification of the globe."[26] Debord claims that pollution of, and by, images, made possible by the reproducibility of objects, even art works – this last a clear legacy of Walter Benjamin's work[27] – prevails everywhere. He aligns five features of the integrated spectacle, namely, "incessant technological renewal; integration of state and economy; generalized secrecy; unanswerable lies; an eternal present."[28]

Scarpa understands how easily reality can be manipulated when everything pertains to the present, especially when reality is projected by media. He offers many hypotheses on why he cannot remember as much as fixer Gelli does. He writes, "I do not pay attention to the present moment" (BF 41; "Io non presto attenzione al momento presente") as "it leaves no trace" (BF 41: "Non lascia traccia"). But a past cannot exist either, for it belongs to individuals like Licio Gelli or Giulio Andreotti, who have made a point of *recomposing* memories as much as they could to become members of history. Temporal space is framed by the characters' own experience, not necessarily in a linear order, because, just like their author, they remember things according to categories and similarities, not temporal sequences. Today is today, and it's a fact, Hume would say. But we cannot be sure tomorrow will come. In hypothesis five, however, Scarpa does say that "I devote all my attention to the present" (BF 41;

"Io presto tutta la mia attenzione al presente"). Literature (to a lesser extent), television, and the internet now are our visual and narrative markers for something we don't know and don't belong to: they define our visual and narrative archives. Unlike what Shakespeare wrote, what's past is not prologue but only the past *tout court*, and it can never return because, unlike figures such as Gelli and Andreotti, we now are painfully aware that we have no role in history. We are not the "redeemed humanity" Walter Benjamin refers to in his third thesis on history. It is "only a redeemed humanity [which] receives the fullness of its past,"[29] and their redemption vouches for their quoting of the past or their owning the legacy of the past, because this humanity finds features resembling the present in it. Eradicating historical knowledge in its spectators is a priority for the integrated spectacle. Like past events, current ones, as Debord suggests, "retreat into a remote and fabulous realm of unverifiable stories, uncheckable statistics, unlikely explanations and untenable reasoning. For every imbecility presented by the spectacle, there are only the media's professionals to give an answer."[30] Indeed, Debord postulated the lack of a past in the integrated spectacle:

> The manufacture of the present where fashion itself, from clothes to music, has come to a halt, which wants to forget the past and no longer seems to believe in a future, is achieved by the ceaseless circularity of information, always returning to the *same short list of trivialities, passionately proclaimed as major discoveries.* Meanwhile news of what is genuinely important, of what is actually changing, comes rarely, and then in fits and starts. It always concerns this world's apparent condemnation of its own existence, the stages in its programmed self-destruction.[31]

The acquisition of information can lead to a lack of actual knowledge and awareness. In *La rabbia*, Pasolini indicates how to defend ourselves from the rhetoric behind the society of spectacle. His poetic commentaries juxtaposed with archival images expose the continuous threat of misreading and misinformation leading to the scandal of unreality. With a similar intent, Scarpa assumes the ethical duty to expose disturbing traits – at once trivial and tragic – that constitute reality and that betray the state of emergency. To this end, he operates a *détournement* of the actual object by twisting signifiers of a social reality into a realist narrative that performs a parody of those very events. The practice and even the definition of conventional realism should not be an element of concern for artists:

> We must ask anthropologists, not narrators, what is realism. Anyway, when I write, I know if I'm forcing a limit, be it "realistic" or not. In *Kamikaze*

> *d'Occidente*, I worked using my diary, my three-month detailed account diary, as bulk material. Then I retold and rewrote everything. *Kamikaze d'Occidente* is the result of rewriting a portion of the "real." That is my actual book in quotes, and then the fiction, in a sense. As in the other books, which seem less realistic, they are a projection of invention. The lack of decidability between reality and invention of *Kamikaze d'Occidente*, in a sense, makes it even more fictional.[32]

Distortion, or *sub*version of reality, is purposeful, since reality as we knew it has departed from what we thought it to be. If the reality in which we live has lost its compass, narration should produce the effect of *dis*orienting the reader when the author posits values different from those conventionally established by images.[33] Scarpa shares with Pasolini the aggressive element, both in verbal and corporeal terms, of the pirate/kamikaze who tries, after *dis*orienting the readers/spectators, to *re*orient them, pointing them in a new direction, since a novel or a poem is not an extension of reality but reality *per se*. Pasolini's pirate writer (*il poeta corsaro*) would struggle against what Sloterdijk calls, in an unfortunate pejorative use of the term, the "feminization of criticism."[34] Scarpa's kamikaze writer knows that "citizens need to be armed with words" (BF 11) to face the threat of the present as the media present it.[35] Again, words *perform*. Scarpa's images of the body and its materiality through sex and bodily fluids, especially sperm as a conduit of life and possible regeneration, confirm somehow Paul Virilio's comment on Debord's theory concerning his omission of sexuality and violence in the fictional staging of life.[36] Through his use of corporeal evidence, Scarpa reifies the artist's ideological disgust with current times that often informs his narratives of contemporary Italy. Scarpa is not so naïve as to consider living outside the society of the spectacle. His participation is indispensable because he would otherwise be unable to perform his gesture of dissidence. This society demands integration into the spectacle. If everything is spectacle and the artist understands the necessity of belonging to what is horrifying, the artist can decide what rules manage identity in the verbal or writing act. Once entrenched in this society, the artist cultivates the full knowledge and understanding of how his or her own acts can be contaminated by "pseudo-intellectual manure" (BF 65). Its power is pervasive, rampant, and falsely condescending. When Scarpa reflects on his artistic acts[37] he underscores how writers are "subjects dispossessed of the action who, nevertheless, are moving strictly within the space of the reaction" (BF 66). But if the writer is granted "lo spazio della reazione" (the space of reaction) while the power possesses the action, we might think that the writer is not free to represent himself, having been "absorbed by the political economy of discourse" (BF 67). Writers intended as intellectuals work alongside the *finzionari* intended as hacks. *Finzionari* might as well be a neologism for those "lavoratori della conoscenza," reminiscent of Pasolini's "clerks of culture," in contrast to the notion of the intellectual. Romano Luperini spells out the contemporary collapse of intellectual independence from political apparata:

> The knowledge-power (*sapere-potere*) of intellectuals dissolves and crumbles within these machineries, with the effect of having these apparata decide or largely affect their fundamental choices. Embedded in these great systems of knowledge-power that respond to a few integrated national and multinational command centres, they have no control over them. They are reduced to simple knowledge workers (*lavoratori della conoscenza*), forced to deal with perpetual instability, flexibility and therefore to develop a high conversion capacity.[38]

The word's expressive possibility resides in the alienating space that denounces an intellectual ineffectiveness against the mediation of aggressive technological apparatuses. Just like numbers, words can be knowingly misread.

Scarpa considers the polls an ideal reading key for a political dictatorship that exists in harmony with the media it owns. The political vote is an instance of misreading and "one of the practices of false line-up" (*schieramento*) (BF 67). Reality can never be narrated in the conventional sense. For Scarpa, in this impossibility lies the danger of putting oneself on the same level as the *narrificatori* and the *finzionari.* Unlike writers who are "erogatori di finzione" (BF 67; fiction providers) the *finzionari* are the "enslavers ... of political fiction and fiction as proposed by the media, the 'fiction makers' of ideology firmly in place today" (BF 67). They are not afflicted by the same anxiety as Scarpa's kamikaze. *Narrificators narrificate* at will, relying on pseudo-literary expressions that resemble non-mediated forms of spoken Italian and TV-show jargon, while mediation is entrusted to the *finzionari.* The unreality abhorred by Morante and Pasolini governs a society marked by the machinations of power that transform reality into fiction, and fiction into reality. This self-referential society logically loves self-description (BF 69). In fact, the intellectual reaction that a falsely democratic power foresees is reduced to a guided manoeuvre. Power determines how this reaction is articulated through plans, themes, and spaces. It is a complete farce: "We fiction authors hold the power of dethroned monarchies, decapitated by the mass media" (BF 75). Power organizes "a wonderful and smart operation of disempowerment giving to the individual a space among many, on the same level as other representative opinions, pretending that it is on their same level" (BF 67). Thus, "the individual and his speech are no longer the space of a break with the absolute, there is no more danger, you let them talk, you do not risk anything. The power does not risk anything!" (BF 67). Such allegations against the supposed tyranny of narrative mimesis, like those against the forced *narrification* of contemporary society, confirm an ideological position that is at times Adornian. The author seems caught in the constant, active pursuit of "articulating the otherwise ineffable contradictions of society" and "transforming art into a mode of behavior."[39] Scarpa's subject argues against the weakening of the individual's own word whereby literature, confined to a social enclosure in which it is purely aesthetic, is reduced to an "opera d'arte che va valutata nel suo valore puramente artistico" (BF 203; work of art that is evaluated only for its artistic merits).

What rules today is an unsophisticated mode of speaking in which literary criticism is a superficial value judgment. Scarpa's intolerance constitutes a manifesto of sorts against dogmatic cultural mediation and the inertial weight of the aestheticization of literature, as a result of critics' seeming unwillingness to engage in a constructive dialogue with writers. "La scena della replica" (BF 195–204; The Scene of the Reply) is a Socratic dialogue between an Author and a Critic. The former articulates questions that await his Critic friend's response.[40] His concept of culture appears hardly in tune with that produced by the liquid society; the culture of non-commitment and oblivion that has replaced that of learning and accumulation cannot suit Scarpa's tenets regarding the political contribution of literature to the community.[41] There is also doubt that Scarpa's reflections claim the attention of his "enemy." Scarpa's individual is an artist who represents himself and the other in an act of solidarity and intolerance towards "the show." Kurt Schwitters's technique of *Schmutzbau*, perhaps claimed by Giuseppe Antonelli when he discusses the use of "*cose* nel senso materiale della parola" (*things* in the material sense of the word), becomes the awareness of having to do with trivial goods, abject in origin, that have now become part of the artist's possible aesthetic world. As Giuseppe Antonelli relates, the difference

> between these items and those obsolete is due to the changing of the context: consumerist fetishism radically changes the nature of material things, and thus their valence. If, for the modern world, the hypothesis was that for which "the *literature* of the societies in which the capitalist mode of production prevails presents itself as an immense accumulation of *anti-goods*," here we face the fulfilment of the "ideological destiny of things after the mid-Seventies, which was to evaporate in signs; signs all the more pure, that

> signify an ever more absent meaning, as the things of writing themselves are all the more de-functionalizing." The list becomes a catalogue, things become trademarks (different x ©, yÆ, z™ marking the decline from *logos* to the *logo*) making possible a provocation such as Tiziano Scarpa's, who titled his collection of short stories *Amore®*.[42]

An act of indignation triggers the repurposing of goods into the composition of an entirely new form of fiction. Though the artist is situated within the integrated spectacle,[43] the authorial gesture exposes disagreement with the spectacle *as is* and constructs an ethical reaction using the tools of art. Wu Ming engaged Scarpa in a passionate dialectics on this subject.[44] Sterile accusations of authorial narcissism often target Scarpa, who sometimes responds with an understandable manoeuvre that nevertheless remains open to criticism. He refocuses the criticism from authorial narcissism to what he calls self-corporeal exhibitionism, an element that Alfonso Berardinelli has criticized harshly. In this intellectual and physical autobiographical take, the subject Scarpa metaphorically sewed his body to his words: "When I put the finger in my belly button, I become the tailor's thimble of myself."[45] Scarpa declares the centrality of his own navel compared not only to the "belly" but as a visual and physical tie to the community for which he speaks and writes. The representational power of a community depends on the artist's bodily thermometer. His political action is pervasive and *dilagante* (widespread, eruptive). It is simultaneously nature and culture. It presents a space that exceeds pre-deconstruction binary oppositions. His biological being, a sparkling set made up with elementary particles, works *within* the social and cultural.[46]

Exhibitionism and narcissism are integral yet not exhaustive aspects of artistic production. Scarpa belongs to the ranks of those intellectuals who, like Roberto Saviano, believe in putting flesh on display in a dromotic reflection of themselves and their community. Paul Virilio looks at disappearance as a notion that relates the vanishing of materiality to the hegemony of a virtual world. This process develops through media technologies up through the cyberworld, and bears consequences with respect to the human body. In this process, speed is inseparable from wealth, which in turn is inseparable from power, and its regime is called dromocracy: we all belong to a racing society where all times – past, present, and future – are blurred.[47] At the centre is the poet's belly button, the gravitational core of his work and writing. Scarpa refuses the dictatorship of the genres. In an explicit condemnation of the constraints imposed by the *editoria del consenso* (cultural industry organic to power, which eliminates dissent),[48] he declares that no work should be categorized in terms of genre, especially the novel, which is polyphonic by nature, "porous and cannibalistic":

> I do not have a structured vision of literary genres. Even less for authors. I am not for an authoristic [*sic*] reading of literature: I mean that you cannot unite the books into categories or genres, even when they are written by the same person. One must evaluate each single book. I think every work is autistic, does not communicate with the other, it is irreducibly singular, unique. In fact, it is no coincidence that I did such a scattered thesis, so heedless of historical sequence and the watertight compartments of individual national traditions![49]

Scarpa reiterates the impossibility of separating one's biological being – one's own *flesh* – from intellectual action. Intellectual action takes on multiple forms and determines the continuous development and production of the artistic creation. Hence, as a sexed, corporeal, thinking human being, Scarpa's intellectual kamikaze is located at the centre of a universe made up by words. The kamikaze acts within the execrated society of spectacle, a society that, unlike what Alfonso Berardinelli claims,[50] Scarpa combats from within, never caricaturing his role as an artist. If he is an exhibitionist, his goal justifies his need to exhibit his dissent in the ample space of reaction. He transgresses outdated diktats of criticism with all the weapons a writer has at his disposal – figures of speech, style, verbal irony – to build a field of tension between himself and his readers. He challenges both the complacency of and the ironic distance from a tradition that he needs to undo in order to hybridize it with his own word and his own flesh. Motivated by moral and aesthetic indignation, Scarpa reaches out to and arrives at the *equal*, the *same* of which Moresco writes. To paraphrase Butler's remarks about the character of Antigone, for Scarpa the act of the word becomes *the* challenge to the state-spectacle, the *duopoly* of television and media. Aware of the impending scenarization of existence, civic indignation prompts his comments. Scarpa recuperates the grounds on which others like him have protested *before* him because he accepts his role as one who fleshes out the indignation against torts that other members of the collectivity feel but cannot flesh out. All possible languages that pertain to power, from the aesthetic to the critical, can be used to destabilize formulas and obsolete strategies. Everything begins in the body: it is the cardinal point of the authorial experience. A corollary to this is the configuration of the comprehension of the physicality of aesthetic action, of the issue of the flesh (*carne*), of our being inside a system that functions by excess. Logo-corporeality represents the symbiosis of word and physicality; Scarpa states that "the proprium, the essence (and also the scandal) of literature are revealed in this way."[51] The ties between the word and the body compose the essence of the scandal that is produced through a fascination with what the desiring subject wants.

The author's focus on his own subjectivity and desire demonstrates an acute awareness of his existence as a thinking individual: he is endowed with logos and is never aphasic. This focus should not be interpreted as narcissism. The subject responds to society's solicitations with wide-ranging feedback, from reactions prompted by shopping at the supermarket and the northeastern Unabomber to the banality of a phone programmed with the default text message "I love you" in *Kamikaze d'Occidente.* Further, his repudiation of the imposition of literary genres exemplifies a positive interpretation of the liquidity of current society, as does his calculated adoption of Bakhtinian categories in the interrogation of the subject. Zygmunt Bauman alerts us to the fact that "the present day recasting of hybridity" is now something denoting "a virtue and a sign of distinction," rather than "a token of *déclassement.*"[52] The tool of a hybrid form of writing allows Scarpa to propose an "I" who interrogates himself through a dialogue on multiple levels and registers that denotes a fissure between the narrating subject and the narrated one. The durability of culture works in inverse proportion to the functionality of what the writings of Scarpa represent in the rejection of an omnivorous culture and its own exaltation. This simultaneous possibility results only when everything is cannibalized. To hybridize does not mean to *mix* but rather to *separate,* to distinguish and discern the different parts of a whole that is still built from the artist's sensorial and sensuous machine, as "la letteratura ... è la parola di chi non possiede altro che la parola."[53] What Kenzaburō Ōe calls *junbungaku* (pure literature) conceives a space in which, for Scarpa, we can still find the word as our weapon and tool. While "(s)iamo cittadini disarmati, abbiamo soltanto la nostra forza di volontà e la nostra parola. Abbiamo la nostra letteratura" (BF 11; we are unarmed citizens, we have only our willpower and our word. We have our literature), it is natural that we respond to socially produced discomforts with what we have (left). In his earlier theoretical text *Cos'è questo fracasso,* his rebuttal to Filippo La Porta's reflections on the contemporary novel, Scarpa stresses how it is "(m)eglio conoscere *gli altri* che la Letteratura" (CQF 19; it is better to know the other rather than Literature), for the latter is "solo un luogo di tutela del discorso individuale nelle società moderne; resta importante perché le sue istituzioni storiche (soprattutto il romanzo) garantiscono al singolo uno sfiatatoio comunicativo" (CQF 19; just a place of protection of individual discourse in modern societies ... it remains relevant because its historical institutions (especially the novel) guarantee a communicative outlet to the individual).

His ongoing collaborative work with other artists and his work on the websites nazioneindiana.com and ilprimoamore.com reinforce the notion that, before being the object of phagocytizing by goods and media, it is better for an artist to exercise agency towards such a phagocytizing mechanism and enter into a dialogue with other artists. Against a process of self-expulsion from politics and the public sphere, something Bauman considers the "modern individual basic attitude ... [by which] the individual, in his alienation from the world, truly reveals himself only in the private sphere and in the intimacy of face to face encounters,"[54] Scarpa's gesture claims the opposite, registering its trademark® for a creative individuality that is sustained by kinship and a sense of collectivity based on similar interests and a similar passion for the word. Scarpa is committed to explaining himself as his work in this blood/flesh relationship with the *other* and the *equal* that Moresco writes about. It is perhaps a histrionic talent that endows Scarpa with his generosity towards the *equal* and the *other*. Or, perhaps, it might be the sense of belonging to a community where, according to Bauman, "each of us is strikingly like the others, in that they must follow the same life strategy and use shared signs – that are commonly recognizable and intelligible – to convince others that they are doing it."[55]

At times Italian critics exhibit impatience towards any text they cannot frame within their own idea of literature. They seem not to listen to writers, even those legitimized by the industry of consent as emerging from the traditional canon. Their fundamental sense of insecurity and lack of trust in their own writers' ability often lead Italian critics to praise mediocre American novels[56] and decree the inability of Italian artists to construct compelling narratives. In turn, this attitude impedes an objective analysis of literary works. Consequently, we suffer an escalating crystallization of the intellectual establishment in an unresolved duel between committed writers and unwilling critics. Without the dialectical approach Scarpa seeks, the danger of a *dis*ideologization becomes a corollary to the intellectual debate. Critics are in crisis, and the *rehabilitation* of a literary criticism that is no longer divided between academic and militant as a form that interprets art works becomes a challenging business.[57] The agent of Scarpa's writing is immersed in his society. He is aware of the ills of his community, and his form of "exhibitionism" does not operate in a vague or vacuous way, for he constantly establishes links between his work and this community.

As Judith Butler states, the importance of a character like Antigone lies in the fact that "she acts, speaks, she becomes one for whom the speech act is a fatal crime, but this fatality exceeds her life and enters the discourse of intelligibility as its own form of promising fatality, the social form of its aberrant, unprecedented future."[58] The "promising fatality" of the speech act to which Butler alludes possesses a perpetually regenerative power. The word of the writer plunges to the bottom of the liquid magma in which we live, and uncovers the *irreparable* to which Butler refers. The word's individuality is a difficult privilege to share if we consider the literary word in a conventional sense. When Scarpa suggests the diary as a literary form, he does so because he solicits a "word of literature that is radically of others": it always reminds us of the collective nature of an individual aesthetic act. Despite our single individual ambition to express our creativity, "siamo tessuti, impastati, fatti (drogati) di altri" (CQF, 22; we are woven of, mixed, made (drugged) of others). Transcribing what someone told us about Scarpa amounts to "uno straordinario strumento di conoscenza" (CQF 22; an extraordinary tool of knowledge) that puts us in direct connection with others. Giuseppe Antonelli suggests re-evaluating the strategy of criticism in order to understand the expressive moves of contemporary writers:

> The challenge is all here: trying to limit, from time to time, the features, variously labelled, underpinning the overall effect of the narrative. In this sense the notion of waste, handled with caution due to the partial easing of the rule, can still be useful. The relevance of each section, however, will be judged not by itself, in the abstract, but by framing it in what Ceserani called "representative rhetorical strategy"; in our case, more specifically: *expressive strategy*. And it is only in relation to the objective of these strategies that the relevance of certain linguistic and stylistic choices can be evaluated.[59]

3
The Fundamental Things in Life According to Scarpa

Scarpa's works, many published during the crucial years of Berlusconi's tenure, criticize and pathologize the system of values in contemporary Italy by the use of the rhetoric of disgust and by drawing on the grotesque. By depicting the subject's intellectual malaise induced by current events, Scarpa's artist draws on his emotions produced by the spectacle of his society. As he resolves to be a member neither of an indistinct crowd of moralizers nor of the mass of indifferent individuals, Scarpa assumes the responsibility for being "a factious witness of his own epoch" like Pasolini, as reiterated by Tricomi.[1] Scarpa's 2003 autofictional novel *Kamikaze d'Occidente* exposes the danger of the easy narratives that replicate, without problematizing, the ills of his time. His disgust with novelistic writing as a banal form of *narrification* – often expressed in his theoretical writings – coheres with his idea that an aesthetic work can always be socially useful.

Kamikaze d'Occidente exemplifies Scarpa's concept of writing as a hybrid narrative without a precise plot (other than the one the artist's everyday life projects) whose effect develops from the skilful alternation of autofictional passages and essayistic prose. The physical text is divided structurally and typographically between the main narrative, a diary of the character's everyday existence, and forty-eight files (*schede*). The latter complement the artist's diary, presenting further personal comments on his act of writing. The character is a relatively well-known writer who is however unable to make a living with his writing; instead he submits his body to sexual acts with female readers who consider it enticing to have wild and disorienting sex with their favorite writer. His sex business is casually finessed by his rationale of self-defence that, to produce culture, he needs some money to scrape by and live in Milan. Sex and culture go hand in hand: his sex-appeal derives from his auratic status as an artist, and his women clients romanticize his sexual performance in this way: "Le donne, penso, mi frequentano perché sono uno scrittore conosciuto.

Per lo meno, abbastanza conosciuto da provocare il desiderio di cercare il mio numero sull'elenco telefonico, ma *non* abbastanza conosciuto da *non* trovarlo" (KO 28; Women, I think, hang out with me because I am a known writer. Known enough, at least, to spark the desire to look up my number in the phone book, but *not* yet known enough to *not* find it; emphasis in the original).

After a series of entries describing his attempt to begin a novel despite a temporary writer's block, Scarpa's fictional alter ego receives a phone call from a Chinese government agent. With the writer nearing destitution, the agent (a former revolutionary Italian who has emigrated to China) convinces him to collaborate on a cultural project about "diffondere in Cina testimonianze di scrittori occidentali" (KO 35; the spreading in China of Western writers' testimonies). The Chinese agent seems to be aware of the artist's economic problems and strikes his blow by demanding an affirmative answer, asking him to write a pamphlet describing the decadence of Western civilization for members of the expanding Chinese empire. The pamphlet, with the clear aim of unmasking Western society to the Chinese people in all its "sfacelo, abiezione, putredine, male assoluto" (KO 35; decay, abjection, putrefaction, pure evil), should possess the specific fictional status of a "romanzo travestito da diario" (KO 34; novel disguised as a diary). As the agent puts it, the pamphlet should be "un faldone che raccolga tutto quello che le succede per, diciamo, due o tre mesi" (KO 35; a binder that collects everything that goes on in your life for, let's say, two or three months). The writer is specifically asked to write not only about what happens to him but also about what he writes, since "per uno scrittore, ogni parola che scrive è un fatto che gli accade" (KO 35; for a writer, every word he writes is a fact that happens to him). In short, the novel should read as a temporal confession of the writer's objectives in both his life and his art. Life, death, ideology, politics, the trade of writing, couples' relationships – everything should be cannibalized by the ironic filter of a professional writer. In this novel, then, the man's life and thought link the moments making up his day like connective tissues, hence generating a picaresque merry-go-round of disparate places and situations. Because of his understanding of Casanovism as an exasperated form of expressing the Self via hyper-sexuality and hyper-philia, but also in order to continue to be true to himself, the writer needs to sell another important part of his body, his "nobile cazzo" (KO 7; noble phallus) for a living:

> Che epoca sto vivendo, io, con il mio nobile cazzo in affidamento alle moine di una lavoratrice del terziario avanzato che prima di andare in ufficio passa a casa mia a rimodellare il suo sorriso inserendovi la mia cappella? Esistono

> nicchie temporali che non sono contemporanee alla propria epoca? Sacche di tempo fossile che si perpetuano a dispetto del calendario? Pieghe in ritardo sui giornali? (KO 173)
>
> (What time am I living, I, with my noble cock in the care of an employee's simpering who before going to the office comes by my house to reshape her smile by inserting my glans? Are there temporal niches that are not contemporary to their own time? Pockets of fossil time that are perpetuated in spite of the calendar? Folds late in the papers?)

From the first page, the writer's penis, this other "instrument" of his creative art besides his brain, is defined as "noble." A pen is often used to metaphorize a penis, but the abundant recurrence of this anatomical element of the writer's body defines a grotesque body that naturally overflows the boundaries of normality. Writing shows its unpredictability – it quite literally lets itself "go" in constructions of paradoxes. As a metaphor for the authorial quill, the artist's penis affirms the presence of the writer in the world as non-representative but equivalent to himself, in which, as in Giacomo Casanova's *Histoire de ma vie,* it is all right to fool fools and fair to help the stupid. The agent finds in the writer not only a symptomatic exponent of Western society but also a member of his society who is only too eager to tell of its physical and psychological complications. Indignation marks the writer's act and turns him into a militant, engaged chronicler whose wit outshines the agent's. To face progress as an impending catastrophe, the writer rigorously applies himself to his job and explains his method:

> Questa mattina lavoro sodo al mio nuovo libro. Imposto la divisione in riflessioni e narrazione. Scelgo una scrittura trasparente, senza giochi di parole. Inserisco testi di servizio, divagazioni e note esplicative in paragrafi separati, che chiamo provvisoriamente "schede." I lettori cinesi potranno saltare le schede senza subire danni alla continuità della narrazione. (KO 43)
>
> (This morning, I am working hard on my new book. I am laying out the division into reflections and narration. I am choosing a transparent writing, without any puns. I enter work texts, digressions and explicatory notes in separate paragraphs, that I provisionally call "files." Chinese readers can skip the files without damaging the flow of the narrative.)

The various files (*schede*) that accompany the main narration of the daily existence of the writer define the various concepts scattered throughout the writer's diary. Of course, Scarpa's humour and playfulness deconstruct the precision behind the division of the text into a narrative and *schede* (files). Days, originally counted with ordinal numbers, and *schede,* originally counted according to cardinal numbers, cease to be counted (for inscrutable reasons) at page 272 and page 276, respectively. The ability to skip the *schede* is also questionable because they are essential to the significance of the main narration. Without the *schede,* readers could not understand the full meaning of the diary; without the diary, we could not justify the presence of the *schede.* The writer is an indignant prostitute endowed with great culture that may emerge at any time, but his presumed working method does not afford any clarity to either his *schede* or his diary. In a complex knot of recounted events and facts, the diary reflects on the international and domestic events that marked the year 2001. The writer prods us to distil meaning from his skilful act of contamination. He wants us alert and vigilant to his actions.

Although physically separated by the font and by the actual space on the page, the two narrative paths composing the body of the book are however non-divorceable in the understanding of the mechanisms by which the writer interacts with his community. The interaction/cross-cutting of narrative and *schede* embodies Scarpa's constant attempt to produce an interdependent body of texts that, as he maintains in his writings in *Batticuore fuorilegge,* tends to abolish a normative idea of literary genres. But his form of indignation lacks hope for actual change as stated by Hessel,[2] and, despite the comic tones of his narrative, his work manifests a sense of grieving for the current state of affairs. Events span from the horrific domestic crime of Erika De Nardo and Mauro "Omar" Fàvaro against Erika's mother and brother[3] to the G8 summit in Genoa and the attack on the Twin Towers. Events constitute the only temporal marker ("le nicchie temporali") that makes it clear he is writing in 2001.

To make a display of his dialectical fireworks built on polemical digressions and dense reflections, Scarpa's narrator needs an addressee, which he finds in the cultural agent of the Chinese government, who turns out to be a former extremist of the Italian left. To control his narrative of desire and to afford quality to his *verbigerazione* (a sort of frantic verbal production), he requires a distinct figure, the agent, to be its repository and custodian of the wreck provoked by the left in Italy. It is to him that he explains his philosophical system while arguing about current events and creating verbal images that feed into the physical and psychological fluids of the artist. The plot, usually a crucial element in a novel, has little or no importance in *Kamikaze d'Occidente*: it is not the sequence of the events that *matters,* for there the way we live defies any linear progression. Any narrative arrangement would not suffice to describe current phenomena. A plot would be of no consequence in the representation of the decline of Western society, not even if it were to come supported by a form of mimetic realism (which Scarpa cannot use, for all the reasons explained earlier). The artist seems to state that novels in our times can hardly be plot-driven or character-driven entities. Corporeality and vitality are as metaphorical as they are literal; they release a creative energy understood as an enjoyable, useful, and spendable energy that is dispensed open-handedly. They compose the real thread behind the text. Unlike Martha Nussbaum's assertion that disgust is inherently immoral because "we connect our vulnerability to decay and to becoming waste products ourselves,"[4] Scarpa's narrative accounts for what Sianne Ngai claims to be "the moralization of the language of indignation."[5] Thus, in Scarpa's use of the grotesque, anger and indignation take on a physical connotation, a rather fitting way to exhibit repulsion as well as enjoyment for what life can still provide. Disgust looks at who is inside the community trying to prevail over the values of that community. Scarpa's subversive verses declare his contempt for prevarication.[6]

In his first conversation with the Italian agent from the Chinese government, the writer protests angrily against the lack of interest in writers in Italy:

> Perché qui, invece, tutti vogliono diventare scrittori, ma nessuno vuole leggere un libro sulla vita degli scrittori! C'è un interesse crescente, diciamo pure un'invidia notevole per il mestiere di scrittore, ma non vuol dire che ci sia altrettanta curiosità per il suo modo di vivere! Ci considerano minuscoli, irrilevanti, microscopici, superflui, parassitici ... il contrario esatto dell'avventura, il contrario esatto della vita! (KO 37)

> (Because here, instead, everyone wants to be a writer, but nobody wants to read a book on the lives of the writers! There is a growing interest in, let's say great envy for, the writer's craft, but it does not mean that there is just as much curiosity about her way of life! We are considered tiny, insignificant, microscopic, unnecessary, parasitic ... the exact opposite of adventure, the exact opposite of life!)

But if the cultural agent demands effort from writers, rather than requiring the figuration of Western decadence from any Italian citizen, his specific request is driven by his knowledge of their weakness and narcissism, because in writers, "quando si tratta di narrare di sé scatta qualcosa di indefinibile. Una confidenza con i fatti, un'empatia fra visione e linguaggio, una magia ..." (KO 36; something clicks when one narrates about the self. Confidence with facts, empathy between vision and language, a magic ...). For the writer, this request represents a unique opportunity to establish a concrete interaction with the reader, requiring what in *Batticuore fuorilegge* he describes as "un atto linguistico vero, culturalmente politico, non artificiosamente evocato dai medium funebri dell'estetizzazione letteraria" (BF 51; a true linguistic act, culturally political, not artificially evoked by the funereal mediums of literary aestheticization). Aside from offering the tempting idea of getting paid, the project of the pamphlet provides an opportunity for the writer to lay out an ethical claim for his work. He abandons his initial novelistic project about the effects of rain in an urban setting and starts working for the Chinese government through his diary on contemporary Italy. Given his assessment of his epoch, he must organize a map of the *Bel Paese*'s customs designed according as much to his ideals as to his frustrated expectations. His system of values is at the forefront of describing his own society. He is only too happy to offer testimony and fiction to millions of prospective Chinese readers under the same regime of meaning. As Scarpa writes in "Come ho scritto *Kamikaze d'Occidente*" (How I wrote *Kamikaze d'Occidente*):

> Potenzialmente, il mio diario sarebbe potuto finire nelle mani di un miliardo e mezzo di lettori, che avrebbero tratto dalle mie pagine un loro giudizio sulla civiltà occidentale di oggi e avrebbero valutato, anche in seguito alla lettura del mio libro, se la nostra società (in particolare la nostra piccola repubblica) sia degna o meno di essere risparmiata. Una tale responsabilità avrebbe paralizzato chiunque. In effetti mi si potrebbe imputare proprio questo: ancora prima di leggere ciò che ho scritto, è inaudito il fatto che io lo abbia scritto, che abbia accettato la proposta. (BF 52–3)

> (Potentially, my journal would have ended up in the hands of a billion and a half readers, who would have drawn from my pages their judgment on the Western civilization of today and considered, partly due to the reading of my book, whether our society [especially our small republic] is worthy or not of being spared. Such a responsibility would paralyse anyone. In fact, I could be blamed for this: even prior to reading what I wrote, the very fact I did it, that I accepted the offer, is incredible.)

The novel becomes a collective map of the author's community that is modelled simultaneously on his kamikaze body, on his geopolitical space within his own country, and on his own society. It could not be otherwise. The uniqueness of a writer's perspective unites with the responsibility of acting politically: a political act of language is entrusted to a culturally correct (true) act of language. The writer can act as a historical agent who explains what happened in the Western world in the year 2001, defining how "politics and art, like forms of knowledge, construct 'fictions,' that is to say *material* arrangements of signs and images, relationships between what is seen and what is said, between what is done and what can be done."[7]

Scarpa's writer's project of explaining Italy to the people of China in *Kamikaze d'Occidente* exposes Italy's current rulers, who must be judged not in terms of their ability to connect their authority with an ancient contract between rulers and ruled, or with a divine bequest of power, but simply on their level of success, or failure, to achieve peace, stability, and prosperity. Scarpa's writer appears to subscribe to what Mario Perniola suggests about the Confucian man. The lack of discipline in ourselves inhibits our ability to establish a harmonious relationship with others. Perniola argues that we encounter the opposite in Italy, because "every attempt to introduce quality instead of quantity in the cultural discourse is labeled as elitist, anti-democratic or even aristocratic."[8] To enable readers to actually *see* things, the old trick of presenting facts to strangers who live far from one's own reality, culturally and geographically, like a modern Marco Polo, always works.

Establishing distance from one's own culture and reality by thinking of the people of China as potential readers produces an estrangement that permits more thoughtful reasoning. The writer can express his intentions in an aesthetic form that is simultaneously meaningful to him and to his distant readers. A narrator – Tiziano Scarpa – who is very close to the empirical author Tiziano Scarpa, voices personal opinions that are quite similar to those of the empirical author. The narrator/character finds an opportunity to present and expose the Italian integrated spectacle the author Scarpa loathes by illustrating how his contemporaneous fellow Italian citizens live, and by highlighting the bizarre path Italian society has taken. A spectacle, indeed, engages Scarpa's fictional character, who is only too aware of his own inescapable condition – a situation that seems to agree with Scarpa's theoretical statements in *Batticuore fuorilegge*. Consider Italo Calvino's idea of visibility as shifting from the word to the visual image ("imagination [is] a means to attain knowledge that is outside the individual").[9] Scarpa's writer in *Kamikaze d'Occidente* conceives images of reality and puts them into words to accomplish his task. He needs the *mise-en-scène* right before his eyes to represent it. The author is responsible for visualizing images, because "alle immagini non basta essere guardate. Le immagini, per esistere, hanno bisogno di essere immaginate. Per questo la civiltà dell'immagine non vincerà: perché punta tutto sulla visibilità, mentre la vera immagine non è quella che si vede, ma quella che si immagina" (KO 113; images cannot just be looked at. In order to exist, images must be imagined. This is why the civilization of the image will not win, because it bets everything on visibility, while the real image is not what you see but what you imagine). *Kamikaze d'Occidente* sets up the fiction of a writer's life against the force of the elements that compose reality. With his own actions, the Western kamikaze proves how the circulation of writing creates a healthy form of disorder, challenging the given distribution of the sensible. The real-life show is on television, which proves to be the best medium to highlight the vulnerability of today's society:

> In questi giorni [post-towers] tutti si raccontano la stessa cosa: dove si trovavano in quel momento, che cosa stavano facendo, *quale attimo della loro banalissima vita è stato irradiato dalla Visione. È l'epopea dello spettatore.* Accendo la televisione, guerra e porno, porno e guerra, stanotte vendono immagini di mani lubrificate che entrano fino al gomito dentro buchi del culo e aerei che entrano fino alla coda dentro uffici a quattrocento metri da terra. (KO 173; emphasis added)

> (These days [after 9/11], everybody keeps telling each other the same thing: where they were at that moment, what were they doing, which instant of their very banal life was irradiated by the Vision. It is the epic of the spectator. I turn on the television, war and porn, porn and war, tonight they're selling images of lubricated hands that enter assholes through the elbow and airplanes that enter inside offices through the tail at four hundred metres above ground.)

"The Vision" suggests a dimly holy reference to the pornography of the images of the fall of powerless individuals. Briefly distracted from our "very banal lives," we are startled by these images. The media blur tragedy and erotic pleasure for sale in a postmodern rereading of the epic *of the* spectator. Scarpa plays with the Brechtian notion of the epic spectator and invites the spectator to take a critical and intelligent role. Spectators cannot identify with fallen heroes, lest they confront death, so feelings of terror and pity and, ultimately, an emotional catharsis, are channelled through sex. Everything is really for sale, like the products mentioned by the *Cannibali* writers twenty years ago. This horde of confused individuals caught in front of their televisions in all their passivity, like the characters Sergio and Michele in Aldo Nove's "Il mondo dell'amore,"[10] make manifest their alienated existence and relative inability to *imagine images.* In this, Scarpa's kamikaze makes his role clear in constructing writing for Sergio, Michele, and all of us. He registers every possible aspect of an extant disavowal of a real civic commitment to something in which we don't believe and to its tragic effects. Rather than castigate the spectators of the Twin Towers attack, he admits his own intrinsic belonging to the society of spectators. He cannot be judgmental! Just like them, he is not in New York experiencing the deaths of 3,000 individuals on 11 September or in Genoa in July 2001 for the G8 riots and the death of Carlo Giuliani. The occupation of a building displaying graffiti depicting Carlo Giuliani's face alerts us to the fact of Berlusconi's domination of the media and generates the narrator's powerful tirade against the current order of things:

> Da pochi mesi è stato occupato un capannone alla fine di via Bramante, dopo cena andiamo a vedere se è aperto. Niente da fare, si vede che anche i centri sociali fanno chiusura settimanale. Ci limitiamo a guardare il grandissimo dipinto murale, in stile anni Settanta, riaggiornato con graffiti e faccioni in stile fumetto manga. C'è il ritratto alto quattro metri del volto di Carlo Giuliani, il ragazzo ventenne ucciso a Genova da un carabiniere ventenne. La sua faccia interrompe l'enorme scritta NO JUSTICE 😐 NO PEACE.
>
> L'uomo più ricco d'Italia si è impadronito della politica attraverso il controllo dei mezzi di comunicazione, è diventato capo del governo e tiene in ostaggio una coalizione catto-fascio-mafio-affaristico-egoista che crollerebbe senza il suo supporto propagandistico. Centinaia di migliaia di adulti pensanti, da quindici a ottant'anni, ricominciano ad affollare le strade per contestare la gestione capitalistica della vita. È iniziato davvero un decennio nuovo. Ci sarà una diminuzione della fiction, cadrà il velo della teleipnosi. Dopo la sbornia di narrativa, fantasia, rappresentazione è tornata la necessità della presenza. Basta rappresentare! È ora di presenziare. Meno metafore, meno mediazioni. Significati diretti. Sensi letterali.
>
> La menzogna dà cenni di cedimento. Negli ultimi vent'anni si sono tenuti celati i conflitti sotto una coltre di irrealtà: ma davvero credevano di poter intorpidire per sempre un'intera nazione a colpi di campionato di calcio, Ferrari, Miss Italia, telequiz, lotterie, Festival di Sanremo? (KO 158–9)
>
> (For the past few months an industrial depot at the end of Via Bramante has been a squat; after dinner we'll go see if it's open. No way, we see that even the squats observe weekly closing. We just look at the huge mural painted as in the seventies, recently modernised with graffiti and big faces in manga comic style. There is a portrait four metres high of Carlo Giuliani's face, the twenty-year-old boy killed in Genoa by a twenty-year-old policeman. His face interrupts the gigantic writing NO JUSTICE 😐 NO PEACE.
>
> The richest man in Italy has taken over the control of the police through controlling the media; he has become Prime Minister, and holds hostage

> a catho-fascist-Mafio-business-selfish coalition that would crumble without his propaganda support. Hundreds of thousands of thinking adults, age fifteen to eighty years, are beginning to crowd the streets again to contest the capitalist way of living. A new decade has indeed begun. There will be a decrease in tv-fiction, the veil of tele-hypnosis will drop. After the narrative-creativity-imagination hangover, the need for presence is back. Enough representing! It's time to attend. Fewer metaphors, fewer mediations. Direct meanings. Literal significances ... the lie gives signs of collapsing. In the last two decades, conflicts were held hidden under a blanket of unreality: but did they honestly believe a nation could be forever numbed by football championships, Ferrari, Miss Italy, game shows, lotteries, the Sanremo Festival?)

What he was hoping for remains what it is: just a hope. Like all other Italians, he too watches events on television and fits in with an increasingly technology-crazed, dehumanized world. In *scheda* number 3, the writer on holiday in Santorini describes his own behaviour in front of the television that projects images of the Genoa anti-globalization demonstrations. Fuelled by indignation, he rants about the riots in Genoa and the inability to develop appropriate strategies to use against the power of the G8: "Idioti!" (KO 20–1; Idiots) is the crude epithet used against the anti-globalization protesters. It is images running before him that prompt his reaction. He shouts at the images on the screen while sitting naked in his hotel room. The character watches the events on the news programs, intercut by sex for sale, and aerial, physical shots of the Twin Towers attacks. This is a spectacle available and visible to everyone.

As a vision, television provides images of the real violence we produce ourselves. How can we explain this to the Chinese people? Can we? A triangle of mimetic voyeuristic desire unites the character, the televised images, and the readers. The morbid grotesque replaces the tragic. Everything happens in a sort of out-of-tune asynchrony; chaos is revealed by an unfulfilled assignment to any classical order. The character watching the televised horror is not even interested in the "symbolic threshold" that the Twin Towers attack represents.[11] The "globalization of fear" does not even strike him.[12] What he registers is the scopophilic gaze – his own, primarily, but also how the cross-cutting between war and sex in television produces a morbid form of pleasure. In *War and Cinema,* Paul Virilio illustrates the ties between war and striptease during the Second World War, noting the prevalence of cinematic voyeurism:

> during and after the Second World War the widespread popularity of striptease, with its allusion to film as well as sexual excitation, indicated the scale of this technophiliac transfer in a society undergoing militarization ... Like

> the soldier, the striptease dancer who undresses on stage becomes a film for spectators, slowly taking off her clothes in a series of takes in which her lascivious body-movements act as the overlapping dissolve and the music as the sound-track.[13]

The kamikaze's gaze in Scarpa's novel brings to mind also Susan Sontag's reflections on the iconography of suffering that usually chooses for representation "those understood to be the product of wrath, divine or human."[14] The act of watching death on live television also raises questions about the allocation of grief in Western society. We are Westerners because we grieve the loss of those individuals falling from the Twin Towers. Judith Butler considers the various allocations of grief and the agents who decide what kind of subject is grieved, and must be grieved. Grieving, far from depoliticizing events, can foment nation-building and, in the case of Scarpa's spectators, promote the building of Western ideals. If we think think of the body as our most private possession, Butler reminds us that, "although we struggle for rights over our bodies, the very bodies for which we struggle are not quite ever only our own. The body has its invariably public dimension. Constituted as a social phenomenon in the public sphere, my body is and is not mine."[15] Television beautifies horror. The Twin Towers attacks remain a pivotal point, iconic of a period in which the kamikaze exists and which he wants to discuss, as it defines his own era.[16] The sexual performer artist and diary writer reacts with violence to the violence of the televised images. Television exacerbates our narcissism and displays our morbid fascination with death and our own vulnerability. As Virilio notes in "The Museum of Accidents,"

> Television – a "museum of horrors" or a "tunnel of death" – has, then, gradually transformed itself into a kind of altar of human sacrifice, using and abusing the terrorist scene and serial massacres; it now plays more on repulsion than on seduction.[17]

In his exasperated voyeurism, the kamikaze satisfies the consumeristic needs of his own society: watching images on television of people falling from the towers or demonstrating against the dictatorial power of the new economy repels him but is an act he commits anyhow. His indignation is collective and has many causes, all belonging to his society and to himself as agent of such anger. The physicality of his bodily reactions, mirrored in his exhibitionistic looking at himself *and* at television, articulates a morbid pleasure shared with his readers. In addition to what Butler calls "the enormous narcissistic wound opened up by the public display of our physical vulnerability"[18] that the attack on the Twin Towers provoked in an immense number of individuals, Scarpa's indignation is palpable and is close to home, to the constant failure of the left to choose the "right" struggles:

> È incredibile questo partito. In nome di una rivoluzione scoppiata più di ottant'anni fa a migliaia di chilometri da qui, di fatto ha svolto la funzione storica di schierarsi puntualmente contro tutte le rivoluzioni, le rivolte, i moti popolari, gli antagonismi conflittuali ... Budapest, Praga, il Sessantotto, il Settantasette, il G8 a Genova ... D'accordo che non si poteva protestare contro un summit organizzato a suo tempo da un governo di sinistra, ma un modo creativo di esserci si poteva pure inventare, no? Invece di lasciare che se ne impossessasse come al solito l'estrema sinistra. (KO 148–9)
>
> (This party is outrageous. In the name of a revolution that broke out more than eighty years ago, thousands of kilometres from here, in fact, it has played the historical function of duly siding against all revolutions, riots, popular uprisings, conflicting antagonisms ... Budapest, Prague, the Sixty-eight, the Seventy-seven, the G8 in Genoa ... Agreed, you could not protest against a summit organized at the time by a leftist government, but they could invent at least a creative way to be there, no? Instead of letting it be hijacked by the far left as usual.)

Scarpa's narrator does not spare his blows. In his discussion of the passions in his *Treatise of Human Nature*, David Hume talks about righteous indignation as a sort of idyllic hybrid of positive and negative emotions that sometimes is just not enough to get the job done, and one must resort to a more (self-)destructive, (self-)annihilating type of anger in order for change to be brought about, in order to create new spaces where what once could not be may now be. When a marginalized individual or group has long fought to have his/her rights understood and accepted, there might be nothing left to do but to let an explosion of calamitous wrath take hold of the situation and obliterate everything in its way.[19] The physicality exposed by the nakedness of the narrator's body and his exhibitionist attitude as he watches falling bodies collide with air, penetrations in clear view for everyone, reveals his own frustration with respect to a party that never seems to "get it right." Death and the death of politics come together aesthetically in an almost Pasolinian way, as in *Petrolio*. *Petrolio* is an unfinished posthumous novel by Pasolini of 522 pages divided into *Appunti* (Notes) with progressive numbering, which are configured in a group of more or less extensive fragments.[20] Carla Benedetti defines the constant presence of the projectual author in *Petrolio*'s "forma-progetto" (form-project) as its very essence and instrumental to "the fruition of the whole text."[21] The narrative fragment is here elevated to a system through which meaning takes shape. The novel is set in Italy in the politically violent early 1970s; the novel's protagonist, Carlo 1, has his double, Carlo 2. A left-wing Roman Catholic from Turin's upper bourgeoisie, Carlo 1 is an engineer for ENI, Italy's oil company, while Carlo 2 is his lower-class "twin." If the unfit, grey character of Carlo 1 represents power in all its ominous mediocrity, Carlo 2 embodies a sexual vocation so consuming that in Pasolini's lexis it amounts to a martyrdom. While Carlo 1 attends to his work or social commitments, Carlo 2 practices incest and, having assumed female form, has sex with twenty boys in a field. When Carlo 2 disappears, Carlo 1 repudiates careerism, sterilizes himself, joins an Eastern mystery cult, and becomes a holy man. Pasolini's critique of the left pervades the whole text, as it shows the basic subservience of the Communist Party to the laws of power.[22] Alike in their loss of faith in a party that no longer exists in Italy, the two writers progressively lose faith in the *kind* of reality that surrounds the narrators of their stories. Everything happens in a discordant synchronicity, chaos revealed in the failure to adhere to any classical canon. The grotesqueness of Scarpa's images echoes the tragic tones of Pasolini's political disillusionment. The sad and bizarre itinerary that our society follows is represented mimetically by the spectacle. Our anaesthetization is what Scarpa denounces so strongly. The work of art does not merely denounce: it can prefigure what is about to come, re-establishing the power of allegory. If we are exasperated, Hessel claims through wordplay (*exasperare* and *sperare*), we need to hope that history can always be revisited by art, and for the better.[23] In its reply to Wu Ming 1's enquiry on new narrative objects,[24] Scarpa's document sets out the logical sense of the prefigurative meaning of the artwork, one that must not follow historicist patterns, rejecting a compulsory adhesion to the system. Adopting a form of anti-narrative must be considered a weapon:

> Noi cittadini armati delle nostre parole, non siamo liberi, né disponiamo di un'autonoma forza prefigurativa: significa ammettere che conta solo la storia del Potere, e noi non possiamo che conformarci a essa, persino quando ci diamo un nome, persino quando dobbiamo scegliere che cosa fare con la nostra scrittura.[25]
>
> (We citizens armed with our words are not free, nor do we have an autonomous pre-figurative force: it means admitting that only the history of Power matters, and we cannot but comply with it, even when we give ourselves a name, even when we must choose what to do with our writing.)

Scarpa introduces a variation on his reflections in *Batticuore fuorilegge*. His "cittadini disarmati" (BF 11; unarmed citizens) stand by the power of their words but are aware that Power represents an almost unsurmountable entity to which we all could succumb. However, artistic works, as Scarpa reminds readers in his comments to Wu Ming 1's *New Italian Epic*, "are not necessarily linked to historical events in a bond of urgent need,"[26] for they are not a mimetic response to them. Unlike Wu Ming 1, Scarpa does not consider art and literature "simple consequences of momentous events,"[27] for this would threaten "the power of allegory to prefigure art."[28] Between art and history, our physicality establishes its consequence. Our body, even if not entirely ours, as Butler contends, regulates exchanges of repeatable emotions like love, affection, anger, and shame. Our body makes our own passions current and eternal. Without providing a mathematical link between art and a historic event, Scarpa engages in the relationship between the artistic and the political act. He does not advance escapist propositions; instead he attempts to uncover what is fundamental in life.

Distilling the essence of life requires an understanding of what constitutes the fundamental values that sustain our lived experience. What makes such a task worthwhile? Values represent a constant, and Aristotelian, motif in Scarpa's writing, for valuable things constitute a good life. What matters, really, in our life? What can we transmit of our epoch that is worth transmitting? And, if words govern us, can they also help us in the always difficult operation of defining oneself to the *postera*? The hyperbolic search for appearances, a quest that aims to hide a repressed reality, becomes the essence of writing. The real, in a Lacanian sense, is situated at the heart of an existence we wish to avoid and that may not be entirely representable. Nevertheless, we need to uncover this "real" to combat unreality. For Scarpa, the constant exchange among the animated thing, the individual, and the inanimate thing retains fundamental importance because it establishes the necessity of contemporary consumerism. This necessity should not frighten the reader but assure him instead of at least one certainty: "The systematic and limitless process of consumption arises from the disappointed demand for totality that underlies the project of life. In their ideality sign-objects are all equivalent and may multiply infinitely; indeed, they *must multiply* in order at every moment to make up for a reality that is absent. Consumption is irrepressible, in the last reckoning, because it is founded upon a *lack*."[29] We constantly consume because we lack the things that we call objects. We consume because, according to Georges Bataille's notion of *dépense*, we need to consume to prevent the disintegration of capitalist society. Consumption is a form of legalized desire because *we ourselves are the objects* we lack. Our own lack of ourselves exemplifies the blamelessness of consumption. We are suffocated by objects because we lack the *fundamental things.*[30] Much of Scarpa's work deals with the paradoxical co-existence of lack and excess in a society marked by a disturbing *horror vacui*, a worrisome aversion to creating a space for thought. Another of its focal points is the contradiction of authorial adherence to and transgression of normative acts. The lack of a physical structure that can order our presence in the world is constantly imagined. It is the essence of the world around us: this is the fundamental obsession, or the desire that no one knows how to fulfil.

What are the *fundamental things* we need to transmit to future generations? At least as early as his 1996 *Occhi sulla graticola*, Scarpa reflected upon what really matters in life. The narrator's addressee is his son, a "future" Alfredo.[31] Some of the *fundamental things* that will later make up the title of his 2010 novel concern studying the "aspirazioni, scopi, senza limitarsi a intuirle" (OG 35; motivations and goals without simply intuiting them) of a person. In studying an individual, he situates the relationship between word and body in the library, the stale repository of the written word:

> (zeta) La biblioteca abolisce e mette tra parentesi il corpo, pretende che l'organismo si spiritualizzi diventando puro paio di pupille ricettive che decifrano alfabeti e numeri di pagine di libri ... è la vendetta dei libri, che sono fatti di linguaggio staccato dal corpo, parole che parlano una volta per tutte senza potersi correggere e ribattere all'interlocutore e alzare la posta in gioco nel discorso e dire l'ultima parola e ridere bene ridendo ultime, come fa invece un corpo che presenzia a una chiacchierata. (OG 37–8)

> ([zeta] The library abolishes the body and puts it between brackets, expects that the organism is spiritualized, becoming a pure pair of receptive pupils that decipher alphabets and numbers of book pages ... it is the vengeance of the books, which are made of language detached from the body, words that speak once and for all without being able to correct themselves and rebut the other party and raise the stakes in the speech and say the last word and laugh well, laughing last, as does, instead, a body presiding over a chat.)

Books become dangerous when they are left to moulder in libraries and are stripped of the corporeal component of our body ("books ... made of language detached from the body"). Relevance does not come only from the style we infuse in our writing then , but through the word's own versatility and its playful and constructive possibilities, along with the sensorial capabilities of individuals. Scarpa's characters *settle* words inside people who fall in love. Another of Scarpa's narrators postulates whether words are created to fill gaps. Are words created to create images that, in fact, "devono essere immaginate"[32] (need to be imagined) as Scarpa writes in *Cosa voglio da te?* In order to imagine, you must first find the words and then create an image (representation) for them.[33] It would appear that the ability to pursue a good life rests on our access to imagination and in our ability to create a constantly changing *imago* with all the words we know. It is only through the power of words that we can afford our survival. As in *Il brevetto del geco,* or even more clearly in *Il cipiglio del gufo,* in which the character Nereo Rossi constructs an ongoing dialogue with words (in his career of TV soccer commentator), in *Le cose fondamentali* words take on the role of actual characters and reveal all their agency in the plot.

Le cose fondamentali further illustrates Scarpa's enquiry into the ethical and aesthetic discomfort of our times. Leonardo, the protagonist, writes a letter to his son, Mario. This text becomes an autobiographical document of appurtenance in an epoch in which what matters, and must be left to our children, is revealed to be unconditional love. Leonardo Scarpa is thirty-seven, a father to one-month-old Mario, and lives in Venice with his beloved Silvana. Leonardo, writes daily letters – literally filled with words – to his newborn son, explaining what he considers the fundamental things in life. At fourteen, Mario will have this paternal document to guide him through life. In *Le cose fondamentali,* Scarpa places his protagonist in a position of necessary interaction with the reader. Unlike in *Occhi sulla graticola,* we now have an actual father, not a prospective one, and an actual, not future, son to whom he says "Come stai, dentro queste mie parole?" (CF 37; How do you feel inside these words of mine?). In one of the many variations on conventional first-person narration, the narrator addresses a "You," who is us. Also, in what could be perceived as an original deviation from the treatment of conventional autofiction, such as a clear reference to the author himself in *Kamikaze d'Occidente* ("Sono la bici di Tiz! Mi porti a fare un giro?" KO 23; I'm Tiz's bike! Would you like to take me for a ride?), Scarpa-the-author does not coincide with the main and narrating character. He aligns him with another character who is not his deuteragonist either, *and* overtly takes on the role of a necessary "complicit reader," or the buddy (male) reader. This is writer Tiziano Scarpa. Just as in *Kamikaze d'Occidente* and, despite what his protagonist claims,[34] also in *Le cose fondamentali* the internal (male) ideal reader is an accomplice to whom the narrating voice can wink an eye during his *virtuosismi.*[35] It is fair to say that the person who wants to help him to understand the essence of the fundamental things is his best friend, Tiziano, who jokes about his homonymy with the writer published by Einaudi. Scarpa explores the limits of realism in this bittersweet novel about paternity and the fundamental things we should teach the next generation. As in previous works, Scarpa utilizes an interlocutor for his protagonist, clarifying what we value most in our existence through writing to another and engaging the other in a dialogue. Children, like the "future Alfredo" in *Occhi sulla graticola,* are ideal addressees because we are forced to process feelings of caring and responsibility. Lives can't be spoiled before they even begin. But the certainties we want to transmit to our children belong only to individuals.

However, although the writer/artist is not the protagonist, he remains an important character through his destabilizing presence and attitude. In the discussions that precede or follow the various moments of his writing, Leonardo calls in or recalls Tiziano and *his* words. Both live in Venice, both are Venetians, and both have the last name Scarpa. Leonardo's and Tiziano's respective presences determine a contraction or an expansion of their will. Leonardo is referred to as Leo, while Tiziano is often addressed as Tiz. Only two things separate them: their occupation – Leo is an employee and Tiz is a writer; and their legal status – the former is a new father, while the latter doesn't want children. These are the first two "fundamental things" in the conception of this novel: the need for fatherhood and the denial of paternity as an element defining masculinity. In *Le cose fondamentali,* the character of Tiziano Scarpa picks up from where the *Kamikaze*'s writer left off. The writer Tiziano Scarpa or Tiz, friend of the protagonist Leonardo Scarpa, claims what the *Kamikaze*'s writer had previously asserted. He has realized the following (fundamental) thing: "Non ho nessun desiderio di avere figli. Devolvere un mucchio di tempo a raccontare fesserie a un marmocchio non mi sembra il massimo delle mie aspirazioni" (KO 65; I have no desire to have children. Devoting a lot of time to telling nonsense to a stupid brat is not my top aspiration).[36] For somebody who uses words to convince, exhort, and denounce, Tiziano Scarpa the character seems inclined to forego the most fundamental qualities of his job. Educating children requires, in fact, a constant use of words that create edifying stories, cautionary tales, and reproach without physical punishment. He is not interested in this aspect of the words. His friend Leo wants to share with little Mario instead the few absolute certainties he has gained in life, as he is aware of the needless secrecy practiced by his parents about certain topics considered taboo:

> Che cos'è l'amore, che cos'è il potere. Che cosa sono i soldi, la malattia, la morte. Gli adulti mi tenevano nascosta la verità sulle cose importanti. Mi sono messo a scriverti per non rifare lo stesso sbaglio. E anche perché non credo che riuscirei a dirti queste cose a voce, faccia a faccia. (CF 6)

> (What is love, what is power. What is money, illness, death. The adults hid the truth about important stuff from me. I started writing to you to not

make the same mistake. And also because I doubt I could manage to tell you these things out loud, face to face.)

With the birth of his son, Leo feels obligated "rifare i conti con le cose primarie dell'esistenza" (CF 44; to come to terms with the primary things of existence). He knows that "finora h[a] vissuto cose di poco conto" (CF 101; until now he has lived trivial things), that he is an employee who does not appreciate the beauty of endless horizons, and who surrenders to those offered by the Lido beach in Venice where he often goes walking. In his perceived awareness of his own limitations, Leo surrounds himself with the few certainties that Tiziano (or Tiz, as this shortening is used interchangeably) constantly challenges. With affection and irony, Tiz tries to dismantle these certainties, or at least tries to make Leo enunciate interesting utterances that will produce an effect in his son once he turns fourteen. Similarly, while declaring his intolerance of children, as a writer Tiz spends considerable time fascinating children with his stories. He instils in them the seeds of doubt with respect to authority. His position against late maternity is antithetical to Leo's. Tiz questions, echoing in this the misogyny of *Kamikaze d'Occidente's* narrator (and many Italian male individuals), the logic of late maternity as an individual who is external to the dynamics of reproduction – not to mention maternity:

> Penso a tutti i figli che le mie coetanee non hanno fatto a ventitré, ventisette, trentun anni. Penso ai figli che precipitosamente, disperatamente vorrebbero fare adesso, a trentasette, trentanove anni. E se ci riescono, li ostentano incredule e pavone, perché finalmente hanno concepito e figliato contro tutto il mondo, contro l'epoca che le voleva sterilizzare in cambio di una malintesa idea di giovinezza, e il bambino se lo stringono, lo strangolano a sé, respirano al posto suo. Fortunato il bimbo che nasce da genitori giovani! (KO 221)
>
> (I think of all the children that my peers have not created when they were twenty-three, twenty-seven, thirty-one. I think of the children who hastily, desperately they would want to make now, at thirty-seven, at thirty-nine. And if they succeed, ... they show them off because they have finally conceived, against all odds, against the epoch who wanted them sterilized in exchange for a misunderstood idea of youth, and they shake, strangle the child, they breath in his place. Lucky is the child born from young parents!)

Reconsidering all Scarpa writes about the dictatorship of hegemonic forms of power, this statement comes as counter to all he claims should be corrected in Italian society. Lack of work, precariousness, and legal rights not easily afforded to women have much to do with getting pregnant at a late age. Easy sexism cannot be the answer to societal issues of such import. Each character takes on a thesis on fatherhood, but he who holds the power of words (regardless of who he intends to use them) relies on one more set of skills. Jealousy is apparent when Leo reveals frustration towards Tiz in his letter to his son Mario:

> La verità è che sono incerto sul da farsi perché ho paura che alla fine ti sarà più simpatico lui. Mi sa che sto costruendo un monumento al mio antidoto, una scappatoia da me, ed è tanto più pericolosa perché esiste, è a portata di mano, non è un individuo astratto, si chiama Tiziano ed io te lo sto descrivendo in tutto il suo fascino antipaterno, proprio nell'età in cui tu starai diventando antifiliale. (CF 79)

> (The truth is that I'm unsure what to do because I'm afraid that in the end you will like him more than me. I feel like I am building a monument to my antidote, a way out from me, and it is all the more dangerous because it exists, is at hand, he is not an abstract individual, his name is Tiziano, and I am describing him to you in all his anti-paternal charm, just at the age when you'll be getting anti-filial.)

These negative feelings partly stem from the rivalry Leo establishes with Tiz. There are those who never feel ready to have children, and also do not want them, like Tiz who, being wickedly creative, achieves great success and garners children's affection, as often happens to men in their forties who have not committed to fatherhood and the responsibilities it entails. It needs to be mentioned that Leo wants to take part in a creative process too. This process will protect Leo from experiencing grief over his son's inevitable adolescent rite of passage that will temporarily exclude him from his son's life. Fundamentally, Leo writes to protect himself, not to seduce anyone, as Tiz constantly does. It is Tiziano who alerts Leonardo to the joys of iPhone use. Tiziano shows him how to write "sul filo dell'orizzonte" (CF 36; on the horizon line) and how to write the word on the image of the screen: "Tiziano scrive camminando, prende appunti direttamente sulle immagini che scorrono: non c'è più un fuori dalla scrittura. La prossimità fra parole e immagini è totale" (CF 36; Tiziano writes while walking, he takes notes directly on the running images: there is no longer anything beyond the writing. The proximity between word and images is complete). But for Leonardo, writing to his child signifies understanding how his son could, fourteen years after the writing of the letter, "stare dentro queste [sue] parole" (CF 37; stay inside these [his] words). As words are us, their meaning is us, Leonardo is aware of his legacy to Mario. Will the son find space inside the space occupied by his father's words? Leonardo writes not to expose the child to his own fraudulent epoch. His good faith and trust in humankind are revealed in several of the parts composing the novel. In part 31, in one of the flashbacks concerning his youthful love for Antonella (an actual subplot to the one about his son's birth), Leonardo claims that, "Il mio amore era diverso, sarei riuscito a smentire l'epoca che mi aveva prodotto. Non ero un eroe, non stavo cambiando le cose, ma quello era il mio primo passo per impostare una vita di verità e giustizia" (CF 71; My love was different; I would be able to disprove the era that generated me. I was not a hero, I was not changing things, but that was my first step to setting up a life of truth and justice). Of course, Leo's expectations are not met in the past affair with Antonella (her twin, Ida, arrives in her place!). But the same sense of moral duty will accompany his adult experience as a father. As he fears his son Mario's absolute certainties about his parents will eventually crumble at fourteen, Leonardo hopes that his words will constitute at least a fundamental aspect of their bond.

Hope is a good passion that sustains a relationship between individuals. It is not simply a matter of blood. What binds Leonardo and Mario is not, as we know, DNA. Rather, it is the ability of the father's words to unite them. His words build a relationship, a bond, a contract with his child. The bond with our children is based on the critical gift of the word, or *logos.* In front of a space as infinite as the horizon, we establish the boundaries for all the things that, in time, children will dismantle and reassemble through the logic of words, our most immense power. To be fundamental, things need to be expressed not simply in words, as the earlier example of the library shows, but with our senses. It is also through our human gaze that words can become something else, can transfigure sense. And Leo is well aware of this potential, for what matters, as we said, is his son's gaze: "Quel che conta è il tuo sguardo. È da lí che arriva la luce, lo sfondamento. Queste parole, da nere che sono, diventeranno trasparenti, trapassate, trapensate, solo se ci sarai tu che le leggi" (CF 37; What matters is your gaze. The light, the breakthrough, comes from there. From their original darkness, these words will become transparent, pierced, hyper-thought-out, only if you will read them). The twist in the story, the secret of Leonardo's paternity, transforms the writer who wonders (always addressing Mario): "Allora a chi ho scritto io? A chi sto scrivendo? Eh Mario? In compagnia di chi sono stato? Non puoi abbandonarmi così. Non puoi lasciarmi solo, qui, dentro queste pagine" (CF 129; So, who did I write to? Who am I writing to? Eh Mario? In the company of who was I? You cannot leave me alone, here, inside these pages); and again: "Mi sentivo padre di un fascicolo di pagine ... Avevo dato corpo a un deposito di illusioni" (CF 150; I felt like a father of a page binder ... I generated a storage of illusions). Such cosmic despair leads nowhere. It also reveals the indissoluble bond between our mind and our words, our senses that declare the victory of the flesh if words are willing to work along with our senses. During Leonardo's moment of disillusionment (which arrived much sooner than the one he was projecting in Mario's future at roughly fourteen!), words have taken over. Like the avenging Furies, they have produced five pages that reveal the real events behind Mario's birth. Words are the only real force we have to express ourselves. They act as characters and, in a long tirade that occupies the whole of chapter 55 (pages 135–42) they urge him to confront the sad reality of not being Mario's real father:

> Leonardo: Leo: non sei che una parola sola: che prende vita solo se si mette in sequenza: se la mettiamo in sequenza noi: fra noi: in mezzo a noi: in fila insieme alle altre: come tutte le altre parole: Leonardo! Leonardo! Ti presenti all'appello? Gli ubbidisci? Prendi ordini dalla tua parola? Dalla parola che ti nomina? Prendi ordini da noi: hai appena scoperto che non sei il padre di Mario: non vorremmo essere sarcastiche con te: ma come fare a non ridere? ... Noi siamo le arpie che devastano il tuo pranzetto. (CF 135–6)

> (Leonardo: Leo: you are but one word: that comes to life only if one puts it in sequence: if we put it in sequence: among us: between us: in line with the others: like all the other words: Leonardo! Leonardo! Are you showing up for the roll call? Do you obey it? Do you take orders from your word? From the word that names you? Take orders from us: you have just discovered that you are not the father of Mario: we would not want to be sarcastic with you: but how can we not laugh? ... We are the harpies that devastate your lunch.)

Confused, hypnotized by the satanic dance of words, which, in the meantime, are taking hold of his mind, Leonardo cannot think ahead. No solution seems possible to mend what seems to be the gravest disappointment of his life.

Once again, Tiz/Tiziano, always lurking, and ready to help his friend, makes Leo discern the pure value of what remains important: the words that make up our entire existence. As the novel nears its end, Tiz/Tiziano arranges what turns out to be a cathartic trip to Basel. Once the truth about Mario emerges, he takes Leo to Basel to experience Hans Holbein's family portrait. The trip is fundamental because Leonardo discovers the real meaning of fatherhood, through art. Tiz shows him a family portrait by Holbein depicting his children, perhaps the first family portrait by a painter. Tiz relies on this ally, the most powerful possible (CF 161) to explain the essence of life to his friend. Leo understands life itself through Holbein's painting: the painter brought his children into his works, thus eliminating the distance between physical and artistic corporeality. Leo is aware that Tiz's writing reflects the image of the world into his own ideas and builds what his friend considers his own fundamental things. He wonders, though, about the validity of the trip to see the actual painting and asks his friend,

> – Ma come ti è venuto in mente? Non potevi mostrarmi un catalogo?
> – Dovevamo vederlo dal vivo. Dovevamo venire qui per capire quanto valore ha questa immagine. Per te, soprattutto.
> – Dovrei farmi convincere da un quadro.
> – Non è semplicemente un quadro. È quello che ha capito lui della vita. Ha visto i soldi, l'amore, il potere, l'angoscia della morte. Uno che ha reso affascinanti i ricchi e le loro monete d'oro, che ha abitato per giorni in una tomba stretta, e poi dallo sfondo nero della morte è riuscito a tirare fuori qualcosa di vivo. Sua moglie non è bella, I suoi figli non sono infelici, ma ...
> – Ma sono suoi! – protestai.
> – Ecco, qui ti sbagli.
> – Hai qualche notizia diversa? Hai studiato la sua biografia?
> – No, e non voglio conoscerla. Mi bastano I quadri.
> – Si vede che i bambini non gli assomigliano?
> – Lasciami parlare. Si vede che li ha dipinti. Capisci? Non gli è bastato sposarsi e concepire due bambini. Li ha fatti entrare nelle sue opere. Devi farlo anche tu. In fondo hai sentito il bisogno di scrivere a tuo figlio.... Se lo dipingi, se lo scrivi, è figlio tuo. (CF 161–2; emphasis in original)
>
> (– But how did you think of this? Couldn't you show me a catalogue?
> – We had to see it live. We had to come here to understand the great value of image. For you, in particular.
> – Should I be convinced by a picture?
> – It is not just a picture. That's what he understood of life. He saw money, love, power, the anguish of death. He was one who made the rich and their gold coins attractive, one who lived for days in a narrow grave, and then from the black background of death was able to pull off something alive. His wife is not beautiful and his children are not happy, but ...
> –But they are his! – I protested.
> – Well, here you are wrong.
> – Do you have any other information? Did you study his biography?
> – No, and I do not want to know it. I only need his paintings.
> – Do you think that the children do not resemble him?
> – Let me talk. You see that he painted them. Do you understand?

– It was not enough to marry and conceive two children. He had them come into his works. You have to do it too. After all, you've felt the need to write to your son ... If you paint him, if you write to him, he is your son.)

What is the scope of this novelistic design? The game consists of submitting to readers, whose opinions must swing between being touched by the sweetness and ingenuity of Leo and warned by the precise observations of Tiz, burdened with the task of trying to understand where, in fact, the higher value of things lies. Remo Bodei suggests that things are invested with values additional to those made evident in the object-in-itself. Things also include "people or ideals and in general all that we have at heart."[37] Mario is likened to a *cosa* by his dad when he still cannot speak or even scream, surrounded by merchandise as "un'aureola di merci" (CF 12; an aureole of goods). For Remo Bodei, the meaning of the word *cosa* (thing) is far broader than that of *oggetto* (object) as "endowed affections, concepts and symbols that individuals, society and history will project, the objects become things, distinguishing them from goods as simple use values and exchange or status symbol expression."[38] Things are also bodies, just like us. In the end, we wonder what Leo really wants to teach his son. We realize that the temporal process of the writing of the letter has also amounted to a period of self-reflection for Leo. Finally, conveniently placed in a paragraph in the text when Leo hesitates to enter his house and watches it from beneath a streetlamp, his character's lines split into indirect speech in the first and third persons, respectively. He reflects on the Self that acts and watches the character who is describing him:

> Leonardo rimase lí, sotto la luce dei lampioni, non so per quanto tempo, a immaginare tutto quello che sarebbe potuto succedere se mi fossi messo sulle tracce di quell'uomo. Fantasticò una catena di avvenimenti, uno piú improbabile dell'altro: riusciva a farsi dare le informazioni che gli servivano dal direttore dell'albergo, rintracciava il padre biologico di Mario. Fantasticare: il mio vizio peggiore è sempre stato questo. Doveva concentrarsi sulla realtà. La realtà era che non avevo il coraggio di lasciare Silvana. Ed ero troppo affezionato a Mario. Aveva paura di perderli, tutti e due. *Preferivo la finzione alla verità.* (CF 166, emphasis added)

> (Leonardo stood there, under the streetlights, I do not know for how long, to imagine everything that could have happened if I'd traced the man. He fantasized a chain of events, one more unlikely than the other: he could get the information he needed from the hotel manager, he could trace Mario's biological father. Fantasizing: My worst habit has always been this. He had

> to focus on reality. The reality was that I didn't have the courage to leave Silvana. And I was too fond of Mario. He was afraid of losing them, both. I preferred fiction to truth.)

Leo understands that preferring fiction to truth means finally understanding what are the fundamental things. Is it true affection – the element one constructs day by day for a son who is not biologically his – or the truth of simple genes he shares with him that should prevail over his feelings, which are just as true? Once again, Tiz/Tiziano underscores the role of the artist and art. Speaking of his dearest friend's intimate drama, he manages to make us understand the fundamental things in life. The act of observing Holbein's painting of his children reconfirms a fact that the words have tried in vain to mystify: art constructs the reality we want it to be, not the reality of things in themselves. By letting his friend experience the actual painting by Holbein rather than its copy in a catalogue, Tiziano intends to reveal to his friend what lies in fiction – the reality we wish for, that is, in order for life to reach its fullest meaning. If I want this son to be mine, I am doing so by writing a long letter to him: my ties, my bond, are what words read through his gaze will become. His gaze will interpret my love, which is real and authentic and truthful.

As suggested by Fernando Savater in his *Ethics for a Child*, "we are not free to choose what happens to us ... but we are free to respond to what happens to us in one way or another."[39] Leo takes charge of what has happened to him by transmitting his own experience to his son. When he reaches the age of fourteen, Mario will consider how his father responded. Struck by the unquestionable reality that Mario's DNA differs from his, Leo prefers his imaginative representation of a Mario who is still his son. He reflects his concept of family through artistic creation as a vehicle of truth, delivering through a simple, touching parable perhaps the greatest gift that a father can give to his son. It's important that Mario, Leo's creature, a baby who was inside Silvana's belly for nine months, a woman Leo loves very much, inherits his greatest gift. His love and his words must outweigh other non-fundamental things. Can words compose a cathedral? Building with words to which we become attached is very important because, just as in the case of a child, they are part of us. The words are our foundation:

> Even philosophical speech act theory teaches us that doing "something with words," to perform an action by talking or writing, that is, is about a thing we do toward others: making a promise, a verbal agreement on a price, a wedding, a complaint. Doing things with words is not just an abstract statement,

> divorced from its communicative situation: you put the face, presence, body, its own history, your own name, your signature. We have to commit ourselves in those words. Its name, the I, our faces are not simply vanity, exhibition, narcissism: are our implication in language. They are not only a mirror in which a performing society seduces us, or just bulky handles that make it easier to catch us police. In particular, the full name is the symbol of the medium convergence writing with the communication medium in the presence, face to face, speech, image, etc. Our own name is a word with no relevant semantic content. Its name has a designative meaning and a pragmatic meaning our implication in language. The name indicates that not just the things we say, but we too belong to the language, we are involved in speech. It is true, so we remain entangled, plotted in the words, and in this way become even more vulnerable to the control of Power. But the price to pay to call us out of the language, and by the appearance, and taking charge for ourselves, is a decrease in the political force of our utterances. No names, no faces, no bodies, no ego, no personal history placed in public and socially shared, we can make fewer speech acts, or make less powerful ones, we can do fewer things with words, and in some cases even we cannot accomplish incisive political action: we decrease or cancel the parrhesiastic strength of our words.[40]

Following the path outlined by Scarpa's powerful statement, preliminary conclusions on Leonardo's take on paternity (of words and children) are in order. For Scarpa, both are important. The birth of a child is made possible by placing the act within a casing that has become almost conventional in the book market: a letter to child, inspired by the title of the famous letter to the son of Marc Bloch. But if it is conventional, the logical consequence is that this entire novel should be read as its envelope. This is where the creative contribution of Tiz is crucial to the design of Leo. On the beach one day, Tiz lends his phone to Leo, who discovers new ways to say fundamental things to his son:

> Ti sto scrivendo questa riga sul filo dell'orizzonte. Mi sono seduto per terra. Tengo il telefono di Tiziano con una mano, poggiato sul ginocchio, sto inquadrando il mare con la funzione videocamera. Con l'altra mano digito le lettere sulla tastierina virtuale, nella parte bassa dello schermo. Le parole compaiono sopra le immagini, e puntando il telefono con precisione sull'orizzonte faccio in modo che il confine fra mare e cielo si allinei con la riga di scrittura.
>
> Scrivo sul filo dell'orizzonte. Il limite del mare e del cielo sorregge le mie parole. (CF 36)

> (I'm writing this line on the horizon. I sat on the floor. I hold Tiziano's phone with one hand resting on my knee, I'm framing the sea with the camera feature. With the other hand, I type the letters on the virtual keypad, on the bottom of the screen. The words appear over the images, and pointing the phone on the horizon with precision I make sure that the boundary between sea and sky lines up with the writing line.
>
> I write on the horizon. The limit of sea and sky sustains my words.)

Writing words over an image, constantly finding out what may be the most complete and complex envelope to frame our words with, that is ourselves, becomes the fundamental thing. Photographs can be "read" much like pages of traditional texts, and words can construct landscapes. Visual textuality turns into a form of contemporary ekphrasis. Words, like diminutive mutants, become us, "Le parole non mentivano, poco fa, si sono impossessate di me, si sono sostituite a quello che sono, a quello che pensavo di essere, sono solo loro che vivono dentro di me, io non esisto, non ci sono" (CF 143; The words were not lying, they have seized me and taken the place of what I am, what I thought to be, it is only they who are living inside me, I do not exist, I am not here).

What is the nature of Scarpa's aesthetic operation? He declares that his is a culturally political act. As was stated in the beginning of the chapter, his writings take into consideration the personal and the collective reasons that prompt healthy anger, or more precisely indignation, towards what is not working in his *epoca.* Anger is thus motivated not (only) by personal needs, but, as in Pasolini's case, also by the author's involvement in and response to his society, one that needs agents of dissent to demonstrate the degree of decadence in which Italy finds itself. What happens in our society must compel us to re-evaluate ourselves and reconsider what is fundamental for our children, even hypothetical ones, like Mario in *Le cose fondamentali.* The posture of Scarpa's fictional writer in *Kamikaze d'Occidente,* as a powerful orator in an ancient polis, speaks volumes about his civic commitment. A writer who prostitutes himself to continue with his art is not living well. Or perhaps, any performer always, somehow, prostitutes his own time and words. Happiness, as such, is not about virtuosity. What role does Scarpa's writer choose for himself? If, as Elsa Morante claims, the writer must have at heart the world and must hate literature [it is] because the writer must be, beyond all mannerism, first and foremost, a poet who introjects the lyricism of his world. The writer must deal with the energies, contradictions, and even the negatives that move the world surrounding him and his community. Corporeal participation means participating with emotions and passions in the struggle that the kamikaze – divine wind – engages in in order to understand the fundamental nature of the things we live for. The images words create reveal their extraordinary ability to find a locus for discussion that is not restricted to the artist's incessant soliloquy (Scarpa's *verbigerazione*). Aware of tradition and aesthetics, Scarpa rejects any mannerism and wields experimental forms redolent with his emotions. The constructive side of an artist's moral indignation produces new forms with which to rethink aesthetics and the means to convey images of a community that has lost its moral compass.[41]

PART TWO

Anger and Spaces of Vulnerability in the Narratives of Melania Mazzucco and Monica Stambrini

The literary and cinematic narratives examined in this part of my book, Melania Mazzucco's novel *Un giorno perfetto* (A Perfect Day) and Monica Stambrini's film *Benzina* (Gasoline), portray domestic violence and sexual politics that see women – full citizens of the Italian republic – perpetually threatened inside their homes and within the space of their city, and made vulnerable by a lack of viable legal support. Both of these works exhibit an authorial preoccupation with the portrayal of the vulnerability of Rome's inhabitants and demonstrate how female artists are not wrapped in their own existence and do not produce self-reflexive narratives based on narcissistic projections of the self, but offer their narratives as the space to voice their concern for current affairs.[1] What becomes apparent in both works is the pragma of a failed process of deterritorialization that exposes the persistence of an inhospitable relationship between women and power within the city. A failed eradication of practices does not vouch for positive changes. Judith Butler studies the process of decontextualization that regulates the set of relational practices between the woman and the city in speaking of Antigone and the polis, and claims that, "as a figure for politics, she points somewhere else, not to politics as a question of representation but to that political possibility that emerges when the limits to representation and representability are exposed."[2] While we often witness a process of deterritorialization divested of any ability to contextualize and represent minority and discriminated groups, we might suggest that space can be deterritorialized and recontextualized in narratives to understand how women can feel as political beings despite the constant threat of limitations to their legal (and human) rights. A threat indicates a notion of vulnerability and fear that assumes historical importance in the fabric of Rome, as deterritorialization does not warrant social change.

I explore vulnerability as a "fundamental ontological condition"[3] that grounds our possibility of responsiveness in static affirmations of the categories of victim and victimization in women's everyday stories set in Rome. By differing from realist tradition, but taking its teachings into account and taking readers *elsewhere* without forgetting the centre, Mazzucco and Stambrini assume the moral responsibility of rethinking vulnerability and victimization, especially for women, within this urban space. They also deconstruct the conventional binary opposition of vulnerability and resistance by demonstrating in what ways the two can be interconnected. Their narratives validate how vulnerability is "not an inherent characteristic of women's bodies; rather, it is an effect that works to secure femininity as a delimitation of movement in the public, and over-inhabitance in the private."[4] Fear appears as an emotion determined by the proximity of danger and violence rather than as an effective bodily response that women project invariably. By restricting women's access to space, by delimiting movement in the public to them, societal norms reveal their oppressive force upon Mazzucco's and Stambrini's characters. In what follows, constructive indignation about violence and homophobia is seen through the compassionate lens of female writer Melania Mazzucco and filmmaker Monica Stambrini, in *Un giorno perfetto* and *Benzina,* respectively. Discrimination and violence against women, lack of legal support, and sexual politics form the common thread. Both authors depict women's resistance to passivity inherent in roles imposed by patriarchal society on victims of violence. Both artists show how vulnerability is a condition fundamentally forced upon female individuals because their bare legal rights, though extant, are rarely defended. The problem lies also with society itself, not just the judicial system, in mindsets resistant to change and a society that nests its conservative ideas in Ahmed's "over-inhabited"[5] domestic hearth.

Ever since Sigmund Freud equated the strata forming Rome with those that constitute our memory, the city's name has been a synecdoche of its mnemonic symbol. Emotional responses to urban monuments release the reality of the city's formative events. As illuminated in feminist readings of ancient Rome, violence against women was foundational to the creation of myths and legends about the city. The forces regulating Rome have been immense. Pier Paolo Pasolini speaks of centrifugal and centripetal forces entering and leaving Rome as he reflects on the ever-changing identity of this city:

> What is Rome? Where is the real Rome? Where does it begin and where does it end? ... Films have helped make it known to those who do not live here. But one must be careful. The Neorealist vein that characterizes the films about Rome is too schematic, too dialectically partial, too filled with humanitarian optimism and darkness to reveal, with its medium gray or pinkish tones,

> the atmosphere of this dramatically contradictory city. The contradictions of Rome are difficult to transcend because they are contradictions of an existential order. Rather than traditional contradictions, between wealth and misery, happiness and horror, they are part of a magma, a chaos.[6]

Stambrini's film *Benzina* and Mazzucco's novel *Un giorno perfetto* utilize the city and the opposing forces that Pasolini describes to compose radically disparate narratives. Within the space (or lack thereof) that Rome offers women, crucial themes of vulnerability and resistance emerge in both works.

The interactive network of human relationships retains great importance in the phenomenon of the alteration of the social fabric of several *rioni* (neighbourhoods) in the multicultural patchwork that connotes Rome at the beginning of the third millennium. Despite the oft-made claim of the immutability of the Eternal City, what Michael Herzfeld calls the "eviction from Eternity" (*sfratto dall'eternità*) of Rome,[7] the physical displacement phenomenon by which entire neighbourhoods have lost their ancient social physiognomy results in a forced transformation that is not only social but also ethnic and identitary. Rome's gentrification becomes a recognizable system of signification and contributes to the rapid transformation of the social and physical fabric of the city, creating a spatial discourse dealing with, once again, possible and real transgressions. Rome proceeds in an ambiguous direction, contradictory in some ways, both for its inhabitants and for the writers who narrate themselves narrating the city. The visual spectacle is so distressing that it may be possible to resolve it only through intuition, by a series of uninterrupted observations that are almost like cinematic shots.

In Melania Mazzucco's 2005 novel *Un giorno perfetto*,[8] a disturbing emptiness dominates the field. Pasolini's combination of "centre-periphery" is no longer a dialectical oppositional model in the construction of the Roman cityscape, this last now conceived by Mazzucco as a narrative image of the shifting grounds of both elements. "The margins and the centre shift and destabilize each other along parallel movements"[9] The stoical character of Roman proletarian Emma reflects an aspect of the aching endemic to women and minorities who are subject to economic globalization as living members of what Michael Hardt and Toni Negri call "Empire." Every day the papers and other media communicate how Italian society has failed to address some of the most basic of women's concerns and rights, not only the right to work, as stated by the Italian constitution, but an even (if possible) more basic one, the right to bodily integrity and freedom from physical violence and oppression. In situating her novel within the space of Rome, Melania Mazzucco promotes a critical reading of literal and actual violence against women that recalls Rome's violent foundational myths. Mazzucco's narrative of legitimacy in an Italian society marred by uncontrolled male rage, transmitted by those whose passions lead them to a position quite distant from Aristotle's good-tempered man, exposes a societal ill of astounding importance regarding the subject who can actually strive for the good life. Vulnerability is an ambiguous term that is often used to define the conditions under which many women (but also children and animals and any other minority) are forced to live today. The situation is exacerbated by male individuals (often, husbands or partners) who direct their deadly rage at women and their children and makes us realize how femicide and family murders contravene the right to life. Mazzucco's essentialist perspective in the representation of the Buonocore family is motivated by statistics that show very clearly that a far greater proportion of crimes are perpetrated by men against women than the opposite.[10] *Un giorno perfetto* challenges deep-rooted practices of victimization and affirms the need to take crucial steps towards a counter-narrative of society and the habitus that constantly confines women to a position of forced victimization.

Postcards from Rome

Compelling readings of the space we live in prompt readers and spectators to activate relations to such space. The *great beauty* of Rome lies in its ability to absorb its multitudinous narrative transpositions and rework them into an acute awareness of the paradox behind such eternal mutability. According to Bertrand Westphal,[11] what is *beautiful* about Rome can be understood in terms of its potential to offer artists porous forms of discourse inherent in spatial representations that determine expansive and current understandings of sociopolitics. Rome represents an emblematic example of a polymorphous city, not only because of the presence of new migrants as characters and a multicultural wave that has transformed its image but also because recent fictional narratives unveil a process of recognizing the social practices that also determine the disavowal of power and agency for other marginalized groups, such as women. If fictional narratives were to crystallize the image of a city into either a welcoming city or a fleeting place, chances are that the very reality they are trying to examine and present would lack credibility in its retelling. Now, if this were to occur, the goal of fictional narratives to make us believe in what they are telling us would be partly unfulfilled. In short, as Westphal relates, we would run the risk of defeating the very purpose of interpreting societal changes, since "truth would be colonized by fiction."[12] But, as Westphal also states, "the risk would occur only if the reconciliation between reality and fiction deprived reality of its verifiable character, if (fictional) textuality 'derealized' the world into absurdity. This is not the case, of course: the writer is neither unconscious nor incompetent."[13]

In the past twenty years, the physical and social landscape of Rome has undergone changes that validate the hypothesis that, after the stage of "acculturation, through the mass media"[14] that draws a parallel between the city and one "of the many small Italian towns,"[15] the city has once again become a "sprawling, chaotic, divided, split, metropolis,"[16] as Pier Paolo Pasolini once described it. Gentrification has contributed to the transformation of the urban assets of the capital. According to Luca Venitucci, the process of gentrification contains traits that are contradictory because the renewed areas, on the one hand, present characteristics of social opening that, for instance, are more inclusive of members of the LGBTQ community and ethnic minorities, but on the other, force the original residents to abandon their old neighbourhoods and move to peripheral areas because of the increased cost of the renovated living spaces. Venitucci likens the phenomenon of gentrification to "the interactions between cultural tendencies and independent artistic ones and market processes."[17] Further, he stresses how "the only instrument of resistance that alternative communities have is the subjective will to not compromise despite their being already a part in this process."[18]

The politics of redistribution oriented around questions of socioeconomic justice often inform narratives in which depictions of multidimensional Rome offer a commentary on its stratified socio-racial-political structure and the ways in which its citizens try to cope with the general sense of unrest shared by many. New categories of characters drawn from real life, such as migrants, are studied in recent narratives as "principal actors at these new points of intersection. By staging their identities in the city, they contribute to a renewed representation of the city as increasingly polymorphous and constantly changing."[19] Narratives can embody ethical acts of resistance, which, while introducing new characters like the new migrants, acknowledge the literary and cinematic legacy that anchors the Eternal City to an illustrious past of its representations while proposing a new socio-anthropological map of the city. Twentieth-century novelistic narratives of the city of Rome described an urban perspective as a spatial category intended to counterpoise that of suburbia. In narratives of the new millennium (*narrativa degli Anni Zero*),[20] the urban perspective becomes a powerful space of investigation to configure capacious models of discourse for reading today's multi-ethnic Roman society.[21] Leaving behind a stale literary image of Rome, writers reflect on the transversal nature of the city's transformations, on the impact of public history on personal lives, and on the static nature of institutions with respect to violence and sexual politics.

Twentieth-century writers constructed narratives in which clear boundaries defined the image of the city. In *Quer pasticciaccio brutto de via Merulana* (*That Awful Mess on the Via Merulana*), Carlo Emilio Gadda's notion of *gnommero* (tangle) alludes to the physical tangle of roads and the destinies of its characters, but its narrative clearly defines the difference between the centre and the *suburra.* In Elsa Morante's 1974 *La Storia: Romanzo* (*History: A Novel*), there is no possibility of inter-class dialogue among the poor neighbours of Testaccio and San Lorenzo, Pietralata and Portuense, living on the peripheries of wartime and post-war Rome, and the urban centre marked by great monuments to the various ruling powers over the centuries. Through deliberate authorial strategy, the centre of Rome never appears, because Morante's narrator must reveal the authentic socio-physical marginalization of the characters Ida, Davide, and Useppe, whose bodies are left to rot in dusty rooms without any intervention from the community. In Pier Paolo Pasolini's works, the city is presented *only* in terms of marginal spaces, like the *borgate,* the then recently built *quartiere* Monteverde in *Ragazzi di vita* (*The Street Kids*). Alberto Moravia's *La noia* (*Boredom*) depicts an anonymous Rome[22] in which the lack of reference to any city landmark frames the existential *angst* of his protagonist, Dino. The portrait of the artist (Dino is a painter) deals with the fundamental question of his relationship with reality: "But could one live in a state of boredom, could one live without any relationship with anything real, and not suffer from it? Here was the whole problem."[23] Dino's relationship with reality is epitomized by a reference to a painting by Wassily Kandinsky: "An empty canvas, apparently really empty, that says nothing and is without significance – almost dull, in fact – in reality, is crammed with thousands of undertone tensions and full of expectancy."[24] Existential angst prevents the author from providing a cityscape of any sort. The history of twentieth-century novels set in Rome, such as Moravia's *Boredom,* is crowded with chastened and disabused idealists whose quest concerns a space of interiority rather than preoccupation with the social. They reject quotidian experience as they pursue emotional states so unfamiliar or so overpowering as to call into question the fundamentally empirical and materialistic nature of the work of art. They raise hopes for artistic catharsis that no work of art could ever be expected to fulfil.

Though invariably referencing the diametrically opposed approaches proposed in twentieth-century novels, twenty-first-century narrative realism explores the uncertainty and instability that Rome's deceptive image attempts to conceal, and describes everyday life in a city that is at once metropolitan and provincial, *Roman* and multicultural. Margaret Mazzantini's *Non ti muovere* (*Don't Move*)[25] and her script for Sergio Castellitto's movie *Fortunata*,[26] Lorenzo Pavolini's *Accanto alla tigre* (*By the Tiger*),[27] and Francesca Melandri's *Sangue giusto* (*Right Blood*)[28] constitute contrasting examples of narratives that reflect the city's image as a disorienting urban agglomerate in which the *limes* (threshold) separating the centre and its margins is muddled, both in time and space. Already within the physiognomy of the city there is a degree of vulnerability that Rome shares with its residents. Rome emerges as a city in which all boundaries seem at times to blur, whether geographical and territorial, social and cultural, psychological and gender-based, historical and metaphysical. These boundaries perpetually shift. Various novels adjust to the notion developed by Brian Massumi, according to which movement should not be conceived as qualitative transformation but more simply in terms of displacement.[29] "When we think of space as 'extensive,'" states Massumi, "as being measurable, divisible and composed of points plotting possible positions that objects may occupy, we are stopping the world in thought. We are looking at only one dimension of reality."[30]

The act of strolling – a trope dear to twentieth-century urban literature – still applies as a means of losing oneself in a tentacular urban complex in order to understand one's own subjectivity in an alienating environment. The purpose of walking, however, does not necessarily reside in finding the other end of an imaginary *fil rouge* of memories and thoughts, but rather in unravelling the existential *gnommero* of Gaddian reminiscence. Within the Roman maze, a heap of problems appears related to an urban context constantly in flux that prompts "storytellers" to narrate its story.[31] Michel de Certeau revisits the notion of walking as a metaphor – as an enunciatory space – in which the text progresses as the character walks the city and eventually finds its own autonomy.[32] Walking is perceived as an activity that holds liberating power, particularly for women, traditionally confined to the sphere of domesticity. Moving is not necessarily synonymous with improvement, because movement, as Massumi argues, is not strictly a linear concept. In *Accanto alla tigre*, writer Lorenzo Pavolini searches through contemporary Rome for traces of a private past he scarcely knows: "L'atollo degli scrittori è un cerchio tanto ampio da svanire all'orizzonte ma resta – per me almeno – un rifugio sicuro, l'ancoraggio migliore della mente, giù nella prateria di posidonia, sulla sabbia bianca della storia" (The writers' atoll is a circle of such dimensions that [it] disappears in the horizon but remains – at least for me – a safe haven, the best mooring of the mind, down in the prairie of Posidonias, on the white sand of history).[33] That "white sand of history" haunts the writer, as he also holds a place within such sands because of his cumbersome legacy. The grandson of Alessandro Pavolini, minister of culture of the Duce, and a writer like him, he searches in his grandfather's writings for traces of a history written on the walls of Rome. To the violence that troubles his own neighbourhood, the Esquiline, the writer opposes a singular state of mental quiet, oriented towards the reflection of his time as his own being within the metropolitan space. An ever-changing Rome presents us in its outlines as a place to be eternally revisited as emerging social transformations compel artists to constantly re-examine sites – like Piazza Vittorio, the *borgate*, or the Garbatella – that have been made famous by twentieth-century literary and cinematic neorealism and realism. In the Esquiline *rione*, CasaPound – the meeting point of the neo-fascists Pavolini writes about in his *Accanto alla tigre* – appears as a deadly bubo in the space disputed by many cultures and ethnic groups.

In *Un giorno perfetto,* Mazzucco sets the living quarters of the Buonocore family in via Carlo Alberto 17 within the same *rione* that Pavolini observes and paces during his strolls. The cityscape reveals its transformations in the temporary survival of old shops:

> Negozi di abbigliamento cinesi e di bigiotteria da quattro soldi, una parrucchiera nigeriana specializzata in acconciature afro, phone center per chiamare il Pakistan e le Filippine a poco prezzo, la botteguccia antiquata di un barbiere, sopravvissuta ai mutamenti del rione, hotel a due e tre stelle per turisti senza pretese.[34]
>
> (Chinese clothing stores and cheap costume jewelry, a Nigerian hairdresser specializing in Afro hairstyles, a phone centre to call cheaply to Pakistan and the Philippines, an old-fashioned barber shop, a survivor of the neighbourhood changes, two- and three-star hotels for unpretentious tourists.)

The act of moving around the *rione* acknowledges drastic changes: Mazzucco's passionate realist novel partly revisits the narrative of *rione* and *borgata* conceived by Pier Paolo Pasolini. Her own empathetic gaze points to vastly complex social issues and sexual politics and directs the readers'gaze in the same direction. In via Carlo Alberto 17, the husband Antonio will kill himself and his son as retribution for his wife, Emma's, leaving him. We are not in a *borgata* but in the heart of the Esquiline. Yet the shrinking of the bourgeoisie as a result of economic decline reveals its effects on the social fabric of Rome as the notion of *borgata* and *borgatari* pertains now to a wider petty bourgeoisie. In the *Anni Zero* novel, the lumpenproletariat and the bourgeoisie are not seen as different from one another, as the *borgata* extends beyond its initial limits and "celebrates with its own existence the crisis of bourgeois certainties"[35] – a crisis that has less to do with new immigrants, gentrification, and multiculturalism than with social decline and unemployment. Yet some accuse new denizens of a violence that lies within the fabric of very Roman families. The representation of family violence registers the mutation in the Roman socio-human landscape and, in some cases, validates the hypothesis of a "juxtaposition of new localistic realisms in a global culture that is by now accustomed to aesthetization."[36]

4
Melania Mazzucco's *Un giorno perfetto*: Domestic Violence on an Everyday Perfect Day

Rome is scrutinized by some as a terminal city where everything flows in a winding, baroque process where we are doomed to death: the "unamendability" of the reality of Rome.[1] The flow appears endless, addressing nothing in particular, and yields to Massumi's idea of movement as a dislocation that does not proceed in any direction. Because of this shift in narration, some of the descriptive categories of realism seen in the Roman novels of the twentieth century, while an important legacy and testimony to the authors' commitment, no longer pertain to the reality of contemporary Rome. For instance, the way the GRA, the Grande Raccordo Anulare, defines Rome's urban layout tells another story about the city and its inhabitants. The GRA is a fragmented, unresolved part of Roman urban planning:

> The strip of asphalt, almost 40 metres wide, up to 100 metres with the areas of relevance, is the only element of relationship [between the enclaves]. Only visual, however. There are no direct vehicular connections. Passing as a pedestrian from one enclave to another means passing muddy countryside, gradients, and ditches if not consular roads or railway lines. Crossing the GRA is impossible. Yet everything is there because there is a connection. The highway is at the same time an urban loop and a determinant of development.[2]

Impossibility and connectedness almost compose an oxymoron that, once again, refers to the Roman maze. Narratives of the disenfranchised, while dealing with the underclass and the presumed atavistic laziness of those who live in this double capital with its decayed beauty, are reminiscent of Pasolini's or Morante's underprivileged. They also confront themselves with a trend situated as a *trait d'union* between the end of the century and the *Anni Zero*: the *Giovani Cannibali* writers, with the notable short story penned by Niccolò Ammaniti and Luisa Brancaccio, "Seratina" (Evening Jaunt), set between the Olimpica and the zoo.[3]

It is against this multi-layered literary background that we measure the contribution of Mazzucco's exploration of violence in narratives of social impact often situated in the urban landscape of Rome. While attending the Centro Sperimentale di Cinematografia in the 1980s, Mazzucco drew inspiration from Zavattini's famous advice that she should examine reality by using public transportation as a privileged (and dynamic) vantage point. In her non-fiction text "Loro,"[4] Mazzucco recounts how she deployed Cesare Zavattini's ideas[5] to study the then-recent phenomenon of immigration. Titled *Gli invisibili* (The Invisible Ones), the documentary Mazzucco prepared along with her schoolmates, Gianfranco and Tarek, developed a visual narrative based on the dynamics regulating a group of African and Arab immigrants. Although Mazzucco never produced her final thesis, the experience she retells in "Loro" became instrumental in the conceptualization of two of the author's most successful novels, *Vita*[6] and *Un giorno perfetto*. "Loro" speaks of the "invisibili" (the invisible ones), the new inhabitants of the city, the new Romans. Mazzucco wants to hear their stories. The opposition between Romans and "Loro" develops from the initial recognition that, to tell of Rome and to understand Rome, Mazzucco needed to reflect further on how her city was changing. Since "Loro," her career has been marked by a consistent interest in social and women's issues. Whoever, like Mazzucco, walks and narratively defines the new Rome, is keenly aware that gendered violence and the culture of violence are certainly not new issues tied to multiculturalism and migration, and many have discussed them through examples from the Latin classics. As classicist Serena Witzke writes, "there is no denying that it was dangerous to be a woman in Rome, given ... the power that *manus* marriages gave to husbands over their wives, and the atmosphere created by the numerous historical tales about rape and murder of women."[7] But while wives were at risk of violence, Witzke argues that the actual victims of violence were individuals already vulnerable, in the sense in which Judith Butler uses the term in *Precarious Life*: these were slaves and free sex labourers who were not Roman citizens and as such did not hold any legal rights in the empire. Mazzucco writes a novel about violence against women in the family well before the Law Decree (D.L.) of 23 February 2009 n.11 (converted into law on 23 April n. 38), which recognized stalking as a persecutory crime, and also before the opening of a mainstream feminist discourse in Italy on the topic. But the problem of securing rights for women is, as Wiztke shows, as old as the Roman Empire.

Mazzucco's 2005 urban epic, *Un giorno perfetto*, is a choral novel whose discourse, notwithstanding the proliferation of plot points and the multitude of characters, centres on the monopoly of discourse sustained by implicit laws of traditional male supremacy and resulting in a general lack of prosocial behaviour and concern with domestic violence. Mazzucco's authorial agency emerges from her clear preoccupation with analysing the ills of Roman society. Family occurrences, as in the case of *Un giorno perfetto*'s conjugal problems, are parts of a whole mosaic in understanding the multifaceted representations of the lives of everyday people, especially women and children who experience anger and alienation. Mazzucco's involvement with her characters and depiction of their grief and emotions constitute a type of authorial intervention in the social fabric that Edward Said calls an "intellectual representation."[8] Her use of conventional realism[9] is appropriate in representing the exploitive spectacle of a woman's physical and psychological victimization and leads readers to consider whether we are powerless in the face of domestic violence or if we can actually understand and act upon the image of women's supposed vulnerability as, instead, an act of resistance to that very threat that would restrict their movement. As Paul Verhoeven's movie *Elle* proposes, we can even think of a rape "victim" as someone turning into the avenger of such violence by contemplating the possibility of revenge. Retribution and compensation for the dishearteningly inadequate and biased legal system when it comes to women are part of the contemporary equation when we consider wronged female characters in fictional works.[10] Mazzucco's narrative evokes questions about why vulnerability has always been part of gender construction for women while the gender disparity in the legal system from which such threats derive is largely ignored.[11]

Scrivere con verità la sconosciuta filologia della vita quotidiana[12]

Ten years after Dacia Maraini's thriller *Voci* (*Voices*),[13] Mazzucco's *Un giorno perfetto* draws the elements of crime and investigation from the detective novel genre and applies them to the themes of domestic and familial abuse on multiple social levels. In its investigation of twenty-four hours in the life of ordinary Romans, *Un giorno perfetto* demonstrates how, for Mazzucco, violence against women is a "philological" matter resulting in "truthful" death. Mazzucco dedicates *Un giorno perfetto* to real women, victims of domestic and sexual violence, whose suffering was not merely a cognitive metaphor but a reality in which they lost their lives.[14] "Barbara S., Angela D. e alle altre che non so" (GP 407; to Barbara S., Angela D. and all the others whom I do not know) are just a few names of actual victims of crimes that, more often than not, go undetected (Simonetta Cesaroni's murder, also known as the "Via Poma murder," is another emblematic instance of injustice for female victims).[15]

Mazzucco employs the classical Aristotelian unity of time of twenty-four hours to conduct her fictional investigation into the family crime committed by Antonio Buonocore. The novel focuses on two Roman wives who are foils for each other: Emma, Antonio's wife, and Maya, Antonio's boss's wife. Despite their different social status, enhanced by their patently different looks, Emma and Maya must come to terms with similar attempts by their respective husbands to limit their agency. While Maya benefits from protection afforded by her affluence and education, Emma's economic status as a precarious worker with no means sees her shuttling between one bus and another, moving through empty spaces in which others like her function like "automatons."[16] The fictional text concerns an everyday story of violence similar to that which can be found in local newspapers. Antonio and Emma's troubled relationship is a symptom of the inability of the lower middle class to cope with unemployment, consumerism, and what Zygmunt Bauman calls the "negative forces" of globalized society.[17] Further, the aesthetic encounter with the everyday and alienating existence that the novel establishes with deft strategies of defamiliarization "pivots around moments of world-disclosing rupture and shock that are contrasted to the homogeneous and soul-destroying routines of daily life."[18] The by now daily occurrences of family tragedies explain the temporal choice of revisiting the twenty-four hours preceding the crime and inscribe a web across Rome by tracing the nine characters' daily routines and movements about the city. In the novel we have two parallel spatial dimensions defined by the actual names of streets and neighbourhoods in which two married women lead their lives: Emma's Rome and Maya's Rome. Both Torrevecchia and Tiburtino, the neighbourhoods where Emma – herself the product of an underprivileged background – spends her days, are working-class, marginal areas that have nothing in common with the exclusive centre of Rome. Parioli's posh Via Mangili is the street where Antonio's boss, congressman Elio Fioravanti, lives in a beautiful villa with his second wife, thirty-year-old Maya, and their daughter, Camilla; the Aventine is where Maya, distraught at the idea of a second and unwanted pregnancy (GP 195), wants to move after her separation from Elio; the Palazzo Lancellotti is situated on Via dei Coronari, where the birthday party for Elio's and Maya's daughter, Camilla, takes place on this "perfect day." These last three spaces belong to a Rome that shares nothing with the Rome of Emma and Antonio, yet, unlike in the twentieth-century novel *La Storia*, where the disenfranchised live on a map that never overlaps with that of affluent Romans, these characters constantly interact because of Antonio's work and because their children, Camilla Fioravanti and Kevin Buonocore, attend the same school. Elio and Maya Fioravanti lead their unhappy life in ritzy neighbourhoods, while the security agent and his former wife lead an equally sorrowful existence in the Esquiline. The scene of the crime in the prologue is described through the point of view of an agent, a colleague of Antonio's, who was sent to check the Buonocore apartment. What we don't know yet is that Antonio, in what media jargon defines as an "act of folly," tries to kill both his children and himself. Somebody might be still alive, but we will know this only at the end of the narrative about the twenty-four hours composing the day and the night *before* the crime occurs. Emma's family is ruined by Antonio's heinous act, while Maya, independent and still young, moves on with her own life. Mazzucco depicts and analyses each hour in the characters' lives, and each character's life, for those crucial hours.

Both stories are framed by the space of the city, which, in Mazzucco's words, deserves indisputably its role as the "tenth protagonist" of the novel:

> The tenth protagonist of my book is twenty-first-century Rome, different from the postcard image and caught in all its nuances: from Parioli to the peripheries, from its most important monuments to its social service centres. A city that is loved and hated at once, seen through the eyes of those traversing it by bus or in an official car.[19]

Busy with grandiose political projects, the mostly male occupants of *auto blu* (official cars) are undisturbed by Rome's funk in their most visible symbol of political power and influence. By contrast, those Romans riding public transportation maintain greater awareness and suffer the consequences of the metropolis's paralysing problems. Through the representation of uneven economic distribution rendered by different modes of transportation in the novel, the city appears to be a conniving character in the exploitation of the disenfranchised, especially women attempting to revindicate their subjectivity. This subjectivity is no alternative to that of men, but rather the right of subjects living in a democracy that fails to fulfil their needs.

What geographical space in the Roman map can best illustrate the stifling problems of the city, circular and eternal, if not the Raccordo Anulare and, inside it, the Tangenziale Est and the Olimpica? Even while modern modes of transportation establish physical proximity, the noise of Rome guarantees deafness to the needs of the other: Romans wander in circles like damned souls. The two circles of the Raccordo and the Olimpica enclose the map of a Rome where security agent Antonio Buonocore, Emma Tempesta's estranged husband, drives erratically before committing his heinous crime. The omniscient narrator follows Antonio Buonocore, a policeman with a powerful and muscular body, during what will be his last day. Emma lives in a tower in Primavalle, "una torre di cemento armato ... un parallelepipedo di quattordici piani, butterato da un accrocco di verande abusive in attesa di condono, padelle di parabole e panni stesi ad asciugare sui balconi" (GP 17; a cement tower ... a fourteen-story parallelepiped, pockmarked by a hodgepodge of illegal verandas waiting to be condoned, satellite dishes and clothes hanging to dry on the balconies). In a melancholic reversal of the fairy-tale princess in the tower, Antonio besieges Emma on what will be his last night, smoking away in the parking lot, lurking below the squalid building where his former wife lives with her mother. Mazzucco's narrator investigates the origins of the assailant's angst and uncovers Antonio's nostalgia for the past, a past that his wife no longer embraces. He does not accept his wife's firm decision to terminate their unhealthy marriage, in which reciprocal physical attraction had kept them together for years despite the numerous instances of reciprocal lack of understanding, physical violence, and abuse. Incapable of accepting Emma's decision to separate – an act of her own will but caused by an abusive marriage to him – Antonio prefers to end his family's life. His love for Emma, at times compared to the adoration of a Madonna, turns to sheer hatred, just as the lyrics of Loredana Bertè's song "Sei bellissima," a favourite of Emma's, are now distorted in his mind: "Lo strano uomo non ti dirà più sei bellissima, sei bellissima. Sei maledetta. Ti maledico, zoccola spergiura – e rimpiangi per sempre ciò che hai fatto alla nostra famiglia e all'uomo che avevi giurato di amare finché morte non ci separi" (GP 19; The strange man will never say again you are gorgeous, you are gorgeous. Damn you, I curse you, lying slut! Regret for ever what you did to our family and to the man you swore to love until death do us part).

The part called "Quinta ora" (Fifth hour) is dedicated to situating Emma in a position of vulnerability *because* of her own act of resistance (GP 42–51). Returning to live in her mother's apartment for lack of means does not amount to an act of emancipation from her previous condition and Antonio's constant abuse. Quite the contrary, it is the reaffirmation of her flouting of social customs that assume the female victim's compliance. Her mother, Olimpia, fully subscribes to the patriarchal mentality and blames Emma for the failure of her marriage:

> Non prendeva mai le sue parti. Per quanto incredibile potesse sembrare, aveva sempre difeso Antonio. Lo giustificava. Addossava a lei, sua figlia, la colpa di tutto. E per molto tempo, dentro di sé le aveva dato ragione. Era lei la causa del loro fallimento, lei l'errore ... Assentarsi. Volare via, per qualche ora. Ma Emma non era un asceta indiano, non faceva il vuoto dentro di sé, la sua mente era una centrifuga impazzita al centro della quale rimbalzava il pensiero di

Antonio, appostato insensatamente giù in strada. La sentenza lo aveva mandato fuori di testa. Questa situazione non poteva durare ... Non guadagnava abbastanza per pagare un affitto. Era in trappola, in quella casa troppo stretta, in quella stanza troppo stretta. In una vita troppo stretta. Da qualche parte c'era una via d'uscita. Ma lei non riusciva a intravederla. (GP 42–3)

(She never sided with her. As crazy as it sounds, she always defended Antonio. She justified him. She blamed her, her daughter, for everything. And for a long time, within herself, she thought her mother was right. She was the cause of their failure, she was the mistake ... To leave. To fly away for few hours. But Emma was not an Indian ascetic, she did not make the void within herself, her mind was a spinning-mad blender at the centre of which the thought of Antonio, parked down the street, was constantly bouncing off. This situation could not last ... She didn't earn enough to pay rent. She was trapped in a house that was too narrow. In a life that was too narrow. Somewhere there had to be a way out. But she could not glimpse it.)

Though refusing to internalize her mother's position vis-à-vis her decision to leave Antonio, Emma's thoughts reflect nevertheless the weight of a common way of thinking. She also reminisces about her mother's opposite opinion when Emma was young and madly in love with Antonio. Her mother's negative comments about Antonio back then accompany Emma through her sleepless night. She is now left to wonder, while reading *Anna Karenina*, a book she found at home because her daughter, Valentina, is reading it for school, if, indeed, she was a bad wife, a bad woman. Putting herself in Anna's place, Emma reflects on her condition. Along with her mad love for Antonio she also remembers him constantly talking her down in front of the children, shouting at her "Di' che non sai fare niente" (GP 47–8; Say that you are a good-for-nothing) for no particular reason. Emma recalls the twenty-third of December 1998 (GP 249) – when, after their umpteenth argument, she waited for Antonio to go to work so she could take the children, leave the house (GP 45–7) and report Antonio – as the turning point of her life, no matter what. She remembers his beatings and his violence, her bruises and her fear. They are forever printed on her traumatized mind. If it spins like a mad blender, there are plenty of reasons for that. Emma knows she can't denounce Antonio for being parked below her building, since "la strada è suolo pubblico" (GP 54; the street belongs to everyone), as her lawyer told her. She is afraid of Antonio's proximity to her and the children, but she is no longer the same woman as she was prior to the twenty-third of December 1998 (GP 49).

Not only the troubled domestic sphere but also the workplace fit Mazzucco's idea of "credibility" for her novels: "If you want to tell a contemporary story you cannot but describe the working world, lest you undermine the actual credibility of the narrative. The dead times constitute people's lives: the eight hours spent in the office, the interminable hours in class, and then the electoral speeches on the city's outskirts, the precariousness of a job in a call centre."[20] Emma works in a call centre, where Antonio calls to hear her voice. He misses that

> voce morbida e suadente che gli scatenava nelle ghiandole una tempesta ormonale e per un attimo lo rendeva felice ... ma lei faceva finta di non riconoscerlo, solo una volta era sbottata, sibilando con voce dura e tagliente: Sto lavorando, non rovinarmi anche questo, lasciami in pace. (GP 37)
>
> (soft and persuasive voice that unleashed in his glands a hormonal storm and for a moment made him happy ... But she pretended not to recognize him, hissing in a hard and sharp voice: I'm working, do not spoil this too, leave me alone.)

The episode, also recounted from Emma's point of view (GP 135–7), is only one of Antonio's numerous acts of violation of Emma's space.

Violence and conjugal abuse become the most significant evidence of a relationship that, for both the Buonocores and the Fioravantis, is no longer constructive. In the case of the Buonocore family, however, it is Emma's decision to end her marriage that leads to the crime that initiates the plot. As in the police blotter of a local newspaper, or even a *noir*, the murder is narrated as a *fait accompli* that will take place in the apartment on via Carlo Alberto 17.[21] In the heart of Rome, in a building bearing a gigantic picture of a famous soccer player to obscure the scaffolding of a restoration in progress, two members of the same family die from domestic violence:

> Prima abitavano tutti qua, ha detto il vicino – i ragazzini facevano un casino d'inferno, andavano coi pattini in terrazzo, protestare era inutile con Buonocore, un prepotente che si credeva il padreterno, poi la madre se li era portati via e non si erano più visti. (GP 13)
>
> (Before they all lived here, the neighbour said – the kids used to make a hellish noise, skating on the terrace. Complaining was useless with Buonocore, a bully who thought he was God. Then the mother took them away and we never saw them again.)

"Before" is a deictic of impressive value in this sentence. It represents the whole temporal lapsus before the murder committed by the head of the family. Discourse is conducted by that very deictic that implies the entire ante-murder family life. The collective aspect of basic unconcern for what happens in other families is defined by the fact that, even though Buonocore displayed his temper inside and outside the domestic sphere, his neighbour only once reported his gratuitous violence (GP 14). He did not confront the man's spurts of rage. He waited, hoping either that the nucleus would eventually break down and the wife would flee with her children or that things between the couple would patch up. Emma left with her children, and it was water under the bridge for everyone in the building. Regrettably, a passive community that refuses to act on behalf of a woman represents a consequential aspect of our everyday life and a mindset that still accepts family violence as a given. Mazzucco questions why neighbours are passive and why they resist intervening. Is this a conventional form of behaviour? How can we think this is the way to respond to violence taking place across the landing from our apartment? Situations like this are so common in Italian society that it is hardly possible to remain impassive when reading of such apathy because we know it's only too real.

Patriarchal discourse usually warns against a *sconosciuto*, a stranger, who can bring violence upon a household, particularly upon children and women, something that Mazzucco's omniscient narrator does not fail to note. The Other disturbs the order in the house, appearing disguised as a stranger who rapes the woman, the mother, and ultimately destroys the family. Almost invariably in domestic crimes, the aggravating individual has his own motives for violence, knows the victims, and is even related by blood to them, like Antonio. As in a case study, Mazzucco analyses one household whose members are stuck in a "vita sospesa, indifferente, oscura" (GP 14; life suspended, indifferent, bleak). The children reared in this environment, Kevin and Valentina, suffer the consequences of domestic violence, nocturnal diuresis for little Kevin, and abandonment syndrome for adolescent Valentina.

While every aspect of contemporary society clamours for the relevance of the *new*, Mazzucco convincingly proposes that Italian society is not necessarily rethinking itself and fictionalizes into the body of her novel the ethical concerns expressed by Rosi Braidotti in her theoretical works. Contemporary society fails to adapt its limits for "the potentially innovative, de-territorializing impact of the new technologies that, in turn, is hampered and turned down by the reassertion of the gravitational pull of old and established values."[22] Rather than rethinking the way they fulfil their duties and rights as citizens within a globalized society, Italians de-territorialize only those areas of society that are connected with consumerism:

> The much-celebrated phenomenon of globalisation and of its technologies accomplishes a magician's trick: it combines the euphoric celebration of

> *new* technologies, *new* economy, *new* lifestyles, *new* generations of both human and technological gadgets, *new* wars and *new* weapons with the utter social rejection of change and transformation.[23]

Citizens appear to be involved in the process of change but do not consider it necessary to form new, alternative communities in which women's vulnerability can be discussed and its terms re-evaluated and reversed. In *Un giorno perfetto,* the violence of physical assaults on women merely exposes the social and historical paradox Braidotti elicits in *Transpositions* and that concerns also globalized Rome: economic growth and a liberal political system do not relinquish or improve social dysfunction; conversely, perhaps, they aggravate the state of things by re-enforcing a victim mythology.

The wave of neo-conservatism that Braidotti describes is an obstacle to rethinking women and their rights. Mazzucco's *Un giorno perfetto* is an ethical and political narrative committed to illuminating Italian society's paradoxical economic development, one that has taken place without the requisite social changes. This novel's conclusions are consistent with Braidotti's reflections: they underscore the dynamics determining women's relative lack of agency, even in a democratic country such as Italy. Not all killings of women are motivated by the victim's gender, but sexual assaults and domestic violence are key elements in the overall picture. Aside from rampant discrimination in the workplace and the *mobbing* phenomenon, women confront their most notable challenges in the domain of family values, especially with regard to the sacred institutions of marriage and motherhood.[24] As Olimpia shows in *Un giorno perfetto,* widespread weakening of the family institution is often blamed on women rather than on other social causes. We are living through times in which a perceived equality of rights allows individuals to express themselves as she does. Alain Touraine's sociological study on women's condition at the inception of the twenty-first century argues that lack of militancy can harm women's legitimate wish for better action against inequality and discrimination. Women's vulnerability is a consequence of a society that simultaneously posits women as victims of a patriarchal system and the institution of marriage while also giving the false impression that it is no longer discriminating against them. More than sixty years ago, Simone de Beauvoir's famous reflections demonstrated the threat to women's emancipation when their role is relegated to that of vessel and caregiver, confining them to immanence.[25] The immanence that, for many, still signifies the static nature of woman becomes a convenient weapon for a community that refuses to grant women an adequate praxis of their democratic rights. When women making complaints at the police precinct are not welcomed, informed, and supported in a way that enables them to escape conditions of subservience and isolation, it means the law is failing them.

In this era of globalization, the original lack of social mobility for women, coupled with a lack of redefinition of their role within the family, produces a further challenge to their democratic rights. Global economics force women back into a cycle of subjection, while laws fail to protect them from abuse. In coping with its transformation, society preserves women's roles as individuals who are not afforded their full rights. Emotionally invested in her characters, chiefly Emma and her children, but also Antonio, the perpetrator of violence, Mazzucco exposes the verbal codes that organize the language of violence against women and suggest powerless victimhood. Media jargon often establishes women as powerless victims, but the problem lies deeper, within society as a whole.[26] At the end of the novel, one is left to wonder if, even more than his estranged wife and children, Antonio himself is the victim of his own haplessness and ineptitude. Unable to change his own life, he does not want Emma to move on with hers. What is apparent, though, is that through Emma's survival despite her husband's vicious and violent act, Mazzucco establishes agency for her character. Like Butler, she believes that "there is some other way to live such that one becomes neither affectively dead nor mimetically violent, a way out of the circle of violence altogether."[27] As we read, Emma too feels that, "somewhere there had to be a way out" (GP 43).

By illustrating brutal episodes of physical and verbal abuse that Emma and Maya endure, Mazzucco reveals disquieting patterns of subjection that expose the myth behind the postcard image of Rome and that are transmitted by a society that *thinks* it provides equal rights to each of its citizens. Mazzucco's postfeminist omniscient narrator inserts fictional investigative reports to argue that public discourse should be directed not at women who are abused or deprived of their rights, stuck in the role of victims, but at men who cannot handle their own ineptitude in coping with social change.[28] Mazzucco's discourse contains media reports about abused and battered women – whether from television or the press – that reveal the stories of men who take out their frustration with their personal failings on their spouses and girlfriends, within an impassive society in which gender equality has advanced so much.[29] Women's bodies give life to men but are also the objects upon which men still to this day discharge their violence.[30] The family, whose protection should be a priority for our society, keeps the man in his usual role and prolongs his childhood. The man celebrates his triumphs as he imposes his failures and frustrations on the female body. Men are not always victorious, Lea Melandri adds, so their destructive rage physically falls first on the bodies of their women, wives, spurned lovers, and children – before they take their own lives.[31]

Mazzucco's representation of the main female characters' travails presents what is almost a platitude: real social emancipation must begin by challenging personal, hence domestic, experiences of violence through legal avenues. The personal defines the political, as the feminist cliché goes. The oft-celebrated domestic hearth is the locus of extreme verbal and physical violence, where women lack the power to speak up for themselves while men inflict violence on those they say they love the most. Silence and inaction prevail over discussion and action on this vexing issue despite statistics that clearly show the extent of the problem,[32] despite the enormous number of cases reported to the police (which appear almost daily in Italian newspapers), and despite the increasing critical interest in the affective dimensions of everyday life, the emotions and feelings that should raise awareness of the social and collective importance of ordinary affects.

Mazzucco's narrator is a social investigator for her characters. She corrects women's aphasia, and discusses physical and mental abuse as Mazzucco has in her historical novel *Il bacio della Medusa.* Overall, Mazzucco argues that violence against women and children[33] (both seen as Others with respect to the patriarchal system) is primarily *discourse* before it manifests in an act of *physical* violence. As a discourse, this violence is connected to media language and juridical narratives. Verbal abuse comes before physical abuse, and certainly before murder. As violence escalates from the verbal to the physical, there seems to be little or no reaction from politics, law, or police – the elements that govern society. Mazzucco's novel resists the common rhetoric that feigns understanding of women's existence, demonstrating how violence against women is an endless family affair passively permitted, even by the law. The novel's prose resists facile rhetoric and reveals a Deleuzian quality: the frail corporeality of the female subjects, best epitomized in Maya's lean body, exposes the wrongs perpetrated by their spouses, companions, and friends. Mazzucco's characters' actions show how "vulnerable and violated bodies can be reconfigured, that is, liberated from the defensive and defeated histories to which they have been consigned."[34]

Mazzucco's verbal images respond to everyday violence with brutally precise images devoid of any morbid pleasure. Physical beatings and forced sex call for serious reflection on Italian society's social implosion. Physical violence effaces victims' power to act and affects them with aphasia. As an essential corollary to her primary concern, Mazzucco engages the female body and its ability to counter recent speculation about the disappearance of active feminism from Italian society and about the rapid loss of the rights achieved through women's struggles in the 1970s. Thus, *Un giorno perfetto* showcases Mazzucco's internalized feminist teachings, encouraging emancipation and drawing attention to women's situations. This novel declares the relevance of feminism beyond facile stereotypes, epitomizing a point of view that goes beyond essentialism and "genderism."[35] While eradicating fossilized and dangerous notions of female acquiescence, this author depicts a growing self-awareness in both Emma and Maya that provides hope for a more equitable future. Mazzucco's ethical responsibility towards women subject to domestic violence, whose voices are constantly muted, reveals her awareness that we need to connect the knowledge and overcoming of precise historical moments to move beyond the ideological impasse of feminism today, and that only then can we fully grasp the parallel relationship between "a depletion of a male power with no authority and the growth of a female authority that can do without power."[36]

Rome and Its Women: Democracy Interrupted

Ida Dominijanni has described "an ancient hostility between the modern State and women,"[37] the animosity that results from "exclusion on the one side and ... extraneousness on the other, which the construction of citizenship has never managed to heal but only to mitigate."[38] The adjective *antica* (ancient) refers to an expansive history of abuse and violence against women. It is Roman history itself that teaches us how women's personal lives are thoroughly political and exploitable.[39] Since antiquity, Roman history has consistently, and famously, braided politics and violence, from the rape of the Sabine women, abducted to replenish the newly founded city and ensure the procreation of Roman warriors, to that of the chaste Lucretia, the founding myth of the Roman Republic. For all its generosity and grandeur, the city of Rome has consistently maintained a troubled relationship with its women. Rome's walls bleed, and too often this blood spills from women's bodies. Beyond antiquity, the rape, torture, trial, and victimization of historical characters such as Beatrice Cenci and Artemisia Gentileschi, as well as a closer model offered by Pasolini's *Mamma Roma,* confirm the association between the history of Rome and the history of violence against women well after the fall of the Roman Empire. In *Un giorno perfetto*, the corporeal quality of violence holds also a misogynistic component of genuine love and adoration for Rome as for her women in the depiction of Antonio, who, at age forty-two, still searches for the complementary image of a caring, maternal Rome that welcomes all men into her womb. In one of his typical swings of mood, Antonio equates his hatred for the city of Rome to that for his estranged wife (and himself):

> Antonio sentì un rigurgito d'odio per la Tiburtina, questa strada alienante, generica, accerchiata dalle fabbriche, dalle aziende informatiche, da

capannoni, costruzioni brutte, una strada nella quale erano brutti perfino gli alberi e i fiori, dove però Emma – *questa Emma nuova che era nata dopo che la sua Emma era andata via* – si destreggiava ogni giorno da quando non viveva più per lui. E ormai odiava anche Roma, questa città femmina dalle forme rotonde, una città materna, fatta di cupole floride come seni e portici spalancati come gambe – il cui segno, come quello delle donne, è vuoto: l'inquietante vuoto romano che mina tutto, è una malattia incurabile. Odiava Roma come Emma, e come se stesso. (GP 218; emphasis added)

(Antonio overflowed with hatred for the Tiburtina, this alienating and generic road, surrounded by factories, computer companies, industrial warehouses, and ugly buildings, a road where even trees and flowers were ugly but where, nevertheless, Emma – *this new Emma that was born after his Emma had left* – managed every day since she no longer lived for him. By now he hated Rome as well, this female city with her round shapes, a maternal city made of domes as buxom as breasts and porticos as wide as legs – whose sign, like that of women, is empty: the disquieting Roman void that threatens everything, is an incurable illness. He hated Rome like Emma, and like himself.)

Antonio is consumed by hatred and, unsurprisingly, sees the entire city no longer as a maternal womb but as a female reproductive organ that rejects him as the *new* Emma has done. But most of all, he hates himself for not having been able to keep his family together, for failing to compel his wife to follow traditional *mores* and family rules.[40] Rather than seeking to become a more accommodating and attentive husband, he blames himself for not imposing his wishes more on Emma. A new construction arises for the fallen dream. The "emotion of hate works to animate the ordinary subject," Ahmed argues, "to bring that fantasy to life, precisely by constituting the ordinary as in crisis, and the ordinary person as the *real victim*."[41] The *old* Emma represented Antonio's ideal, which the *new* Emma has ruined. Rome and Emma, Emma and Rome: in showing the beauty of ancient Rome to his children during their last walk together right before his crime, Antonio, originally from Calabria, realizes how little he still knows about this city. Touching the Bernini elephant statue in front of Santa Maria sopra Minerva, he equates his ignorance of the city with his ignorance of his wife:

un capolavoro barocco di imitazione della natura. Mai visto nemmeno questo. Quante cose ho ignorato. E vivo a Roma da vent'anni. Ma cos'è, Roma? È la città cui Emma mi ha incatenato. Roma si fa amare esattamente come una donna, perché ti piace, perché stai bene con lei, perché ti capisce, ti accoglie e ti risponde. Perché, malgrado i difetti e le mancanze che rendono irregolare la sua bellezza, quella bellezza supera ai tuoi occhi tutte le altre. Ho sposato Roma come Emma. Una bellezza che ho goduto, ma che mai mi è appartenuta. (GP 333)

(a baroque masterpiece imitating nature. Never seen this either. How many things have I ignored. And I have been living in Rome for twenty years. But what is Rome? It is the city that Emma chained me to. Rome makes herself loved exactly like a woman, because you like her, because you find yourself at ease with her, because she understands you, she accepts you and responds to you. Because, despite the defects and faults that make her beauty irregular, that beauty surpasses all others in your eyes. I married Rome as I did Emma. A beauty that I enjoyed, but that I never possessed.)

"Rome makes herself loved exactly like a woman, because you like her, because you find yourself at ease with her, because she understands you, she accepts you and responds to you," Antonio ruminates. But we know that, despite all the comparisons made between the city and a woman, Rome's history runs parallel to the history of violence against women. In *Un giorno perfetto,* violence functions to depict, metaphorize, and explain the glory of the Eternal City. History seems to repeat itself by showing that the violation of women's bodies is as much a part of the "new-era" globalization process as it was a part of ancient and Renaissance Roman society. It is not unusual to connect the politics of gender with that of subalternity and violence, for the Western tradition has "naturalized" the notion of erotic violence and rape in its foundational tales. Western authors employ erotic violence and rape in beautiful myths "that simultaneously articulate and hide the socially constructed story of male and female sexuality difference and power that makes women 'essentially' vulnerable and mute."[42] The Western tradition has always acknowledged what Lynn Higgins and Brenda Silver call "a paradigm of rape and silencing [for] they go hand in hand."[43] While in male authors we witness the elision of scenes of violence – particularly rape – and the subsequent, institutionalized acceptance of gender oppression, Higgins and Silver instead urge their readers to see how, when it comes to representations of rape and violence, it is almost impossible to dissociate "poetics from the politics of gender."[44] Indeed, in their view, "the entire Western lyric tradition and the quest for beauty, truth, and knowledge associated with the 'Grecian spirit' allow for sexual violence to become a myth, an aesthetic locus."[45] To demystify this troubling tradition, feminist artists must critique it and reinstate the violence and rape of women as literal rather than metaphorical events. They must take these acts in their factual sense and represent them without the symbolic value that confines violence to a realm of sublimation. Mazzucco, and Stambrini to some extent, divorce the notion of essentialism and stasis from that of vulnerability, and propose a renegotiation of agency for violated women.

"A Good Map Is Worth a Thousand Words": A Geography of Violence

Literary maps, according to Franco Moretti, demonstrate or reveal "the *ortgebunden*, place-bound nature of literary forms: each of them with its peculiar geometry, its boundaries, its spatial taboos and favorite routes."[46] Furthermore, maps

> bring to light the *internal* logic of narrative: the semiotic domain around which a plot coalesces and self-organizes. Literary form appears thus as the result of two conflicting and equally significant forces: one working from the outside, and one from the inside. It is the usual, and at bottom, the only real issue of literary history: society, rhetoric, and their interaction.[47]

Moretti's reflections on the productive synergy existing between geometry and the novel prompted my conceptualization of a map of Rome for *Un giorno perfetto* – a map that reflects the finely textured narrative of a day in the city's life. A map of the characters' wanderings about a city can materialize the interaction between the internal force of the literary form and the external force generated by the interaction of society with rhetoric. This interaction produces both the plot and the themes that inhabit the novel. The map of *Un giorno perfetto* identifies the many distinct layers of modern-day Rome. In this novel, the city's geometrical geography of streets, squares, and circles inhibits conceptualization of an elegiac, classic, and serene Rome, suggesting instead an intricately textured place that is arduous to decipher. This map contains the bundle of subway and bus lines through which Emma commutes between her mother's narrow apartment in the impersonal cement dormitories of Primavalle, near Torrevecchia, and the call centre on the Tiburtina road where she faces and succumbs to the threat of age discrimination. The precariousness of work mirrors also the precariousness of Emma's subjectivity and physical lack of space for herself. Emma is struggling to keep her job in a call centre. The 2001 map of Rome propounds a sheer static chaos for which, not incidentally, Aris – a graffiti artist with the name Zero and son of congressman Elio Fioravanti's first wife – likens the city to a "meraviglioso pantano" (GP 114; a wonderful swamp). To Zero, Rome appears as "una città decrepita e immobile" (a dilapidated and inert city), too burdened by her past to flourish in the future. To him, this is a city in which "abitanti giravano in cerchio, come dannati" (GP 114;

inhabitants wandered in circles like damned souls). Sasha, the professor of Antonio's and Emma's daughter, Valentina, also depicts Italy in terms of periphery, thus admitting similar concerns for contemporary Rome:

> [L'Italia è] una colonia neanche di importanza strategica ormai che il muro di Berlino è caduto. È una periferia, e anche parecchio degradata – dal punto di vista culturale, si intende – nella quale ogni talento e ogni autentico slancio espressivo vengono repressi e soffocati e appiattiti in una consolante uniformità. (GP 272)
>
> ([Italy is] a colony with no strategic importance now that the Berlin Wall has fallen. It is a periphery, rather degraded – culturally speaking – in which every talent and every authentic expressive impulse are repressed and suffocated and flattened in a comforting uniformity.)

The map of the city reveals a destructive energy that dooms Rome to repeat its history of chaos and violence. The rhetoric of this past, which many still consider glorious, signifies the city's basic inability to adapt to the future and globalization, failing to respond to the new demands for, in Braidotti's terms, "an interrelation of the centre with the peripheral."[48] In response to Zero's denunciation of the state of the city, Mazzucco's narrative hardly depicts Rome as somnolent and lazy; instead it exposes problems integral to Rome's emergence in the era of globalization. "The historical era of globalisation is the meeting ground on which sameness and otherness or centre and periphery confront each other and redefine their interrelation"[49] – a characterization that allows Mazzucco to appropriate the geographical space of the city and underscores how "producing a cartography is a way of embedding critical practice in a specific situated perspective, avoiding universalistic generalizations and grounding it so as to make it accountable."[50] Resisting such generalizations, Mazzucco wants to write with truth the unknown philology of everyday life. What Rita Felski calls "the quintessential quality of taken-for-grantedness"[51] of everyday life unfolds in disquieting ways in which we witness the encounter of "a mundane social world and a phenomenological relationship to that world."[52]

Everyday violence in a mundane social world cannot be an act of love. Violence is about possession and the inability to cope with another's agency. The investigation of Antonio's physical violence against Emma and his family and his boss's psychological abuse towards his young wife, Maya, reveal causes that transcend the personal. Buonocore and Fioravanti represent two sides of the same coin: the pursuit of happiness based on old social mores and materialistic goals and a sense of self that cannot take account of women's right to an autonomous existence.[53] However, the different endings for these families rest on the notion of class, the distinction between those who lead a privileged existence and those who do not. Buonocore's violence and rage develop in a manner altogether different from those of his congressman, Fioravanti. The latter undergoes his own personal downfall – as a husband, because his wife is leaving him; as a public figure, because his own political leader is withdrawing his support; and as a father, because his son, Zero, disowns him. That "solidità virile" (GP 95; virile solidity) that Fioravanti found so reassuring in Antonio's "collo taurino" (GP 95; taurine neck) crumbles when both men face their inability to make anyone happy, even their own relatives. Without condoning the husbands, Mazzucco demonstrates that discussions about sexual violence should not be limited to what Janice Haaken calls "a debate between agency and victimization"[54] nor to notions of consent. It is important to understand society's role in the surge of hopeless violence experienced by Western families. As suggested by Lea Melandri in *Amore e violenza*, Mazzucco's lengthy descriptions of Antonio's state of illness lead us to conclude that, according to the omniscient narrator, violence against one's own family is a distinctly male expression of impotence and haplessness, of men's inability to live up to their own expectations for themselves.[55] Antonio recognizes his ex-wife's superior ability to resist an alienation that he can only repress through physical violence. Responding to Emma's extraordinary strength in leaving him to begin a new life for herself and her children, Antonio faces an ancestral fear of, and envy for, her vigour and tenacity, which leads him to attempt to capture and rape her. As Mazzucco puts it, there is no act of folly to justify this character's crime: "Antonio Buonocore's story is not that of a man [who is a] victim of a raptus of folly, as we frequently read in newspapers, but that of an average guy in crisis over the end of his marriage. His internal emptiness stems from the fact that his woman has taken away a part of him along with his kids. For this reason, he decides to use people's bodies as blunt instruments. He does not go suddenly crazy."[56] So, the everyday life of Antonio is shaken by his emotions that no longer find a match in Emma's. His "taurine" neck can hardly sustain the blow to his male pride: "Bodies are not defined by their genus or species, by their organs and functions, but by what they can do, by the affects of which they are capable – in passion as well as action."[57] Bodies produce affects, according to Deleuze and Parnet and, as Kathleen Stewart asserts,

> ordinary affects are the varied, surging capacities to affect and to be affected that give everyday life the quality of a continual motion of relations, scenes, contingencies, and emergences. They are things that happen. They happen in impulses, sensations, expectations, daydreams, encounters, and

> habits of relating, in strategies and their failures, in forms of persuasion, contagion, and compulsion, in modes of attention, attachment, and agency, and in public and social worlds of all kinds that catch people up in something that feels like something.[58]

"Persuasion, contagion, and compulsion" motivate Antonio's blind ire, which has nothing to do with a constructive form of indignation but echoes that of countless irascible and aggressive tragic male literary figures. When looking at, or perhaps stalking, the stoic and resilient Emma, Antonio feels psychologically inferior and weak. Antonio cannot accept his ex-wife's agency and move on with his life because, according to him, Emma destroyed the perfect picture of his family. Antonio wants to forget his daily life with her: "Oh, Signore, aiutami a dimenticare tutto questo, dimenticare lei, i bambini, la casa. Aiutami a svegliarmi domani senza questa nostalgia andata a male come un surgelato scaduto – libero" (GP 20; Oh, God, help me forget all of this, to forget her, the kids, the house. Help me wake up tomorrow morning without this nostalgia gone awry like expired frozen food – free). He cannot see himself as an independent adult, which is not the same as a free man. He wants to feel liberated from his dependence on Emma and their everyday life together, but something prevents him from furthering what remains only a dream, a mental subterfuge to escape his now squalid reality:

> Poteva incontrare un'altra donna. Poteva innamorarsi, sposarla, costruirsi un'altra famiglia ... Allora, cullandosi al pensiero di essersi liberato di lei, di loro, di se stesso, Antonio s'addormentò ... Consapevole, subito senza scampo, di non voler rivivere quel passato né fuggire in un qualunque futuro. Di non volere una donna nuova, una vita nuova. Voglio stare dove sono già stato. L'unica novità che cerco: tornare con te. (GP 20)

> (He could meet another woman. He could fall in love, marry her, have another family ... Then, lulling himself with the thought of having gotten rid of her, of them, of himself, Antonio fell asleep ... Aware, immediately hopeless, of not wanting to relive that past or to escape to another future. Of not wanting a new woman, a new life. I want to stay where I have already been. The only novelty I want: to be with you again.)

Nostalgic recollections of their courtship, the handsome couple's great love, inscribe what turns out to be a temporal map of prolonged acts of violence. Antonio's repeated acts of violence, ever since they camped on Lipari beach twenty-one years before that tragic fourth of May, 2001 (GP 222), lack even the slightest hint of romantic jealousy. They are exposed for what they signified to Emma: trips to the hospital where shame would take over a sense of justice towards herself. She was sent to the Policlinico hospital twice, where the second time, the nurse Rosa, in a gesture of solidarity, silently placed a flyer for battered women on Emma's lap. Emma, just as countless women before and after her, had always forgiven the violence she endured from Antonio, her own "Gentleman or Beast."[59] Violence defines their relationship and everyday existence for years before Emma finally leaves. Once, outside a club, Antonio responded to her threat to call the authorities by screaming "sono io la polizia" (GP 230; I am the police). In this instance, jealous rage determines his act: "l'aveva trascinata per i capelli tra le pozzanghere e le macchine in sosta ... l'aveva presa a calci e schiaffi, perché voleva sapere cosa cazzo aveva in più di lui quella specie di ballerino negro" (GP 230; he dragged her by the hair through the puddles and parked cars ... he kicked her and slapped her because he wanted to know what the fuck that black dancer had that he did not). This is not a fantasy of violence but a real attack that confirms the fact that Emma is a member of a society that grants the use of of violence to its men precisely because these men make the word of authority ("sono io la polizia" GP 230) their own. Within the neo-patriarchal system, Emma cannot be exempted from the common belief that wives do not denounce family abuse and violence, lest the character lose credibility. But slowly she convinces herself of the unsustainability of this way of living: "si era liberata dai sensi di colpa e non si guardava più attraverso i suoi occhi" (GP 231; she had freed herself of guilt and no longer looked at herself through his eyes). This is the *new* Emma.

Mazzucco's omniscient narrator exposes the flaws of patriarchal authority and legal discourse, the first elements of discrimination against women, along with the rhetoric of family. The need for changing discursive practices becomes apparent when patriarchal discourse that pretends benevolence informs the *maresciallo*'s thoughts about Emma, when she denounces Antonio for the last time before his crime. Women's inequality is underscored by his reflections on the recording of the first charges she brought against her husband on 13 November 1998, and then withdrew. Her incorrect Italian jeopardizes the comprehension of the statement to the police, and "la denuncia faceva acqua da tutte le parti" (GP 252; the police charges were unreliable):

> Emma Tempesta sembrava alquanto instabile, durante la faticosa redazione della denuncia aveva fumato tre sigarette. Interrogata sulla sua professione, aveva rifiutato di spiegare quale fosse, perché una persona non è il lavoro che fa ... Inoltre, la Tempesta non aveva saputo spiegare la dinamica del presunto tentativo di omicidio. Era salita di sua volontà sull'auto del marito.

> E il poliziotto aveva il porto d'armi ... La Tempesta non ricordava com'erano andati i fatti, o non voleva dirlo, magari aveva addirittura avuto un rapporto consenziente col marito – un fatto molto comune, in casi analoghi ... Indagini delicate, da effettuarsi con la massima discrezione. C'erano di mezzo dei bambini. Altro non poteva permetterle. Se non la certezza che guidava ogni suo giorno. La legge è uguale per tutti. (GP 252)
>
> (Emma Tempesta seemed rather unstable; during the difficult drafting of the charges, she had smoked three cigarettes. Questioned on her profession, she had refused to explain what it was, because a person is not the job that she does ... Moreover, Ms Tempesta had not been able to explain the dynamics of the alleged murder attempt. She got into her husband's car of her own will. And the police officer had a gun license ... Tempesta didn't remember how the facts developed, or she didn't want to say it, perhaps she even had consensual sex with her husband, a very common fact, in these cases ... Delicate investigations, to be carried out with the utmost discretion. There were children involved. He could not allow her anything else. Only the certainty that led him through every day. The law is the same for everyone.)

The sarcasm inherent in one of the greatest fallacies ever pronounced, "the law is equal for all," underscores the futility of Emma's denunciation, because if the law is the same for all, its interpretation is not. Despite the imminent threat, Emma's voice remains unheard. The *carabinieri* do not believe that the law is equal for everybody. For one thing, Antonio is one *of them,* as he claims in his favourite mantra, "sono io la polizia" (GP 230; I am the police). Furthermore, there exists a basic reluctance on the part of the authorities to address prejudice towards women. Women's voices – their linguistic power – fade into aphasia because they are not heard. Legislative discourse and its practice are not the same for everybody. Whenever society denies women their rights, the very notion of democracy is in danger.

When Emma denounces her ex-husband for the last time, on this *perfect day*, the *maresciallo di zona* (the local chief of the carabinieri) discredits her report. His is a voice of authority, and like Antonio, he "is the police." Prior to her attempted murder on the fourth of May 2001, Emma had, when they were living together, already denounced her husband at the carabinieri of Esquilino on 13 November 1998. However, she had withdrawn her report, surrendering herself to the fixed idea that women and their bodies are victims and sites of vulnerability. The *maresciallo* asks her, "Ma perché? ... Cosa possiamo fare per voi se non ci aiutate ad aiutarvi!" (GP 250; But why? ... What can we do for you, if you do not help us to help you!). Use of the plural "you," the Italian second person plural pronoun "voi," indicates the multitude of women Emma represents – the many women who justify their man and his violence over and over again. Emma says, "io lo amavo, era mio marito, il padre dei miei bambini" (GP 250; I loved him, he was my husband, the father of my children). Hers is not merely shame; it is the feeling that he who says he loves us cannot harm us.

We have two possibilities here. If we consider vulnerability as a fixed concept, Emma is the symbol of women bound to systemic violation by men like Antonio. If she has internalized Antonio's violent feelings and blames only herself for his behaviour, her body, like that of her children, will be subject to continued violation and exploitation because, as Erinn Cunniff Gilson states, "to be vulnerable is to be en route to harm and violation by virtue of one's compromised status."[60] However, some forty days after the first unsuccessful rape attempt in 1998, Emma leaves her husband, a man who cannot cope with the breakdown of his own moral codes determined by his own failure to think of his marriage in a different manner. Antonio believes, due to his jaundiced and stereotypical opinion, that Emma will end up "una megera fallita come la madre" (GP 233; an old failed hag like her mother). In theory, Antonio is convinced that he wants to rescue her, dutifully, from the "tradimento della vecchiaia, dalla decadenza e dall'infelicità" (GP 233; the betrayal of old age, decay and unhappiness), since only he can make Emma beautiful. In actuality, he patronizes his estranged wife, diminishing her into a position of submissiveness. Lacking both the ingenuity and willingness necessary to reconsider his role and self-expectations, while internalizing hegemonic perceptions of gender and sexuality, Antonio submits to extreme measures. In his mind, it is not he but Emma who fails to adhere to sacrosanct laws.

One Last Perfect Day

Antonio Buonocore concocts his horrendous crime in the Church of Sant'Agostino while waiting for Elio Fioravanti, who was committed to daily prayer in front of Caravaggio's *Madonna dei Pellegrini.* Antonio had never entered the church before, and the solemn beauty of the painting intimidates him. He also cannot help but compare the austere and yet solemn church of the Augustinians to his mother-in-law's eerie church, "di cemento armato, costruita negli anni Ottanta, completamente priva di arredi: le file di banchi fatte di seggiole incollate fra loro, rubate a un cinema di periferia ormai chiuso da tempo. Non c'erano né altari né quadri: le pareti erano nude" (GP 105; made of concrete, built in the eighties, completely devoid of furniture; the rows of pews made of chairs stuck to each other, stolen from a suburban movie theatre now closed. There were neither altars nor pictures: the walls were bare). In its title, *La Madonna dei Pellegrini* carries the notion of wandering connected with Mazzucco's Rome: pilgrims travel to the Holy City, but pilgrims are also imprisoned within its perimeter marked by the roads the popes built for access to the basilicas. The realism of Caravaggio's painting – the sensual and barefoot Madonna, modelled on a *popolana*, holds Jesus at the doorstep of a modest home – apparently leads Antonio, now afflicted by hallucinations, to see a connection between Mary and Emma, based on what he believes is their striking resemblance. The imagined likeness between the two women leads Antonio to reflect on his present condition, which he blames on Emma:

> Era una donna, con un bambino. La donna era bruna, fiera e semplice, come, come, come ... Il bambino aveva tre, forse quattro anni. Poteva essere Kevin, o almeno il Kevin di cui Antonio aveva memoria, prima che lei glielo portasse via. Prima che distruggesse la sua vita, trasformasse l'agente speciale in un lacché, i suoi bambini in due estranei. (GP 107)

> (It depicted a woman with a child. The woman was dark-haired, proud and simple like, like, like ... The boy was three, perhaps four. He could have been Kevin, or at least the Kevin Antonio remembered before she took him away from him. Before she destroyed his life, turning the special agent into a lackey, and his two kids into two strangers.)

While his boss, representative Fioravanti, prays to the young Madonna for protection and help in the upcoming elections, Antonio draws inspiration from Caravaggio's *Madonna* to plot his family's murder. Antonio's frenzy results from an irrational jealousy that is not simply erotic. He resents his wife for gaining custody of their children and for not being what women should be, thinking "le donne non sono più quelle di una volta" (GP 104; women are no longer what they used to be). Despite his six guns and three rifles (GP 363), Antonio unconsciously locates Emma's superiority in her ability to escape their abusive relationship and his extenuating jealousy, and responds with verbal and physical attacks. For Antonio, killing Valentina and Kevin amounts to his revenge against Emma for all that he believes she stole from him:[61]

> Anche ora, immaginava di agire come se lei fosse presente – e, benché non potesse impedirgli nemmeno un gesto, potesse vederlo. Agiva come se Emma fosse la spettatrice del film che andava girando. Il film della loro

> vita, nel quale lei aveva cercato di ridurlo a una comparsa insignificante – mentre era, e sarebbe rimasto per sempre il protagonista. Gli venne in mente che avrebbe potuto davvero filmare la scena, e allora lui e i bambini sarebbero morti milioni di volte. La pistola avrebbe sparato all'infinito, e all'infinito lei avrebbe voluto salvarli, e non avrebbe potuto farlo. (GP 366)
>
> (Even now he imagined himself acting as if she were present – and, although she could not prevent him from making a single move, she could see him. He was acting as if Emma were the spectator of the movie he was shooting. In the movie of their life, she tried to reduce him to an insignificant bystander – but he was, and forever would be, the protagonist. It dawned on him that he could have actually shot the scene, and then he and the kids could have died a million times. The gun would have been fired infinite times, and infinite times she would have wanted to save them, without being able to.)

In his hallucinatory "certezza di una giustizia superiore" (GP 336; certainty of a superior justice) Antonio is about to kill his own children "a million times." He will become prey to the violence of his own world and doom his own existence, for the pillar on which he built everything, *la famiglia*, no longer exists. By shooting his family, he wants to "ricucire lo strappo che li aveva separati, annullare la lontananza, far tacere il dolore" (GP 365; mend the rift that separated them, cancel the distance, silence the pain). Although his wife is psychologically stronger, Antonio, in his disturbed view, believes that Emma, like her mother, is necessarily passive – a woman of little means in a society that denies equal rights to uneducated women of low social stature. Antonio, albeit in a convoluted way, fights against the notion that women, as Touraine asserts, are catalysts for change in contemporary society. Touraine insists that contemporary women's consciousness and social mutation are no longer separable items, insofar as women constitute a cultural movement more than a social movement. While men reduce their existence to an endless videogame of violence in which their own children are the actual protagonists,[62] women locate a site of change in alternative manners of conceiving sexuality and the heterosexual couple.[63]

Mazzucco reveals how violence against women is still a striking societal problem, through disheartening narrations of spousal violence juxtaposed with the narrative sequence of Antonio's car speeding towards the Farnesina via the Olimpica road and the depiction of nocturnal conjugal rape, as the second wife in the novel, Maya, succumbs to Elio Fioravanti, her ambition-driven husband. As Patricia Joplin writes, despite marriage being "the proper use of woman as sign," where she should have "the power to speak,"[64] this power continuously fails to materialize. Perhaps this explains why Mazzucco creates a character such as Maya to counter or complement Emma's agency. Woman-as-sign leaves a mark on us, and Emma's body never escapes our attention, not so much because of its undisputed sex appeal, but because it exudes the kind of strength that transforms Emma, a modern proletarian, into a new kind of *popolana*, a revisited Nannarella. Sensual, determined, and passionate, likened by Antonio to Caravaggio's *Madonna dei Pellegrini*, in all her voluptuous beauty, Emma stands out as the author wants her agency to emerge in the narrative, to provide justice to those women who, in a system in which agency is incompatible with vulnerability, are still better equipped than Antonio, and men like him, to face the quotidian symptoms of social malaise. Emma successfully presents herself as a subject susceptible to modification, resisting a twisted yet ingrained concept of the victim. Emma defeats the "dominant concept of victim, which is static, dichotomous, and unambiguous,"[65] by demonstrating that her experience reflects the variable reality of victimhood.

But how can one negotiate personal, including bodily, boundaries between the self and the everyday, represented in this case by one's own *family*? "Ethics," Braidotti observes, "is related to the physics and the biology of bodies. That means that it deals with the question of what exactly a body can do and how much it can take."[66] Maya, Elio's unhappy wife, repeats her mantra, "*Sono* felice, *sono* felice" (GP 84; *I am* happy, *I am* happy; emphasis in the original). When Maya meets Emma in front of their children's school on the day of her daughter Camilla's party, she is amazed by the sense of security projected by the mother of her daughter's sweetheart, stuttering Kevin. Emma's vulgar yet attractive appearance inspires Maya to find a strength that her own perfectly shaped and slim body cannot provide. Emma, whose fatigue emanates "qualcosa di erotico" (GP 85; something erotic), also radiates "qualcosa di indefinibile" (GP 85; something indefinable), a quality expressed involuntarily in her "sorriso, nello scintillio dello sguardo" (GP 85; smile, in the sparkling of her eyes). While Maya looks like "Audrey Hepburn dei Parioli" (GP 112; a Parioli Audrey Hepburn) in her glamorous yet understated look, Emma dresses in a "pelliccetta sbottonata e una maglia troppo aderente" (GP 86; unbuttoned fur and a too-tight sweater), and flaunts badly dyed hair, the natural colour apparent to Maya after a quick but thorough assessment. Maya instinctively wants to keep her distance from Emma "perché era priva di relazioni sociali. Perché non viveva più col marito ... Perché era una donna carnale e provocante" (GP 91; because she did not have social relations, because she no longer lived with her husband, ... because she was a sensual and provocative woman). Yet

Maya wants to ask her how and where she found the courage to leave her husband: "come fa una donna con dei bambini piccoli a ricominciare una vita da sola" (GP 92; how a woman with young children manages to start a life anew by herself).

Maya is astounded by her brief encounter with Emma: "l'incontro con Emma Buonocore l'aveva scombussolata. Scoprire che una madre di famiglia tutt'a un tratto pianta il marito, piglia i bambini e se ne va. Quei due sembravano così affiatati. Una così bella famiglia" (GP 112; the encounter with Emma Buonocore confused her. To discover that a mother all of a sudden dumps her husband, takes her children, and leaves. Those two seemed to be so in harmony with each other. Such a beautiful family). While sitting in an expensive hair salon, Maya ruminates over the image she has constructed of Emma's family. Perhaps thanks to that serendipitous encounter with Emma, Maya, a woman strapped into an uncomfortable Prada dress and strangled by social conventions, which comparisons to the iconic and ultra-slender Audrey Hepburn only reconfirm, finds the strength to leave her husband. Maya's comfort in her own body is threatened by her inability to know her own needs. She feels confined by that Audrey Hepburn-like body, the image of a woman, of herself, that she now resents for its passivity. Maya sees the vigour in Emma's body and the agency it projects. Unlike the class differences between the equally failed Antonio and Elio, the relationship between the two women's bodies exemplifies a connection that transcends class difference to highlight one woman's reliance on another woman's example, however unexpected their encounter might be. Mazzucco effectively uses them as their respective foils, as the proletarian Emma inspires Maya to stop feigning happiness and take control of her own life. While the legal system does not believe Emma, as shown through her interactions with the police, Mazzucco believes in the strength of her female characters, for with all their faults, with all their problems, the unhappy wives Emma and Maya do indeed build new lives.

Despite themselves, wives like Emma continue to be the victims of men's inability to cope with a society that is transforming its models and adapting to a global cultural shift with respect to women and their roles. The powerlessness and fear of these fathers and husbands are manifest in their physical and sexual violence against their own families, their women and children. The family, the foundation of Italian society, reveals its inability to cope with the pressure of globalization, with the insecurity and uncertainty of the future. Drawing from Max Scheler's theories, Zygmunt Bauman describes this state as deriving from the "inner unresolvable contradiction of a society that for *all* its members sets a standard of happiness which *most* of those 'all' are unable to match or are prevented from matching."[67] Antonio's reflections during his wait in Sant'Agostino, on a society approaching suicide, explore women's sacrifice as necessary to maintain a precarious status quo: "la società si sta auto-terminando, non ha futuro, perché tutti inseguono una felicità egoistica, immediata, sterile, e bisogna porre un argine anche legale a questo disfacimento" (GP 104; society is suicidal, it has no future, because everybody searches for an egotistical happiness, immediate, sterile, and we need to place a check, even a legal check, on this dissolution). But Elio Fioravanti's indifference to his agent's usual litany notwithstanding, we wonder why the ultimate ideal of the self-sacrificing woman is still appealing to Antonio.

The vulnerability of the bodies Deleuze discusses refers to the vulnerability of those dreams of happiness available to everyone. Such dreams appear shattered by what Bauman refers to as most people's inability to meet society's standards for happiness. Antonio's idea of happiness harks back to a pre-second wave feminist society in which women undertook any sacrifice and silently accepted any form of exploitation to keep the family together. With the advent of populist ideology and its constant references to capitalism as the means for obtaining the "good life," everything (as in Berlusconi's *game of work)*[68] must seem easy and obtainable. For the wives of the new Italian society moulded by the power of the integrated spectacle, summer vacations at "exotic resorts" like Sharm-el-Sheik appear as a tacit reward for domestic abuse. The fact that a contract binds a woman to a man in marriage warrants too many behavioural, psychological, and physical mishaps – all in the name of a passion called love, but one that can too easily turn into hatred. If the woman submits to the contract without believing in it, de Beauvoir argues,

> she can thus propose to do nothing more than construct a life of stable equilibrium in which the present as a continuance of the past avoids the menaces of tomorrow – that is, construct precisely a life of happiness ... The ideal of happiness has always taken material form in the house, whether cottage or castle; it stands for permanence and separation from the world.[69]

Mazzucco's narrator slowly unveils Emma's need to gain an agency that is not defined by the passivity that often leads women to endure abuse in exchange for acquiescence and a home. Happiness – a long-term serene relationship with the companion of your life – reveals its limitations to Antonio, for he lacks the means to obtain it for himself and his wife. Mazzucco shows how Emma and Maya (Maya through Emma's example) have understood the dichotomy between selfhood and sacrifice, enabling them to become aware of their self-defeating behaviour, once and for all. Acquiescence in unwanted marital sex leads to graver crimes against oneself – namely, unhappiness.

The epigraph to Mazzucco's novel, taken from one of U.S. President George W. Bush's speeches about family values, is compellingly pertinent to Bauman's words on family: "la famiglia è il luogo in cui dimorano le speranze del nostro paese, il luogo che fa spuntare le ali ai sogni" (GP 7; Family is that place in which our country's hopes rest, the place that allows the wings of dreams to spread).[70] Happiness is hoped for to allow a family to "spread the wings of dream," words echoing what Leon Battista Alberti, himself an illegitimate child, wrote about the family well before George W. Bush. Mazzucco is aware that, if there are happy families, their fictional treatment might not satisfy her readers' thirst for intellectual investigation. Leo Tolstoy's oft-quoted initial statement in *Anna Karenina* – that while all happy families resemble one another, each unhappy family is unhappy in its own way[71]– speaks volumes about the role of affects in narrative strategies. Unhappy families are especially interesting in terms of narrative representation, as their individual unhappiness conceals societal ills but also personally moves us. Not coincidentally, Emma is discovered to be reading her daughter's copy of Tolstoy's novel (GP 45). Recommended by Sasha, Valentina's teacher, the novel builds a bridge between the mother, who reads the novel for pleasure, and her daughter, who is required to read it for school:

> [Sasha] sfogliò *Anna Karenina*, che gli era rimasta fra le mani. Con una certa disillusione, si rese conto che non lo stava leggendo Valentina. A segnare le pagine, qua e là scarabocchiate col pennarello da una mano infantile, c'era un foglio di quaderno con una serie di numeri scritti a matita. Il conto delle spese del mese di aprile. Le uscite superavano abbondantemente le entrate. Lo imbarazzava spiare nella modesta guerra quotidiana di Emma con la vita. E ancora di più lo imbarazzava il pensiero che Emma avesse cominciato a leggere quel romanzo solo perché lui lo aveva raccomandato alla figlia. (GP 325)

> ([Sasha] leafed through *Anna Karenina*, which was lying in his hands. With some disappointment, he realized that it was not Valentina reading it. There was a piece of paper with numbers scribbled on it to mark the pages underlined here and there by a childish hand. April expenses. Monthly expenses exceeded income. It was embarrassing to pry into Emma's daily modest struggle with life. Even more embarrassing was the thought that Emma had begun reading the novel merely because he had recommended it to her daughter.)

One might be tempted to think that Emma Tempesta, whose given name is, after all, that of Flaubert's heroine in *Madame Bovary*, is empowered by reading Tolstoy's novel about an unhappy wife. It is reasonable to suggest that she identifies with the doomed woman, and that her act of reading allows Emma to create a parallel between her state of being and Anna's. Of course, Emma jots down expenses on the margin of the page, because for a humble temp like her there is no real escape from financial instability. However, what is innovative in Mazzucco's reference to Tolstoy's opening sentence is the parallel she draws with Bush's 2004 State of the Union Address. Through Emma, she develops a historical connection between a globalized topic and a nineteenth-century novel that is relevant to her analysis of violence and women's vulnerability in Roman society. This epigraph establishes a globalized parallel to confirm that Italian society, despite all the discussions about family values, bears a striking resemblance to American society, suggesting that violence against women, starting with the family, is an eternal, global, and all-too *familiar* matter. Another sentence in Bush's speech illuminates an even broader problem: "The same moral tradition that defines marriage also teaches that each individual has dignity and value in God's sight." Bush's speechwriter underscores the importance of understanding that not only in marriage, but also in individual existence, one must avoid losing his or her own dignity – an essential notion that many characters of this crowded novel seem to have lost, even if only temporarily.

The Victim: A Victimist Positioning

Media discourse addresses the lack of effective change in how women's bodies and minds receive attention in patriarchal forms of discourses. Recent research shows that "the language choices available for women who have experienced sexual violence are influenced by the dominant culture's construction of sexual violence."[72] Linguistically, in this case at least, English is a far more precise language than Italian. *Ratto*, from the Latin verb *răpere*, not only means sexual violence (usually against women) but also defines the (quick) act – *răpidum* – of taking somebody away from where they were.[73] Nymphs in Ovid's *Metamorphoses* are usually depicted as fleeing from their assailant. There is a dynamism about the act of rape that does not correspond to the submission of the woman's body to the man/god's will. However, what is similar in both English and Italian, is the origin of the term "victim," which comes from *vinta*, "won over." This word

> emphasizes a woman's lack of control and innocence in the situation, and permits her to talk about the traumatic event. At the same time, it perpetuates the myth that women are powerless and need protection, thereby

asserting the male-dominant culture's authority over women. The term *survivor* seems to give the user power and control over her life, but it may limit her ability to discuss the event if and when she needs to. All of these paradoxes highlight the need to examine how women come to claim certain labels over others, if they do at all.[74]

An alternative might be to reverse the terms of discourse about violence. According to Giordana Masotto, we should reverse the terms by which we speak, denounce, and decry rape and violence against women. Rather than stating that the victim of a rape was, or is, a woman, Masotto suggests that we should emphasize that men have acted upon a victim:

> In this history, there are some normal human beings, in all their variety, and they are women. Not particularly fragile, but actually quite resilient, in short normal. And then some human beings, men, have a problem: a potential for violence. We women are not the problem, stop speaking of us. Instead, I would want the problem to be recognized for what it is. I would want, therefore, not to read anymore a newspaper's headline stating "another woman has been raped" or beaten, but "another man has lost control," the nth male has attacked. I would want men, all men – journalists, intellectuals, and politicians included – to begin to think of themselves as carriers of something that can become very dangerous and with which only they can deal. Something that, when they mean well, they try to censor, that they pretend not to see and don't want to face. A problem they refuse even to name, preferring to express their pity for the poor female bodies. Something so evident and macroscopic that it disappears, that it cannot be seen unless there is a precise will to name it.[75]

Masotto plainly states that a general, rather than individual, attitude needs to change. She attributes to male journalists a distorted and destructive handling of male violence in their descriptions of crimes. Masotto emphasizes their "uncontrollable tendency to reconstruct and re-compact on any level *the male cohort* [which] impedes a healthy mending of the problem."[76] More generally, one cannot help but agree with her that women want neither protection nor violence from men. Women wish for relations based on respect and awareness of their identity, of who they are. Taking into consideration soaring figures for incidents of violence, there should be little surprise at the apparent inability of Italian society to reverse the terms in which we discuss violence and the rape of women. While women are the object of violence and rape, the perpetrators of such acts receive scant attention in the news, whether in the disturbing descriptions of found bodies, or even in discussions of the motive, which too often concentrate on a pre-existing relationship between victim and assailant. Leaving the site of violence is often dangerous for a woman and her children, but it is an important gesture towards resisting vulnerability. As Judith Butler declares, "we are first vulnerable and then overcome that vulnerability, at least provisionally, through acts of resistance."[77] Within a patriarchal system, such as the one Antonio believes is crumbling before his eyes, a woman's speaking out is tantamount to a betrayal of the father of her children, laying her open to social blame for his faults, as shown through Emma's futile attempt to denounce her husband to the police.

If the novel lacked the narrator's political stance against the inequity of everyday life in contemporary Rome, we would witness the threat that, within its story of violence, *Un giorno perfetto* "perpetuates the traditional tendency to sanctify the silent victim."[78] However, the author and the narrator make political statements informed by their compassion for all women victims and survivors of domestic violence, as is confirmed by Mazzucco's extensive dedication to violated women. Her personal and political indignation at these crimes leads her to investigate the dynamics leading to such violence and to bring truth to the philology of everyday life. The literary rhetoric in Mazzucco's terms resists, albeit ambiguously, the image of women's *memento mori* at society's altar. *Ambiguously* is an apt descriptor, because Emma's character presents two reactions that could be considered antithetical to Antonio's violence. On the one hand, Emma represents what Phillips and Lamb call the "true" victim – the "culturally approved victim,"[79] endowed with the conventional features of the abused and battered woman. Emma refuses to be pathologized for her condition because it would direct attention away from Antonio and, above all, from the social conditions that enable his behaviour. By affirming this concept, we understand how Emma is bound to a position of non-agency. In such a situation, her role as victim extends beyond her relationship with Antonio to her relationship with Valentina, her daughter, and with her mother. A victim-blaming rhetoric ensues that raises the question of whether the author is playing with the conventional sense of victimhood or if she is convinced of it. On the other hand, Emma establishes an alliance with Sasha, Valentina's gay professor of literature, a member of another marginalized group. Emma learns how to see her own situation in a different light by spending time with him. More concretely, she even saves her own life by accepting his invitation to leave for the weekend. The question remains whether Mazzucco problematizes the character of Emma (Emma as a "pleasing woman" or Emma as a "together woman") as a means to strip away conventional ideas about victimization that consider women and sexual minorities as vulnerable, or because she herself lives in a society where static and active notions of female vulnerability are constantly at play. Perhaps, as Butler writes, "vulnerability is neither fully passive nor fully active, but operating in a middle region, a constituent feature of a human animal both affected and acting."[80]

Postmodern narratives have been steadfastly developing the double bind that results from the norms of victimization, dismantling white male invulnerability as a stable, fixed structure, while trying to give voice to the vulnerable.[81] The household remains the space in which such dismantling rings most alarmingly and reveals its corroding illness. Literary representations of families have always depicted significant symptoms of malaise. Female aphasia and atavistic compliance with rules make us conceal our activities and grief. Often described as shame, such feelings suggest women believe that, once their victimization becomes apparent to others, their susceptibility to exploitation increases. In this way, "the conventional concept of victim construes victimization and vulnerability as wholly incompatible with agency."[82] Society no longer limits its requests to reproductive and domestic activities; it adds a responsibility outside the domestic sphere. The necessary catalysing reforms have not been implemented, even if politics has indeed attempted to assist women who face violence, abuse, and exploitation in the form of unpaid work inside and outside the house. The *lavoro di cura,* such as Emma's care for the retired general, in addition to her domestic chores, involves a form of caregiving that extends well beyond the affective sphere and familial role of a woman. Motherhood, we know, is so much more than mere reproductive activity, even as notions of women revolve around responsibility and family. The fragmentation of feminist culture is at the core of this societal dysfunction, in which politics is subservient to a representation of the world that is still emphatically gendered in its norms and ethics.

Mazzucco's *Un giorno perfetto* suggests that Italian feminism has not disappeared, insofar as it has been instrumental in fuelling and motivating authorial intentions and effects. Taking a postfeminist perspective that reconfirms the agenda of feminism and does not merely look at establishing visibility for the individual female, Mazzucco effectively argues that women are potentially better equipped to fight the negative effects of modernization than their uncertain and deluded male companions. With its obsessive narratives about corruption and displacement, this novel offers Mazzucco's readers a Rome that is oppressively conformist and that persists in denying women opportunities to change society – a denial that Italian women have often internalized, as exemplified by Emma and Maya. A feminist mode of demystification must include social criticism, and Mazzucco engages in such criticism by creating female characters who are only superficially subservient to their societal roles.[83] Women still have the ability to reconceive the Self. If the subject disappears, or liquefies, the cause must be found in the multitude of signs that surround him/her. In Emma's case, these signs also compose the map of her own city, Rome. Mazzucco tries to rescue the *reality* intrinsic to a discourse of violence against women from a distant intellectual and male perspective that has traditionally framed it as myth and metaphor for loftier topics. Mazzucco reflects on the negative affects that often regulate bodies by locating these bodies in the quotidian world of Rome. She offers further evidence for Rosi Braidotti's reflections on society by panoptically showing the reality of both privileged and marginalized Romans. In the end, readers can only hope that Emma and her daughter will escape the lethal consequences of Antonio's decision to eliminate a family he can no longer hold together, whether through the power of their will or by sheer chance. Ultimately, serendipity intervenes for Emma as she accepts Sasha's invitation to visit the Saturnia baths, though her decision does indeed indicate agency. Her daughter is spared, barely, because she is still breathing when paramedics arrive at the crime scene. Emma and Valentina survive Antonio's rage and homicidal raptus, while pregnant Maya leaves her husband and starts a new life, accepting the challenge of becoming a single mother to her unborn baby. Mazzucco's narrative voice envisages the ethical duty of women authors to expose the violence still oppressing and repressing Roman women and, consequently, Roman society. "Vulnerability," Butler states, "is not the opposite of agency[,] and undoing the binary between the two terms is a 'feminist task.'"[84]

5
Pushing Boundaries: Road Movies and Gas Stations in Monica Stambrini's *Benzina*

S'il est difficile de vivre, il devient de plus en plus impossible et inefficace de mourir.

– Antonin Artaud

Every cubic inch of space is a miracle.

– Walt Whitman

Lesbians are runaway, fugitive slaves.

– Monique Wittig

Elena Stancanelli's 1998 *Benzina*[1] represents lesbian practices of love while illuminating the lack of acceptance of such relations in Italian contemporary society. Stancanelli's novel did not receive much critical attention. In fact, the novel was rather quickly dismissed, and it is only in the past few years that it has gained significant critical consideration, particularly with Charlotte Ross's, Patrizia Sambuco's, and Claudia Karagoz's studies dealing with Pierre Bourdieu's theories on the bourgeoisie and social *habitus* and the theme of the mother-daughter relationship, respectively.[2] The strong visual matrix led critics to relate Stancanelli's short novel to the writings of the authors who, at the time, were conveniently grouped by Italian media and press under the generic umbrella of *Giovani Cannibali.* The reasons for such critical assimilation lie primarily in the time of publication, 1998 being the year of publication for (then-dubbed *Cannibali* writers) Aldo Nove's *Superwoobinda*,[3] Isabella Santacroce's *Luminal*,[4] and Tiziano Scarpa's *Amore*®. The alienating setting that denounces familism as one of the most taxing problems in Italian society, in sharp contrast to the stereotype of strong Italian family values, also contributed to the critical reflections of the time that considered *Benzina* another example of *Cannibali* writings.

No other Italian writers used more blood and gore and violence in fiction than the *Cannibali.* Blood certainly drips and soaks through many of the narratives by Ammaniti, Nove, and Scarpa. The frequent use of blood and violence in Stancanelli's novel – often an integral part of an entertaining storyline – played a key role in the critical assimilation of her work to the narratives of social, if not political, distress of the *Giovani Cannibali* works.[5] Each of these aspects is relevant in her work, but her use of "splatter" is only superficially close to the pulp scenes that lent notoriety to Aldo Nove and Niccolò Ammaniti, literary sensations of the mid-nineteen-nineties. Gory effects construct dissimilar imagery and interpretation in Stancanelli's novel, for what is underscored here is not a generic displacement of individuals in society but rather a particular one: the unambiguous dislocation of the lesbian protagonists of the story in relation to the tight weave of Italian society. Nove's characters are alienated spectators in a consumer-oriented society. Their existential queries belong to a more universal order of alienation that finds no specific relation to gender societal constructions or to the desire to modify them according to non-normative identities. Similarly, though symptomatic of a societal malaise, Ammaniti's boys remain on the other side of the Italian social "barricade," re-affirming contemporary Italian neo-conservatism through every expression of their existence – even in their permitted "evening" transgression.

Stancanelli's 1998 novel reveals scopes and effects distinct from those articulated in the *Cannibali* works. During one night and one day, the protagonists, Lenni and Stella, accomplices and lovers, roam the Roman beltway to get rid of the body of Lenni's mother, killed by tragic mistake during a squabble. The two girls want to reach a space in which they can live their unconditional love without threats. Rebellion, societal rejection of their lesbian love, revenge against maternal patterns, and matrophobia compose the themes of a fairy tale told in a dry yet engaging way with a tragic and poetic ending. *Benzina* focuses on the desire to freely communicate a form of sexual subjectivity that Italian society remains reluctant to acknowledge and accept. Since the notion of troubled gender does not enter the equation of societal mutations, Italian society fails to make space for those women who don't fit into the male-female polarization and construction of a gendered identity that still dictates the norm and preempts the agency of the subject. In Judith Butler's words, we perform or act certain behaviours because of understated and/or oppressive pressures:

> If gender consists of the social meanings that sex assumes, then sex does not *accrue* social meanings as additive properties but, rather, is *replaced* by

> the social meanings it takes on; sex is relinquished in the course of that assumption, and gender emerges, not as a term in a continued relationship of opposition to sex, but as the term which absorbs and displaces "sex," the mark of its full substantiation into gender or what, from a materialist point of view, might constitute a full *de*substantiation.[6]

Aware of the imposition of social meanings upon their subjectivity and rebelling against a gender construction that is no longer viable, Stancanelli's queer women struggle to compete for the cohabitation of spaces within the GRA of Rome. A need for better integration of those individuals who aspire to peaceful shared living is at the core of the novel. In contrast with the characters of male-authored *Cannibali* stories, the young women of *Benzina* become visible only as Others, separate from the society of the Same, hence providing readers with a point of view that problematizes the treatment and ending of Italian bourgeois stories. Through Lenni and Stella, these characterizations illustrate the constraints experienced by both the stereotypical bourgeoise girl and the working girl, while deconstructing and problematizing another precarious binary stereotype, the lesbian butch/femme couple, which Italian media and mass culture embrace to proscribe any queer individual from normative life.

Monica Stambrini's 2002 cinematic adaptation further elaborates the issues presented in Stancanelli's novel and emphasizes the visual quality of *Benzina*'s narrative. Stambrini's *Benzina*[7] analyses the attempts a lesbian couple make to locate their place outside the boundaries of the Roman beltway. Their geographies are symptomatic of the lack of space for them within a social system still chained to the stereotyping of gender roles. In both narratives, a constructive anger acts as a powerful agent for the aesthetics of an engaged denunciation of social problems regarding women and sexual politics. *Benzina* imagines the visual as an ideal contestation site for women. In revisiting the fields of space within a capitalist society and the struggle for representation of sexual identity, it successfully deploys strategies wherein the visual narrative confirms its ability to be a site where subjects test distinct possibilities of their existential corporeality. Rather than present crystallized subjectivities, *Benzina* analyses the attempts a lesbian couple make to find their place within a social system still bound by traditional discursive practices. *Benzina*'s cinematic adaptation convincingly extricates questions about vulnerability and bodily exposure in Italian society. The idea of the explosive nature of a feminist geometry, at once social and personal, was prompted by my memory of American painter Ed Ruscha's diagonal compositions entitled *Gas Stations*. Just as Ruscha sees the disenfranchised in American society as setting up a long itinerary of gas stations, Stambrini uses the visual image of a gas station to elicit the incendiary power of resistance in vulnerability. Exposure is dangerous, as it can elicit a form of uncontrollable anger. While we agree with Butler that "there is always something both risky and true in claiming that women or other socially disadvantaged groups are especially vulnerable,"[8] it is important to understand how contemporary authors construct such precarious images to illustrate how women's disempowerment is still possible.

Critical attention, though of a mixed and even contradictory nature, was primarily focused on Stambrini's film. Instead of dismissing the film because of its splatter effects as several Italian critics did, American and British film critics have often underscored the innovative notion of the visual in its construction. Perhaps such critical divergence is generated partly by the existence of Anglo-Saxon feminist film theory, which allows for more serious consideration of films by women directors. It is a fact, though, that until recently, there were very few Italian women directors who undertook narratives of lesbian couples and their positions within society. Stancanelli's film *Benzina* is permeated with the desire to read queer (lesbian) sexual identity as a non-restrictive and a non-normative one that allows queer individuals to inhabit social spaces in less rigidly conformed typologies and without being subjected to pathologization and harassment. For instance, splatter effects depict the cold-blooded attitude of Lenni and Stella towards Lenni's mother and towards the threesome that eventually disrupts what had been their tranquil world. The mother and the threesome (in the film, two men and a woman whose relation to each other remains unclear) are members of the society that ostracizes Lenni and Stella. Stambrini's film actively proposes a space for reading their desire as a part of such a society, albeit on different terms. We should always be mindful that "identity markers," as Butler writes, "are not prerequisites for political participation."[9] Both Stancanelli and Stambrini take issue with discrimination against lesbians and queer people in general. The saliency of discrimination and widespread homophobia within Italian society compels them to use their works to raise consciousness about intolerance especially against lesbian women. They create compelling images of individuals trying to affirm their subjectivity in literary and visual exposés of harassment for the marginalized Lenni and Stella.

From the Novel to the Film

The novel succeeds in providing spectators with the motives behind the crime to open the story as a *noir*. *Benzina*'s dialogic use of dead characters recalls theatrical and cinematic effects, revealing at once the influence of French playwright Antonin Artaud's *Suppôts et supplications* and *Sunset Boulevard*'s deceased narrator, while simultaneously reminding readers familiar with the notion of the Kristevian *abject* of its unquestionable visual dramatic powers.[10] The representation of a "different" kind of youth and response to a bourgeois lifestyle focuses on one couple and on the mother of one of these two women. This is a strange ménage à trois in which the dead character[11] assumes the same importance as the two living characters.

Elena Stancanelli co-wrote the script for the film with director Monica Stambrini, openly approving of how Stambrini adapted *Benzina* for the screen. Indeed, the novel and the film reinforce one another by capturing the essence of gazing at what is difficult to stare at: a corporeal space that cannot be situated within the norm, within regulatory geographic and topographic spaces, because it has been and still is culturally marginal. The essence of both works is as pervasive as the actual gasoline that appears in all its incendiary, destructive, yet liberatory relevance in the finale of the two works. Gasoline, a combustible fluid, is used as a metaphor to explore the relationship between the treatment of the theme as offered by the visual effects of the novel[12] and by the literary effects of the film, the latter revisiting the pre-existing imagery of alienation, isolation, and suburban squalor to repurpose visual references that partly provide the film with its queer and liberating qualities.[13]

In Stambrini's film, the so-called transgression and the transversality of lesbian love are narrativized and organized according to a subjective space that suggests to spectators both the characters' failure to achieve a space in Italian society and the possibility of a rescue from it. The film asks spectators to take a position on the matter, partly feeding into Butler's notion of identity markers as "not prerequisites for political participation."[14] The geometric construction of narrative and visual diagonal lines that regulate the text both in the positioning of the characters during dialogues and in the perspectives of scenes aligns much of the film's content with Elizabeth Grosz's theoretical contributions. This film effectively conveys the notion of a corporeal space conceived as non-universal in opposition to the normative in a rigid binary combination.[15] Stambrini's *Benzina* critiques previous dangerous figurations of lesbianism as a confined and antithetical space of discourse. Figurations of the butch/femme dyad, aesthetic props defining the two identities, and markers of female attractiveness are problematized rather than presented in the stereotypical fashion we have come to accept. While representations of lesbian couples are not infrequent in recent Italian women's novels, from Dacia Maraini's *Lettere a Marina* (1981) to Melania Mazzucco's *Il bacio della Medusa*, or in films that depict a female dyad (i.e., Stefania Rocca's and Angela Finocchiaro's happy couple in Cristina Comencini's *La bestia nel cuore*,[16] or Sabrina Ferilli and Margherita Buy in Maria Sole Tognazzi's *Io e lei*),[17] Stambrini's critique purposefully unearths a more expansive and meaningful approach to sexual diversity, avoiding sexual polarization and the construction of an *either-or* space for her characters. It aims, more particularly, to prevent the performative act from becoming, once again, an agent of confinement rather than freedom for women who don't adhere to the norms of identity construction. Indeed, the forecast of an impossible "future-in-becoming" lurks on the horizon, but this representation carefully avoids any binary opposition that is detached from reality. As Elizabeth Grosz states,

> Sexuality, pleasure, desire need not be represented only through oppositional or binarized divisions between self and other, subject and object, heterosexual and homosexual – just as ontologies need not be understood only in terms of the divisions between matter and mind, nature and culture, the biological and the psychological, the natural and the historical. While this binary structure has long been recognized as a pervasive form of containment of the subordinated term through its negative or contradictory relation to the dominant term, there are a number of strategies developed to problematize its conceptual dominance.[18]

Stambrini's goal to avoid creating pernicious binary structures articulates the visual narrative of this lesbian couple, whose outrage at being doubted, ignored, or shamed into silence prompts their reaction, and eventually their defeat in this life. Stambrini's characters will conquer in the afterlife what they couldn't on Earth. The issue of vulnerability and victimization is skilfully incorporated into the layers that compose the images of the two girls struggling against agents of disruption who appear at their gas station. The arrival of people at the gas station is central to the development of a plot that otherwise would remain restricted to the still-important topic of the mother-daughter relationship for queer couples. When members from the same society as Lenni and Stella arrive and start shooting a movie about their life, they treat the women like caged animals and display clear resistance (not indifference, otherwise they would not be there) towards accepting queer individuals. Their very act of shooting an amatorial movie centred on Lenni and Stella elicits the fact that, in Italian society, a queer couple represents a strange spectacle that exists outside the realm of everyday life. The two women cannot overcome their own vulnerability through acts of resistance, as Judith Butler suggests,[19] because harassment is for some still seen as just a joke to make with friends at another's expense. Thus, Stambrini's sequences of violence, like Mazzucco's passages in *Un giorno perfetto,* address the lack of social support for individuals who try to resist discrimination. Indeed, Stambrini's visual images send a stronger message to her audience than did Stancanelli's novel regarding the urgency of establishing norms that can be hospitable for everyone, for Stancanelli preferred a more poetic and less violent approach to the depiction of the same events. Stambrini's incendiary editing and images reveal a masterful organization of the economy of vehement and deadly passions structuring the entire plot. The reified *death drive* of Lenni and Stella, if an outcome of the inexorable social ostracism that makes their ride a pointless one, both reveals the mechanisms that articulate the girls' righteous indignation and exposes the dynamics of how vulnerable victims disempowered by society act in the face of unjust treatment. Social inscriptions do not disappear just because we are aware of them.

In Stambrini's film, issues are deeply embedded in the very nature of the cinematic representations, but they question the normative principle of inclusion within a regime of visibility. Visual images erode assumptions about the state of psychological confinement where Italian society wants to put affluent women such as Mazzucco's Maya. Lenni's mother is credible through the depictions of her frigidity and frantic attention to her looks, but images make us see what we don't see. Within such a premise, the mother-daughter relationship is revealed in all the weaknesses and strengths that love and hate bring to the relationship, a "fierce attachment"[20] that demands alternative spaces to dismiss obsolete representations of mothers and (lesbian) daughters. The maternal issue does not disappear with the death of the mother, showing how hesitancy to take up the mother's point of view is no longer part of a feminist narrative. The mother returns as another character in both the novel and the film. Her death does not indicate her disappearance – quite the opposite, in fact[21] – and revisits the possibility that the mother-daughter relationship might become a non-oppositional one.

Benzina or the Paradox: An Aristotelian Work

Stambrini's film depicts the events in the story in the same chronological order as in the novel. As in Mazzucco's *Un giorno perfetto,* the story takes place within a twenty-four-hour Aristotelian time frame, symbolically beginning on the eve of Ferragosto, a holiday specific to Italian society, one that marks the high point of the August holidays and, ever since the advent of the Roman Catholic church, the assumption of the Blessed Mother to Heaven. After the initial scene of Giovanna arriving at the Fiumicino airport, the first shot is the back of the mother – dead – on the ground of the gas station, the main setting and contesting site of the film. The first line in the movie pertains to Stella, who theatrically confirms what we suspect to be a *fait accompli*: "È morta!"[22] (00:56; She is dead!). A clear refusal of cheap suspense ensues. Spectators view the body of a woman who is already dead, as someone watches her alongside us, and the opening statement, as in a *noir*, announces a crime that is, perhaps, waiting to be solved. After the first, factual frame of *un crime accompli*, the film introduces a scene obtained through the careful editing of two different scenes. No dialogue (if not for some remarks of the cab driver) accompanies the visual text. The words said by Lenni to Stella upon seeing her mother arriving are muted. The initial cross-cutting situates the crime and prompts spectators to speculate on the reasons behind it. The initial frenzied and synthetic narrative, achieved by cross-cutting between the mother's arrival at the gas station and the gas station *after* her arrival, with running titles superimposed, culminates in the mother's sitting at the table chatting with Lenni (01:01–5:46). An embarrassed Lenni hesitates to reply to her mother's questions. The dialogue goes awry, and Lenni drily asks her mother for the money she asked for in the letter. The beginning sequence contains a series of abrupt cuts between the bar that Lenni runs, adjacent to the gas station her lover Stella owns on the GRA, the *Grande Raccordo Anulare* (the Roman beltway), and the taxi transporting an anxious Giovanna to the gas station. In a pertinent montage between a squabble at the bar and Giovanna's arrival at Fiumicino/taxi ride to the gas station, viewers experience this obsessively rhythmic presentation of what leads up to the accidental matricide. Cross-cutting links the most significant actions in the movie, which do not occur simultaneously but are intricately connected. As in the novel, we learn of Lenni's lifestyle, her three-year estrangement from her mother, and her Florentine prison house, through the quarrel between mother and daughter. Giovanna's death and Lenni's and Stella's subsequent attempts to hide her body help spectators understand what lies ahead.

Extreme close-ups of Lenni's face, her mother's face, and Giovanna's red and white spiked-heel shoes (the same colours of her dress and blood) juxtaposed with the mother's voice as she screams, argues, and furiously smokes are inserted among the scenes of Giovanna's arrival at the airport and later Lenni's bar on the *Raccordo Anulare* – clearly, this is not the beginning of *It's a Wonderful Life*. The supernatural element of the mother's voice functions as a theatrical apparatus that serves the entire plot, but, as we shall see, the mother is not her daughter's guardian angel – she is no Clarence Odbody sent to help George Bailey in his hour of need. Her voice belongs to the unheard, to the women who unwittingly endure a restrictive, normative life with rules as unclear to them as to those, such as their daughters, on whom they attempt to impose such rules.

In the bar, shots and counter-shots of mother and daughter, quite literally framed in their squabble, unmask the impending complications of this relationship that they still entertain, even after all these years (8:00–9:27). The camera visualizes for the spectators the weight of the traumatic adolescence that still weighs on bulimic Eleonora, or Lenni (played by the actress Regina Orioli), by shooting Giovanna's beautiful body, draped in a white dress, from above with an overhead crane (9:38–9:48) (see figure 5.1).

Lenni's shamed verbal defence, marked by heavy stuttering, cannot compete with her mother's long-rehearsed tirade about her daughter's basic lack of compliance with the rules she has laid out on how to be the perfect bourgeois woman, maintaining a lean figure and submitting to men's needs. It should not be overlooked that Lenni's acceptance of her mother's insults is due to the fact that the girl needs money to restore the bar and the gas station, the two spaces that she and her lover, Stella, occupy and make their universe beyond the GRA. Silent until this moment, Stella, a woman abandoned by her mother at her first cry, appears outside the bar with trepidation and growing anxiety about what has become a row between her lover and her lover's mother. The scene depicts Stella igniting the bottom of her boots with her lighter, smoking, and staying put to show her indignation and ignorance of mother-daughter relational practices. She is extraneous to such a relationship and does not know how to break the tension between the two. As the two women's altercation grows louder, Stella enters the bar to defend her lover, and Giovanna falls and hits her forehead on the bar, dying an accidental death. Lenni's mother is unintentionally murdered. Matricide, however grotesquely random, has been committed, and Stella's act to defend Lenni seems to fulfil the latter's unspoken desire to get rid of her "Mommy dearest." The bizarre aspects of this scene underscore what is not accidental: the story begins and ends on Ferragosto, the day of the Virgin's Ascension, and revolves around a matricide. The two girls are not *just* killing Lenni's mom, they are killing the Mother:

> The qualities associated with [the mother archetype] are maternal solicitude and sympathy; the magic authority of the female; the wisdom and spiritual exaltation that transcend reason; any helpful instinct of impulse; all that is benign, all that cherishes and sustains, that fosters growth and fertility. The place of magic transformation and rebirth, together with the underworld and its inhabitants, are presided over by the mother. On the negative side the mother archetype may connote anything secret, hidden, dark; the abyss, the world of the dead, anything that devours, seduces, and poisons, that is terrifying and inescapable like fate.[23]

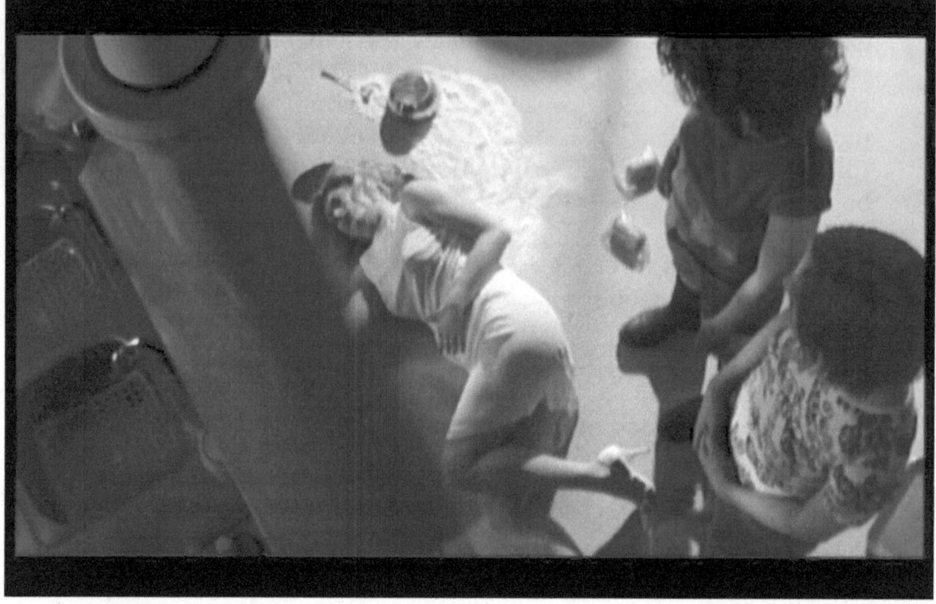

5.1 *Benzina* (9:47)

From the ambivalence of the mother archetype elicited by Jung's statements and its dual-nature historical examples emerges the "Virgin Mary, who is not only the Lord's mother, but also, according to medieval allegories, his cross."[24] *Benzina* deploys the two antithetical aspects of the Jungian Mother archetype to expand its scope in making manifest Italian social asphyxia. While the Mother of all in Italian patriarchal culture ascends to Heaven, Giovanna dies and must disappear before it's too late. She is the Cross that has hampered her own daughter's subjectivity.

Already at its outset, then, the film's abundance of gruesome passages reinforces an emotionless rendition of the unintended matricide. However tragic, the visual effect borders on the grotesque: the splatter effects in the intercut scenes at the beginning of the film rely on the visual sensation of the thickness of Giovanna's deep red blood running across the bar's linoleum floor along with the sugar that fell out of a bowl placed on the counter during the fight. Extreme close-ups show Stella's dog beginning to lick the seeping blood, and Lenni's vomit which resulted from the sight of her dead mother. The camera assumes a dry, almost stern, approach by unsympathetically composing and presenting the shots of Giovanna's beautiful body lying on the floor, in a perfectly fitted white dress. Cross-cutting accentuates an authorial desire to avoid empathy, to avoid identification with any of these women; rather, it dispassionately problematizes conventional notions of women's reciprocal trust while asserting a frankly antagonistic view of the mother-daughter bond, which it takes to its extreme. The screen is inundated with a deep red, the red of Giovanna's blood (9:48–9:49). Lenni can only state "Che belle gambe! Ha sempre avuto delle belle gambe" (10:10; What great legs! She always had great legs). Cut.

Bodily Fluids

Though we know that at the core of this casual murder lies Lenni's unspoken desire, a forbidden fantasy of many abused children, to metaphorically kill her mother, we also realize that Giovanna's death is the catalyst for the story to unfold. The presence of the body reveals how the dead mother will never leave her daughter and her lover alone. Even dead, a mother like Giovanna cannot conveniently be placed in any site where dead people are usually put to rest. Daughters can't get rid of mothers like her. "Such waste drops so that I might live, until from loss to loss, nothing remains in me and my entire body falls beyond the limit – *cadere*, cadaver"[25] eloquently shapes this scene which depicts Lenni lying motionless on the floor near her mother's corpse. Death as a fall, as the word *cadaver* comes from *cadere*, decrees the first authentic connection between Giovanna and Lenni. Though Lenni is seen in an act of mourning, incapable of pulling away from the body, Giovanna's blood serves as a visual antecedent to the protagonists' tragic ending, eliminating any superfluous pietism from the images unrolling, another directorial reason for the initial cross-cutting. The frame provides a space in which intangible aspects of the mother and daughter's affective commitment can be examined. The frame also recuperates Melanie Klein's notion that the primal mother is the idealized primary narcissism and primary experience of abjection that partly informs Kristeva's theories in *Powers of Horror*. The presence of Lenni's vomit next to her mother's blood reinstates an economy of disgust as determined by contingency and proximity. As Sara Ahmed writes, disgust is "defined in terms of the 'contact' between objects" (or individuals in this case).[26] Also, "for their implicit association with femininity, with maternity, with the corporeal, all elements subordinated to the privilege of the self-identical, the one, the unified, the solid,"[27] it is apparent how the cultural irrepresentability of vomit and fluids like menstrual blood leads spectators to the proximity of the *abject* to waste fluids, which Kristeva argues is the connotation of the relation of the individual with the maternal. Just like bodily fluids, gasoline is a liquid that "resist[s] the determination that marks solids, for they are without any shape or form of their own."[28] "What is disturbing about the viscous or the fluid," Grosz observes, "is its refusal to conform to the laws governing the clean and proper, the solid and the self-identical, its otherness to the notion of an entity – the very notion that governs our self-representations and understanding of the body."[29] Gasoline acts as a disturbing fluid and produces fear in the manner that the visual and the audible associate with bodily fluids in this film. The incendiary power of gasoline conveys the idea that fluid identities, when not regulated by norms, constitute a threat to normative society. This trope represents the very combustibility society still attributes to same-sex relations. The indeterminacy of female sexuality escapes the laws of society, and its power to revisit social frameworks lies in its forced marginality.

Soon afterwards, Lenni and Stella engage in escapist sex, finding temporary comfort in the touch of one another's body and buying time to think about what they will do next, while Giovanna's white-clothed corpse lies on the floor nearby covered with blood and sugar. The stark colours of the diagonal lines that compose the Dutch frame of sex scenes between Lenni and Stella connect symbolically the three women *and* the confined space of this struggle: an emotional reaction ensues at sight of the deep red of the blood on the floor, which matches the red of Stella's shorts, while Lenni's shirt and the sugar are the colour of Giovanna's draped white dress (11:28–11:31). The two bodies of the girls lie diagonally in a frame that concretely admits awkwardness in the display of normal emotions – awkwardness in a world that assumes lines must be straight and clear, awkwardness in a world that requires a clear definition for the individual and pressures non-conforming individuals within a space labelled "transgressive." Sexual pleasure, desire, and pain cohabit in this Foucauldian *autre espace* defined by the bar. Lenni and Stella's positioning is not as fluid as gas *yet*, or even Giovanna's blood, which they now must clean up. Colour establishes lines of connection between the three disjointed characters as they all lie on the floor, already overwhelmed by the recent happenings. The white of Giovanna's dress and the sugar represent freedom against the red of the blood, symbol of destruction but also of resistance. Images regulated by colour control the production of subjectivity throughout the scene in all its problematic complexity. This threesome is about to enter a no man's land.

An Accidental Death, an Accidental Mother

Giovanna's accidental matricide is indispensable to the rethinking of the three women's position within the symbolic order. As Patrizia Sambuco argues in her analysis of Stancanelli's novel,

> the unpremeditated, clumsy and "comic" murder of the mother acquires relevance in the critique of patriarchy and in the re-conceptualization of a female sense of self, which is, however, only available to the mother in the surreal dimension. Through the killing of the mother figure, as well as through the ironic depictions of the bourgeois woman, Stancanelli underlines her rejection of the maternal. Yet the mother's death allows the rebirth of a woman who uncovers a sense of self previously unknown to herself. Thanks to the death of a body framed into a patriarchal structure, a new woman, closer to other women, emerges. The mother's death has the function of distancing class distinctions and the difficulties that separated the mother from her daughter.[30]

With her death, with her body placed as it is in the trunk of the girls' car, Giovanna paradoxically has more time to hear, and talk to, her daughter and comes closer to understanding her convictions, while slowly gaining insight into the forced construction of her own femininity. Giovanna comes to realize how embedded in her entire existence and relationship with Lenni was a forced definition of their gender as a societal pressure. In turn, such pressure prohibited her from understanding Lenni's needs for what is only human: acceptance and equal rights for everyone. The constraints of an "unlivable life," Butler affirms, are a product of categories that do not warrant all citizens a life worth living. LGBTQ movements task themselves with "distinguishing the norms and conventions that permit people to breathe, to desire, to love and to live, and those norms and conventions that restrict or eviscerate the conditions of life itself."[31] Giovanna's posthumous body, freed from her beautiful clothes and placed into the trunk of the girls' car, represents the possibility of a post-mortem grasp of her vacuous arranged marriage and her Florentine *vita di società*. Her body in the trunk makes evident that all she lived for was an impediment to Giovanna's interactions with her own daughter. What Giovanna took for granted when she, herself, became a mother gets in the way of a true understanding with her daughter. The authorial message that all things are crooked, not positioned according to a Cartesian orthogonal axial system, justifies the obsessive use of the Dutch angle, and comes across quite strikingly when this now defunct Florentine lady interacts with her daughter. From being a "victim," Giovanna will become the girls' accomplice.

In the staging of absurd brutality that reveals its strong debt to Antonin Artaud's theatre of cruelty, Giovanna's redeeming grace is that, now dead, she can finally hear what her daughter has to say and how she feels. Through the paradoxical agitation of what is now her dead body, the mother hears all about Lenni's galloping bulimia, the daughter's constant queasiness while living with her. Only now Lenni makes explicit how Giovanna's constant desire to make her daughter "fit" the mould of Florence's bourgeois world, one in which her name was Eleonora, inspired her defiance and resistance to social inscriptions. The diagonal bundles of light project the bodies of the three protagonists in space, while they finally see and listen to each other. Initial stereotypical hatred and lack of understanding between a beautiful mommy and an ugly duckling are renegotiated in the space and time of the film. The ironic use of Giovanna's condescending voice-over serves as a commentary on the situation that ensues after the young women's clumsy moving of her body into the trunk of their car, in a spoof of familiar scenes from gangster movies. *Benzina* eviscerates the women's triad by constructing a polyphonic text based on the alternation of the three characters' points of view. The montage permits a clear understanding of this three-way discourse in which the deceased mother is as present as the living women. Undeniably, the composition of the frames – as in the sex scene between Lenni and Stella on the floor next to the dead mother – visually explains the complex theorem that frames these characters as the artist's message.

Along with corporeal proximity, the relationship amongst the three women comes equipped with a paradoxical feeling of estrangement. Shots, frames, and panning make evident the way in which issues can be perceived not only internally, through the characters' distinct points of view, but also from the outside of this intricate triangle composed by Stella and Lenni, and Eleonora-Lenni's mother, Giovanna-Mamma. How different can the issues of Stella and Lenni be with respect to those of a heterosexual couple? In the novel, some local bullies come to gas up their car and heavily harass the girls. In the film, this external presence is reinterpreted to balance the triangle of three women with a heterosexual threesome, composed of two men and a woman. Stambrini adds a woman, Pippi, to the two men who engage in the fight with Lenni and Stella, to represent a heteronormative perspective on the search for subjectivity. We see Pippi shoot a video with a handheld camera of the scenes we are watching.Their struggle emblematizes that between the "normal" world and the girls' world. This tension, initiated by the violent way in which the *ragazzi* pretend to fill their tank even though the gas station is closed, lasts until the culminating moment of the final explosion. *Benzina* can be a "film indeciso fra il videoclip e il Dogma 95" (a movie oscillating between a videoclip and Dogma 95) as Francesco Alò states, when we rethink Pippi's recording of the violence inflicted on Lenni and Stella by her buddies, as her handheld camera delivers a free-form and spontaneous style reminiscent of Dogma 95. Pippi's visual angle composes scenes in a slow, amateurish manner that is in no way feminist, but in its evident voyeurism rather attests to a visual field where Lenni and Stella are perceived as perverse and estranged heroines destined to arouse pleasure *because* they are queer. Spectators, such as the three individuals arriving at the station, are made visible to us, the actual spectators. In Stambrini's adaptation of the novel, the heterosexual threesome exposes the confusion that can exist also between couples considered "normal" vis-à-vis those labelled "transgressive" because of their sexual orientation. Spectators might begin to sense that the laws of heteronormativity do not necessarily guarantee a "normal" existence. In fact, we do not know the relationship entertained by Pippi with her two male companions. As receivers and evaluators of the visual and literal explosion of negative societal forces that lead to the end of the three main characters' story (or the beginning of a better one), spectators are made aware that, far from creating a stale version of *Thelma and Louise,* Stambrini's visual narrative deconstructs and recomposes the themes and strategies of the women's anti-road movie, already in itself a deconstruction of the classic road movie.[32] Stambrini's aesthetic approach appears "dictated by an entire set of beliefs and desires and by a set of coded languages and generic apparatuses"[33] that are applied to debunk previous representations of lesbian movies and ménages à trois. The external triangle's French car, a Renault, might allude to Stambrini's own fascination with François Truffaut's 1962 adaptation of *Jules et Jim*'s triangle, another film adapted from a novel that ends with the transgressive characters falling to their death from a bridge in a car.

Many are the influences revealed in this film. In his rather condescending review, Bill Chambers bills Stambrini's *Benzina* as a "Hollywood movie."[34] Chambers is correct for reasons other than those he suggests. To negotiate the problematic discourse of lesbian love and motherly discursive constructs, Stambrini's *Benzina* draws visual inspiration from several California-based sources. David Lynch's films come to mind right away, but what we need to list, instead, are the ways in which Stambrini breaks from the Hollywood female road movie genre and hybridizes it with same-sex love stories such as *Heavenly Creatures,* from *Boys Don't Cry* to *Wild at Heart* and *Butterfly Kiss. Benzina* has been consistently categorized within the two-women movie or women's road movie subgenre. Its originality lies in the way Stambrini problematizes the women's road movie in dealing with Stancanelli's story of queer love.

Stambrini's film delegitimizes the palpable societal reasons for revenge and revisits the chain of violence that engenders more violence beyond the death of the American heterosexual heroines Thelma and Louise. Her film offers a cathartic death that redeems Lenni from her world and frees her from the estrangement imposed by the bourgeois *habitus.* The spectacle of a contemporary society unable to come to terms with a notion of diversity appears here in all its disturbing force. *Benzina* depicts violence, love, and solidarity among women as a more nuanced and subtle business than its American, and even Australian, predecessors as in the case of *Heavenly Creatures.* Displacement takes place on multiple levels, most notably at the gas station run by two women, in the notion of "static runaway," and through gasoline that takes on *full* signification as a tool to escape from reality. Finally, transverse lines of love that do not rely on trite references to lesbian singers such as Sinéad O'Connor's or Gianna Nannini's tunes, as happens alas in the novel, provide spectators with powerful points of visual reference and interpretation. In *Benzina,* gasoline acts as a deceptive device for such an escape from reality, only to become the liquid essence that annihilates and destroys the couple's aspirations towards freedom. In short, gasoline fuels no escape; it drives the women nowhere.

Fuga Statica: An Oxymoron

As script co-writer and director, Stambrini claims that the central idea of the movie concerned the static flight, or *la fuga statica* of the two heroines.[35] The oxymoronic *fuga statica,* or static escape, alludes to the entire discourse of the film and how this anti-road movie illustrates Lenni's and Stella's final opportunity to escape after the shocking murder, as it is grounded on the notion of paradox. Is the road genre a way to gain enlightenment? Did Jack Kerouac ruminate over the same issues as Dante did when he began working on his own road trip piece? With evident differences, perhaps both artists shared a common desperation. Perhaps they gained knowledge of the world. What matters is that travel, a trip, in literature as in cinema, almost invariably points, to a varying extent, at disaffected characters who are engaged in life renewal and whose actions are often motivated by some form of indignation. The voyage Lenni and Stella (and Giovanna's body) take is, for all intents and purposes, a runaway journey. Initially misled by cinematic competence, we ultimately realize that even though *Benzina*'s characters' real crime is, as in the American film *Thelma and Louise,* a claim to "subjectivity,"[36] since characters "become outlaws the moment they seize control of their bodies,"[37] Lenni and Stella don't actually "move." In the GRA, the ring that limits Rome and connects the city to the national Italian turnpike Autostrada del Sole, the two women with Giovanna in the trunk drive in circles, towards nowhere, and finally return to their gas station.

Indeed, the space of American road movies cannot exist in this anti-road film. Its atmosphere is as claustrophobic as that of David Lynch's *Blue*

Velvet, a movie whose visual influence recurs in Stambrini's cinematography and camera use. Characters do not *move* at all. As Massumi writes, there is *dis*-placement in their movement, as the act of moving has no scope or trajectory.[38] In an atmosphere dictated by significant haze, Lenni's and Stella's footsteps are heavy and resounding: these two girls appear crushed by the external gaze of a society that produces language, mass media, and norms. And they are haunted. Their chase advances notions of velocity, as does any act of movement, but it lacks a rebellious theme that finds resolution at the end of the chase. *Benzina*'s scenes in the gas station and the subsequent chase in a confined space that frames the protagonists bring to mind Ed Ruscha's celebrated series of *Gas Standard Stations* paintings and his *Twentysix Gasoline Stations* book.[39]

Ed Ruscha painted this series, of which *Standard Station, Amarillo, Texas* (1963) is one of the best examples (figure 5.2), and published the book of photographs in the early nineteen-sixties as an expansion of his critique of the capitalist world that gas, cars, and roads signify. In Ruscha's domain of visual representation, namely painting, those oversized lines of the bright lights of Hollywood become flames, while his carefully designed diagonal compositions celebrate roadside architecture and signs. Interestingly, Ruscha claimed he wanted to be a director. His wish, though not uncommon in Los Angeles, is a testament to the allure of film frame composition, which is similar to that of painting but dilated in its kinetic possibilities, even as it is capable of more than a single painting. Cinematography in *Benzina*, set in a gas station as it is, more or less unconsciously draws visual strength from Ruscha's source of inspiration and reference to films. By bringing into the production of the visual the essence of the literary, Stancanelli's novel, and the pictorial, Ed Ruscha's "deadpan serial displays of filling stations,"[40] Stambrini's film incorporates theorizations on visual culture partly derived from American pop art in its photography, while revisiting the American women's road movie genre as exemplified in the past fifteen years[41] in a complex exercise of hybridization.

Director of photography Fabio Cianchetti, who also directed the photography for Bernardo Bertolucci's *The Dreamers*[42] and *Besieged*,[43] utilizes red and turquoise hues to evoke Ruscha's gas stations: the initial bar scene is an exemplary instance. After painting gas stations, Ruscha moved on to constructing books of photographs of his gas stations. Then after defining a narrative in his visual, Ruscha moved on to writing in his paintings. Investigating the power of the word *within* or, better, *superimposed* onto the image, Ruscha establishes a set of reciprocal references/influences on the word-image relation and how topography influences the language. The citation of objects related to consumerism is

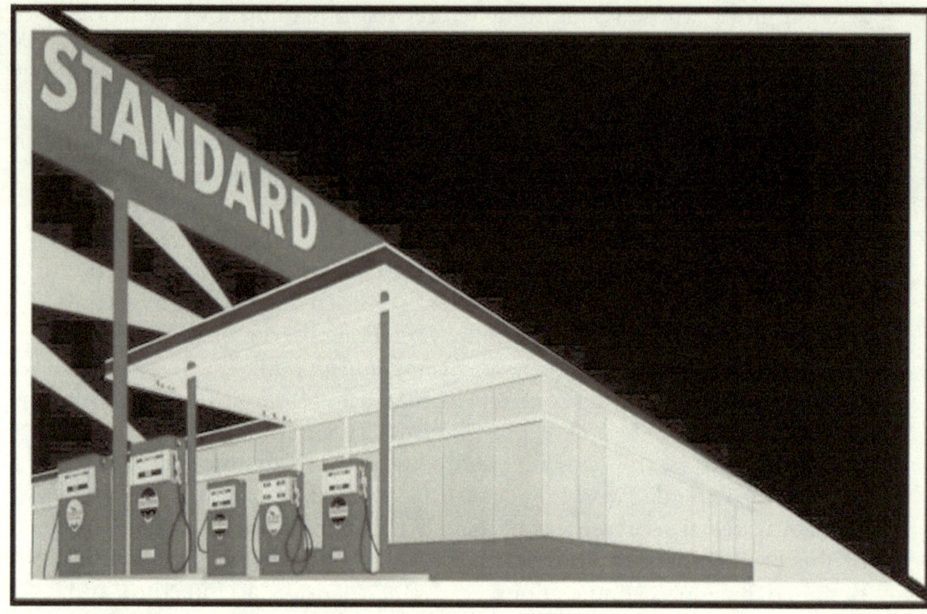

5.2 Edward Joseph Ruscha, *Standard Station, Amarillo, Texas,* 1963, Oil on canvas
Hood Museum of Art, Dartmouth: Gift of James Meeker, Class of 1958, in memory of Lee English, Class of 1958, scholar, poet, athlete and friend to all; P.976.281. © Ed Ruscha

not limited to placing untransformed items of capitalism within works of art, or making art out of them. On the contrary, Ruscha defines the squalor of capitalist society by showing the displacement of such objects. Unlike what Baudrillard thought about signs, as stated in his *On America*, for Ruscha, gas station advertisements are historically contextualized, and they directly refer to capitalist consumerism and marginalized people: the displaced, the homeless, and the vagabonds who people the shoulders of American highways. Signs are neither self-generating nor self-referential, and Ruscha's words attest to their contextualization. The thrusting diagonals and vanishing horizons that are visually apparent in Stambrini's film are present in *Benzina* the novel as a geometric irresolvable rendition of the negative forces of Italian family relations. Ultimately, the intricate relations between a mother, her daughter, and her daughter's lover rule over the other visual elements in the film.

In hybridizing the genres to which the film pertains, namely the road movie and the lesbian thriller, along with pictorial references, Stambrini constructs diagonal forms of discourse through the figurative representations of lesbianism and the mother-daughter relation that constitute the thematic matter of the novel, within a crooked world where things don't stay where they should, as her movie demonstrates. In the novel *Benzina,* all things are crooked: the moon, the stars, and the sky, as Lenni points out to Stella at the end of their static journey. When Stella gives Lenni a snorkeling mask for their vacation in Tunisia,[44] Lenni gazes at the stars. Through the distorted lens of the mask, Lenni discovers that, as well as the stars, the moon also is not what she thought – "è tutta storta la luna"[45] (the moon is all crooked) – as is the sky – "tutto storto anche il cielo" (BE 151; the sky is also all crooked). When Lenni and Stella wear the snorkeling mask while waiting to die, the entire system in which they have been living is revealed to be crooked. The mask has multiple meanings: it is a device to portray who you are not and an object used to enter, and move through, different environments. It distorts our vision precisely to allow us to see new things in new ways. The diagonal lines that Stambrini uses to construct the frames of *Benzina* reveal how crooked the world is for Lenni and Stella once they leave, or try to leave, the gas station on the GRA. The gas station is strategically placed at the boundaries of the Eternal City, approximately where one could imagine the shantytowns described by Pier Paolo Pasolini. Long roads that trace diagonal lines evoke distinct trajectories, suggesting paths of freedom as promoted by twentieth-century road movies and capitalist tools like cinema and gas stations – stations on which the whole of Western civilization depends to fuel our journeys of pleasure or evasion, at least until the discovery of new energy sources. By default, gas stations also posit the power of capitalism as a bedrock of norms that artists, through their "transgressive" characters, resist in order to express their individual aims and beliefs, their conceptualization of sexuality and subjective corporeality.[46]

In *Benzina,* Californian or Texan gas stations at the sides of highways, like those depicted by Ruscha (see figure 5.2) are replaced by a squalid Roman suburban gas station. California highways are replaced by the *Raccordo Anulare.* In his *Gas Stations,* Ruscha traces the road from California to Texas, rendering the pictorial space dynamic, devoid of a true, realistic landscape of any sort, while Lenni's and Stella's diagonal lines converge into a clogged and suffocating circular landscape, the Roman beltway. It *looks* like a turnpike, but is not. Just as the lines on Stella's hands look like an "autostrade senza uscita" (BE 65; a turnpike with no exit), in this beltway there is no exit. To use a Lynch title, this indeed is a *lost highway.*

While Lenni and Stella drive in search of a getaway (see figure 5.3), the GRA takes on its full meaning as a deadly ring that holds and controls the trajectories of individuals, forcing the characters to return to the gas station, the space where they thought they could find refuge and that symbolized their haven, or heaven, but has been violated.

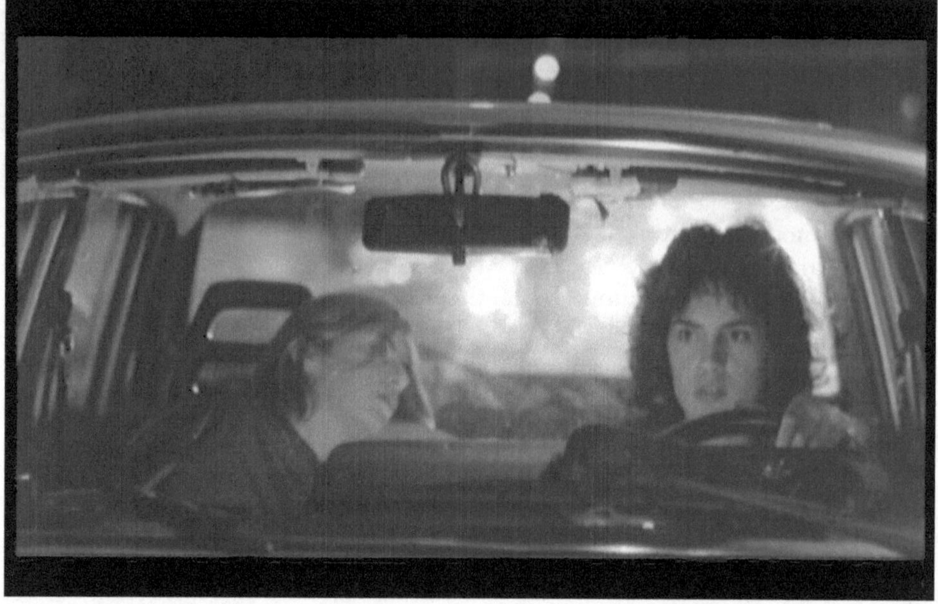

5.3 *Benzina* (27:33)

This anti-road movie depicts a suffocating societal space regulated by a gratuitous violence and rage that Lenni and Stella want to avoid but are powerless to modify, and that they end up replicating with the accidental killing of Giovanna. That they will never reach their destination is not merely a small "deviation from clichés," as Chambers claims, forcing the film's meaning to align with foreign mental and cultural patterns that are familiar to Hollywood or American indie productions. On their road trip, Stella and Lenni *can't* move far beyond the gate for reasons that visually wed a personal impotence with social restrictions and general homophobia. In the film, their *non*-trip further corroborates the closure expressed in the novel. Far from denoting a sense of movement, the "road" and the semantic field connected with it point thus to stagnation and isolation[47] for the women. Reversed in meaning, the road movie as a genre, deriving more from travel literature, makes visible Lenni's and Stella's lack of freedom, despite the spaces they try to claim for themselves: the gas station and the road around it.

Stambrini's sequences depict the gas station as a fixed theatrical stage, as there is no landscape around the station and the lines do not indicate any departure points, similar to how Ruscha's paintings with long diagonals produce the visual effect of a static escape from consumerism in their absence of landscapes that can in some way depict California or Texas. All lines seem to converge on the gas station, as in the Twentieth-Century Fox logo, depicting a place that exists only in our imagination. In this physical setting, "distinguishing [between] the norms and conventions that permit people to breathe, to desire, to love and to live, and those norms and conventions that restrict or eviscerate the conditions of life itself" becomes an arduous task.[48] What Butler suggests could be achieved by a more collective interest in the goals of queer studies cannot quite yet happen inside the Roman beltway. Space exists for the two girls provided they don't transgress and trespass the limits of the station. Once they do so, they are damned. In the novel, the gas station is likened to an island, "un'isola felice dove dimenticare le preoccupazioni" (BE 58; a happy island where worries can be forgotten) in which "il marciapiede doveva segnare il confine tra il bar e la loro vita quotidiana" (BE 58; the sidewalk was supposed to mark the threshold between the bar and their daily life). "Doveva" means it was supposed to but did not. The gas station can hardly signify a place where Lenni and Stella can be themselves, as it indicates only more deceptive space. The gas station is a physical cage in which two subjects are confined and live, quite literally, on the border, or at the limits of society. Deconstructing the significance of a gas station into an emblem of confinement for the "transgressive" couple brings Stambrini's work closer to reversing the meaning of an object in pop art. The transformation into an icon of an everyday object of American consumerism estranges its own sense, makes it foreign to its own use. As the love story of Lenni and Stella is not considered a "normal" love story, their space is bound to "non-spaces": the station as their island/oasis; the car as their vehicle, which takes them back to the gas station, with Lenni's mother's corpse in the trunk. Love is not permitted; it is "interrupted." Positive change is forbidden for Lenni and Stella. The very oasis they created in this *terra franca* will be their curse.

While the mother's death marks the beginning of *Benzina*, Lenni and Stella's death marks the end of it. The beltway is the perfect ring of death to frame the story. The mother's death is essential to the development of the plot, while in Stambrini's intentions the two women's death is to be viewed as cathartic and liberating. The final death serves as an emotional cleansing. Neither death scene invites easy empathy from spectators.

The *Big Bang*, or the explosion in the final scene, once again reminiscent of Ruscha's stations, recalls other cinematic explosions. Lynch's *Blue Velvet* and *Twin Peaks* influence the construction of *Benzina*'s frames. Lynch's steel sheet background or use of fire are mirrored in frames such as the already mentioned one in which Stella lights the sole of her boot, or the one in which she burns the clothes worn by the girls at the time of Giovanna's death.[49] Extreme close-ups suggest the materiality of each face; the lines and shapes of their features are juxtaposed with the absurdity of the siege to which society subjects individuals, as absurd as the police siege that determines *Thelma and Louise*'s fatal leap into the canyon. In the novel, the gas station appears like an island surrounded by a dark sea of gasoline. The station is named "la casa delle sirene" (BE 155; the mermaids' house) in which "le due nuotatrici erano volate via, galleggiavano sopra le loro teste," (BE 155; the two swimmers had flown away, suspended over the policemen's heads).

The film presents this image by way of debris slowly rising into the sky (see figure 5.4), alluding to the souls' ascent to Heaven, a universal judgment of a different kind, with the camera moving vertically from the terrain space to a "higher" one. Can we read this as an *homage* to Antonioni's *Zabriskie Point* (via Lynch)? At last, Lenni and Stella finally reach *the* place – Paradise. They arrive at a beach, which, in their eyes, metaphorizes Heaven. "Io sto zitta e penso che tutta questa benzina sparsa diventa sabbia e al posto delle pompe sdraiate in terra ci sono le dune, come a Skiathos" (BE 148; I stay quiet and think that all this shed gasoline becomes sand and instead of the pumps on the floor there are dunes, as in Skiathos). "Quassú" (up here) is now the space where they find themselves, along with Lenni's mother, who waits until the girls' death to ascend, while the "laggiú" (down there) life remains in the hands of the policemen, metonym for official power, who are frightened by the girls' laughter from *quassú.* Finally,

> La rincorsa è finita, e non ci sono piú denti per azzannarsi né tempi per crescere e invecchiare, e ora le possiamo ridere tutte le storie, e lasciarle dondolare una dietro l'altra, piano piano, fino a quando non toccano terra. (BE 156)
>
> (The chase is over, and there are no more teeth to tear each other to pieces or time to grow up and age. Now we can laugh at all the stories, and let them swing one after the other, slowly, until they touch the ground.)

Stancanelli's and Stambrini's characters exist in a world *renversé,* where the sea rises above ground. All materiality loses solidity at the end of Stambrini's film. Birth into a perfect world is possible for Lenni, Stella, and Giovanna, but can happen only once they give up their earthly roles, those that society formed. They have turned into "liquid" the space that confined them, as it insisted that conformity provided the only escape. The ultimate explosion, though problematic in authorial intentions, provides a rebirth to the three women, in spite of the strictures of their

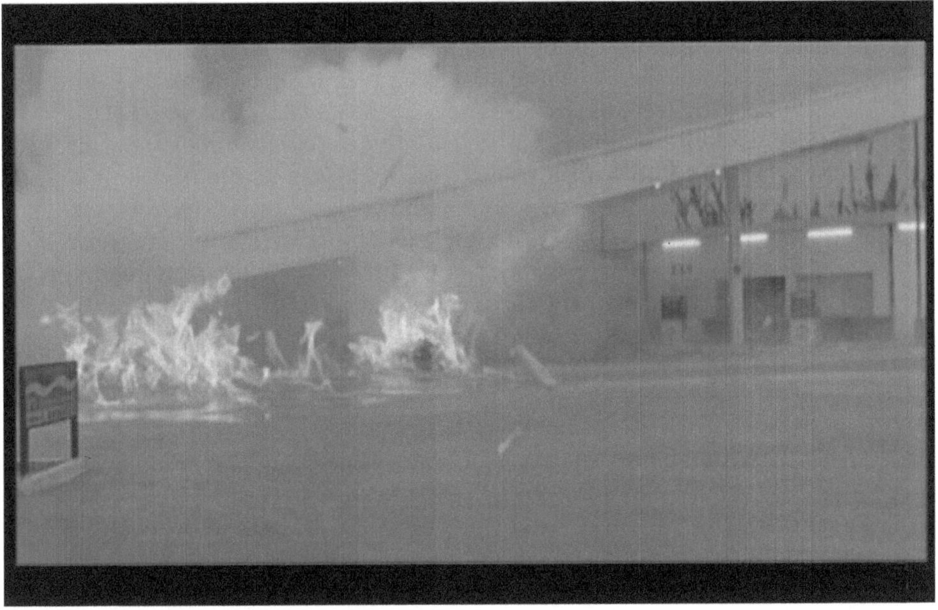

5.4 *Benzina* (19:32)

society.[50] The final explosion is the materialization of the proliferation that the wearing of the mask entailed in the first place (1:18:05–1:20). Affective change starts abruptly: it's explosive and deadly. We can become others. The ontological nature of chaos reveals its power.

Where can Stambrini lead her spectators after her hybridization of these references to Hollywood, Ruscha, Lynch, and *Thelma and Louise*? Stambrini shapes her take on Italian society's restrictive views in an aesthetic visual text that denies in all its subtexts the terms by which we usually refer to a road movie, denying, too, a space, even such an isolated space as a gas station, to those who deviate from heteronormativity. Far from fuelling the acceptance of diversity, gasoline remains an object on which capitalistic wealth and conformist norms are built. Paradoxically, no freedom is gained; no fuel leads the girls to freedom. What "is marginal is located as a site of danger and vulnerability."[51] Lenni and Stella remain marginal, as there is no law enforcing their rights. Fluids surge and move, but one is left to wonder, "Che cosa diventa una storia dopo un'esplosione?" (BE 153; What becomes of a story after an explosion?). The film deals with the confinement of space for volatile bodies, with bodily fluids that connect women to other women in a bordered, restricted society in which same-sex love can be practised only when confined. In short, the film is the opposite of a road movie, for it warrants the lack of space where gender can be negotiated and performed on one's own terms: all women die. A character's death can never be perceived simply as a tool for freedom, as we know from *Madame Bovary* and *Anna Karenina*. Unless attempts are made to critique society, unless new discursive practices find a space in which diversity can be situated, lesbian love and kinship cannot *go* anywhere but towards death, in a gigantic and purifying pyre, reminiscent of the sari rituals by which Hindu wives burn alive to escape the shame of widowhood. Once women are burnt, society is once again purified, as the fire's energy cleanses the emotions of humans still living. We return to Girard's theory of the scapegoat. But, in fact, women's situations take pains to find spaces of insertion. Utopia, or dystopia in the case of Margaret Atwood's *The Handmaid's Tale*, does not transform society effectively. Dystopia is another place where solutions are relegated to the limited space, however interesting and aesthetically appealing, of a film or a novel.

The legacy of the dead, what they leave to the living when dying, is heroic and noteworthy. The two *Benzina*s demonstrate the insufficiency of the notions on which the cult of the dead is built in dealing with the representation of women's subjectivity and their position within society. A corollary is the fact that existence, whether in this world or in that represented by the terms "Paradise" and "Hell" in patriarchal discourse, seems to be an extinct notion, as is the manner in which they venture up "there." In this voyage to another world, neither mentors nor saints appear for the girls. The universe described by Stancanelli and Stambrini as one in which "non esistono madri generose, né figlie devote" (BE 114; neither generous mothers nor devout daughters exist) justifies the final scene, which consists only of the gas station explosion, for the energy produced by the burning gas could also provide energy to renew the world as these women have experienced it. This vertical and dynamic explosion undermines Baudrillard's notion of *implosion*, drawn from McLuhan. Can we be sure that, as Baudrillard writes, "death, as a fatal or symbolic event, must be erased. Death must be included only as virtual reality, as an option or changeable setting in the living being's operating system"?[52]

We Don't Need Victims

It seems paradoxical that, to improve the condition of women and to truly grant them their legal rights, the only effective weapon seems to be a weakening of the very notion of gender. It is hardly surprising that, in many respects, gender is still perceived as a "cage," and this problem isn't helped by archaic notions that men represent culture and women nature – a nature bound to reproductive power.[53] The old model of gender division does not hold, either. Being "woman born" constitutes a form of identification that women choose for themselves as "affirmation of their desire to be women."[54] From a political standpoint, what matters is the meaning of this desire for affirmation *as* women for *all* women: how such affirmation is constructed and perceived and, further, how it resists any ideological interpretation of *being a woman*. Above all, *being a woman* signifies the acknowledgment of one's subjectivity, the notion of the thinking subject, and the ability to have rights and laws. These "three components," Touraine argues, are "inseparable from democracy."[55] Democracy can only exist when the rights of individuals and of social actors can be defended within an institutional space, the law. A democracy affords a form of positive individualism when the singular experience of a woman can give rise to a collective form of revindication of rights. Although we live in a society accustomed to collective rather than individual expressions of struggle, Touraine believes that women can exercise a form of resistance that is distinct from "class struggle."[56] Further, the sociologist states that women revindicate the right to construct their own selves in a different, existential manner that men's desire or power cannot restrict.[57] Lessons from 1970s feminist movements have allowed contemporary Italian women artists to propose models of resistance and to counter stereotyped literary and cinematic depictions of social perspectives regarding Italian women, offering narratives that expose and politicize societal problems while denying women the status of passive individuals. Contemporary women authors' investigations of violence take the form of an indignant authorial voice that denounces violations of, and violence against, women. Underreported aspects of women's lives within their own families beg for analysis and discussion, rather than silence and rhetorical images. The profound examination of the social status quo one enjoys in these narratives displays the artists' empathy for those women who, regardless of their sexual orientation, are often victims of violence – in particular, but not solely, domestic violence. Accepting these women's everyday reality as unshakeable and unchangeable is no longer a viable project. Repudiating vulnerability signifies accepting victims' agency as a possibility for change. Advocating for norms that eliminate the category (and possibility) of what is considered "vulnerable" implies the advancement of society. But in order to do that, vulnerability must be recognized, for, as Butler states, "We cannot posit this vulnerability prior to recognition without performing the very thesis that we oppose (our positing it is itself a form of recognition and so manifests the constitutive power of the discourse)."[58] A correct theoretical and legal framework needs to be in place for "norms of recognition" to be "essential to the constitution of vulnerability as a precondition of the 'human.'"[59]

Without the physical and financial safety of marriage, women in ancient Rome had no legal protection and were forced to become regular sex labourers, Serena Witzke affirms. Their vulnerability was caused by the difference between the legal rights afforded to women who were citizens and those available to women who were not. While citizen women were indeed subject to Rome's culture of gendered violence, non-citizen and slave women most commonly suffered its consequences. In contemporary Rome, the lack of the norms that Butler advocates for changing the condition of vulnerable subjects seems to come from within the very legal structure that should protect women from violence, not just in terms of culture but also in terms of actual threat within the domestic space. *Un giorno perfetto* exposes the incendiary problems within a family unit when a woman tries to react to the victim-oriented mythology of the all-suffering wife. But when women try to escape from the domestic space because they want their lives to reflect their agency, other problems arise, as *Benzina* aptly illustrates.

To conclude, women writers like Mazzucco rely on the power of the literary form to make their voices heard. During the years of Berlusconi's political tenure, women thinkers and feminist activists, already oppressed by the ideological backlash, were discouraged from reacting and acting against the establishment. But there were always reactions and intellectuals – like Mazzucco – who strove to renegotiate healthy political reflection and literary praxis on femicide and undetected crimes against women.Mazzucco knows that, as Rancière states, "the real must be fictionalized in order to be thought."[60] Mazzucco's characters coincide with the realist narrative of the time and period in which the story takes place. The author, however, frames her social criticism more acutely within the dynamics between Roman society and women. She places her characters within a broad human landscape that her omniscient narrator engages with sociologically in frequent commentaries on the city. In *Un giorno perfetto* constructive indignation rests on the assumption that women must reject traditional forms of politics and social struggle and reclaim their rights. While a new generation of women has achieved awareness of the cultural transformation that confers new roles and new dignity upon them, there is little real awareness that certain patriarchal norms of conduct hinder their actual chances of reaching equality in terms of legal rights and a status within political discourse. Mazzucco employs an omniscient extra-diegetic narrator to project the character of Emma, who, despite her regrets about dismantling her own family, resists moralizing critiques of her behaviour and invokes a new course of action for women, one where they become agents of their own existence.

On a cinematic level, Stambrini demonstrates how gasoline is a fluid that does not conform. In addition to its deregulating liquid, "essence," the French word for it, it is extremely dangerous, for it also burns the objects it saturates as it does the space where it lies ready to fuel a future explosion. However, gasoline is also a propelling liquid that ignites the possibility of escape. In road movies, gasoline assumes the role of the enabler: characters are shot while filling the tanks of their cars, pick-up trucks, and motorcycles. Perhaps we should give credit to what Stambrini considers the cathartic power of the final explosion: it is a visual element that triggers a liberating outcome for her characters. Within the GRA, a progressive notion of history seems to keep failing when it comes to women and their rights as individuals. Or, perhaps, we are left to think that the space for such asymmetric fates is confined unless female characters conform. Nevertheless, Mazzucco and Stambrini denounce in different ways social practices that must be amended through narrative visions and visual images that affirm the existence of an aesthetic regime, taking into consideration societal failings at revisiting discourse practices.

PART THREE

Anger and Love in Spaces of Otherness in the Narratives of Paolo Sorrentino, Simona Vinci, and Veronica Tomassini

The third part of *Righteous Anger* concerns three narratives about an individual's existence when modified by an erotic love that lies outside conventional relationships and triggers a different understanding of the passions of the soul. The analysis of the individuals locked in the hotel's different sub-sets of Paolo Sorrentino's *Le conseguenze dell'amore (The Consequences of Love)*, Simona Vinci's hotel room in *Stanza 411*, or the caves of Veronica Tomassini's *Sangue di cane* considers the heterotopias where these individuals experience an erotic love that will forever alter their lives while investigating such constraints and ills of contemporary society as the Mafia, abuse against women, and discrimination against migrants. I construct parallels between cinematic narratives and literary narratives, and I am also aware of generic hybridization as a necessary aesthetic tool to express the variables of an ever-changing reality depicted in spaces intended as *other* spaces, hotel rooms as caves in Ortigia. I am particularly interested in the persistent, though variable, cinematic narrative treatment of the woman as a disruptive element in a man's life as compared to the perspective provided by female writers and directors, whose narratives evidence new ways to refigure interiority with respect to exteriority and to promote the characters' agency. If interiority is not seen as a form of interiorization, it can then illuminate the relation between the inner space of the protagonists and the outer space with which they interact under the influence of a particular emotional state – that of being in love. When dealing with narratives of love, the anger that finds its cause in this passion is presented in various ways. However, there is a tendency to assume that individuals are somehow revealing the anguish and troubles caused by their condition, or the seeming contradictions of love, rather than expressing the temporary happiness provided by the state of being in love. Angry motions of the soul that result from being in love are often determined not so much by the interaction between the two lovers as by situations that are socially constructed, such as those that result from crime, inequality, and injustice.

These authors' reliance on realism makes apparent how reality needs, first and foremost, to be imagined and deconstructed in the defined time and space in which protagonists live. Aesthetic interpretations of reality do not lead to misinterpretation or to the assumption that "all reality is socially constructed and infinitely exploitable and that truth is a futile notion because solidarity is more important than objectivity" ("tutta la realtà sia socialmente costruita e infinitamente manipolabile, e che la verità sia una nozione inutile perché la solidarietà è più importante della oggettività"), as Maurizio Ferraris states in his *Manifesto del nuovo realismo* (Manifesto for a New Realism).[1] My findings show how the "unamendability of reality" seems, on the contrary, to be reinforced by the narratives here examined precisely because these fictional interpretations never abandon the examination of social and political issues, the matter of which reality is actually made. Time and space, fundamental elements of any narrative, are scrutinized in these authors' interpretations of reality in ways that are often anti-naturalistic in their use of *estrangement* to underscore the individual's indignation.[2] The fictional narratives analysed in this part investigate the emotional life of characters facing the pressure of strenuous situations that originate in erotic passion. The constant shifting between inner and outer spaces identifies interiority as a spatial construct that allows the subject to express agency versus passivity when it comes to love. As with indignation, love and its many facets require the presence of another individual to be set into motion.[3] Love's principle of action also works as an indicator of social anxieties that affect the individual's relation to the community. Relationality and the relational aesthetics conceived by Rancière[4] emerge in the following pages as an apt theoretical framework, for artists construct spaces and relations concerning their ethical responsiveness and relationship with the territory of the common. The texts analysed in part 3 articulate counter-narratives to conventional renderings of love, through reflections that stem from an individual love story but expand to include society. Vinci deals with abusive love, Tomassini with discrimination against minorities, and Sorrentino with love as potential escape from an existence devoid of any meaning.

As I have chosen narratives of love situated within stifling closed settings or spaces, Michel Foucault's concept of heterotopia guides my theoretical framework. Paolo Sorrentino's *Le conseguenze dell'amore*, Simona Vinci's *Stanza 411*, and Veronica Tomassini's *Sangue di cane* analyse space by investigating forms of heterotopically and heterochronically framed erotic passions.[5] Foucault defines at least five principles that characterize spaces in which deviations from the norm occur. Other spaces, in his definition, are

> something like counter-sites, a kind of effectively enacted utopia in which the real sites, all the other real sites that can be found within the culture, are simultaneously represented, contested, and inverted. Places of this kind are outside of all places, even though it may be possible to indicate their location in reality. Because these places are absolutely different from all the sites that they reflect and speak about, I shall call them, by way of contrast to utopias, heterotopias.[6]

According to Foucault, a hotel room in which activities like a honeymoon or an illicit affair happen out of sight defines real places rather than that particular transition zone that Marc Augé calls "non-place."[7] What distinguish *other* places from *real* places and *non*-places are the particular situations occurring in them that transform the individual's perception of his or her own existence and eventually perturb his or her awareness.[8] In addition to the otherness of places, Foucault theorizes the otherness of time: a museum can be simultaneously heterotopic and heterochronic, as it is a space hosting objects spanning eras and styles. The very existence of these objects is duplicitous because they exist in the time we see them but they also have an eternal physicality that resists temporal attacks. Heterotopias align with Foucault's concept of non-linear history and non-ontological notion of power, the latter a web of relations attached contextually to the site at which power is exercised. Engaging with social issues as presented within heterotopias establishes the possibility of exploring the physical connections to the author's subjectivity. How does the author relate to the community in which his or her ethical-aesthetic commitment might stem from an unexplored place whose variables do not quite fit into either the real-real or the imaginary? If, as Rancière suggests, ethics is a field for the disruption of the status quo, as it promotes "the kind of thinking in which an identity is established between an environment, a way of being and a principle of action,"[9] heterotopias are simultaneously ethically endowed with a private and yet public aspect. In turn, when heterotopias create settings for characters in literary and cinematic narratives, they illustrate how art can contextualize its origin within the author's social structure. By disrupting places that are at once real and imaginary, heterotopias permit an oblique critique of society through a subtle denunciation of its values. They underscore the constitutive ethical matter by which the relational aesthetic process is shaped while revealing the vulnerability of practices of power previously believed to be impregnable. It is within these spaces that passions might resolve what Martha Nussbaum calls, thanks to Proust's sentence, "the upheavals of thought" and through powerful counter-discourse expose normative criteria that concern the relationship of realism with the real.

My assessment of Italian artists' outcomes concerns almost invariably the analysis of their commitment in terms of constructive and dispassionate re-presentations of society that shy away from flippant self-denigration. Their adoption of realism is a critique of society, for the very process of rereading it within a narrative can never be a normative matter. Genres are troubled from within. As I previously stated in the case of Scarpa's narratives, the novel form is a hybrid and still the most suitable way to approach the narration of reality. Novelistic narration strikes Raffaello Palumbo Mosca[10] as the most apt for a truth quest that "can not only be factual" because its scope "is, in fact, to unveil the hidden connections between facts and the universal."[11] Faced with the loss of values, the opposition of individual/world (personal/universal) predictably offers, with humans as part of a material universe that ceaselessly retells itself, a fictional hypermodern text that contrasts alternative narratives of the time and space occupied by humans and all other living beings with conventional ones. Diffractive readings in the fictional hypermodern text validate Bertrand Westphal's statement about the active, as opposed to the strictly representational, role of literature whereby "fiction does not mimic reality, but it actualizes new virtualities hitherto unexpressed, which can then interact with the real according to the hypertextual logic of interfaces."[12] In the productive interaction between reality and the literary fiction that proposes its re-presentation (reality presented again but in a subjective way), fictional depictions of places and times promote a better understanding of real-world places. They also reveal the relationship between perceptual and cognitive structures and the material and spatial structures of the physical world. What appears, on the surface of the text, to be a matter circumscribed in the private space of the characters instead reveals the great relevance of its social context. In addition, reality is never too distant. For instance, the genre of the novel releases expressive transformations that appear "manifest in the type of images that each novelistic text builds to question the state of things (the universal, the social)."[13] We examine two things here: the emergence of a subjectivity that tries to create space for its expression within the structural container called "narrative"; and the transformed point of view of a sexed subject who interprets passions, emotions, misogyny, and gender construction in alternative ways from the past. As Ida Dominijanni states,

> strictly speaking, the subject of sexual difference is no longer an 'individual' as conceived by the lexicon of modern politics ... Equality, freedom, fraternity, power, authority, representation, right and rights, community

> and common all turn out to be marked by the neutralization of sexual difference and need to be rethought in the perspective of the embodied and sexed subject.[14]

Individuals move within heterotopias as complex constructions, as Foucault claims, shifting between the functions of an anthropological place where they have a certain identity and that of a non-place. Based on what authors declare in these narratives, we can think that an *other* space, a hotel room for instance, might warrant their characters' freedom from the constrictions of their immediate environment. As Simona Vinci writes in *Stanza 411*, "nessun altro posto al mondo fa sentire liberi quanto una stanza d'albergo" (no other place in the world makes one feel as free as a hotel room).[15] Its space does not provide the individual with another possible existence but offers a temporary respite from external pressures. In the narratives analysed in this part, spaces function as physical reminders that the passions of the soul, especially love, when not mitigated by a good passion such as reason, tend to isolate us from the rest of society while still bearing the effects of being part of it. Individuals construct something real that lies outside their habitual space; they deconstruct their reality to understand it. Being a member of a community (I am in relation to others) but living temporarily outside its centre (in this instance I cannot quite relate to a group for my moral concerns are directed towards one individual) affects the individual's constructive relationality and limits the ability to respond to any social change. In turn, by questioning normative criteria established for the setting and the reasoning behind erotic love, Sorrentino, Vinci, and Tomassini demonstrate an ethical concern for better intersubjective relations and gender roles.

These literary and cinematic narratives appeal to us by means of the sincerity with which each author – either in the quasi-autofictive mode of Tomassini's and Vinci's novels, or in the visual *conte philosophique* of Sorrentino's films – analyses the impact of an erotic passion on individuals. Their characters' lives appear not to be solely regulated by diktats of progress – for instance, by the need for self-defence and the precariousness of work that hamper Mazzucco's Emma's already evident vulnerable position. In their temporary position of *beings in love*, these characters act within heterotopias and inform narratives that counter the ordinary without pure abstraction. These are not fairy tales but realistic narratives that – though asking "what if we could change things simply by loving somebody?" – are also prepared to examine the possible consequences of giving a free rein to one's passions. The Mafia's presence in *Le conseguenze dell'amore*, the migrants' situation in *Sangue di cane*, and women's condition in *Stanza 411* are topics that *matter* in these narratives but that deal primarily with a vulnerability that differs from the one witnessed in Mazzucco's *Un giorno perfetto,* because the vulnerability these artists observe in their respective characters originates from love rather than hatred and fear. The functional presence of the passion of love triggers a poetics of affects that, by partly relying on heterotopic settings, lends itself to innovative narrative solutions. My preliminary conclusions concern the will to experience erotic love, independently of reason's warnings about the sometimes literally deadly consequences of erotic passion. The common denominator for Sorrentino's, Vinci's, and Tomassini's love narratives lies in their uncanny ability to elicit the potential that animates the ordinary of the quotidian into something extraordinary. Since erotic love involves only two individuals, their stories of unconventional love show its basic impracticability, as something deceivingly divorced from an indignation that promotes ethical reasoning. Despite their most obvious and immediate differences apparent in their genre and style, these narratives hold social implications and defy moral and/or representative clichés serving as unusual parables for what love can do.

6

A Recipe for the Advantages and Disadvantages of Love: Anger and Misogyny in Paolo Sorrentino's *The Consequences of Love*

Il cinema rappresenta la realtà. Ma se la realtà fosse così bella non ci sarebbe il cinema.[1]

–Jean-Luc Godard

This chapter discusses the ways in which passion animates the last crucial days in the otherwise dull existence of Titta Di Girolamo, the protagonist of Paolo Sorrentino's film *Le conseguenze dell'amore.* Titta, skilfully played by Toni Servillo, is a Mafia middleman[2] who has stoically endured isolation for eight years, confined to an aseptic hotel in Lugano, just so he could provide for his family back in Naples. He only has one job: to deliver money every week to a local bank on behalf of his Mafia bosses. As Pauline Small notices, this Mafia movie is unusual in its "marked absence of explicit political contextualization."[3] Such absence allows Sorrentino to focus on Titta's entrapment in a hotel and other spaces rather than on his dealings with the Mafia. Titta, a victim of his own illicit connection to Cosa Nostra, seems to be on the verge of succumbing to a state of apathy. Sorrentino's twist to a Mafia movie consists of showing spectators that the most excruciating and dangerous of all feelings, love, can trigger a way out of inertia. At the outset, viewers may or may not root for Titta Di Girolamo, who later surrenders to a deadly love for Sofia, the beautiful though modest and unpretentious bartender of his hotel. All he wants is for her to be happy: that's true love.

We are first introduced to Titta in a back shot followed by a frontal shot. We see him feigning indifference at the sight of Sofia in the back room of the hotel bar. Here Titta is presented as having achieved an enviable state of composure, as a man above passion. He is a fifty-year-old commercial accountant who, for many reasons, has been reduced to complete emotional withdrawal, as he knows a strong passion might result in deadly consequences. The protagonist's voice-over overlays the first scene in which Sofia watches him while fixing drinks, as he smokes. Now framed by a frontal take, Titta stares at the camera. His sphinx-like voice-over expresses in a free indirect speech his worst fears:

> La cosa peggiore che può capitare ad un uomo che trascorre molto tempo da solo è quella di non avere immaginazione. La vita, già di per sé noiosa e ripetitiva diventa, in mancanza di fantasia, uno spettacolo mortale ... Io non sono un uomo frivolo. L'unica cosa frivola che possiedo è il mio nome, Titta Di Girolamo. (2:50–3:31)

> (The worst thing that can happen to a man who spends a lot of time by himself is not to have imagination. Life, already boring and repetitive, becomes a deadly spectacle when lacking in imagination ... I am not a frivolous man. The only frivolous thing I have is my name, Titta Di Girolamo.)

A funeral carriage passes by as a reminder of the death Titta, like all mortals, feels is foredoomed. In the second scene, from the balcony of his room, Titta sees a man pivot to gaze at a young woman – who could be Sofia leaving the hotel – and slam into a light pole. The connection between Eros and Thanatos is presented almost immediately. All the while, Sofia tries to strike up a conversation with Titta, but he does not answer, refusing, for the time being, to give in to his imagination (see figure 6.1).

In a subsequent scene in the subset represented by the hotel bar, however (this being a heterotopic location where all the most important moves of the game happen), Titta observes Sofia, who has knowingly left the door of the back room where she is changing ajar to let him watch her undressing. He remains seated and jots down a thought: "Progetti per il futuro: non sottovalutare ..." (31:20; Future plans: do not underestimate ...). The camera (and the spectator with it) caresses Sofia's shoulders as if it were Titta's hands (see figure 6.2).

When Sofia leaves the bar for what spectators will later learn is her driving lesson, she finally catches Titta's eye. Or at least this is the first time that spectators see her catching his eye. Though we are aware that something is about to happen between the two, Titta does not approach her. Sofia gazes at him as the camera slowly returns to the notebook and displays the end of the message that Titta scrawls. Titta's completed thought is finally revealed: "Progetti per il futuro: non sottovalutare le conseguenze dell'amore" (31:49; Plans for the future: do not underestimate the consequences of love) (see figure 6.3).

A single image appears afterwards, a sort of "Kodak magic moment," showing Titta's wife, Giulia, in her wedding dress, smiling after the marriage ceremony that had taken place many years before (see figure 6.4).

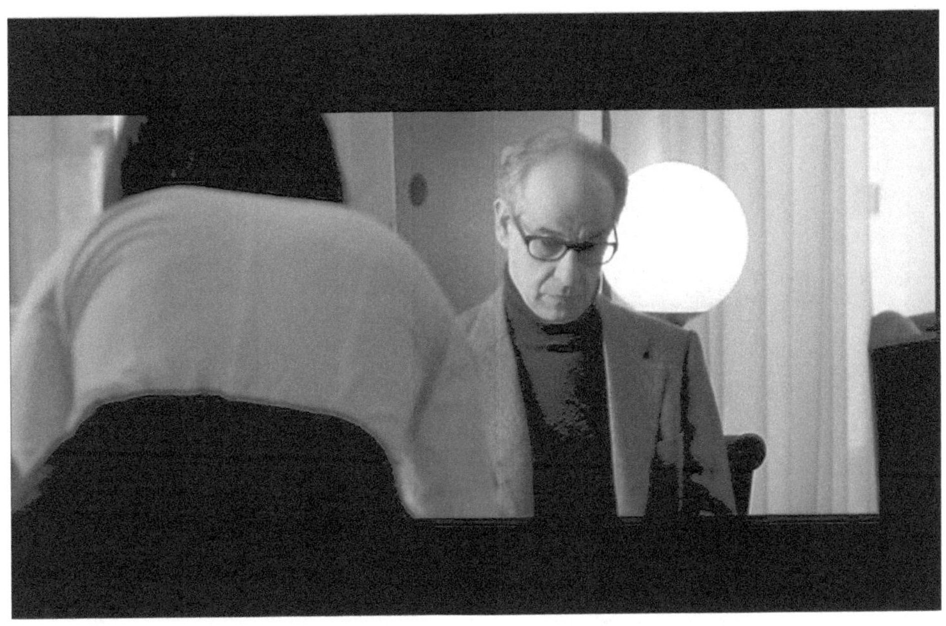

6.1 *Le conseguenze dell'amore* (30:38)

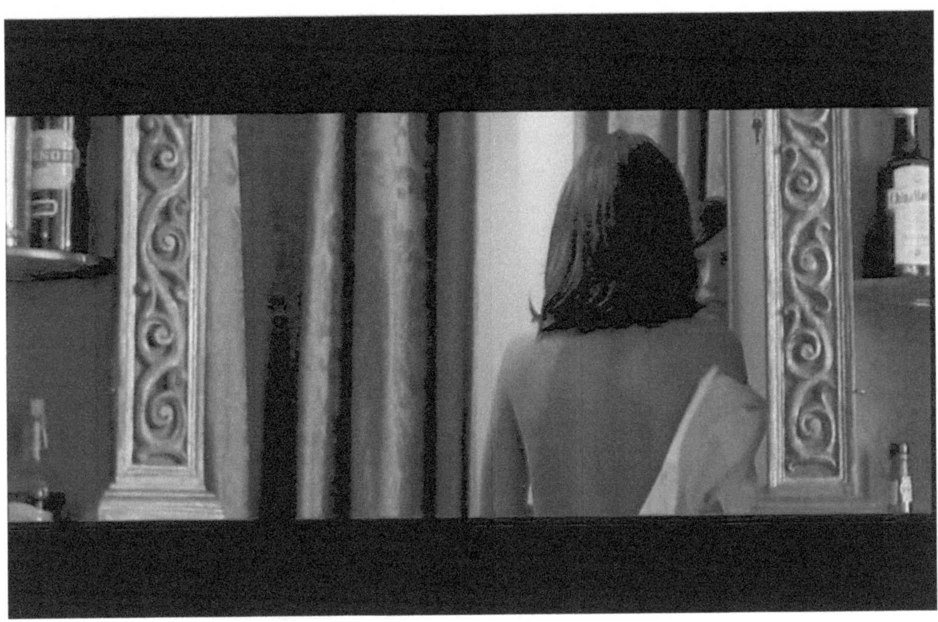

6.2 *Le conseguenze dell'amore* (31:49)

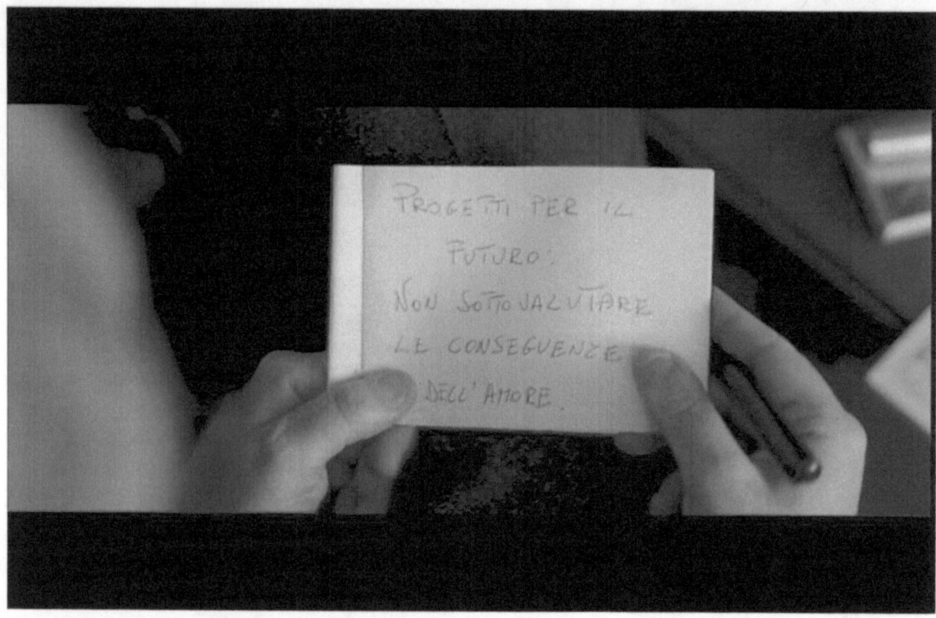

6.3 *Le conseguenze dell'amore* (31:50)

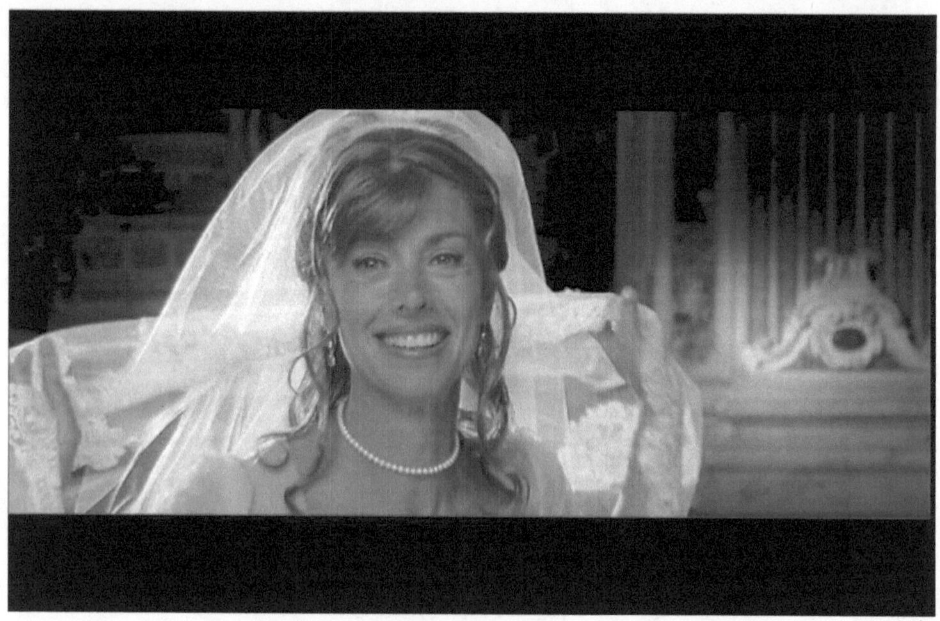

6.4 *Le conseguenze dell'amore* (31:53)

The connection between the two seemingly unrelated scenes is revealed. The sudden flashback recalls the great affection that Titta had for Giulia on their wedding day twenty years earlier, and presents itself as an apparition of what he could still *feel*. The image reifies Titta's feelings in a direct way. The same connection with that moment returns during the two instances of sexual impulse presented later in the film: Titta's masturbation act in his room, intercut with shots of a gorgeous woman he had glimpsed earlier in the mall (32:34–32:40) and flashes of Sofia's beautiful breasts. Sofia's body is slowly exposed: the take from Sofia's shoulders establishes a trajectory by which we see Titta gazing straight at Sofia's delicate breast (59:28–59:42) (see figure 6.5).

After a visit by his brother, who strikes up a conversation with the bartender, Titta overcomes his shyness and initiates minimal interaction with Sofia. The short flashback, a single image intercut with details of Sofia's body, marks the moment when he submits to passion while writing his death sentence. As he peers out of his room's window, the sunset reveals a crane. Until then, he had exhibited stoicism, but at that moment, Titta gives in to passion.

The equilibrium he had maintained between his repressed feelings and his current life gives way to a need for love, a need of which he is perfectly conscious: "I have never been loved by anyone," says Titta to the director, while paying his final bill, an account for eternity. And as Ornella Vanoni sings in an extradiegetic song that introduces the scene of Titta's fall and subsequent death at the hands of the mafiosi like a *malacarne* (a low Mafia figure usually in charge of killing), in life "it takes passion, a lot of patience, raspberry syrup, and a bit of nonchalance ... it takes a page from your playbook, Latin sensuality and a minimum detachment." That "bit of nonchalance," of deliberate unconsciousness, Vanoni sings, will bring enamoured Titta to the rite of the last scene. Immolated on the altar of love, an altar in pure liquid cement offered to him by Cosa Nostra, Titta will finally end his purgatorial existence. His death, Hume would say, amounts to the terrible consequence of following your passions without proper discernment. Put another way, Titta pays for the error that transformed his life into a perpetual connivance with the Mafia and a condition of emotional immobility. He pays for stealing money from Cosa Nostra. He pays for falling in love at his age and in his situation. As he tells Sofia, he is well aware that "the most dangerous thing [he's] ever done in [his] life was perhaps entering this bar" (41:43). We return to the image from the beginning of the movie of the funeral carriage, ancient and vaguely Neapolitan in style, passing on the street in front of the hotel. Its shape reveals Titta's looming fate, functioning as a visual prologue

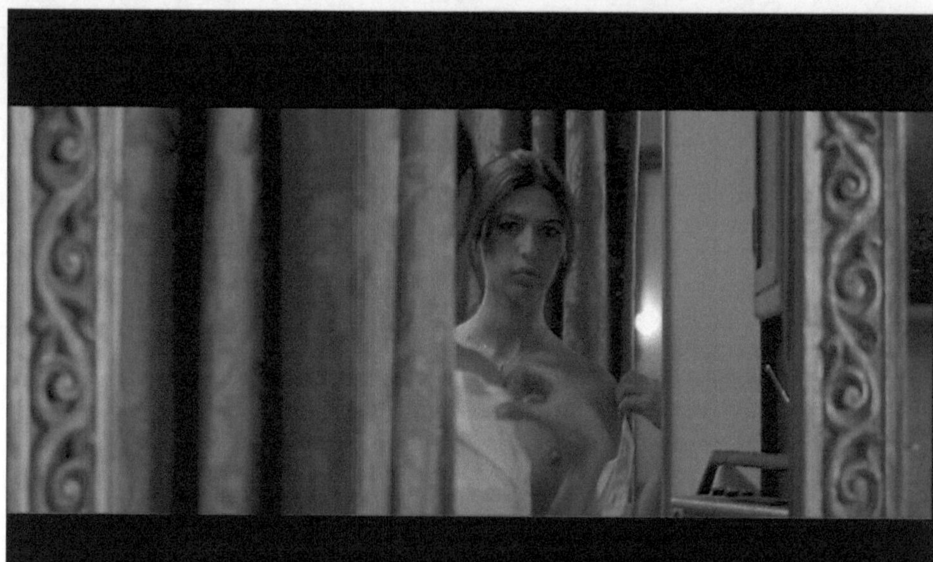

6.5 *Le conseguenze dell'amore* (59:28–59:42)

to his ill-fated destiny. It is a harbinger of a death. Titta lives in his own "aquarium," in a Swiss hotel that, in the imagination of many Italians, corresponds to a closed and silent place, *just like* an actual aquarium. What lesson are we to take from Titta's tribulations with love? What will his giving in to his passion produce? Is love something very generous in nature? Or is it something we rather feel as a way out of our own misery? As David Hume states in the section "Of the Passions," from his *Treatise of Human Nature*:

> Benevolence or the appetite, which attends love, is a desire of the happiness of the person belov'd, and an aversion to his misery; as anger or the appetite, which attends hatred, is a desire of the misery of the person hated, and an aversion to his happiness. A desire, therefore, of the happiness of another, and aversion to his misery, are similar to benevolence; and a desire of his misery and aversion to his happiness, are correspondent to anger. Now pity is a desire of happiness to another, and aversion to his misery, as malice is the contrary appetite. Pity, then, is related to benevolence, and malice to anger: And as benevolence has been already found to be connected with love, by a natural and original quality, and anger with hatred, 'tis by this chain the passions of pity and malice are connected with love and hatred.[4]

It is appealing to be able to discern the value and the exercise of passions with the same sagacity as Hume. However, can we all administer our passions in the manner the Scottish philosopher traces? The element of relationality in cinematic narratives is apparent, because the need to investigate the tenuous borders between genres uncovers how conventional categories of narrative analysis no longer suffice and how hybrid works emerge. Roy Menarini speaks of directors Matteo Garrone's and Paolo Sorrentino's ingenious "re-elaboration,"[5] which produces hybrid cinematic texts. Menarini stresses the innovative presence of these two directors in Italian cinema in their daring re-utilization of cinematic genres. Their contribution to genre hybridization reveals aspects of originality in its outcome and also elaborates a thick layer of references, as Alfio Leotta notes with regard to Sorrentino's *Le conseguenze dell'amore.*[6] For Menarini, Garrone's Bloomian "anxiety of influence" relates to Claude Chabrol's use of composition and emplotment in his *noirs,* particularly in his earliest productions. Garrone is also more cinematic than Sorrentino in his approach to plot, as he rarely begins from the script, while Sorrentino states that for him everything begins with literature and the act of writing. In speaking of the story behind his first feature film, *L'uomo in più* (2001), Sorrentino explains that he does not have a specific plan in mind when he writes a script. He creates stories that inspire him and that present themselves to his imagination without too many "intellectual calculations."[7] Also in his interview with Gary Crowdus for *Cinéaste,* Sorrentino reiterates his method for conceiving a story line from a storyboard for individual shots and entire scenes:

> I'm not able to compose a shot, to improvise, during the shooting. I prefer to previsualize so that when I go on the set I can concentrate on working with the actors. I prefer to separate the two things. Consideration of the camera angles and shot compositions comes before work with the actors. This method, which provides me with a solid base from which to work, then enables me to incorporate into the film any impressions I have on the set. As a moviegoer myself, I love the directors who do storyboards, such as the Coen brothers and Martin Scorsese. I like a very precise composition of the shot and I don't think that's easy to achieve on the set, so it's important for me to have worked out a sort of plan.[8]

Sorrentino owes some of his boldest techniques and visual allusions to Federico Fellini's anti-naturalistic works; he also borrows from postmodern pulp and pastiche examples offered by directors Sam Mendes and Quentin Tarantino. He establishes with their precursors a series of shifting relations that stresses the singularity of his oeuvre while acknowledging his influences. As Peter Wollen argues in his work on the auteur theory, "the director does not subordinate himself to another author; his source is only a pretext, which provides catalysts, scenes which fuse with his own preoccupations to produce a radically new work. Thus, the manifest process of performance, the treatment of a subject, conceals the latent production of a quite new text, the production of the director as an auteur."[9] Sorrentino's storyboard carefully defines the importance of an *other* space as a locus for the investigation of an irrational passion leading to disaster.

The Folly of Love: Misogyny and Frail Men

In a posthuman society that markets internet relationships as remedies for loneliness, on-screen representations of an actual – non-romanticized – love should move us, as the force of characters' passions appears to deactivate the harmful simulations of existence we see on reality shows (amongst others). To be compelled by passion – they seem to tell us – is still worth living for. But we (as much as the characters) are relatively unprepared to witness/experience the devastating, and deadly, consequences of such feelings. What matters in Sorrentino's movies is (as often happens) the male character: how much he loves, the folly he commits, or when he dies. Love and fascination with the female body are passions perceived – and actively illustrated for the spectators' enjoyment – as a cancer, an illness and inescapable source of failure and disaster for the male protagonist(s). Female characters function as a means by which men can escape apathy. At the same time, woman is a creature not to be trusted because she leads men to commit unethical acts, to their ruin. Nonetheless, men keep falling for women, because women provide the motivation for imagining other places/spaces in life. The idea that habits function as "trouble savers"[10] is particularly suggestive for a reflection on the characters of Sorrentino, for, until the end of his films, we are left to wonder if habits are not indeed the deadliest of weapons rather than a repository of serenity.

With past literary examples in literature such as Ovid's *On Women's Cosmetics*, or Tertullian's *The Appearance of Women*, misogyny results in indifference towards violence against women and the marginalized. Earlier in this book, Mazzucco and Stambrini were shown to be involved mediators of this societal ill. Sorrentino seems to perpetuate, while presenting it, the motif of a woman's presence in a man's life as a threat when it comes to amorous passion. While his cinematography might be innovative, his way of thematizing the presence of a woman in a man's life is rhetorically and visually bound to traditional takes. Drawing on Nietzsche's ideas of love as meaning to be immensely creative and fundamentally mendacious just like an aesthetic object, Chiara Piazzesi argues in her study that Sorrentino puts on the stage the ontological refusal of the person in love to undergo the docility of meaning:

> Folly, therefore, is neither *in* the desire nor *the* desire, but it is what is done by *acting* in the name of it. Folly is in the consequences of love, in translating the passion into *strategy* (that is, an *if… then* with which it seeks to mimic the world of rational action, ending inevitably in looking crazy), ostensive. Here is the «catastrophe» (Barthes 1977, p. 45) of Titta: because love holds absolute value, and because of such value, everything falls under the imprisonment of meaning, therefore within the fundamental, crucial question – *then* a negative sign is not just an incident but alludes to the absolute of *all or nothing*, and so the *Incident*, the Catastrophe ensues.[11]

Le conseguenze dell'amore and *L'amico di famiglia* (2006) (as well as his contemporary Matteo Garrone's *L'imbalsamatore* [2002] and *Primo amore* [2003]) depict a complex mingling of misogyny, anger, and love by wielding the grotesque as a narrative mode suitable to present the subjective experience of love. "It is in the grotesque," notes Roberto De Gaetano, "that Italian cinema seems to rediscover the natural destiny of the *split and deformed body of Italian society, its separation from a tradition and a common project, its estrangement from the (epic) narrative of History*."[12] The use of this narrative mode as a way to understand reality produces what De Gaetano claims is "the great paradox of Italian cinema: a constant presence of reality without any realism, a 'de-realized' presence of a real that is constantly converted into a dream, a nightmare, a hallucination."[13] Reality for both Garrone and Sorrentino reveals its unstable and unavoidable relationship with human beings, as they are subject to reveries, dreams, nightmares, and apparitions. Who is at the centre of this hallucination? Who sustains the weight of such estrangement from the epic narrative of history?

Misogyny often intervenes in the narrative of this "deformed body of Italy," with its apotropaic look at women's roles in cinema. Not only voyeurism constructs Garrone's and Sorrentino's female roles but also the inability to gain a perspective on women that could enhance their presence in the narrative, whether they are muses or perturbative elements in men's lives. Misogyny, or the disturbing aversion to women coupled with the fear/attraction that love's inevitable consequences produce, colours these films' narratives. Garrone's first films share with Sorrentino's *Le conseguenze dell'amore* and *L'amico di famiglia* a lavish concern with the theme of erotic obsession that produces, in turn, storylines imbued at times with the morbid and extreme aspects of sexuality. In both directors lies the preoccupation with understanding greed, or to put it another way, a collective Freudian connection between sex and money, the unresolved fascination with such an exchange, and the power that arises from it. The erotic woman emerges from these motives and is held responsible for the collapse of the hero, as her encounter dictates the course of his existence. As De Gaetano contends, Sorrentino's narrative constructs a de-realized presence of reality endowed with the problems that afflict Italian society. The Mafia influence is one problem, but the argument here is that Sorrentino only imagines erotic love as a disruptive element in a man's life. We are confronted by representations of women in misogynistic terms, reflecting an inability not only to look at all people in terms of their individuality, as Ida Dominijanni would note, but also to achieve normative gender relations. Sorrentino proposes a variation on the theme, however, in that he isolates his protagonist Titta in a specific heterotopia that utilizes the space of the hotel and its rooms as mental spaces for his slow agony and projects the possibility that only an upheaval of emotions stemming from his love for bartender Sofia might liberate him from such agony. Hence the strategy of love is depicted as a powerful disturbance from the stillness of one's own existence.

A neo-romantic, Wertherian-like mode depicts Titta's love, and its effects make it essential to look closely at how the character of Sofia, the woman he falls for, is constructed. The woman as perturbative agent emerges from a long tradition of characters designed to destabilize the male protagonist's agency. It is not so much their mesmerizing beauty that is the agent of perturbance as it is a distinctive power to disrupt men's codes of behaviour and control over their passions. Postmodern depictions of women do not conform to the portrait of *femmes fatales,* while the male characters are not attractive either. Some of the male characters are even grotesque, a feature that, in Enrico Carocci's view, aids Sorrentino also in showing Italy's sense of "fragmented collectivity."[14] Stricken with hideous physical features, as in the case of the character Geremia de' Geremei, his men are often ugly and almost invariably lonely individuals, divorced from anything that remotely resembles and recalls the predicaments that arise from social and familial participation. They are de-realized in this respect. Sorrentino's *L'amico di famiglia* stages, for instance, the impossible love of a grotesque usurer, Geremia de' Geremei, perennially affected by migraines, who lives afflicted with the hallucination that he can be loved by the beautiful daughter of a waiter who comes to him for money to pay for her wedding. His descent into love's hell takes him through every level of aberration or, better, exposes his disturbed mind to spectators. Grotesque in his features and physical defects, short, with bandages and potato slices on his head as a remedy for chronic migraines, Geremia de' Geremei shares little with the community except for the money he lends. He lives in surreal, metaphysical places rendered through the eerie cityscape of a town in the Agro Pontino (likely Sabaudia), while the dwarf protagonist of Garrone's *L'imbalsamatore* connives with the Mafia. Quite literally, they both belong to what De Gaetano calls a "deformed society." In the de-realized presence of the real, male characters embody frailty and insecurity with respect to their appearance, and, above all, their feelings. They do share, however one formidable element: the ability to still fall in love with someone who, in the director's view, is unworthy and detrimental to the character's existence, making us realize that it is not just women we are afraid of but love in general as the cause of our individual downfall. Again, on the subject of misogyny, Jean-Luc Godard, one of Sorrentino's influences, provides telling and inherently misogynistic comments on women and cinema:

> The cinema does not question the beauty of a woman; it only doubts her heart, records her perfidy (La Bruyère wrote it is an art of the whole person, that of placing a word or an act that deceives), and does not see anything but her movements. We do not smile at such passion that logic inflames. Undoubtedly, what ensures its value is that it always deals with loving or dying.[15]

As in Godard's statement (which by extension works also for the queer relationship in *L'imbalsamatore*), Sorrentino sees only beauty in the object of love. However, in the bidimensional and flat representations Sorrentino renders of women, it would seem that it is their perfidy as their crippled hearts to construct what Roberto De Gaetano calls "intensive bodies," "bodies crossed by thresholds and not made of organs, are those that suspend the organic. Bodies that are treated like intensive surfaces."[16] The algid actresses Olivia Magnani and Laura Chiatti perfectly embody the sex appeal of the inorganic, to use Mario Perniola's famous sentence. Women's crippled hearts do not depend so much on their own feelings as on what the male character wants from them. Titta's falling for the bartender in his hotel, the beautiful Sofia played by Olivia Magnani, validates Godard's reflections on love as De Gaetano's notion of a theatralized body. By inference, such passion could signify either Titta's rebirth – validating his efforts at scheming against the Mafia out of his desire to have a life after discovering love through Sofia – or his death, an ending the film proposes as a more realistic scenario. Titta's attraction leads him to lose his bearings, to give up momentarily his non-harmful masculinity – which had kept him alive for years locked in the hotel – thus causing his own death or martyrdom. With its still waters, the Lugano Lake forebodes for the protagonist of *The Consequences of Love* a transfixing destiny that changes his role from Mafia middleman to martyr on the altar of love. It is suggested that love is a mistake that men should never commit. Yet Titta yields to love and is doomed for his passions.

In his interview with Sorrentino, Guido Bonsaver claims that, along with its hedonism and luxury at all costs, the Italy of Berlusconi that is represented in *L'amico di famiglia* reveals the society's "soft and dirty belly"[17] through the character of a loan shark who tries to squeeze out of a woman the happiness that his deformed body denies him.[18] While appreciating Sorrentino's psychological study of male characters, Bonsaver was one of the first critics to argue that female characters suffer in Sorrentino's scripts from a lack of "depth of psychological introspection and characterization."[19] According to Bonsaver, this detail should not distract us from the true force of Sorrentino's cinema, its "visual impact, in its attempt to blend colours, shapes, sounds and movements into a staged choreography that is not an end in itself."[20] In many works by male authors, the conceptualization of the *femme fatale* is the integral trigger of the plot, especially in *noirs* and hard-boiled thrillers. The female characters appear devoid of psychological depth but retain their dangerous power, to the extent that they often lead the male protagonist to his own ruin, confirming the negative effects of a woman on a man's life. The ghost of moral and pedagogical lessons on how and why a man should never fall under any female subject's spell lurks behind the plot.

Femmes fatales are conventionally drawn with very shallow and bold strokes. Spectators should be concerned with the motives behind the presence of female characters with such trifling roles. What creates this negative aura is not so much their limited speaking parts as the negative effect they provoke in men who fall in love with them. When he falls in love with a *femme fatale*, a man becomes aware of the full extent of his vulnerability, which leads him to ruminate on death, and makes the presence of reified beauty central to the plot, a recurring trope in Sorrentino's oeuvre, as the apparition of Miss Universe in his *Youth* (2015) reiterates. By the time the male character has figured this entire process out, alas, it is too late. We are at the end of the narrative. In short, the crux is not so much the woman in her role of the irredeemable corruptor as the man's perception of her as a catalyst for feelings that he should never experience in a life ruled by reason. However, emotions rapidly develop into potentially deadly passions. A woman viewed as a mantis, even if in a de-realized way, Sorrentino's Sofia fits into the category of those roles that define how, in Peter Wollen's words, "man is woman's 'prey.'"[21] Men actually succumb to their *own* emotions: Titta looks like Sofia's metaphorical prey, but in actuality he is his *own* prey. Sorrentino's understanding of a woman's role is conservative and not merely dictated by a conventional use of voyeurism. If women behave well, they are sentimentalized, and perhaps gain more speaking opportunities. Otherwise they remain a strategic presence for the development of the male character and his eventual ruin. In what looks like a modern rendering of a cautionary tale for the sequence of actions the protagonist goes through and the lessons learned from them, *Le conseguenze dell'amore* instead reveals an ambiguous approach to the treatment of male characters when they fall in love.

The reasons for the lack of further development of the possibilities that erotic love always creates perhaps lie in the misogynistic undertones of Sorrentino's narrative. In *A History of Misogyny in Literature*, Katherine Rogers takes a Freudian approach in discussing the cause of misogyny in Western writers from Aristotle to Ernest Hemingway. Rogers provides a pragmatic summary of the male psychology of patriarchy and restates the possible motives of misogyny. Misogyny stems from a multitude of causes: bad experiences with women, projection of one's own failings onto an innocent other, consequences of the normal frustrations of men and women living together, and fear of women's power. In trying to answer the question of why men become misogynists, Rogers emphasizes one important point: the inherent fear men feel that, if women were ever to be freed from their current restrictions, they would become men's masters.[22] More recently, Tania Modleski further reconsiders misogyny as something determined by the sheer volume of objectified women in movies rather than their mere bidimensional presence.[23] It is not one isolated case that causes misogyny; rather, its expansive representation turns it into a permanent and crystallized feature of our (conservative) society. It's difficult not to take issue with how Sorrentino isolates his characters within the confining space of misogyny, because his perspective runs counter to the postcolonial notion by which we consider the individual as always being "in transit." According to Iain Chambers, being in transit implies not only the notion of a physical displacement but also that of turning "every place and every language problematic, continually exposed to all queries coming from elsewhere."[24] If Sorrentino problematizes Titta's displaced position within his heterotopic setting, one wonders why his investigation of erotic love falls short with Sofia, who is never provided with agency. If the individual's surroundings are a place whose compositional elements can be scrutinized and re-evaluated in their representation, how can one explain the auteur Sorrentino's use of stereotypically misogynistic images and roles for women that consist of practically no lines and never showing, as

Godard said, "anything but [their] movements"? Each female character for Sorrentino tends to act as a (negative) muse rather than being an active participant in his scripts. Displacement occurs only for male characters, while women are relegated to roles with barely a few lines. Not only the movie in question reveals this stance, but also how Fanny Ardant appears to Jep in *La grande bellezza* (2013; The Great Beauty) or, for different reasons, the aforementioned presentation of a silent Miss Universe in the pool scene in *Youth* (2015). Rather than illuminating epiphanies, Sorrentino's movies propose women's appearance in terms of an arresting beauty charged with a significance that only the male protagonist can unravel. Misogyny, coupled with the fear of the inevitable consequences of love, fills the narrative of Sorrentino's films. Erotic obsession, a storyline that verges on the morbid, and extreme sexuality illustrate a preoccupation with trying to understand a collective anxiety about feelings. However, Sorrentino's narratives always stop short of illuminating the other (female) side of the relationship, as Titta's love is a one-way street. Titta wishes to escape passion's upheavals, yet is allured by even the prospect of temporary happiness. All too human, Titta abandons his firmness of resolve in paying attention to the consequences of love before a bidimensional Sofia.

In his study of passions, *Geometria delle passioni*, Remo Bodei rethinks the categories of passion and reason as two "pre-judged terms ... that define each other (by contrast or difference) only within determined conceptual horizons and specific evaluative parameters."[25] Passions, according to Bodei,

> prepare, preserve, memorize, rework and exhibit the "reactive meanings" most directly attributed to people, things, and events from subjects who experience them within certain contexts. Passions elicit the forms and metamorphoses of such contexts. Passions actually leave to "reason" itself, posteriorly presented as provisionally overwhelmed and seduced, to determine the purpose and range of their action, identifying the objects on which to pour themselves, measuring the point at which the impetus must halt, dosing the virulence of dissipative attitudes.[26]

Bodei's statement points to the interdependence of reacting to passions and using reason to control them. In a general way, Bodei accepts an account of passions similar to Hume's. In fact, Bodei's account of reason accords with Hume's doctrine of the intractability of the passions to governance by reason. Hume's dictum that "reason is and ought only to be the slave of the passions, and can never pretend to any other office than to serve and obey them"[27] clarifies how for the Scottish philosopher following only reason does not lead to virtuosity. Reason alone has no reason to exist. Reason can preside over passions, but only when the very existence of passions causes the existence of reason. Hume and later Remo Bodei both assert the importance of similar actions of control by the good passion of reason over more uncontrollable ones, such as erotic love. However, one cannot admit to the inadequacy of the concept of passion as a blinding force. Passions are feelings but only because they are internal motions in a material being. They are part of a construct that disregards discernment only on the surface of things. For Hume passions are unreasonable only if "founded on false suppositions"[28] and if the individual's capacity to access his/her potential defence has not been assessed. If passions can be a blinding force, they are nevertheless *useful*, in that they "shake the experience from inertia and monotony, make life palpitate despite pains and sorrows."[29] Bodei's interrogation of the value of a life without passion, "of what is it at 'heart' to us, and of which we fear the loss,"[30] could call for an answer that states passions are worth living for, even if they reveal themselves to be deadly. Philosophy can only reveal a part of reason; it can only convince us that part of our life needs reason. It cannot convince us that reason is the sole producer of happiness or that philosophy can satisfy our understanding of how we conduct our existence:

> If you come to a philosopher to be inculcated how you should choose your ends, Hume is saying, to know what desire to gratify, what passion to comply with, what appetite to indulge, you stand to be disappointed; for the lesson of philosophy is that nothing is entirely desirable or valuable in itself. There is no means of deciding what the best life for human beings is ... The best remedies for unhappiness are easy and obvious, with nothing distinctively philosophical about them.[31]

The effective merit of a controlled life without passion is undisputed – but a life without passion ensures boredom. Bodei concludes by questioning whether "total apathy, lack of feelings and resentments, inability to rejoice and to get sad, to be 'full' of love, anger, or desire, the very disappearance of passivity, understood as a virtual and welcoming space for the appearance of the other, would not perhaps be equivalent to death."[32] Anything is better than apathy, already in itself a move towards death, as the prefix "a" added to the word "pathos" negates the life of passions. Reasoning about love cannot quite match the ecstatic feeling of it, something Mario Sesti affirms in his comments on *L'amico di famiglia*, as the characters "seem to defend themselves from life because they are able to unravel their every illusion with language ... Why then do they abandon themselves to love?"[33] Sesti's query concerns the "rabbia remota" (remote anger) of Geremia originating in his being an illegitimate child and bearing the burden of a difficult childhood.[34] But the abandonment to love of frail male characters begins with *Le conseguenze dell'amore* and reveals the vanity of resisting the passions. Paradoxical ambiguity is exposed by how problematic seems to be the exercise of controlling the upheaval created by passions and the need for their control by reason in order to survive, but at the cost of not living a full life.

Rationality, often proclaimed by male protagonists, is more often than not a *safe* burden for the lives of Sorrentino's protagonists. Carrying on an illicit business – one works for the Mafia and the other practices usury at the expense of poor neighbours – Titta Di Girolamo and Geremia de' Geremei, a clear derivation of the Italian Paperon de' Paperoni (Disney's Uncle Scrooge), work their way through emotions almost as a means to ascend to Paradise, or at least to some form of Purgatory, for their previous existence was stained by business and dirty money. An interesting element of Sorrentino's investigation concerns the misogynistic approach that renders female characters (nearly) mute. After years of attempts at revisiting old gender binaries we witness the return of *femmes fatales*, as they are depicted by Sorrentino's mischievous cinematography. I argue that Sorrentino identifies love – including the irrational decisions love triggers – as an indispensable passion. But Sorrentino's claim comes charged with notions of misogyny that are inherent in Italian culture, and not even his brilliance manages to dismantle them. He is a full member of his society and, as such, his female roles are, in my view, more revealing than others of where things still stand as far as giving voice and space to a woman in a man's film in Italian society. Sorrentino, nevertheless, crafts an original tale about the universal experiences of love and lost opportunities to develop our potential. For instance, Titta's anger relates more to his own forced inactivity, which makes him a person who cannot and does not want to dare, at least until the day his own "Albertine," in the person of Sofia the bartender, unveils the secret of love: making us courageous and bold despite the consequences.

Misogyny plays a key role in the theme of control of the passions, for men are believed to maintain control over their emotions and women to give in to their shifting and excessive feelings. What matters in *Le conseguenze dell'amore* is not only the setting of the story in a secluded hotel, and what a heterotopia can make us realize about the character inhabiting that space, but also the original sense of confinement of Titta's passions. His fatal resolution to release those passions stems from his encounter with what I consider an apparition, Sofia, a character who is not fully fleshed out and who approximates De Gaetano's idea of the "inorganic body." We know little about her, yet her presence is central to Titta's story, since she triggers his final gesture towards ending his purgatorial existence in the hotel. The space of the hotel represents the central setting but signifies both public and private spaces,[35] a semantic field the auteur has established *a priori*. There is a direct correlation between the rooms of Titta's mind and the interior spaces of the hotel. What fills these spaces is the author's[36] understanding that a woman's presence is a "catalyst"[37] in a man's story, a story that is otherwise infused with camaraderie (*Youth*'s friendship between the filmmaker and the orchestra conductor) or limited to business relations (Titta and Cosa Nostra). A woman's presence and her subsequent death give pungency to life, but the romance seems to be primarily between men.[38] Dana Renga argues convincingly that

> Sofia's seemingly irrational death is necessary for Titta to transcend his depression and the confines of his Mafia-made prison so as to eventually reach a state of enlightenment ... To be sure, Sofia's erasure from the narrative is without consequence, while Titta is redeemed through death.[39]

I am not entirely convinced that Titta is redeemed through death, but it would be difficult to disagree with Dana Renga and Pauline Small that Sofia's presence is a catalyst in thrusting the dangerous ingredient of passion into a man's otherwise apathetic life – after which her character simply vanishes from the screen. If love compromises male reason, this time it is for a good cause. The word (*la parola*), originally the weapon and unlikely tool through which an accountant such as Titta displays his control by speaking an impeccable Italian unlike the heavily accented Sicilian vernacular spoken by the mobsters, fails miserably against his emotional response to Sofia, a woman he barely knows. But his love for her redeems him from his passivity and turns his forced captivity in the hotel into a last chance to win over Cosa Nostra by outwitting the two hitmen who went to kill him. Sorrentino makes play of thriller conventions by presenting at first his colourless Titta Di Girolamo as the embodiment of the classic model of the Aristotelian "in-irascible" man, whose defective extreme of anger triggers the philosopher's interest.[40]

Titta's character is constructed at the outset to embody the "in-irascible" man. Smartly clad in a well-tailored jacket and cashmere turtleneck, he appears composed, even phlegmatic. He sits quietly in the hotel bar and observes the muffled movements of people around him, his posture resembling that of Hume's Stoic. With his detached attitude to existence and to social relations, Hume's Stoic embodies a refined system of selfishness. Hardly a positive characteristic, the "in-irascibility" of the

Aristotelian man suggests his apathy, his detachment from a world of which he is no longer part, having succumbed to the Mafia and money's easy allure. His voice-over (with a condescending tone) is yet another attribute that reinforces his image. Stoics consider good people to be those who avoid emotions such as compassion and erotic love (and, surely, anger), since they do not warrant a "morally acceptable life."[41] Then why does the stoic/in-irascible Titta decide to attract Sofia's interest? To prove perhaps that erotic love can be part, as Nussbaum relates, of a morally acceptable life? Is it because of the awareness that his morally *un*acceptable life cannot justify entrapment and seclusion? Two elements may provide answers: first, the Mafia removes meaning from a man's individual existence as his actions are subject to the central power of the system, regardless of his social status, and second, that women have been the ruin of men since Eve's time. Both are central themes in thrillers and Mafia movies, and yet Sorrentino reverses all the significance we usually attribute to them. Titta morphs into a man who is far from controlled, as we will see. Though aware that Sofia is, as Albertine is for Marcel, "both outside of him, impossibly distant, unpossessable, and inside him, an internal object that disturbs what is deepest in his sense of life,"[42] Titta feels a need for her that envisions sexual desire but has more to do with establishing a relationship. Sorrentino's reflections on the upheaval of the mind by love deploy open references to Louis-Ferdinand Céline's Sophie to construct the character of Sofia or, more accurately, to construct the main character's sense of apprehension at spotting Sofia in the bar. Two girls are reading the Céline novel *Journey to the End of the Night* out loud in the room:

> But let's get back to our Sophie! Her mere presence seemed a feat of daring in our sulking, fearful, unsavory household ... The joyful strength, precise yet gentle, which animated her from her hair to her ankles troubled us, alarmed us in a charming sort of way, but definitely alarmed us, yes, that's the word.[43] (21:40–22:06)

The quotation from the Céline novel might have been the kernel of Sorrentino's treatment of love. Via the conduit offered by this quotation, Sorrentino creates a brilliant parallel between Marcel and Albertine of Marcel Proust's *Remembrance of Things Past* (*Swann's Love* especially) and Titta and Sofia. Like Marcel, who is obsessed with Albertine, Titta senses he cannot do without his love for Sofia. Indeed, Sorrentino's interpretation of the auteur theory, in his understanding of setting a specific *other* space for his characters (*metteur en scène*), encourages the construction of contemporary myths, which is why the nexus between misogyny and the consequences of falling in love holds specific validity. What led Titta – the in-irascible man – to risk the ire of the Mafia was the perception of Sofia's "joyful strength." Her strength "alarms" Titta but also rejuvenates him. Regardless of the consequences, passions can be miserable but valuable because their effect produces emotions that are worth living for, even if only for a short time. And it is actually the duration of vehement states on which literature greatly relies for its own construction because "the time span of rage and its immediate consequences, the time span of falling in love and its immediate consequences, of grief and its immediate consequences, happens to match the particular kind of timescale on which literature operates best."[44] Fisher argues in fact that an episode for literary or narrative use "has only a certain scale, which matches, among other things, the scale of an experience of the outburst, consequences, transformations, and settling into the calm of a passion."[45]

"Non confondere mai l'insolito con l'impossibile" (Do not ever confuse the unusual with the impossible), a key phrase in *L'amico di famiglia*, could be the subtitle for the treatment of passions in Sorrentino's *oeuvre*. While fear is not necessarily always included in the list of passions established by philosophers (for example, Descartes excludes it in his essay on passions), falling in love – as a mere apparition, an episodic moment, and something unattainable – triumphs as an indisputable example of passion, one that is vital to all humans. What seemed impossible for the stoical Titta, pictured in empty Swiss shopping malls, becomes unusually real through imagination. We slowly understand Titta's character's transformation: if his love for Sofia is unreasonable it is because only something utterly unreasonable could shake his existence.[46] After years of stoic numbness in which the Mafia has slowly excluded him from all elements of ordinary life – work, family, social connection – Titta *feels* something again. If irrational, his love is however constructive, allowing him to break free from the Mafia's hold over him, one that he has tried to manage through rational thinking and that now inflicts an extreme punishment on him. His death amounts to the protagonist's suicide. He announces this death himself in a short note: "do not underestimate the consequences of love." But the death must be extraordinary.

Love's weight is intolerable, but for a reason. Titta will suffocate in the quick-dry cement: a reverse crucifixion for love. And the image of the steel cables suspending him over the liquid cement ready to absorb his flesh, while his last memory is of Sofia's face, intercuts with the shots of the steel cables on the snowy mountains where his only friend, Dino Giuffrè, works. We learned earlier from Titta's conversation with his brother that Dino is a schoolmate from Salerno whom he has not seen for twenty years. Feelings, not reason, dominate Titta's mind at this moment, as when he gives the luggage containing nine million dollars to Carlo and Isabella, the former owners of the hotel. Sorrentino cross-cuts these two scenes to confirm how a conventional Aristotelian male friendship retains an uncontaminated value that is as pure as the snow.[47] "Once you are friends with somebody you are always friends," Titta says to his brother. Friendship connotes a bond between men that is never broken and almost righteous if compared to the passion of love. It is a value whose purity is symbolized by the icy whiteness of snow on the mountains where Dino works.[48]

In *Le conseguenze dell'amore*, Sorrentino's homosociality generates the modes of exploitation of the woman on screen, something that is perceived not only through the character of Sofia but also through that of the maid and of the mysterious red-haired woman. A kind of low voyeurism, according to Kenneth MacKinnon in his study on misogyny in the work of director Brian De Palma, defines the existence of the woman "only in relation to castration," which she "cannot transcend," as Laura Mulvey had already theorized in 1975.[49] In this kind of visual pleasure there exists, of course, the pleasure of the protagonist, which the spectators share with him in looking at the woman. The scopophilic gaze largely structures Sorrentino's *mise-en-scènes.* His fascination with the follies men commit for women prevents him from developing a female character. He focuses on the love of looking at a woman who can hardly speak, since her character has few or no lines to define her agency. But there is something else that complicates scopophilia in Sorrentino's films: a form of narcissism that is limited by the woman's presence on the screen. The visual presence of a woman, Mulvey writes, "tends to work against the development of a story line, to freeze the flow of action in moments of erotic contemplation."[50] Sorrentino's desire to let his protagonist play the card of the passion of love as an existential reaction to stagnation is ambiguous. His ambiguity – unresolved empathy or lack thereof – cannot grant his characters redemption. Spectators are entangled in the director's ambiguity when they consider Titta's actions. Can we reveal our empathy towards the character or not? Can we share what he is going through or not?

Suzanne Keen has defined three possible kinds of narrative empathy: bounded strategic empathy (stemming from experiences of mutuality), ambassadorial strategic empathy (cultivation of the empathy of others to a specific end), and broadcast strategic empathy (a collective call to empathize with characters). Empathy, more than sympathy, triggers prosocial behaviour, but Keen considers three different ways to exercise empathy. The auteur's own ambiguity in projecting his feelings about his characters and how they behave with women produces a characteristic "empathic distress."[51] This is what readers/spectators feel, Keen writes, when their moral code is at odds with that of the characters. With empathy, you feel *like* the character, and it triggers a reaction and emotion that is very different from sympathy.[52] Sorrentino is an auteur who, unlike Garrone, does not base his stories on actual news or literary works, but imagines situations that, scene by scene, develop a trivial story linked to facts that could belong to everyone, challenging the notion that an everyday life is banal.[53]

It is the episodic moment of falling in love described by Peter Fisher that decrees, as Taviani suggests, the shift of the everyday into an epiphany for the film's protagonist. An event of short duration – an episode – can forever modify the course of one character's existence. Destinies are subject to a different kind of scrutiny under the close watch of the auteur who conceptualizes the film script as a conduit from his ideas to the cinematic and has markers throughout his body of work that define his ongoing themes.[54] Spectators become accidental moral judges of Geremia's and Titta's actions. The women for whom men lose their minds usually appear to be without a soul. But Miss Agro Pontino Rosalba relieves her parents from wedding debts by exchanging sex for the money they owe to Geremia, thus demonstrating how, in a poor family, the daughter's body always equates to a monetary asset and tool of exchange. Her giving in to Geremia's lust reveals her feelings for her parents while angrily conforming to class and societal expectations. Sorrentino's ambiguity and camera use allow us to understand the bankruptcy of reason that results from trying to tame passion. Sorrentino demonstrates a palpable Humean scepticism towards life values. When coming to terms with their distorted reality, protagonists can only expect a rude awakening from their momentary illusion. The final punishment of the protagonist actualizes a misogyny that, instead of exemplifying itself in the devouring or instrumentalization of the female body, works against those who experience it. The upheaval of the mind resulting from love is liberating and produces an existential break from the apathy of everyday life. It also causes the cessation of physical existence for Titta, while for Geremia it eliminates the possibility of believing in his own delusionary expectations.

Experiencing love amounts to an irreversible mutation of one's existence *ante quem*. There is however, no real parallel between Sorrentino's characters and Stendhalian or Foscolian antecedents, for romanticism *tout court* cannot enter these narratives. Sorrentino's narratives compose *his* story, a fruit of his imagination that nevertheless involves emotions that his spectators can relate to and share to a certain degree. We experience a very real sensation that makes us feel "full of love," as Bodei writes, but we remain dubious of its outcome. Paraphrasing James Harris's words that it is the duty of a philosopher to seek to understand where happiness lies, if you come to an auteur to ask for direct advice on how you should choose your role in life, you will be disappointed. For, as Sorrentino himself explains, rather than choosing straightforward and direct takes on events and life stories, he looks for ambiguity, both in meaning and visual techniques. We allow ourselves to think of Sorrentino as Hume's sceptic reincarnated, as he does not attempt to alter the economy of passions in his audience or to persuade them of the loftiness of things other than what they desire. His hope is, perhaps, that his viewers will reap a tangible benefit from trying to understand the rationale behind his protagonists' choices, as his fictional characters reveal the fiction of reality. Watching Titta's or Geremia's anguish might evoke a reaction that moral philosophy and cinema do not aim to provide for their basic acknowledgment of the fact that the lively knottings that tie together the world we inhabit do not always rely on an "objective" notion of common sense. The key is to grasp, as Piazzesi states, that

> Sorrentino's film sees the incommensurability of causes and consequences, namely, an overwhelming subjective sense that does not open to objectivity, does not reconcile itself with the meaning and concatenation it would like to confer upon it. Obviously, it is a weird affair: how can Titta love a person he does not know (the girl often repeats it to him, who doesn't know *who I am*)? ... he can. Purely: yes. Because in love, the experience of the world of the loving subject is totally irreconcilable with the meaning that can be given to the General, the objective, to common sense.[55]

Titta needs *a* particular kind of wisdom (hence the name "Sofia") in his life at that very moment. He needs to peer at her breast not just out of mere voyeurism but because the most conventional gaze a man can offer a woman can alter his existence. Spectators see him looking at her breast and become intrigued by the object of his interest, always subjective. Hence, Sorrentino manipulates our conventional reaction to let us into the mind of a man who wants to alter the terms of his own existence. This man needs to fall for Sofia to end his purgatory. The upheaval of the mind serves as a salvific emotion. We could reframe Sorrentino's ambiguous message on the necessity of love in life according to Nussbaum's notion of love as "a particular kind of awareness of an object, as tremendously wonderful and salient, and as deeply needed by the self. The project of possession (or of helping) is then a response to that awareness."[56] Titta requires his love for Sofia and her radiant beauty (Céline's "joyous strength"), regardless of its consequences, or perhaps *because* of its consequences.

Sorrentino's films never provide happy endings. However, they always speak of the stasis of political and ideological passions, of the emptiness into which Italian society is slowly sinking. This waste of human lives underscores how the passion of the heart makes life worth living. Titta decides against reason, as he assesses the possibility of the disaster that hangs over him, reified by the arrival of a person who awakens a spark of feeling in him. It is apparent that soon this vital moment when passions overcome reason will be deadly. Love is salvific precisely because it leads to the individual's earthly end. Falling in love disrupts Titta's way of life, and his stoic compliance with Mafia rules ceases to exist along with his death. It is a no-win situation: if you don't submit to passion you remain passive, like Jep who continually reminisces about his youthful love in *La grande bellezza*; if you let yourself be conquered by passion, you risk your life, like Titta. Running the risk of ruining your life affirms its existence, and constitutes a victory over apathy. The scope of the domain of passion is that of internalizing social and cultural imperatives, immunizing the individual against any form of imbalance that can be detrimental to his functioning within society, even that of the Mafia.[57] Do we want to cling to the few things we can still control, or can we relinquish them? If we do relinquish them, we might be able to change the storyboard. Titta changes his own life by abandoning his firmness of resolve and his fear of the consequences of love.

7
Society, Simulacra, and Love: Simona Vinci's *Stanza 411*

For David Hume, love is an indirect passion, an impression generated by the complex intertwining of direct passions, with desire as only one of its components.[1] By restraining imprudent or immoral impulses that love can trigger, we appeal to reason as a good passion capable of controlling intense (erotic) affections. However, the more we try to activate reason, the more likely we are to fail, because the origin of love – the original impulse to love, that is – can hardly find a proper rationale for its own being. "Since reason alone can never produce any action, or give rise to volition," Hume states, "the same faculty is as incapable of preventing volition, or of disputing the preference with any passion or emotion."[2] Reason, in short, can neither originate nor hinder any act of volition. Simona Vinci's creative energy and imaginative writing frequently address the topic of love and the use of reason to temper the disadvantages that such passion seems to impose on women in particular. In her work, love is a signifier for human relations whose sustainability is measured in the breakdown of social bonds between the individual and society.[3] The fictional protagonist of the love story recounted in *Stanza 411* coincides with the writer Simona Vinci: her own subjectivity becomes her object of enquiry and is intermingled with the analysis of the case studies (sexual, marital, relational) that the narrator presents within the context of heterosexual feelings of love. The novel's discourse on love has inspired my analysis of the ties between a subjective and intimate topic such as the confession of a love story as a book of life and its narrative rendering in a book whose content weaves together the private matters and general pathemic dynamics that motivated Vinci to further investigate abuse and violence in contemporary Italian couples. This text not only presents love as a passion bearing significance for the relationship between the two protagonists of the story, but also shapes love as a psychological space for Vinci to reflect on the society in which she is an active member and commentator. In a construct that juxtaposes metanarrative and narration, Vinci describes the reaction of her protagonist at the end of her self-defined first true love by tracing its development. Vinci expands her field of enquiry to gender issues in Italian society as a whole to contextualize her own story against the backdrop of a collective and uninterrupted form of social misogyny that still justifies male behaviour and condemns women who do not submit to social rules. Self-reflection reveals its thematic and formal significance throughout the text, and a self-reflective mode appears to be convincingly functional to the structure of the text and to its outcome, allowing for a narrative that constantly transitions between inner and outer spaces of discourse, expands its radius of inquiry from the writer to other individuals, and establishes new knowledge of the manipulation of love in Italian society.

Succinctly put, *Stanza 411* is an exposé of an erotic relationship with a non-fiction narrative mode playing with autofiction.[4] While the front matter defines the book as a novel, its content reveals, in fact, an overexposure of the author's presumably actual existence that interlaces Vinci's enquiries on societal gender dynamics. The narrator possesses the physical traits of Vinci and shares her profession. In addition, some of the events narrated in the book coincide with real events in her own life, such as a love affair (the two protagonists are both writers) that Vinci actually experienced. One could venture to say that their passion began and ended with the act of writing, a not-unusual literary theme.[5] The two writers first fell in love with each other's words, and their first physical encounter, which occurred in a hotel room in the centre of Rome after a long exchange of e-mails, resulted from their correspondence. The fictional representation of this brief but intense love with "V.T.,"[6] the dedicatee of her love letter or novel, partly transpires from an interesting parallel between Vinci's thin physical image, almost resembling an Alberto Giacometti sculpture (S411 33), depicted in the hotel room's mirror. Another of Foucault's heterotopias, the mirror holds value in showing the body of the woman and, through her body, exposing the intensity of her feelings of love for the writer. The narrative suggests parallels between this love and the Pantheon. Love anchored to the solid shape of the Pantheon reads as a visual and concrete possibility to rationalize and contextualize enquiries concerning the nature and essence of a passion, or lack thereof. When love is represented in a literary text as a monument, the author states all its private but also collective relevance.

Vinci's cautionary tale draws from both the novel and the autobiography to subvert current discursive practices, to discuss erotic love as a synthesis of body and soul, and to expose Italian misogyny. Though the reference to monuments as simulacra representing the passion of love in literature is hardly a new trope, the Pantheon, one of the most renowned monuments of ancient Rome, takes on a new significance for Vinci's character, who chooses it as an ideal correlative of her passion. Whether we admit a Platonic representation of reality, either faithful or distorted, simulacra have long served as images of real entities and refer to them in a subjective way.[7] Among all the monuments, Vinci chooses the Pantheon because its structure and function before the advent of Christianity make it physically and symbolically representative of the sense of completeness that only deep love, however short and complex, can offer a person. By situating her *Stanza 411* firmly within the city of Rome and by comparing her love to the Pantheon, Vinci puts her anger to work, even as it seems that she falls prey to a vindictive desire to expose her former lover's weaknesses.To recall Hume, one does not fall in love out of reason nor can one fall out of love because of reason. But anger can be put to work to expand and elaborate one's own grief and put it at the service of others. In essence, in *Stanza 411* Vinci transforms the vehement passions that follow the end of the protagonist's love into what I consider a healthy and constructive form of indignation towards the wrongs committed against women by society in general, while showing the complexities of creating a monument out of that love. The Pantheon is emptied of its original meaning and slowly becomes a simulacrum of love. Via such a universal passion, the protagonist's self-reflective mode converses with the outer space of her collectivity, and eliminates the danger of a hypertrophic authorial ego. The feelings arising from introspective thoughts expanding on the outside of her world concern a social use of anger, or righteous indignation.[8] The ethical edifice, her book, shapes a narrative where, after a description of the details of the love affair, the sublimation of erotic passion turns into a sociological investigation about the use and abuse of power in relationships. The social import and force of conviction resulting from passion deal also with the analysis of the protagonist's bodily connection to her passion. Corporeality lies thus at the core of the analysis of behaviour towards women that Vinci witnesses in the Italian community, and her assessment is less than encouraging.

My reading of *Stanza 411* here differs from that of the critic Alfonso Berardinelli, for I believe he missed the connection between Vinci's book-*verité* and a larger discussion on the economy of exchange in heterosexual relations. While Berardinelli's reading is tied to Vinci's actual identity and to her actual affair with V.T. and liquidates the authorial effort at coming to terms with the violence involved and produced in what is called love with a "get over it already"[9] series of remarks, I believe that Vinci's text is situated in a time and place that cannot lead a female writer to admit even the possibility of "getting over it already." The simulation of a male reaction used to reframe in literary narrative personal and social problems that reveal instead a specificity of gender in order to avoid male critics' blasting remarks should no longer be needed. If Virginia Woolf spoke in rather different terms about the difficulties confronting women writers, the same urge fuels contemporary writer Vinci to express her (gendered) point of view:

> It is probable, however, that both in life and in art the values of a woman are not the values of a man. Thus, when a woman comes to write a novel, *she will find that she is perpetually wishing to alter the established values* – to make serious what appears insignificant to a man, and trivial what is to him important.
>
> And for that, of course, she will be criticized; for *the critic of the opposite sex will be genuinely puzzled and surprised by an attempt to alter the current scale of values,* and will see in it not merely a difference of view, but a view that is weak, or trivial, or sentimental, because it differs from his own.[10]

While it seems implausible to read words that liquidate Vinci's work in the way Berardinelli does, it is crucial to analyse how the writer exposes existing values in Italian society when it comes to "love."

Heterotopias, Hotel Rooms, and Aggrieved Women

Measured and sublime in its effort to keep anger under control, *Stanza 411* is a love letter by the first-person narrator to her former lover. Like many letters, *Stanza 411* does not follow a linear chronology; blank spaces frame digressions or reflections. The introspective mode is enhanced by an authorial gaze that allows readers to see the two lovers through the keyhole of a private setting, echoing the image of the child, Pietro, spying on his mother and her lover in the beautiful and desolate villa of Vinci's *Come prima delle madri.*[11] The woman analyses herself and her body with the same merciless lens offered by the reflections on sex and death of one of her favourite writers, Georges Bataille.[12] Elements from Vinci's stories in *In tutti sensi come l'amore* can also be traced in this analysis of women and their corporeality.[13] Vinci connects her truthful version of events between the two lovers with the social dynamics of sex exchange. The passion of anger arising from the ending of love triggers the process. When we are angry we learn something about ourselves as well as about others. "That we are often surprised by wonder or surprised by anger is one clue to the fact that something new is disclosed to us in states of vehemence. The object's demand for attention that makes up one detail of wonder lets us see that we do not choose the objects we end up thinking about. Something catches our attention."[14] Subjective feelings, punitive emotions in particular, transform the writer's feelings from anger (something relatable to the individual such as a love gone awry) to indignation (something that always concerns a consortium of at least two or more individuals) towards women's subjection to power. This shift from personal anger to collective indignation promotes her social investigation in the second part of *Stanza 411,* as her narrative constructs the necessary bridge between a purely personal account of her passion and her interest in action towards the community. Vinci's character affirms itself like a subject trying to maintain a "sguardo neutro" (S411 7; gender-neutral gaze) while looking at her body "se è possibile ...," as the character notes, "lo pulisco, lo mondo dai residui" (S411 7; if possible ... I clean it, I clean it from residues). But it is only her body she can watch impassively (perhaps). Her character knows instead that love is a subjective process; she understands that the dynamics of passion get us involved and disrupted. It is from this extreme push against immanence that the stimulus to writing arises: the aspiration to transcendence – also in an aesthetic sense – of living.

Vinci dedicates her book in the form of a letter to the other writer, "V.T.," whose initials, if we agree this is an autobiographical writing, coincide with those of Italian writer Vitaliano Trevisan. The epigraph is charged with meaning, as the quotation is taken from one of the letters composing Ovid's *Heroides.*[15] Ovid's imaginary epistles sent by abandoned and aggrieved women – Dido, Penelope, and Medea – point to love as a struggle in which a woman rarely finds her feelings recognized. In Vinci's epigraph, she chose Phaedra's lines addressing her stepson Hippolyte: "Anche il nemico legge gli scritti inviatigli dal nemico" (S411 3; Even the enemy reads his enemy's writings).[16] The two peritextual elements – the dedication and the epigraph – assert unequivocal authorial intentions. Despite her love, or perhaps because of her love, the author is aware that her words can threaten her former lover, another writer. Words brought them together and now are her weapon. Rhetorically, she lessens this threat near the end of her book: "Vedi come sono le lettere: avanzano in cerchi concentrici, eludono la trama, mescolano i tempi. Sono appunti di guerra. Schemi di battaglia scarabocchiati su un pezzo di carta. Sono irritanti le lettere, ma che male possono fare, alla fine? Sono solo parole" (S411 120; Look at how letters work: they move in ripples, elude the plot, confuse times. They are war notes. Battle plans jotted down on a piece of paper. Letters are irritating, but what harm can they bring in the end? They are just words). Denying any power of harming her reader with her words is a rhetorical device, as her feigned refusal to acknowledge their importance merely marks her exactly opposite belief.

Love results in physical fatigue but also physical awareness of the context in which the passion was born and in which the two individuals have, for some time, shared thoughts and sex. Love reveals its own impossibility to continue when two individuals, though intellectually and physically attracted to each other, want different things. The woman affirms her right to make public what they had together. She is convinced that what she must say to her dedicatee is an individual truth that, once pronounced, belongs to the collectivity:

> Questo scritto ti dispiacerà da subito. Dall'inizio, provocherà in te irritazione. Ti disturberà. Dovrai leggerlo fino in fondo lo stesso. Perché dice la verità. Certo, è una verità che appartiene a me, ma in un certo senso ogni verità singola appartiene a chiunque, una volta pronunciata. (S411 5)

> (This text will upset you right away. From the beginning, it will rankle you. It will disturb you. All the same, you will have to read it through to the end. Because it tells the truth. Of course, this truth belongs to me, but, in a sense, once pronounced, every individual truth belongs to anybody.)

Wherein lies the origin of such intellectual overconfidence in thinking that one's truth, once uttered, can belong to anyone? How can a truth belong to everybody in the age of simulacra, in the age, that is, in which the only truth, as Jean Baudrillard has repeatedly said, is the fact that there is no truth? The book has made public something that is private by definition, love. It also shows what Maurizio Ferraris criticizes about the myth of objectivity as a social construct according to which "la verità è una forma di volontà di potenza" (truth is a form of the will to power).[17] However, Vinci strips love of its ornaments to enquire into the life of other heterosexual couples, including her own parents. Affective poetics addresses and concerns the physicality of love and its pains in a naked way, without sentimentality, without farce, without parody. On the other hand, the writer will question every truth she states in the text. Further, while Vinci does not reveal the identity of the woman who speaks, many elements suggest that *Stanza 411* is a long autobiographical epistle she has written to a man, a literary genre that justifies the text's frequent references to Ovid's *Heroides.* The autobiographical aspects of *Stanza 411*'s narrator – such as her declared profession as a writer and the physical descriptions of herself and the man with whom she was in love – confirm the juxtaposition of the narrating protagonist with Vinci the author. For Vinci, any enquiry into the contribution of emotions to ethics must confront the ambivalence and excess of erotic love and never be divorced from the societal norms forced upon the protagonists and their collectivity. While it is true that "there is erotic love at the root of all [adult] emotions,"[18] one must "show that even erotic love can be part of an ethically acceptable life."[19] But love can also be a trauma unto itself. The protagonist has decided to tell her former lover her own truth regarding their love. And this experiential moment in its limited duration prompted the writing of the text. As in the case of Titta's falling for Sofia, it is useful to remember Fisher's observations about the importance of these experiential moments in literature:

> The episodic, incandescent moment of the occasioned passion ... must be the central matter, while needing to be kept distinct from the inclinations. It is by means of the vehement states and their causal power that we derive one clear model of what "having an experience" looks like. Literature's reliance on moments of experience, rather than summary, generalization, or long perspectives of time, gives to vehement states an important position as one central matter for literature.[20]

One episode becomes a decisive moment in the life of an artist who, in turn, relies on her feelings occasioned by that very episode to elaborate on the experience. As in the case of *Le conseguenze dell'amore*, in *Stanza 411* the setting for the moment of experience leading to a narrative about love is a hotel, this time in Rome and initially confined to room 411 where the two writers first meet in person:

> Dentro la stanza 411 ci sono due letti accostati. Lenzuola color crema e pistacchio. Tappezzeria negli stessi toni. Sul soffitto, stucchi verde pallido e avorio. Una scrivania. Un grande specchio. Molto spazio. Una finestra che dà su una piazza. La piazza è enorme. Delimitata da posti di blocco. La città è Roma. Poco oltre, c'è il Pantheon. (S411 13)

> (Inside room 411 there are two beds. Creamy and pistachio linens. Upholstery in the same tones. On the ceiling, pale green and ivory stucco. A desk. A big mirror. A lot of space. A window on a square. The square is huge. Blocked by police barriers. The city is Rome. Just nearby, there is the Pantheon.)

Places like a hotel room can belong to anyone, like the truth the author wants to pronounce in her book. Their story has taken place almost all in hotel rooms or in the

> palcoscenico di stanze in affitto, luoghi instabili che non sono vere case, luoghi dove ci siamo ritrovati senza difese, senza storia. Nude presenze.

> Maschere da commedia dell'arte che abbiamo tentato come potevamo di riempire con i nostri gesti, i nostri corpi, le nostre parole. (S411 37–8)

> (setting of rented rooms, unsettling places that are not true homes; places where we found ourselves vulnerable, without history. Naked presences. Masks for the *Commedia dell'Arte* that we tried to fill in as best as we could with our gestures, with our bodies, our words.)

In this impersonal setting that only simulates the sense of privacy of one's own room but never belongs entirely to the individual (hence, paradoxically, the sense of freedom that this discovery unearths), we find a kernel of Vinci's piercing social critique. Her description compares the love affair to a masquerade, a spectacle played for a finite time while each was wearing a "mask." She writes that it is not by chance ("forse non è un caso") that their love was consummated inside rooms with little or no significance for the two lovers. Hotel rooms or rented rooms represent "counter-sites" – sites, that is, that "simultaneously present, contest and invert"[21] real sites in which, the moment you cross the threshold, you become a stand-in, the archetype of a story (S411 37; "uno spazio nel quale non appena varcata la soglia ti tramuti in una comparsa, l'archetipo di una storia"). For Foucault, a mixed kind of "other space" lies between a utopia and a heterotopia: the mirror. Indeed, Vinci repeats this motif to represent interiority in her novel as well as to depict herself in that framed piece of special glass, as painters have done in the past. In discussing heterotopia, Foucault considers the mirror as one counter-site that stands between utopia and heterotopia:

> The mirror is, after all, a utopia, since it is a placeless place. In the mirror, I see myself there where I am not, in an unreal, virtual space that opens up behind the surface; I am over there, there where I am not, a sort of shadow that gives my own visibility to myself, that enables me to see myself there where I am absent: such is the utopia of the mirror. But it is also a heterotopia in so far as the mirror does exist in reality, where it exerts a sort of counteraction on the position that I occupy.... The mirror functions as a heterotopia in this respect: it makes this place that I occupy at the moment when I look at myself in the glass at once absolutely real, connected with all the space that surrounds it, and absolutely unreal, since in order to be perceived it has to pass through their virtual point which is over there.[22]

In a mirror of the hotel room, the protagonist looks at her body situated in that very room, a space that affirms its importance as the "counter-site" and after which the novel is titled. She ponders how no one can see her waiting for a man who will never come back: "Sono io che piango, e allo stesso tempo no, la donna dentro lo specchio è un'altra donna. Ma chi?" (S411 67; It's me crying and not me at once, the woman inside the mirror is another woman. But who is she?). Reminiscent of Anna Banti's incipit of *Artemisia*, not by chance a *Kunstlerroman*, the narrative explaining the process of a woman doubling herself via the mirror leads her to engage in a dialogue with her former lover in order to give form to her feelings of anger. Verbalizing feelings provides a thread that only a narrative built around them can provide. No matter how much Vinci tries to illustrate her former lover's qualities, her explanation proves insufficient because we cannot identify the moral reasons behind such passion. Perhaps she cannot see them herself at this point, realizing that he has so profoundly internalized a normative picture of heterosexual relationships that she begins to dismantle his persona starting from the criteria by which he moulded their relationship and then expanding them to the social sphere. Exploring a love lost or addressing the letter to him means choosing a literary genre to probe her point. However, such a choice does not necessarily persuade readers that she is able to control her passion through reason.

In a way, Vinci makes Hume's point that reason is one of the good passions. She investigates the cause of her grief, she deconstructs the moments of her love, and she asks why she fell for this man. But the process of estrangement that the motif of the mirror in the room provides for the protagonist in a successful *mise-en-abyme* seems at times insufficient to give her the necessary distance from what happened in her life because of her passion for the writer. In short, we fear she cannot manage to let prevail the "calm passions above the violent."[23] If the mirror is a heterotopia in that it occupies a place opposite to that of the subject looking at herself, her self-reflective mode shifts to imagining for herself a counter-image. The possible role as a spectator of her lover's love-making with another woman is perhaps the most evident manner in which she can observe her own image reversed through somebody else. The other woman functions as a mirror for the female writer and narrator. In her wish to witness her lover's sexual act, she claims to have sought two things:

> dimostrarti che un amore profondo come quello che provavo per te non poteva essere turbato nemmeno da questo, da un'altra presenza, un altro corpo. *Essere con te, di più: essere te. E volevo vedermi. Vedere me. Come una donna sconosciuta, un corpo sconosciuto, un corpo qualunque che avrebbe potuto essere il mio.* Vedermi da fuori, per comprendermi. Riversarmi sulla pelle di un'altra, riempirla con le mie sensazioni, fare della sua pelle la mia, del suo

sesso, il mio. Allontanandomi da me, finalmente sapere qualcosa di me. (S411 85; emphasis added)

(To show you that a deep love such as the one I felt for you could not even be disturbed by this, by this other presence, by another body. To be with you: being you. Moreover, I wanted to see myself. See me. As an unknown woman, as an unknown body, any body that could have been mine. Seeing myself from the outside, to understand myself. Pouring myself over the body of another woman, filling her with my sensations, making mine her skin, her sex my sex. Going away from myself, to finally know something about me.)

In this process of self-awareness, she tries to tie her feelings to those of others. The impact of her writing lies in the choice of the genre,[24] in the literary motifs and rhetorical figures as well as in the arresting tones through which she discusses gender politics.

Of Monuments and Love

Stanza 411 refers to a room in a downtown Roman hotel. For a brief time, the world lies in room 411 of the Hotel Nazionale in the Piazza di Montecitorio, Rome. A room in the vicinity of the Pantheon, on whose site should be found, Freud claims, not only the Pantheon of Hadrian but also the original building erected by Marco Agrippa in 27 BCE. The Pantheon is the point of reference for this woman who speaks of love by situating her own body in that hotel room in Rome. With its massive presence, the Pantheon seems to set the coordinates of the city in which her love blossomed by creating a kind of "spatial persecution"[25] between the individual and the city. In the first part of the novel, the discussion of its imposing mass lies on the vertical axis on which Vinci's writing elaborates love as a passion. The writer's emotional response to the monument is clear and, as in the case of the room, the monument provides her with a sense of security and freedom because, "solo all'interno del Pantheon mi sento in salvo, al sicuro, come se mi trovassi nell'occhio del ciclone, nel punto preciso dove le forze contrastanti si annullano, e infine si disperdono" (S411 14; only inside the Pantheon I feel safe, safe as if I were in the eye of the storm, at the exact point where the opposing forces annul each other and finally disperse). However evident her response is to the physical presence of the monument, her obsession with it is not quite clear even to herself. The writer seems to respond to the "always reversible tension between the physical eye and the inner eye," in the words of Federico Bertoni in his *Realismo e letteratura*.[26] She relies on the famous oculus of this monument that, by still standing tall in the centre of the city, is testimony to the history of a collectivity.

In the novel, the Pantheon connects the protagonist's love and the community – the Pantheon and Love. The writer lingers in that Roman palimpsest and scrutinizes her emotions. If it is true that an ethical mind must be able to control the motions of erotic love because "l'amore va contro ogni logica" (S411 100; love defies any logic), the monument represents the fulcrum of her efforts to rationalize her feelings on a page that consists of only this paragraph:

> Non so perché ti sto scrivendo di questo. Di un monumento. Un tempio. Un luogo. Uno di *quei posti carichi di energie* alle quali siamo incapaci – almeno, io lo sono – di dare un nome preciso, una definizione. Forse si tratta solo di bellezza. Pura e semplice estetica. Genialità architettonica, e ingegneristica. O forse, è anche che *l'amore somiglia a un tempio*: è *la prima volta che mi trovo al suo interno*. Sono proprio sotto il suo occhio ciclopico attraverso il quale entra la luce del mondo. (S411 16; emphasis added)
>
> (I do not know why I am writing this to you. Of a monument. A temple. A place. One of those places filled with energies that we are unable – or, at least I am – to give a precise name to, a definition. Maybe it's just beauty. Pure and simple aesthetics. Architectural and engineering genius. Or maybe it is also that love resembles a temple: it is the first time I am in it. It is just beneath its Cyclopic eye that filters the light of the world.)

She certainly knows why she writes about the Pantheon. She needs this physical presence to endow it with all the meanings traditionally attached to it, only to deconstruct them and present the void of a lost love. Deconstructing the monument's layers becomes "un'ipotesi che non si può evitare. L'amore è una stratificazione di sentimenti contrastanti, è governato dai cinque figli di Venere, Amore, Antero, Paura, Terrore e Armonia" (S411 17; a hypothesis that we can't avoid. Love is a stratification of conflicting feelings, governed by the five children of Venus, Love, Antero, Fear, Terror and Harmony). Love needs to be rethought in view of the connection Vinci establishes between her love and the monument, against the threat of "partiality" and the "exclusive character of love" attributed to it by Adam Smith, who "considers [erotic passion] an enemy of social interest,"[27] since erotic love "forms no part at all of the moral equipment of the judicious spectator."[28] Through her connection, readers can grasp instead how love "gives us understandings of value that we then translate into other spheres."[29] In *Civilization and Its Discontents,* Sigmund Freud uses the Roman palimpsest to identify the processes of the psyche: the "fantastic hypothesis" that, rather than as a "human habitation," allows him to speak of Rome as a "psychical entity ... where nothing that has come into existence will have passed away and ... all the earlier phases of development continue to exist alongside the latest one."[30] Freud's reading of Rome's strata as a metaphor for the unconscious emerges in the images Vinci compares to her love:

> Il Pantheon è il monumento meglio conservato della Roma antica, ha attraversato quasi indenne secoli di Storia ... È il progetto a contare, la costruzione, come i materiali poggiano gli uni sugli altri, come si amalgamano. (S411 107)
>
> (The Pantheon is the best-kept monument of ancient Rome; it has survived centuries of History almost intact ... What matters is the project, the construction, the way in which the materials lie one on top of the other, their amalgam.)

In its perfectly symmetrical structure, this famous monument alternates its shapes between the square, symbol of rationality, and the circle, symbol of the universe. Its structure interlaces the two, as if to claim that such a relationship is inescapable. It is also a solid structure, almost impossible to divest of meaning and significance, representing at once the human and the divine, the need for reason and for a supernatural force. As the admiring protagonist says of its solidity,

> Forse, vale la stessa cosa anche per i rapporti d'amore. Cosa c'è di più fragile dei sentimenti? Perché durino è il progetto a contare, la costruzione, non i materiali iniziali; anzi la genialità sta proprio nel riuscire a inventare un progetto capace di supplire alle mancanze basilari. Noi non siamo stati capaci neanche di costruire un'impalcatura. Ci siamo arresi subito. (S411 107)
>
> (Perhaps, it is true also for love relationships. What is frailer than feelings? What matters for feelings to last is the project, the construction, not the initial materials. Actually, the genius lies precisely in succeeding at inventing a project capable of making up for our basic shortcomings. We have not even been able to build a scaffolding. We surrendered immediately.)

Vinci regrets the fragility of their love, one that could have possessed the Pantheon's stability only if the pronouns "I" and "You" had become "Us": "Non esiste un Noi, solo un Me + un Te, un Io + Tu. Noi è una fusione impossibile" (S411 107; An Us does not exist, only a Me + You, an I + You. Us is an impossible fusion). The physical reference to the monument relates directly to the sense of strength that Vinci attributes to it. Vinci could not construct the meaning of her discourse even if she had divorced language and architecture. In the monument, she finds the stability and the perfect scaffolding her protagonist would have liked to see for her love. Its literary, and therefore also linguistic, reconstruction of her love must start with the Pantheon. To put it in Claudia Brodski's words, "the making of reference through architecture of some kind, the forming of a place to which perception returns, on which imagination lingers, and language renders its 'own,' – that is, both inherently *and* externally, or historically, significant,"[31] marks Vinci's discourse of love. Her referent is forever extant; the writing of her love through her aesthetic act of publishing a letter allows for its unending presence. The Pantheon, a world-renowned monument, echoes the knowledge of the passion of love that bridges cultures and boundaries. Leonardo's Vitruvian man, inscribed in a square, attempts to fuse the forces of emotion and reason and defuse the outburst of erotic anger in both writers. However, reference to architecture through language, the physical referent of a monument, remains incomplete without the figures allowed by literature. When merged, the two separate elements of language *and* architecture can accomplish what is impossible when they operate in isolation:

> It finds a founding of the referent in the conjunction of two materially different, inherently artificial forms, forms that, unlike birdsongs and beehives, have no basis, other than that imagined by desire or ideology, in nature.
>
> Each internally articulated and externally malleable, intertwined with living and its memorialization, with sensory experience and its demise, language is never and building is always contingent upon a specific part of space, bound to a ground: a "here" that can never "take the place" of language inasmuch as language itself can only "take place" figuratively; a "here" that, ... unable to speak for itself, joins the word that takes no place in history.[32]

Freud strengthens his initial point regarding the layers of memory with the hypothesis that the preservation of the whole of the past applies to psychical life on the condition that "a trauma or an inflammation"[33] has not damaged the psyche. He compares "destructive influences" that change a city to "causes of illness," as "demolitions and replacement of buildings occur in the course of the most peaceful development of a city."[34] He also states that a city is "unsuited" for a comparison of this sort "with a mental organism"[35] and looks at another possible comparison with the body of an animal or a human being. Transformation also occurs in a human body, and "early stages are not preserved."[36] For Freud there is "rather the rule than the exception for the past to be preserved in mental life."[37] Not everything is destroyed – in Rome you can still find layers of historical buildings below new ones. Freud's ideas precede Nussbaum's stances on both the ethical implication that an emotion assumes when enacted and an emotion's power to alter the course of events. Provided that the past is not destroyed completely, as memory traces a part of her recent past, Vinci's "oceanic" emotions focus on love and offer explanations about what structurally ties the protagonist's construction of her narrative to the edifice of the Pantheon.

In Vinci's text, the construction of the memory of her past love and the comparison of its features to those of a monument afford the unnamed woman the opportunity to move beyond her personal experience to reflect on the social. Vinci uses the Roman monumental architecture of the Pantheon as a visual and symbolic source that opposes with its eternal solidity the state of emptiness to which her love binds itself. Towards the end of *Stanza 411* it becomes apparent that the Pantheon is emptied out of the meaning she previously attributed to it with regard to her former love and appears deconstructed into its simulacrum, fitting in with John Muckelbauer's definition as intended by Plato's *Sophist*:

> The Simulacrum's ... internal structure is composed of a necessary relation to the outside, to a subjective perspective, making it seem impossible to actually locate. The Simulacrum does not exist either in the image of the subject who perceives the image, but in a nonlocatable movement between the image and the subject: both are internally implicated in its structure. In other words, the Simulacrum is not simply an object that produces an effect on a subject, but a subject-object complex that is characterized by a differential movement between the two.[38]

The Pantheon triggers the "differential movement" Muckelbauer discusses, and Vinci chooses the Pantheon to become her simulacrum/monumental symbol of love because she realizes the concrete possibility of a "differential movement" between two lovers when feelings rest on solid ground. Just like a building in which layers of brick create volume and thickness, the two lovers could have endowed their love with a solid and durable structure. Though this did not happen, not all is entirely lost in the larger context that literature always provides to writers. The square part of the Pantheon's structure, which stands for the rational mind, offers another purpose to Vinci's narrative in this differential movement.

Stemming from the recollection of her personal experience, Vinci's discourse on erotic love shifts to the analysis of the social dynamics that regulate heterosexual relations. Narrative discourse in *Stanza 411* moves in a circular way towards concerns relating not only to her personal reminiscences of a lost love but also to the employment market and the family environment as an examination of sex trafficking. Her own mother's economic dependence on her father, something that must have left a mark on Vinci as a woman seeking independence through work, is also scrutinized. In short, the elements concerning her narrative of a lost love function with a ripple effect as *research tools* to investigate love's effects on individuals and society, resulting in rationalization of her angry emotions. Contrary to what the protagonist writes to her former lover, "non so perché ti sto scrivendo di questo"(S 411 16; I don't know why I am writing to you about this), she knows exactly why she inserts her personal description of the image the monument creates in her. Her self-reflective mode and the use of simulacra are functional to her narrative about the impact of society on relations in which women find vulnerability rather than strength. The immanence of the Pantheon allows the writing of the self to become a writing of others. The protagonist's subjective memory is useful to her thematization of love because, as Mario Domenichelli notes,

> we are surely what we have lived, but also, if not in particular, what we remember or don't remember of the experience. And what we remember is an affect, an emotion which takes on the form of a representation. Each memory of what we have lived, thus, is not what we have lived, but its representation. It takes on its shape through the imaginary as a function, and constitutes a fragment in connection with the whole in a pattern that involves a myriad of possible connections for the relationship between personal memory and its image and collective memory and its image.[39]

Love is a site of energies, because a site of need, as Freud describes, creates a distinct meaning from Vinci's retrieval of the Pantheon as an objective correlative.

The two separate elements of creative writing *and/as* building (as narrative re-presentation of an experience), when merged, can accomplish together what is not entirely possible when they operate in isolation from each other. For the protagonist of *Stanza 411*, the Pantheon constitutes the ideal referent for analysis and investigation of a love story limited in time and space, a sort of pathemic chronotope. The Pantheon, with its massive round shape, establishes the coordinates of the city in which this love lives and exhausts itself, creating a sort of spatial persecution correlative to the object of the protagonist's love with its open, if reparative, central oculus, and directs the writer's efforts through the physical force radiating from the oculus, which maintains the imposing structure of the dome. As Tracey Winton notes about this monument,

> Rome's devious streets displace your beacons: the Pantheon particularly seems to migrate rapidly through the city, repeatedly confronting you anew with a kind of spatial persecution, mocking your prospects of navigating by choice. By a continuous renewal of strangeness, meaning erupts in a quotidian turbulence, which is not banal, but idiomatic and splendid.[40]

It is precisely by benefiting from centrifugal force that the oculus propels its visionary energy. From that wanted laceration between internal and external space, the writer takes on for herself a role not unlike Ovid's in his writing about famous or imaginary women. While Ovid looks at myths of famous literary women, Vinci draws inspiration from her own witnessing and annotations regarding current women's living. Freud's famous "flight of imagination"[41] hypothesized that Rome, rather than being a human habitation, was a psychical entity. It could have "a similarly long and copious past – an entity ... in which nothing that has once come into existence will have passed away."[42] Freud's imaginative flight accommodates Vinci's purpose in relating the city and the Pantheon to her reconstruction of love's physical entity, with all five components, and the layers of civilization that guided her through aesthetic creation.

Several problems arise from the metaphor of the act of love as a building in *Stanza 411*, not least the drama concerning "the need and the incompleteness"[43] of childhood, because "erotic love implies an opening of the Self to an object"[44] that can only occur when traumas already have been handled. Vinci's protagonist is a successful writer. The woman, thanks to her writing talent and piercing eye, extends her analysis of love as a binding force to contemporary women in Italy, beginning with her own mother and moving on to prostitutes. However, the treatment of both relates to the mercantilist relationship between sex and money. The economy of the gift does not quite enter that of exchange. In other words, Vinci's contempt for certain male behaviour is not merely of a self-referential type. Contempt – not *per se* a properly punitive emotion,[45] since it is understood as a cold emotion – triggers the individual to consider the possible threats directed at an individual. However, when contempt leads to anger, it functions like a magnifying lens and highlights the inferiority of the person who has caused this anger.

Rather than limiting such contempt to the object of her individual affair, Vinci's protagonist manifests the collective side of her righteous anger – indignation, according to Hume, which is stronger than contempt – by recounting many events in which her contempt is triggered by violations of social norms. For instance, her righteous anger becomes punitive when she recounts how she witnessed a man hitting his female partner on the street and knocking her to the ground. The protagonist records her own physical reaction to this act of violence: "Urlo, uno scatto di tutto il corpo che mi slancia in avanti come davvero fossi in grado di volare fuori dalla finestra e raggiungerli lì dove stanno, per portare pace" (S 411 98; I scream, an outburst traversing my whole body thrusts me forward as if I could indeed fly out of the window and reach them where they are, to bring peace). Witnessing a physical attack on a woman profoundly affects the protagonist and triggers what Suzanne Keen calls "broadcast strategic empathy" (a collective call to empathize with characters).[46] She empathizes with her characters, but she also wants us as readers to commit to, and share, her empathy.

The threat posed to that woman is internalized by the protagonist and made her own. Just as she saw another woman in the mirror a few pages earlier, she now sees herself mirrored in this woman. The protagonist's emotional response accords with everything she had written before, and will write after, in recounting that act of violence. As Benoît Dubreuil writes, "strong violations attract our attention ... [to] the blamable action itself and thus elicit the visceral emotion of anger."[47]

An overview of women's condition presents discrete points through the protagonist's reminiscences of observed injustice, thus confirming anger as "the most primitive and spontaneous evidence of an innate feeling for justice and injustice within human nature."[48] The protagonist slowly processes an anger that could be seen as visceral in some passages. Reasoning with and through her anger leads the narrator/author to define patterns of maltreatment against women that she feels are directly related to her personal love story. Perhaps the upsetting scene that relates most directly to her own life concerns the embarrassing economic dependence of her mother. She has personally witnessed her mother's position of subordination:

> Mia madre è stata mantenuta da mio padre per tutta la vita. Casalinga. Dunque non *mantenuta,* ma pagata per prestare un servizio senza limite orario e non garantito da nessun sindacato: domestica, cuoca, segretaria, assistente, tata, badante, stiratrice, puttana. Queste – e quante altre? – le mansioni di una casalinga. Ancora adesso, la mattina, quando scende al piano di sotto e entra in cucina per fare il caffè, il primo sguardo di mia madre è per la mensola sopra la quale mio padre prima di uscire lascia, infilate sotto una tazzina, le banconote che devono servire per la spesa ... Ogni spesa per sé dalla crema per il viso a un paio di mutande è soggetta a contrattazione.

> Non è mai stata libera, mia madre, di uscire di casa e comprarsi un vestito senza dover rendere conto a mio padre. (S411 81–2; emphasis original)

> (My mother has been kept by my father for her entire life. Housewife. So, not *kept*, but paid for a limitless service and unsecured by any union: housewife, cook, secretary, assistant, babysitter, caretaker, ironer, bitch. These – and how many others? – the job of a housewife. Even now, in the morning, when she goes downstairs and comes into the kitchen to make coffee, my mother's first gaze is at the shelf on which my father before going out, drops down, under a cup, the banknotes she needs for expenses ... Every expense for herself, from a face moisturizer to a pair of underwear, is subject to bargaining. My mother has never been free to go out and buy a dress without having to account for it to my father.)

This is a negative model for a couple whose dynamics hit too close to home for Vinci to ignore: the writer feels disgust and contempt for her father's behaviour, while her mother's lack of economic autonomy fuels her shame and indignation. Shame because it concerns her own parents and indignation because she is consumed by a sense of injustice about what she witnessed that she knows is not unique to her own household. This is partly why she wanted her own independence, both economic and professional. Negative feelings are instrumental in showing the boundaries that allow the distinction between subjects and objects and how they can be undone as an act of rebellion against societal patterns.

Vinci describes various situations that share the commodifying connection of women and their bodies with their common dependence on sex as a spendable and non-enjoyable, or material, part of their bodies that is considered an indispensable element for bartering, with the case of the Nigerian prostitutes the most impactful and obvious. The exchange is far from equivalent to a gift of the self to the other, as she would like it to be for every woman, but rather it comes articulated in utilitarian terms: "I soldi, tra mia madre e mio padre, sono sempre stati il centro attorno al quale far ruotare i litigi ... Spendi troppi soldi. Chi li porta i soldi in questa casa?" (S411 82; The money, between my mother and my father, has always been the centre around which to turn the quarrels ... Spend too much money. Who brings the money in this house?). Her contempt for male conduct does not simply result from self-referential instances related to a disappointing father. It concerns the very idea of the exchange that any love entails, what you give and what you receive: "è questo che ho sempre odiato – senza peraltro riuscire a sottrarmene – dell'amore: la sua mentalità da bottegaio" (S411 72; this is what I have always hated about love – without being able to escape from it, its shopkeeper's mentality). Contempt extends to the abject condition of those who pay to gain pleasure, and go "a caccia di un corpo da marchiare per un istante e poi dimenticare. Un corpo da possedere, da comprare" (S411 81; hunting for a body to be branded for a moment and then forget. A body to possess, to buy). While research suggests the number of men paying for sex is increasing, it would seem that Vinci's attitude towards prostitution still retains the notion that women are forced into selling their bodies as a means of survival. It is not so much just the sadness at seeing a woman having to sell her body as that the transaction puts the man in a position of social and financial superiority over her. The social construction of sex is primarily of a commercial type, apparently. This form of contempt leads the writer to comment upon something obscene, hence disgusting, the product of a world that capitalizes as much on sex as love. A body is "branded" because it must indicate what a person can purchase with money in the fleeting act of exchange. Though in Vinci's discussion there is a slight confusion between what one gives in exchange for sex and what one gives in exchange for love, her point is clear: we maintain certain expectations when we offer something that is ours, whether it be our emotions or our flesh. Expectations for Vinci amount to the possibility that love can be a generous thing, not a reductive *quid pro quo* that is never far removed from verbal or physical violence.

The Body and the Body of the City

For Vinci, drawing on past images of idyllic and selfish love is not compatible with her beliefs about the writer's role in society, for the past amounts to an accretion of things that are needed only to promote larger reflections on the present. Vinci's character is frozen in an eternal present where little is collected from the past because it is deemed irrelevant unless the current topic under scrutiny (intimacy between men and women) relates directly to childhood events.[49] In this perennial present, if the body has recognized the permanence of seemingly lost events, it still has enough memory to flesh them out in its act of writing. Vinci is aware that stories happen to people who are made of flesh:

> any story, in its deeper meaning, is something that happens to bodies: men, women, horses, even boats, that are like bodies. The difference between information and true stories, stories that happen to bodies, lies in the perspective, in the optic of things. It's a matter concerning how the story is narrated. As a story, not facts. But, in order to observe what is physical, to observe the essence of narratives, it is necessary that the true and own body

of the narrator be on site or in its immediate surroundings. You cannot observe on a screen.[50]

For Vinci, the physicality of the narrator is key to the believability of what is narrated. Her statement provides the narrator with the authority to create a narrative that transfigures facts. Composed of distinct elements and senses, the body validates its anguished exploration of a time that seems indistinct and equivalent to everyone else. Vinci expands this moment in her customary skilful manner to focus on human behaviour in a merciless sampling of base instincts and feelings that could never find a better space than in literary narratives. The only material element that defines time now lies in the value of the word that sublimates its meanings in the novelistic scaffolding. The word is *inside* the woman's body: in this way, the body of love finds space in a woman's body. Her body, slender and cared for, bent momentarily to the will and desires of a man, inscribes itself into all that is now gone: love. The monument alone is not sufficient to attest to this, so the body lends its support. Love, no matter what, must hurt because it never fulfils one's expectations. While we enjoy it in a time of finite duration that can forever modify our own being in the world, at the same time, we must talk about and deal with it as a reality that is as irrepressible as its mechanics of exchange: "non posso sottrarmene" (S411 7; I cannot escape from it). The body searches for "uno sguardo neutro" (S411 7; an impartial gaze) that can narrate an unbiased story for it. A woman affirms herself as a subject in her attempt to gain an unbiased gaze "se mai è possibile trovare uno sguardo neutro per osservare se stessi" (S411 7; if you can ever see yourself impartially). According to Freud, who saw when visiting Italy the country's constant display of Eros and Thanatos at work, "a feeling can only be a source of energy if it is itself the expression of a strong need."[51] He attributes to the human body the possibility of being the only physical space where layers of memory can really function, for cities are subject to destruction and reconstruction. From the physical bulk of the Pantheon then, doubly present as a symbol, or a simulacrum, of love, *Stanza 411*'s apparent and relevant display of corporeality reminds us of Vinci's constant attention to corporealityin all her works.

Attention to the human body is one of the oldest narrative elements, as "getting the body into writing is a primary concern of literature throughout the ages."[52] When speaking of love as a passion close to the self, the narrating "I" acts upon her gaze and cleans up a body that needs cleansing. She cleans it from "dai residui, dalle domande, dalle incertezze, dai complessi" (S411 7; from residues, from questions, uncertainties, complexes) that, like anyone else, she has carried over "dall'adolescenza – piú indietro ancora, dall'infanzia" (S411 7; from adolescence, even further back, from infancy). But her narrative voice emerges from the body of an adult woman who desired and was capable of mature love. She wants to discuss an adult love, a ruthless, joyless love that caused her suffering. Women scrutinize the exquisitely physiological experiences of their body and emotions: these motives often construct the entire plot of their works. Can one draw ethical implications from such scrutiny? Alberto Casadei argues that in the Italian contemporary novel its ethical stance or

> the possible ethics of a narrative work must first be understood as its ability to provide a prototype of behaviours and actions that have not yet been evaluated. Here the hermeneutical space is opened: it is the analysis of the rhetorical complexity of the plot to draw attention to its nuclei of meaning. And the reading of the ethical configuration becomes an integral part of the meaning to express.[53]

If we accept Casadei's comments about the ability of the plot to draw attention to its nuclei of meaning as ethical sites of creative refiguration, *Stanza 411*'s plot, with the multifaceted social behaviours it addresses, makes it hard to fix our gaze on any single aspect. Vinci's love affair – Vinci's observation of reality as of her own body – produces a series of tropes and possible meanings that points to how, in the posthuman era, corporeality and the body constitute the best starting point for investigating the dissolution of reality and determining its current value. As Roberta Tabanelli notes in studying three short stories from Vinci's *In tutti i sensi come l'amore*, her protagonists redefine their corporeal topography through mutilations as transgressions of social norms, as resistance to the relationship with the opposite sex and to the codified and mercantilist idea of a woman's body.[54] In *Stanza 411*, the writer stresses how not only the external, but also the internal, parts of the body survive:

> Il mio corpo è fatto di ossa. Muscoli. Tendini. Ci sono le vene azzurre, un reticolato di fiumi che mi attraversano. Le vene grigie, dossi di materiale vischioso, in rilievo. È un arazzo segreto che puoi contemplare solo da vicino, dopo aver tolto i vestiti. Dentro le vene, il sangue. Ancora piú a fondo – immagina la lama del chirurgo che fende gli strati, li lacera uno alla volta con perizia – ci sono gli organi. Sotto il seno sinistro, appena piú grande – e dunque piú odiato – del destro, c'è il cuore. Sotto lo sterno, c'è lo stomaco. A sinistra la milza, a destra il fegato e la cistifellea, e piú sotto l'intestino, l'utero, le ovaie. C'è ancora tutto. Niente è stato toccato. Sono ancora intera. (S411 9)

(My body is made of bones. Muscles. Tendons. There are blue veins, a network of rivers that cross me. Grey veins, bumps of viscous, embossed material, in relief. It's a secret tapestry that you can only contemplate closely after taking off your clothes. Inside the veins, the blood. Even deeper – imagine the surgeon's blade cutting through the layers, tearing them one at a time with skill – there are the organs. Under the left breast, barely bigger – and therefore more hated – than the right, there is the heart. Under the sternum, there is the stomach. To the left the spleen, to the right the liver and the gallbladder, and more under the intestine, the uterus, the ovaries. There is still everything. Nothing has been touched. I'm still whole.)

Vinci's bodies, as Nathalie Marchais points out, are not those full and curvy bodies of the classic Italian woman. Vinci's female creatures are lean and slender, on the verge of anorexia. Their bodies "express malaise, fear, along with the trouble of being woman."[55] Betraying the angst of being characterized by her body, Vinci's woman is obsessed with the liberating condition of permanent thinness[56] while submitting to her sexual impulses and allowing her body to be mutilated while enduring other physical violence. Thus, the impossibility of controlling passions in a rational way haunts Vinci's woman because she is capable of violence as well. It might seem that there is no possibility of getting someone to understand and appreciate virtue as a beneficial option for human beings.

The writer who remembers looking at herself in a hotel room in the middle of Rome is detached and mercilessly studies her body in all its details – this is the body of an adult woman. This is the body of a woman not only willing and capable of loving the body of the other writer, but also capable of scrutinizing empathically and formulating reflections on the condition of women in Italy when it comes to the constraints of love. Her body is ready for adult love, past childhood, past the contempt for her own body that has lost its gentle childhood form along with its progressive disillusionment with her parents. This body goes on remembering, and aches in the act of remembering such love. This body insists on the ethical necessity of telling "the truth" to its interlocutor, and as such, utilizes the writer's writing, an *unamendable* body of writing that has matured after years of apprenticeship in the trade of uncovering truth. Regardless of how problematic it can be, she and her body are dedicated to telling a "nuda, quella ruvida, fastidiosa" (S411 23; naked, rough, bothersome) truth. Truth is difficult to reveal because love can turn language into something treacherous and duplicitous:

tutte queste parole che ho appena scritto, sono vere, e allo stesso tempo sono bugie: l'amore sa travestirsi, convincerti di essere qualcos'altro. Si

> rivela a distanza di anni, in gesti che credevi di avere rimosso, in lacrime che ti sembravano poco sincere, in volti che hai creduto di poter dimenticare. E ogni volta, ci si reinventa una prima volta. (S411 24)
>
> (all these words that I have just written, are true, and at the same time they are lies: love can disguise itself, can convince you to be something else. It is revealed years later, in gestures that you thought you had removed, in tears that you thought were insincere, in faces that you thought you could forget. And every time, we reinvent ourselves a first time.)

Love forces us to "reinvent ourselves" every time we reminisce about it. Energy transforms us every time its recollection emerges. Just like a body of writing, the human body metamorphoses, constantly changing its appearance. The body

> è plastilina che si modella giorno dopo giorno, istante dopo istante, e tra me e lui non c'è più nessuna unità, c'è solo una battaglia che infuria tra le cellule del cervello e quelle di tutto il resto. Il mio corpo non mi appartiene più, esiste solo in funzione del tuo desiderio. Respira per potersi accordare al tuo respiro, si muove per assecondare la tua volontà di movimento, resta immobile quando tu lo vuoi immobile. (S411 75)
>
> (it's clay that one shapes day after day, moment by moment, and there's no unity between me and him, there's only one battle that rages among the cells of the brain and of everything else. My body no longer belongs to me; it exists only according to your desire. It breathes to be able to match your breath, it moves to support your will to move, it remains motionless when you want it immobile.)

The body becomes a tool of self-torture that the woman, for the sake of love, has not hesitated to adapt to her lover's needs to the point of assimilating it to that of a "bambola di gomma senza bisogni cosí volgari e fuori luogo come il cibo o gli escrementi" (S411 76; rubber doll without a need for such vulgarity and out of place like food or excrement). In the physical encounter, she seeks control of herself as she seeks that of the other. Sex becomes a willing interpreter of one's own desire for annihilation and erasure, the desire to become "uno spazio vuoto, una stanza impersonale in una città sconosciuta. Una pagina bianca. Un segno in un alfabeto che nessuno conosce fino in fondo" (S411 31; an empty space, an impersonal room in an unknown city. A white page. A sign in an alphabet that nobody knows entirely).

In Vinci's posthuman narratives, the body constitutes the room that we inhabit, just as the room inhabited by the two bodies is comparable to the city. *Stanza 411* is a self-contained universe, like Rome. The room could be understood as the simulacrum of a love destined to die, and yet eternal in the layers of writing. Love's layers were worn in that room (and in many others, always rented and never owned) in that very city. However, any reasoning starts from the body and the body of love to form its simulacrum. The carnal reality and the emotions that arise from it in the intervals of reminiscence pervade the space of writing. Entering your body into the body of Rome means witnessing such a search, such a path, to confirm that constant and productive tension between the body and the mind.

The ultimate misfortune for a writer is to have another writer imagining him – the *imago* of which identifies his narcissistic psyche. In other words, the depiction in intimate physical detail of the writer "V.T." in *Stanza 411* reveals, paradoxically, Vinci's admission of having loved someone who does not exist at the same time as she catalogues his flaws as an example of all the wrongs Vinci's protagonist attributes to men. To this flawed man, she opposes the image of a man "che non esiste. L'altro che tutti aspettiamo da sempre e che non può arrivare" (S411 121; who does not exist. The other we all have been waiting for forever and who cannot come). She constructs a man according to her own imagination but based on his true features, offering an example of this great challenge of the realist mode. She wants to show life "as it is"; but fiction cannot quite accomplish that task, presenting as it does a discourse that by definition contains the element of fictionality. The hatred that comes after love is the definitive marker of what is left to Vinci of her male protagonist – that V.T. who makes his limitations clear. Essentially, Vinci remains faithful to her style by exploring what happened to her (her experiential factor) as defined at that time, in that room, through that love lived by her own body as narrator, which, though objectively real (the room exists, the city exists, love exists), can no longer make the very object of such a narrative exist. In short, the details of the love story provide a verbal weapon that allows the writer to fight the addressee of her letter, the enemy in a text that is fictional but based on autobiographical data.

Perhaps, what is most relevant in Vinci's treatment of love is her ability to draw inspiration – as in breathing, taking in air – from interior malaise to relate her own experience and feelings to those of a multitude of women. Far from being selfish, this love produces a moral anger that prompts Vinci to launch a tirade against a society that manipulates women's love in the service of men. David Hume considers stoicism a refined type of selfishness, and Vinci's writer is endowed with scepticism towards any philosophical system that might regulate life. In Hume's four essays on happiness, the Sceptic is not convinced that happiness lies in moral virtue. However, the Sceptic does not witness wrongdoing in a static society either. This short novel deals not only with Vinci's experience, but with that of many others, acknowledging and yet refuting the innate selfishness of love. From her own mother to the prostitutes who, as in the ancient *lupanari*, exercise the oldest profession from dire necessity, the protagonist-writer handles an extreme challenge facing woman: the need to construct the image of a man to love, a man who does not exist. Like the centrifugal force of the Pantheon's oculus, Vinci's writing places readers in a situation that extends to other women by being introspective and connected to the contingency of a room and of a man. The room that is no longer "one's own" concerns the destiny of many others; and what happened there, once represented through Vinci's writing, "dice la verità. Certo, è una verità che appartiene a me, ma in un certo senso ogni verità singola appartiene a chiunque, una volta pronunciata" (S411 5; tells the truth. Of course, this truth belongs to me, but, in a sense, once pronounced, every individual truth belongs to anyone).

Within the autofictive discourse, the narrator's statements lead us to question the veracity of the narrated fact. The first statement of this kind is that the text speaks the truth, but it is immediately specified that this truth belongs to the narrator, a truth which is therefore subjective. On page 18, the narrator says, "Non è la verità, ma quasi" (S411; It is not the truth, almost). What was stated before is only partly being denied here, as a certain degree of approximation is evoked by virtue of that "almost." Later, the narrator seemingly contradicts her initial assertion by insisting "Ti sto dicendo la verità" (S411 23; I'm telling you the truth). This alternation of statements finds its synthesis later when the narrator declares "Tutte queste parole che ho appena scritto sono vere e allo stesso tempo sono bugie" (S411 24; All these words I have just written are true and at the same time are lies). Here is the short circuit of an autobiographical agreement the author never actually made with the reader. What is authentic, however, is Vinci's preoccupation with rendering how feelings are dangerous for women. Immanence is not a natural state for women; rather, it is an imposition that society has brought upon them. Therefore, while love is by its own nature selfish and preoccupied with itself, *Stanza 411* reveals how even the end of it can spur a prosocial analysis in a committed author such as Vinci. From a room that is no longer only "her own," Vinci produces a wider and generous exposé of women's condition, sexual politics, and body politics.

8
Wounding the Individual: Dynamics of Diversity and Anatomy of Love in Veronica Tomassini's *Sangue di Cane*

The autobiographical circumstances that generated the writing of *Sangue di cane* (Dog's Blood), a 2010 novel by Sicilian writer and journalist Veronica Tomassini, appear rather ordinary: an educated Sicilian woman falls for a Polish alcoholic immigrant, Sławek. Their love, despite marriage and the birth of a child, proves to be difficult for reasons that transcend the typical relational dynamics of a couple. The two lovers' attempt to establish what the narrator calls "normalcy" and to fit into the city's symbolic order becomes a sad parody of domestic life. Sławek's subjectivity, often compared to that of a wild warrior, fails to be *reorganized* into that of a "normal" husband, as he cannot become a member of the narrator's community. The author, however, elaborates on the trope of the stranger and expands her field of analysis to entrenched practices of segregation and discrimination within her own community, practices that greatly affect the immigrants, the new residents of Syracuse. Indignation and compassion for their existence shapes the narrative space the narrator inhabits, and now sees from a distinct perspective. Filtered through fictive practices of appropriation of real events and other rhetorical strategies, Tomassini creates a dissonant space of meaning in the novel's construction and fictionalizes Syracuse's inhospitable response to current immigration.

Tomassini's politics of location establishes a cartography of her own subjectivity vis-à-vis the moral values and the politics of Syracuse's citizens. It provides an understanding of how her protagonist's own problematic relation with her community shapes her story about the marginal identities of the Polish residents. The ethos of her community, as well as the relative confinement of the coordinates of space and time of Syracuse, anchor Tomassini's scrutiny of an Italian peripheral community to reflections from which the lack of compassion for the Other (the immigrants) transpires. The community does not want to be concerned with the Other and confines migrants to a space that lies beneath the surface of the city, rendering these new inhabitants virtually invisible. Her scrutiny concerns the dynamics of hospitality and hostility that are addressed in Jacques Derrida's reading of Immanuel Kant's *Third Definitive Article of a Perpetual Peace* in his essay "Hostipitality." By virtue of a Latin etymon that relates *hospitality* to *hostility* (this last parasitizing the first),[1] we see how the former could exclude the very possibility of *welcoming* strangers. The notion of sub-alternity reveals its own pragmatic everyday meaning in the failure to accord respect to newcomers while manifesting the discrimination existing in a globalized world.[2]

The narrator's deceptive effacement – her name is never revealed – makes the story in *Sangue di cane*, the first instalment of Tomassini's long narrative, more about Sławek and the Poles than about herself. My study considers the failed heroic tale of Sławek in *Sangue di cane* as a starting point for Tomassini's broader investigation into the conditions experienced by both the Polish immigrant Sławek and the different communities of *imperdonabili* (unforgivable) that continues with a second novel, *Christiane deve morire* (Christiane Must Die), and a third novel, *L'altro addio* (The Other Good-bye).[3] In a fragmented narrative featuring frequent flashbacks, *Sangue di cane* recounts a love story in which the author also examines the *imperdonabili*, those individuals who either cannot conform to the rules of society, or do not want to. As in Vinci's case, the entire text is presented in epistolary form, but in Tomassini's, the letter is written at Christmas, a significant time for many. The confused tones underlying the text illustrate the impact of the trauma of the narrator's tragic experiences with Sławek, seemingly preventing the narrator from properly ordering the various segments of her love story. She entrusts her fragmented memories to the format of a narrative written while preparing for Christmas in her parents' middle-class home. Even though she is an "adulta e può raccontare" (adult who can tell) readers about the phases of Sławek's Calvary, she struggles to find a coherent order for them: "Sai che non so piazzare gli accadimenti?" (Do you know I cannot place the facts?).[4] Instead, they are offered in an accumulation of episodes about the couple's difficult love, alternating with the narrator's reflections on the *imperdonabili* and the human condition under strenuous circumstances.

Two narratives run parallel in the novel: the narrative of the love story of the narrator and Sławek; and the narrative of the failure of the community to grant to the undesirable guests – the immigrants – the "right to hospitality"[5] that would enable them to integrate into Syracuse's community. While Tomassini's fictional narrative centres on human beings and their complex relationship, the characters grapple with the external forces of a morally oppressive society. The relative flexibility of the textual form appears to alter the modalities of novelistic expression by which the aesthetic act speaks to us. Partly based on autobiographical facts, the fragmentary narrative constructs the dissonant space that allows for ethics and compassion to participate in the story as readers are encouraged to reflect on the author's indignant mode. If, as Derrida argues in his discussion of Kant's essay, "universal hospitality arises from an obligation, a right, and a duty all regulated by law,"[6] the author records the limits that her community imposes on such laws. The text reads like a personal accusation directed at the town for letting the newly formed subcommunity of Polish immigrants rot and die, disappearing from the visible surface of Syracuse into the caves underneath the island of Ortigia. Endowed with the structure and the breadth of a Greek tragedy that historically refers to the space of the colony, the novel allows only a very few characters to appear in the foreground, while a tragic chorus of desolate characters stands in the background. As the narrative registers their casualties, readers witness their death, its causes rooted in wrongheaded politics on global migration. While this extensive mortuary theory of marginal characters reads as a commentary that frames the love story between the Sicilian woman and the Pole Sławek, it stands for something else as well: the long list of casualties forms the subcommunity of unwelcome members who suffer exclusion. Shut out of the community, stripped of the most basic human rights, they are doomed to die. The relevance of Sławek's disillusioned epic lies not only in the botched love story with the protagonist and narrator of his negative heroic existence and their mutual attempt to lead a "normal life." It also lies in evidence that suggests a greater problem linked to the failed politics of conventional hospitality demonstrated by the Syracuse community when confronted with a new and unfamiliar Polish community.

In Tomassini's novel, the concept of the *communitas* plays an integral role in the narrative, along with her representation of the inhospitality of the Syracusans. Within the space she inhabits, the protagonist develops a problematic reading of her own role within the community, as she takes pains to consider herself a member as well. The concept of *munus* is problematic in her rendition of her community dynamics vis-à-vis the new immigrants and presents the inconsistency Lorna Weir considers challenging in Roberto Esposito's reflections on the notion of the gift. The "*munus* tests the expansive limits of the gift" because it lacks the notion of "apparent voluntariness."[7] While the *munus* (gift) is the basis of the social tie and of our sociability – the "transcendental form of political obligation"[8] – Weir finds Esposito's take on the gift to be inconsistent. If the *munus* is to be understood as the simple obligation to give, for

Weir such action would imply a "logic of donors without receivers."[9] The *munus* implies reciprocity, but, Weir asks, "how is reciprocity logically possible where actors are bound only to the obligation to give and not receive?"[10] She proposes two forms of gifts in communities: the impersonal gift (to the gods or community) and the reciprocal gift that is given to, received by, and returned by other members of the community.[11] But without a gift received, there is no obligation to give. In *Sangue di cane*, the protagonist feels no need to return a gift, as the community has not given her one, thus eliding any benefits from her being a member of the community. She is unburdened by the economy, suspended by the need for reciprocity, yet bound to this community in which she occupies space. She cites the ostracizing of the Poles as evidence of the failure of Syracuse to be a hospitable space for anyone who does not conform to the laws of the community. And the community fails to accept the rules of hospitality because strangers are perceived as enemies of the city order.

The Love Letter as a Novel

Tomassini's *Sangue di cane* resists conventional definitions of genre because of its formal fluidity, causing us to reflect on the potential of the aesthetic act. The text makes apparent that, "although deriving content from reality, the aesthetic act (a true experience, not merely a perception) manages to appropriate issues sifted through the means of mimesis and rhetorical strategies."[12] In Tomassini's hybrid novel, a sense of physical situatedness in time demonstrates how a literary text reflects on the *hic et nunc* of the author's corporeal reality and its experiential data (its feelings), while appropriating narrative techniques to expose dramatic current facts that are tied to geopolitical issues. That is, *Sangue di cane* proposes texts and contexts that appear different yet are related by what shapes contemporary life in its author's town. Tomassini recognizes the terms of the connection between the love story that structures the main narrative and its social context. At the same time, she makes a larger, almost universal, case for acceptance and hospitality for those who do not belong and cannot receive a *munus*.

A social passion sparks the aesthetic act that shapes the reality in the characters' fictional depiction. This fictional depiction explores the possibility of borders breaking down as each individual's passion towards his or her own society results in a unique retelling of that society. For example, acts of misunderstanding or injustice against oneself, like those against the community in which the author lives and works, trigger anger, an indirect passion that results in moral indignation and self-expression. Indignation, itself an indirect passion according to David Hume, comes endowed with bad and good qualities,[13] offering the possibility of a shared, multi-level reading of the individual and of the space in which the author affirms the right to express his or her corporeality, being, body, and mind while dismantling the myth of spatial uniformity. Bearing a message, authorial ethics in the pragma, the literary text imposes an act of participation and identification (or refusal) on its readers/addressees. The aesthetic sets in motion our reaction to the poetic, lyrical, evocative, compelling effect the reading offers. Only by analysing personal passions that spill over into the social can we understand the tenuous boundaries between what I consider "my world" and "The World."[14]

If I analyse my indignation – a passion that is social by construct, since it always needs someone other than me but close to me in order to be triggered and affirmed – I also analyse the limits of my world. Only after this analysis, by which we establish a connection with our identity, can we say that the perimeter of our world has dwindled: we need action to recover the surface and attempt analysis because our state is no longer an *impassionate* one. The aesthetic relationality transforms the matter of the fiction into an act of ethical reflection upon reality. As seen in the previous narratives analysed in *Righteous Anger*, the author's outrage sponsors a new claim for a paradigm of human worth and dignity, suggesting a possible role for equity concerns. Vehement states move us to understand and utilize our inner sense of justice, something that might precede reason but necessarily considers it. An inner sense of justice becomes an ally of indignation that, originating from the personal experience of a tormented love, can move an individual towards analysing hospitality and hostility in the community. Indignation isolates a specific time in the narrator's immediate past and organizes the entire narrative around it. While personal anger eventually fades as the love story is recounted, albeit in a fragmented way, the other narrative – the one concerning the *imperdonabili* – generated by a compelling urge to avenge injustice, remains and permits readers to investigate the dynamics that prevent a conventional sense of hospitality towards marginalized groups in Italian society. Keywords will be useful to build a map of Tomassini's techniques and themes in *Sangue di cane* that unravel the micro-intersubjectivity of the love story and the macro-intersubjectivity of the relationship in the space inhabited by her community alongside the immigrants' sub-community. The practice of autofiction, already analysed in Scarpa and Vinci, the adoption of the love letter as textual speech as in Vinci's *Stanza 411*, and the chronotope that overturns the linear order into displaced moments reconfigure materially and symbolically the territory of the common. The "common" can no longer be what the town of Syracuse was before the arrival of the Polish immigrants.

Their massive presence determines a social alteration that designs a new space. Within such territory, an economy of love and exchange overlaps with the essential relation of hostility between the physical bodies of the Poles and the host city.

In *Senza trauma*, Daniele Giglioli argues that autofiction is "a text in which contractually one must always come to terms with the *imago*, if not with the real figure, of the writer."[15] In Giglioli's understanding of the term, "textual reception shifts towards a pact of Lacanian flavour between the text and the reader who accepts the verbal system that makes up the text whose words are pronounced by a real voice, a real person who has a real name and last name."[16] By virtue of the name, the author understands the law that binds him or her to the relationship entertained with the matter of his/her narrative: "Even assuming everything is false," Giglioli affirms, "it is *my* falsity that I am subjecting you to. And since it is mine, it is authentic nevertheless."[17] Tomassini herself talks of *Sangue di cane* in terms of autofiction, partly encouraging its interpretation in Giglioli's terms:

> What I narrated (in the novel) was about me, then, what happened on the narrative level has been the mediation between the needs of autofiction and literary influences (certain influences). That kind of metauniverse that I stumbled upon concerned – and I do not think much has changed today – a sort of army of shattered heroes, humiliated and offended by history, a tale of outlaws, generated by upsetting times and borders that are still wary and deceptive. I met these indigestible (*indigesti*) heroes, wearing their heavy immoral burden, and yet nationalist, in a sense, the vodka, a real social pillar, proudly, mercifully proud of their demanding belonging (the proscription), harnessed with a centuries-old ache, a perennial tedium.[18]

The recording of her personal grief and indignation at a specific time of her existence along with the weight of "certain literary influences" constitute the synthesis that perfects the tie between the matter and the form of her personal adoption of the autofictive mode. According to Isabelle Grell, autofiction defines

> a story characterized by a socially recognizable and engaged style, fully recognized by an "I," which is the author. To avoid the term *novel* or *autobiography*, this story is connoted by its style, because it is its style, the subtle poetic music that any author perceives when s/he writes, that distinguishes *autofiction* from classical "autobiography," which is inscribed, rather, in the recording of a lifetime. It is socially recognizable and engaged, because an *autofiction* does not tell the story of the whole life of the protagonist, but

> only a part, which is "in situation," if you want to borrow the expression of Sartre. Finally, *autofiction* is "fully recognized by an I," as the writer bears the same name as the narrator and assumes the responsibility of this name up to defending himself before the law.[19]

The similarities among Tomassini's stories, the personal and the fictional, and the use of dialogue that reveals the stories' source in the author's life allow us to believe that an autofictional aspect of the novel resembling Grell's definition does exist. In fact, Tomassini's *Sangue di cane* builds a narrative that is fictional yet "socially recognizable and engaged" and "does not tell the story of the whole life of the protagonist, but only a part." *Sangue di cane* is an autofiction because the narrative extends beyond the limits of a chronological rendering of events in the author's life (as in St Augustine's *Confessions*) and locates in a specific time of her life the matter that becomes a fictional narrative by its own decomposition and re-composition in an array of prolepses.

A larger question emerges by virtue of these autofictive techniques: are we sure that the entire novel is not about the inability of the author/narrator to *fit into* her own non-fictive world? Is it, rather, her failure to accept the conformism of her community that ultimately draws her to talk about herself and her falling for Sławek? Ultimately, I claim that her intuitive (re)consideration of the signification of cosmopolitics, as a regulatory tool for inclusive communities that are aware of the contemporaneous complexities of geolocalities, drives her to deregulate fictively the values of her town as a way to achieve self-awareness. The author proposes the trope of the wronged stranger and the indignation that arises from such a spectacle to represent her dissatisfaction with established practices of her own community. The effort to show "the complexity of the global condition"[20] filters through the pages of Tomassini's text. Indignation paves the way for a re-evaluation of where and how we live now, of where and how we argue now for freedom even to be in a community. The story goes full circle: from the subject discussing her community of origin, to her inability to accept the politics of subjection this community imposes on the new migrants. The narrator and protagonist cannot accept such an oppressive politics, feeling that it applies as much to herself as to the immigrants. She ultimately rejects her original community to adopt the immigrant community because, in her view, a community should have flexible borders, and should be constantly evaluating the possibility of accepting new members. It is her acceptance of the new reality of the Poles of Syracuse that problematizes all loci concerning geography and power politics related to this space that is unequally inhabited by the Italians and the immigrants. The story is not situated in a nowhere land: it is firmly rooted in the reality of Syracuse.

Geopolitics: Syracuse

> Siracusa è una città straordinaria, contiene sottomultipli del suo barbuto lignaggio di insospettabile provenienza. *Sottouniversi* polacchi, russi meno, albanesi meno. Sottouniversi polacchi ed è ciò che mi interessa di più. Il nostro sottouniverso intercalava tra gli uni e gli altri ed era compreso tra via Marconi, via Carducci, via Crispi. Iniziava e finiva entro e non oltre, con estemporanee appendici del tutto irrilevanti. E io fui presa al laccio, fu la deviazione folgorante nella mia vita, la svolta quella vera, quella che dà il colpo di mano, che radica e divelle, che demolisce per poi ricostruire. E noi contribuimmo ai lavori, costruimmo la nostra cattedrale nel deserto, il nostro amore (SC 73; emphasis added).

> (Syracuse is an extraordinary city, containing submultiples of its rough lineage of unsuspected origin. Polish *sub-universes,* with some Russians, and fewer Albanians. Polish underworlds, and that's what interests me the most. Our sub-universe alternated between the former and the latter and was delimited by Marconi Street, Carducci Street, and Crispi Street. It began and ended within and no further, with impromptu appendages that were completely irrelevant. And I was taken to the snare, it was the dazzling deviation in my life, the turning point, the real one, the kind that triggers a spasm, that entrenches and eradicates, that tears down to then rebuild. And we contributed to it, we built our cathedral in the desert, our love.)

How does one interpret inhabited space? Of course, space can be read in many ways, as when we analyse a panorama and realize that the concept of a landscape depends entirely upon a human agent who observes the elements that compose nature. Animals do observe nature, but they always need a human narrator willing to translate what they see. The agent who observes nature modifies it in the very act of observing it. This is a mirroring effect that can be found when a city takes on so much relevance in the construction of a novel. To comply with the term "inhabited," a space that defines a city requires its inhabitants to be the agents who activate its analysis. Inhabited space is subjective because we don't all look in the same direction when we look at the city, nor do we feel the same sense of being with the community in which we live. Further, in referring to the terms of marginality and centrality in analysing cultural and physical peripheries, geography takes on equal relevance with time and space, but cannot be the same. Taking a cue from Gilles Deleuze,

Roberto Esposito observes how geography is not synonymous with space, because "geography is not limited to provide history with elements, features, localizing foci – it is not history's spatial component – but something less obvious and more incisive."[21] Esposito ascribes to geography the ability to take the concept of "simple progression" away from history and provide it with a specific environment. History here stops at the threshold of a love story that deals with its own birth and tragic finale; history here stops at the threshold of the original nucleus of Syracuse, the island of Ortigia, and makes clear the dialectic between territorialization and deterritorialization that refracts fallacious boundaries and makes friable all borders. Right at the intersection of via Carducci (likely the actual via Malta in Syracuse), the city, at the crossroads of Roman and Greek civilizations, witnesses the encounter of the two main characters, the author and the Polish immigrant. When geocriticism and corporeal female passions meet, as Elizabeth Grosz argues, they validate a literary analysis of permeability and defy the idea of historical progression that Doubrovsky in fact claims to be one of the most evident differences between the autofictional and the autobiographical mode.[22]

Syracuse is not interchangeable with other Italian peripheral towns, being rarely depicted in literary works. Syracuse's uniqueness – a Sicilian town, home to the most important Greek theatre outside of Greece, and a Mediterranean port – becomes, by necessity, an added and equally important layer for understanding the treatment of love in our times. For the writer, the peripheral town amounts to the epicentre of personal emotional eruption and the questioning of her own community's moral purity (as well as of her own actual *belonging* to it). *Sangue di cane* plays out around the construction of a space inexorably divided into two halves: the caves where illegal Poles live, and the surface of the streets on which the everyday life of the Syracusans seems to be conducted, mostly in cars. Rhetorical strategies allow for Tomassini's novel to be composed of two horizontal spaces, Hades, or the underworld, where the Poles hide, and the streets of Syracuse, the visible locus populated by Italian citizens. At the threshold delimiting the two spaces, a couple in love tries to make sense of this division as one of the aporias intrinsic to the concept of hospitality. The tragic tone of the novel is reflected in the structure of the city; Ortigia is isolated from the "modern" city, and its caves are presented as the "logical" site of the Poles' private Inferno. They cannot be left in sight.

The novel reveals the permeability of the city as its layeredness. Its layers of construction far exceed those of renowned tourist sites. The city itself is compared to, and represented as, a disproportioned *latomia* with ambiguous geometries that resemble the odd shapes of the ancient quarries described by Thucydides in his *History of the Peloponnesian War*. Thucydides' descriptions of the cruel Syracusans forcing Greek captives into quarries turned into concentration camps come to mind when reading about Tomassini's porous Syracuse.[23] Tomassini's poetic prose carves physical geometries with laconic and repeated reflections that conjure up images of death: "Siracusa era un cimitero di polacchi" (SC 72; Syracuse was a cemetery of Poles). Tomassini exposes today's similar necrotic side of the city. Syracuse reveals its palimpsest of strata in this respect as well. The *latomie* – the quarries used to imprison the Greek soldiers – are like the caves beneath the island of Ortigia that function as both an encampment and a cemetery for the Poles. For the Polish community, Syracuse is indeed a city of the dead. The two spaces delimit two different social classes and the status of the two protagonists: the woman is Italian and middle class; the man, Sławek, is Polish, and his history of violence and abuse carves a visible mark in his present existence. The two spaces also define the entry of the Italian woman into what the narrator calls "la saga polacca" (SC 15; the Polish saga). By falling for Sławek, she explores her irresistible attraction for his world of exploited immigrant subjects. Her infatuation with this man leads her to become enamoured of the fierce pride of the Poles. Polish history becomes an obsessive mytheme, almost a subplot, of the love story: the word "Poland" amounts to a "porzione irriducibile di un mito" (SC 55; an irreducible portion of a myth). Veronica Tomassini tailors her narrator's position vis-à-vis her community to displace the essentialist ideology of individualism that turns the "self" into an atomized private entity. The relationship affirms Roberto Esposito's tenets on the relationship between the individual and the community:

> In the community, subjects do not find a principle of identification nor an aseptic enclosure within which they can establish transparent communication or even a content to be communicated. They don't find anything else except that void, that distance, that extraneousness that constitutes them as missing from themselves; "givers to" inasmuch as they themselves are "given by" [*donati da*] a circuit of mutual gift giving that finds its own specificity in its indirectness with respect to the frontal nature of the subject-object relation or to the ontological fullness of the person (if not in the daunting semantic duplicity of the French *personne*, which can mean both "person" and "no one").[24]

The narrator positions herself as a subject who does not find a principle of identification within her own community. Her personal role situates her as the messenger of each world to the other, respectively[25] at the intersection between the city of the dead and the city of the living Italians who ignore, if not loathe, the former.

The Traffic Light: We Do Not Know What Hospitality Is

The two spaces of Syracuse are divided by a semiotically important traffic light, the threshold where the narrator meets the young Pole and experiences love at first sight. Their existences are not meant to meet at any point because, though occupying the same space, their trajectories are socially demarcated. She, a bourgeoise, he a "figlio di zoccola certificata" (SC 20; son of a certified whore). To a friend who accuses her of not having a "bourgeois conscience" because of her feelings for the Polish immigrant, the narrator replies:

> Perché, di grazia? Perché quel semaforo lì, quello che era lo spartiacque tra noi e il senso comune, il sentire retto, onesto, conforme, aveva il calco della *deregolamentazione*; forte e primitivo il simbolo, una battaglia etica perfino, da giocarsi sul tempismo intelligente di un tabernacolo luminoso. Chiamasi distanza sociale. Io mastico l'espressione e non vi trovo valore. Distanza sociale: un bolo che rumino e rumino e che non sputo volentieri ... Chiedere soldi a un semaforo per miseria, è una balla superata da sopraggiunti luoghi comuni. Chi ci crede più? Un cancro dell'anima ti divorava, era la mia convinzione, non è che fossi proprio fuori strada. (SC 21; 53; emphasis added)

> (Why, pray tell? That traffic light, or the divide, that is, between us and common sense, had the cast of deregulation; strong and primitive symbol, an ethical battle even, to be played on the intelligent timing of a luminous tabernacle. The light signalled social distance. I chew over the expression and find no value in it. Social distance: a bolus that I ruminate and ruminate and don't spit gladly ... Asking for money at a traffic light out of poverty, this is horseshit outdone by new clichés. Who believes it anymore? A cancer of the soul was eating you alive, that's what I thought, and I was not that much off.)

What for her friend amounts to a sort of betrayal of her status reveals for the narrator the shades of an ethical battle. The "distanza sociale" (social distance) is not an obstacle; quite the contrary. Of course, it is not by chance that the man and the woman meet at a street light. Within the contemporary Italian social panorama, perhaps nothing comes across as more stereotypical than the image of the immigrant asking for money at the light. Yet, *Sangue di cane* problematizes the signs constructing this image and turns them into the elements of a symbolic and possible intersection of two spaces that do not communicate: a light indicates a crossing of two roads, showing which way traffic should go, who should proceed, and who should wait. While confirming the validity of stereotypes related to the Polish community in Italy, from begging for money at the street light to drunkenness, the narrator also investigates the causes and origins of such poverty and degradation. In her narrative, she transfigures the negative portraits released daily by the media into those of epic characters. While the media dwell on the shocking effect that the display of the fragility of what Kelly Oliver calls the *"othered"* triggers in readers, the narrator points to the opposite. It might be a platitude to underscore that the simile of a tabernacle is rather suggestive of the Christological aspect that the narrator wants to construct for Sławek's Calvary. The narrative problematizes the violence that abjected individuals like Sławek bear as a cross and considers it impossible to look at any "dynamics of oppression without considering its psychic dimension."[26] The traffic light is emblematic of the threshold between the two worlds; the community of citizens (people who can afford a car and drive on the surface of the city) and the community of strangers (people stripped of their legal rights and seen as unwanted foreigners) attempt to inhabit the same space of the city by crossing "the threshold the line of which can be traced."[27] Deregulation, defined as the "abolition or reduction of state controls and supervision over private economic activities,"[28] is used as a term that could hinder a healing project for something far larger than the love story itself, something that defines the nature of the space allocated to different kinds of "humans." For the narrator, this traffic light becomes a "luminous tabernacle," a light that, by generating the encounter with the Polish man, will spawn the narrator's healing process. . The author calls upon the city of Syracuse to testify about its own rejection of the new people:

> Siracusa si irrigidiva piuttosto che fremere, non fu una scoperta per Siracusa la vostra identità, non agli inizi, perché Siracusa si fece un baffo della vostra identità, salvo poi piazzare bandiera su un plausibile avamposto, il vaniloquio a posteriori, una ciancia con i caratteri della ufficialità, pubblica e persino cortese, per cui la Polonia fu inchiodata a terra di badanti e di pitocchi. (SC 85)
>
> (Syracuse would stiffen rather than shake; your identity was not a surprise for Syracuse. Not in the beginning, because Syracuse laughed at your identity, except to place a flag on a believable outpost, nonsense in retrospect, a tittle-tattle with the appeal of the public and even polite official status, by which Poland was pegged as a land of *badanti* [caretakers] and lice.)

The sub-universe (*sottouniverso*) of the Poles becomes the object of investigation for the narrator at the very moment she *falls* – an apt English term for *innamorarsi* – for the man at the traffic light. Encountering Sławek means encountering a community that was, until then, almost invisible and unknown to her. Her own subjectivity had been shaped by her unhappiness with the response of Italian society to the Other: indifference, tolerance (in a pejorative sense), a feeling of unease at the growing changes and transformations of Italian society – the *badante* (caretakers), for instance, being a new element in a society in which, until relatively recently, family members had been responsible for taking care of ill or older relatives. "Love is compassion," she repeats like a mantra. This modern couple wanted to be normal: "Volevamo la normalità, Sławek, non c'è altro da aggiungere ... Regolamentare: poteva essere un passaggio successivo, fortunato. Regolamentazione invece di deregolamentazione: quel 'de' ci atterriva. Su tale prefisso ci scavammo una cloaca ripugnante, dentro allevammo i nostri demoni" (SC 48; We wanted normality, Sławek, there is nothing else to add ... To regulate: this could have been our next step, a fortunate one. Regulation instead of deregulation: the 'de' there terrified us. On such a prefix we dug a filthy sewer, we raised our demons). The dynamics of oppression could be broken by their claim to normality: "E questo rivendicare normalità fu la grande rivoluzione, la nostra provocazione" (SC 116; and revindicating normalcy was the great revolution, our challenge). While they both seek the comfort of normalcy and the everyday life of a couple – marked by ordinary things such as sharing a house, getting married, and having a baby – everything seems to work against them. The more the narrator navigates Sławek's muddy waters to attain normalcy for their love, the more it seems this goal cannot be fulfilled. Why? In my reading of this novel, Sławek, in all his abjection, embodies the only element that will heal her condition of "noia esistenziale che non conosceva colori intermedi" (SC 23; existential boredom that ignored nuanced colours). Hers is a *nausée* of living that can only be cured by the earthquake and quagmire of passions that the catalyst of his presence causes in this young woman rebelling against the precepts of petty-bourgeois life. While the entire novel can be read as a letter that she writes to her vanished love after his return to Poland, she also addresses the people of Syracuse: "Non sono mai stata amata così. Non possono negarlo" (SC 45; I've never been loved so much. They cannot deny it). Who is the subject of "they cannot deny it"? Who denies the intensity of Sławek's feelings for the woman if not the people of Syracuse?

The lack of compassion that the Sicilian community displays towards the *othered*, the immigrants from Poland, constructs a powerful narrative of exclusion. As Poles arrive already tainted by their endemic addiction to vodka, like a negative birthmark,[29] their process of removal from the surface of the city is relatively simple. The question of space is fundamental to understanding the erasure and rejection of the Poles of Syracuse. Permitted by the intimacy of the personal relationship already established with readers by autofictive strategies, the narrator reasons with them, and herself, about the power dynamics that regulate the spatial frame of Syracuse and the impossibility of her love. While the protagonist writes a love letter to her disappeared Polish lover, she also vows to have compassion towards the proscribed Polish. In this act, she deliberately inscribes herself within their group, thus confirming her discomfort with sharing what she considers an unwelcoming space, Syracuse, with the people of the city. Her instinctive reluctance to share the gift of the community is now enhanced by her knowledge of the reasons why she cannot identify with or share the values of her community.[30] In Georges Bataille's words, she "delinquishes" her original community and disavows her own group, which in their eyes amounts to a crime.

Righteous anger results: the artist's indignation inscribes the text within a literarily constructed passion that unveils the aporias of hostipitality through the language and devices of fictionality. She understands love as an epistemic passion, and through her love for the Pole she unfolds the story of his sub-community. This passion, translated into a letter-confession, makes readers reflect on the possibilities by which the notion of community can deflect its original norms and implode in current Italian society.[31] This implosion takes place when it is almost assumed that the stranger's arrival is not welcomed, but forced. As such, the *munus*, the dutiful gift individuals must bestow to be recognized as members of the community, is not deemed necessary for these strangers because it would imply that they have been accepted by the community, which the inhabitants of Syracuse are not likely to do.[32] In fact, throughout *Sangue di cane*, the concept of rejection and exclusion from the space of the city is physically reiterated. Poles live in Dostoevskian settings: residing in caves, the "Casa dei morti" (House of the Dead),[33] working in hidden rooms, hiding in bushes. Further, the constitutive relation with violence of the *communitas* that erects the borders of an imagined community based on assumptions about the collective coherence of the *siracusani* – "Noi italiani, voi polacchi" (SC 20; We Italians, you Poles) – reasserts itself perpetually. Crime, or the criminal underground, exists in the foundational moment of a community. The protagonist's moral indignation reveals how communities determine the lack of rights and, ultimately, the death of individuals and scapegoats. As Braidotti writes, "contemporary necro-politics has taken the form of the politics of death on a global yet regionalized scale."[34] The vulnerability of the immigrant slaves lies in the paradox by which they are now free to move in communities that "do not know yet what hospitality is,"[35] thus exposing their corporeal vulnerability.

Love as Episteme

A frequent mytheme in contemporary thought and literature, the apparent, but never real, impossibility of verifying truth, totters when it confronts the epistemology of the passion of love. Love constructs knowledge through abstract theoretical schemes applied to ethical problems. The passion appears as more real and more physical if encountered in a literary text. The author does not regard love as a disproportionate act of madness but as an epistemological envelope in which the narrator prompts the analysis of pertinent issues. As the narrator admits, "l'amore semplifica molte cose perché erudisce nella sconsideratezza. Col mio *trasporto cosmopolita*, dentro il prodigio coltivato da animo slavofilo, il mio, mi addentrai nella saga polacca" (SC 85, emphasis added; Love simplifies many things because it educates in its thoughtlessness. With my *cosmopolitan abandon*, within the wonder cultivated by a Slavophile soul, mine, I entered into the Polish saga). She claims to have learned much about Poland because of Sławek. But one might question whether she was predisposed to the passionate urge to learn more about a country that she discovered by reading about it and not by living in it. She, the *ex*-communicated, the one living *outside* her community but sharing its space, owes a debt of gratitude to the man who left her. The dynamics of oppression concern them both and encourage readers to embrace the connection the ethical narrator creates between the narrative of their love and the narrative of the *othered*:

> Entrambi vivevamo con la falsa percezione di un rifiuto a priori, roba da sfigati. Tu perché vivesti da figlio di zoccola certificata nell'orfanotrofio di Konskie fino a dieci anni, poteva andarti peggio tuttavia, poi una madre ti è venuta in soccorso, l'alter ego di colei che abdicò. Io piuttosto incline al melodramma, con una precisa opinione rispetto all'elemento fato, fato senza pathos. Ma soltanto fino a un po'. Fino a quando non incrociai la via dei dannati, cioè la tua. (SC 20)

> (We both lived with the false perception of an a priori refusal, stuff for losers. Because you lived as a certified whore's son in the Konskie orphanage until you were ten, it could have been worse, then a mother came to rescue you, the alter ego of the one who abdicated. I, rather prone to melodrama, holding a precise opinion with respect to the element of fate, a fate with no

pathos. But only up to a point. Only until I crossed the path of the damned, yours, that is.)

Her healing depends on her Polish warrior: "Si, misek, mi hai guarito. E insieme abbiamo attraversato un ponte. Bisognava mostrare coraggio, e io, a mio modo, lo dimostrai, non retrocedendo" (SC 21; Indeed, misek, you healed me. Together we crossed a bridge. We needed to show guts, and I did it my way, by not recoiling). The protagonist, and narrator, is fully aware that her feelings for Sławek are entangled with the discrimination levelled against the Polish community, saying, "Il nostro amore non può esulare la saga polacca" (SC 84; Our love cannot lie outside the Polish saga). Her love story is inextricably connected to an act of justice towards the proscribed group of Sławek.

Love is presented as an act of piety and of compassion (*cum passione*) towards the Other. For the protagonist, love is an all-encompassing passion, intense and extreme on the part of both the loved and the lover. It cannot be restrained by conventions or norms, for reason can hardly negotiate its role in their lives. In fact, the kind of love exemplified in *Sangue di cane* calls into question the expression "transgressive love" used by Julia Kristeva in her *Tales of Love* when it is applied to a *communitas* like that of Syracuse. The narrator ponders the interpretation of Sławek's sudden disappearance offered by the female psychologist ("amica psicologa"): "Figlio di puttana, dunque figlio di un abbandono. Memorizza, l'amore è equivalenza, amore e abbandono, se lui amerà sarà ancora figlio di puttana. Mica l'ho abbandonato io? Semmai il contrario" (SC 65; Whore's son, son of abandonment, that is. Remember, love is equivalence, love and abandonment; if he will love he will be again a whore's son. But I did not abandon him, quite the opposite). How can one explain abandonment? How can one always return to blaming the mother to explain a man's treatment? Out of love for him, the woman endures her community's scorn and accepts the nickname "puttana d'Albania" (SC 65; Albanian whore) as the price she has to pay.

The epigraph of the novel quotes Curzio Malaparte's *La pelle* (*The Skin*): "Why can't you understand that there must be thousands and thousands of Christs, among all those corpses? Even you know it isn't true that Christ saved the world once and for all." In a private communication, Tomassini explains the significance of those lines: "Malaparte's words give us the sense of compassion and mercy that pervades the landscape and the narrator's own voice. In any dirty, abject, miserable individual, the narrating voice of *Sangue di cane* recognized the meaning of existence, the almost mystical meaning of pain. Yes, as the Gospel says – in every face wrinkled by grief, she recognized the face of the Christ."[36] The love letter to the proscribed reveals the Christological aspect of the martyrdom of the discriminated against. She appropriates this non-novelistic discourse, a form of hagiographic discourse, and weaves it into an icastic novelistic text in which the civil passion and the sense of outrage against the proscription of the Poles in the city of Syracuse seep through the subjective experience of love. But if we recognize the humanity in the face of the Christ, by corollary, Žižek claims that "*we, humans are not.*"[37] The "inhuman core in all of us humans, or, that we are 'not-all human'" is kept away by politeness "toward the inhuman Neighbour's intrusive proximity."[38] Politeness, itself an ambiguous concept, can be likened to what we call civility, or compliance with the structure of our society. Intrinsic to civility are the unwritten rules that *de facto* condition freedom while affirming its existence. Discrimination works against the new martyrs of globalization, as Tomassini calls the Poles, but also against those who expect them not only to comply with but also to actually *like* our rules.[39]

If the new martyrs are to reach the coveted "normality," perhaps obtainable by adopting the rules imposed by the community that does not accept them, they require advocates who can speak for them in real life, paralleling the novel's astonishing feat of exposing discrimination and social compliance in such a poetic way. These agents empathize with these new subjects and know how to counteract the community's repressive strategies. Unless a stronger passion – compassion – counters the contempt that the city displays, the Poles of Syracuse will be destined to live in the Hades of limestone caves near and underneath Ortigia. Attention to these anti-heroes, these marginalized everyday characters, is fundamental to the depicted landscape. This landscape oscillates between life and death. The representation of the death and the corpses of Yurek, Danuta, and Piak (SC 13; 101), the martyrs of globalization whose valiant acts the narrator praises – all these images reinforce the theme of abjection. And moral indignation mounts:

> Indecoroso restare ancora, rimandare una dignitosa partenza. Meglio il nulla. Non c'è il nulla. Avrei voluto consolarli, non c'è il nulla, c'è il regno dei nuovi martiri, sapete. I nuovi martiri hanno il viso caliginoso, sono le maschere della metropoli, sono i topi degli underground. Siamo un pochino noi. Io per una questione di luce riflessa, riflettevo il vostro tormento, assistevo sgomenta alla riffrazione di una tragedia corale, da cui rimasi esclusa in parte, un requiem a metà. Era la vostra tragedia corale ... Voi eravate i poeti del dolore, i poeti, muti e ciechi. (SC 10)

> (Unseemly to remain, to postpone a dignified departure. Better nothing. There's nothing. I would have liked to comfort them, you know, there is

> nothing, there is the kingdom of the new martyrs. The new martyrs have misty faces, they are the masks of the metropolis, the rats of the underground. This is us a little bit. I mirrored your torment by a reflected light, I watched in dismay the refraction of a choral tragedy, from which I was excluded in part, an unfinished requiem. It was your choral tragedy ... You were the poets of grief, the poets, mute and blind.)

Sangue di cane reveals the impossibility of producing a "vital" grotesque – for instance like the one theorized by De Gaetano. The masks of the new martyrs only reveal their tragic condition of sub-humanity, something quite distinct from membership in the proletariat. Deprived as they are of their socio-spatial destination and means, this sub-humanity seems to define

> not only the zero of any psychosocial depth of the subject but ... the reduction of the organicity of the human to a primordial instinct, where the "primitive" character of the drive (pulsion) refers only to itself, without going through the mediation of the signs, without becoming perversion, that is. The sub-human occupies the space between the human and the animal ... [and] is an area of indiscernibility for which a human body – stripped of any psycho-social identity – has much more in common with an animal body than with other human bodies.[40]

The performative role of many acts appears reversed. When Sławek tries to set himself on fire, while the narrator claims that "conclusa, compiuta la strage, innocenti sulla pira della menzogna, innocenti strinati dalla brutalità del mondo" (SC 172; the slaughter was concluded, finished, with innocents on the pyre of the lie, innocents scorched by the brutality of the world), the arrival of the police and crowds on the scene reveals the opposite of what was announced. For Sławek, this attempted self-immolation amounts to salvation. The ethical outrage of the narrator colours these lines: "Il tuo risveglio si mostrò nell'ultimo atto di questa tragedia slava, nutrita dalla menzogna, nella crepa di una diaspora congenita, impressa nella carne del tuo popolo" (SC 172; Your awakening revealed itself in the last act of this Slavic tragedy, fed by lies, in the cracks of a congenital diaspora, imprinted in the flesh of your people). Tomassini's tragic characters not only occupy the space that De Gaetano locates for these individuals between the human and the animal; they also elicit compassion through depictions of their inexorable descent to the abyss, a process that is emblematic of what has become a regular practice: the posthuman approach in which we study humans not *as such* but because of the different treatments and understandings we give to the term "human." Tomassini's anger helps us understand how our categories of analysis must be revised and reassembled, since human behaviour towards animals also reflects the treatment of the dispossessed, people relegated to the lowliest place in society, the new martyrs of globalization.

The Abject

Lei è una ragazza qualsiasi. Lui è un abisso.
(She is just any girl. He is an abyss.)

– Veronica Tomassini

This novel is governed by the tones of a tragedy and the narrator's restless quest for truth. What burned inside the narrator while she loved the Polish immigrant still burns inside her at the moment of composition. It is Christmas time, a time to be happy and serene – but not for the narrator, who feels constantly monitored and judged by her community. We know that, in the eyes of the community *above ground*, she is an Albanian whore. She defines herself as such in the third person (SC 118).What is the meaning of this label? Her attachment to Sławek detaches her from her community of origin and turns her into a foreign whore, an "Albanian," an adjective that still today holds negative connotations among Italians. She is linguistically *ex*-communicated from her community.

In the letter to Sławek, the narrator discusses the deaths of many Poles who arrived at the margin of the continent, Sicily, only to die there. Sławek's body is the primary site of the abject. For Hal Foster it is "this category of (non)being defined by Julia Kristeva as neither subject nor object, but before one is the first (before full separation from the mother) or after one is the second (as a corpse given over to objecthood)."[41] Tomassini suggests these tremendous conditions throughout the novel, in which the narrator details the vomit and other bodily excretions, the blood literally pouring out of Poles who come to Syracuse to die, as if it is an elephants' cemetery. As Foster suggests regarding the representation of the abject, we see how Tomassini's images "tend towards a representation of the body turned inside out, of the subject literally abjected, thrown out. But this is also the condition of the outside turned in, of the invasion of the subject-as-picture by the object-gaze."[42] But the question is why? It is tempting to work with Kristeva's abject when dealing with Sławek's character because the narrator offers much evidence that his abjection finds its roots in his intersubjectivity, corrupted even before it had a reason to exist. His possibility of relationality is doomed from the start because his relationship with both the biological and the adoptive mothers (and by inference with the motherland, Poland) is not extant. The obscenity in the scenes of violence in the novel suggests an attempt to transcend the visual in understanding the saga of the Poles. The place of the abject is where meaning loses its properties. Just as there cannot be political action in isolation, according to Arendt, Oliver warns that "one's sense of oneself as a subject with agency is profoundly affected by one's social position [as] we cannot separate subjectivity from subject position."[43] The issue of suffering lies at the core of subjectivity "and its concomitant sense of agency when ... [people] are abjected, excluded, or oppressed."[44] It is important to start with the subjectivity of the "othered" because, "without taking into consideration subject position we assume that all subjects are alike, we level differences."[45] So, if the development of individuality cannot be explained apart from its social context, neither can a social theory be formulated to explain the dynamics of oppression without considering its psychic dimension. Thus, we can see how the social context within which the love story is embedded is one in which the *former* member, the narrator, also becomes oppressed. Even prior to meeting Sławek, she was oppressed and excluded by her *communitas* – *ex*-communication was inevitable.

The novel emphasizes the point that, as psychoanalysis forms social theory, so intersubjectivity regulates our subjectivity.[46] Indeed, when the protagonist yielded to her cosmopolitanism she was already proving her exclusion from her community, for "subject positions, although mobile, are constituted in our social interactions and our positions within our culture and context."[47] The dynamics of her encounter with the Other and his sub-community are demonstrated through her love for a community she does not know. The attraction to the abject that Sławek represents determines the outcome. If relationality is primary – neither one subject nor the other – and precedes intersubjectivity, a possible response could be that responsivity "is both the prerequisite for subjectivity and one of its definitive features."[48]

Relationality lies at the core of this woman's quest into her recent past: how to come to terms with her expectations; how to define the process of intersubjectivity that relates her to Sławek, and by default to the *othered*, the sub-community of Poles she meets in her saga. Also, with respect to Sławek, his suffering subjectivity unleashes rage and ire, two negative passions that in the articulation of his character are illustrated in a conventional manner, through contempt or unhappiness. The agency of his subjectivity – as an individual who is abjected, excluded, or oppressed or othered – renders him incapable of relationality, even with those who love him. He is incapable of uttering, or verbalizing, and of constructing. He lacks words to express his feelings, and the woman who loves him finds them for him. The abject is a threat to the community, and as such he must be excluded from where the subject lives and works. He must be deposed on the other bank of an imaginary limit. The reference to the minute descriptions of the Polish corpses reminds us of our position at the threshold between life and death. This is a constant leitmotiv of Tomassini. Her narrator unearths problems related to her lover's upbringing and the difficult relationship with his two mothers – the first a prostitute who left him in foster care, the second profoundly disappointed by Sławek's criminal life. His separation from the semiotic, from his mother(s) and his motherland, becomes the narrator's site for struggle. She, in turn, takes over the place of both, at the cost of renouncing her own motherhood. In fact, when she gives birth to their child, her own mother will take care of Grzegorz.

She symbolically substitutes herself for both of Sławek's mothers, attempting to resurrect her personal Christ from his life of abjection and grief. Aware that his love for her represents a gift, *un dono,* she strives to provide him with stability. His gift to her is that of snatching her away from her existential boredom with his excesses and his ex-centric (as an outsider) style of loving; her gift to him is herself and a share of the normalcy, the stability, her family provided for her. Further, the subject experiences abjection in relation to the separation from the semiotic. Sławek's tormented relationship with his own mother, as with his motherland, furthers our understanding of his character structured as the unwanted. The stranger and the narrator's love for him might function as a pharmakon –a remedy – for the abjection. Two people – two worlds – meet to provoke a destabilizing of barriers whose threat is Sławek's condition as abject. Her attraction to him (the *abject*) is emblematic of the mixture of fascination and repulsion caused by the abject as theorized in Kristeva's *Powers of Horror.* In the case of Sławek and his narrator-wife, we are reminded of Esposito's comments regarding the *not-being individual* of the relation. From a continuum, we derive our individuation within a community in which our individuality is only affirmed because "community is what is most properly our 'own' [*il nostro piú proprio*]"[49] – an entity to which we belong and are attracted by a force strictly counterpoised to the survival instinct. Paraphrasing Esposito, this is the wound that we inflict, from which we emerge, when we alter ourselves by entering into a relationship not only with the other but also with the other of the other, prey to the same irresistible expropriative impulse.

Anger and Love: Partial Conclusion

Love is a passion that should stir all the loftiest feelings. And yet, as the three works examined in part 3 demonstrate, authors use pure imagination and personal experience to connote their narratives. Theirs is an act of investigation that assumes the ethical responsibility of declaring one's own interest, not merely for what concerns us in the abstract or in relation to ourselves but because love stories provide us with a different context to recognize the ever-friable material of which society is made.

Sangue di cane deploys social investigation, autobiographical fiction, and reflections on the transformation of the social fabric, of border writing (*scritture di frontiera*), in a love letter written to Sławek by his wife. She is a Dido left by her warrior husband, a man in search of new adventures with which to defy normalcy and claim transgression as his most prized trophy – hence the tragic mood of a novel that does not allegorize current reality but renders it in poetic language. Similarly, Vinci's *Stanza 411* reveals an act of social concern that goes outside the limits of that room, thus showing how *other* spaces give us pause and make us think of the human condition. Sorrentino's *Le conseguenze dell'amore* finds a way to combat Cosa Nostra with means that are virtually unknown to Mafia movies: love wins it all. But love indicates a degree of wisdom in Titta's ability to give himself entirely to the project of having a life, that life that Cosa Nostra took away from him. It is only through the presence of Sofia that Titta's life turns upside down. And so, the creative mind of Sorrentino, though putting too many aphorisms in his character's dialogue, manages to show the revolutionary power of love and the anger that sets in motion all the best instincts of an "unhappy" and "shy" accountant.

Good passions, including a constructive use of anger, are the engine of aesthetic enterprises. Good feelings impel artists to create works that identify values for which it is worth living, or dying. Aiming for happiness is only natural. Love, when it does not lead human beings to destructive consequences, represents surely the most noble of passions. In its third part, *Righteous Anger* has examined representations of passion and erotic love in film and literature that share common ground with ugly feelings: anger, envy, stupidity, and low impulses are often juxtaposed with conventional displays of love. We are all aware that in real life passions are never situated in a clear binary opposition. We need to explore the intricacies of passion in order to appreciate the value of constructive anger in our artists' reassessments of society and attempts to come to terms with it.

Afterword

Righteous Anger constructs a framework for the analysis of specific contemporary Italian literary and cinematic narratives originating from a genuine authorial concern for socio-political issues. This framework could not exist without a clear understanding of the ethical role of anger, gleaned from an analysis of the artists' intentions in the composition of their narratives, as a twofold element that becomes a prosocial behavioural tool to guide the texts' reception. Passions, especially supposedly negative ones such as anger, play an integral role in the way fictional texts promote an understanding of reality that challenges the status quo. The collective aspect of indignation becomes a tool for the community of which artists are active members. The individual artistic act of protest, made explicit through the expressive means of rhetoric, hybridization, and genre parody, in novels as well as in films, generates counter-discourses that expose and deconstruct distinct societal ills and their underpinnings. As Peter Fisher states,

> In anger I insist and declare that I will maintain a certain perimeter of my own worth. Acts that injure or imply the diminishing of what one can expect from others will be noticed, pointed out ... Anger, when noticed by the other, announces to him and to onlookers that, in my eyes, an injury or slight has occurred.[1]

Indignation, as we know from Hume, sets in motion a greater understanding of the "injury," one that is as much ours as it is others', since such passion "bestow[s] a new force on all our thoughts and actions."[2] *Righteous Anger* explicates the role of constructive indignation and vehement passions in the formation of literary and cinematic narratives as they guide themes and images centred on what "injury" means, and of which the artist is profoundly aware. This book underscores the concept that, just like power, literature is innervated within the social body of a community. As Wu Ming 1 stresses in his debate with Scarpa, the socio-political context from which a book emerges remains fundamental to our understanding of it. As we cannot conceive, according to Foucault, an ontological construction of power as anything more than a series of dynamic and ever-changing relations, the same relations occur between the social body and aesthetic expressions that comment upon it.[3] The legacy of postmodernism, that of "escap[ing] from concepts as logically monolithic as the 'political,'"[4] demands a separation of the formal aesthetic from the ideologically engaged act that for some artists revealed the shackles of a forced action and immersion of art into a space that was too confined. This caesura produced detrimental results from acts of misreading.[5] The works studied here revisit the political commitment of yesteryear and warrant a renewed desire to "collect and combine as much as possible into a new vision"[6] that does not necessarily produce dystopian or utopian narratives. Aesthetics – the distribution of the sensible – reveals its inability to transform art into an actual tool to remedy the ills inherent in the living community – or, as Rancière stresses, "what aesthetic education and experience do not promise is to support the cause of political emancipation with forms of art."[7] However, if art is not political in itself, by way of "the very distance" art entails with regard to "conflicts or identities," it is political because it creates a particular "type of space and time," as well as because of the "manner in which it frames this time and peoples this space."[8] Art "reframes the material and symbolic space. And it is in this way that art bears upon politics."[9] We understand that aesthetic education and experience cannot support "the cause of political emancipation"[10] since, as Rancière maintains, the politics of the arts is "a politics that is peculiar to them, a politics which opposes its own forms to those constructed by the dissensual interventions of political subjects."[11] Passions and emotions constitute an ideal field for studying the relationality between the subject and society, in that they provoke deeper evaluations of the ethical dimension of our actions. The actions of artists can and do "make a difference in the course of their life as in the world in which that life is lived."[12]

In investigating its consequences, aesthetics tries, once again, to propose a synthesis with ethics by tying Rancière's "knot." Aesthetic actions have become vessels for Italian artists, relaying their desire to locate a new harmony for ethics. The very matter of the aesthetic act raises the issue about the non-reversible dynamic between fiction and non-fiction today. Hybrid practices have in turn produced the so-called hybrid narratives composing a practical response to the need for a more flexible canon. Wu Ming 1 has elaborated an expansive list of works that constitute what he calls the New Italian Epic. But, if "everything is fiction, not everything can become non-fiction,"[13] warns Raffaele Donnarumma. The lack of reversibility between narratives brings us back to the divergence between the narrative of events and the narrative of images drawn from them but constructed with other goals. The fluctuating condition of genres, something for which the term *scritture di confine* (border writings) is often used, leaves us wondering whether our reception of literary and cinematic narratives is still regulated by the guidelines enforced by postwar militant Italian criticism, a reception that, until recently, had understood the realm of literature (and to a lesser degree that of cinema) in terms of a programmatically ethical, committed, and strongly ideologized body of aesthetics, while more commercial fiction simulated discommitment and delved into other elements of meaning construction.

Other factors intervene in our reception of these *scritture di confine.* Corporeality is not a matter exclusively of the flesh. Corporeality regards also our feelings and what *scritture di confine* resolve to do with them, with the body intended as human, with the posthuman, and with the things we deal with on an everyday basis. In Rancière's words, "art – a form of knowledge itself – constructs 'fictions,' that is to say material arrangements of signs and images, relationships between what is seen and what is said, between what is done and what can be done."[14] A cinematic or a literary narrative constructs a fiction that is only too authentic and veracious. The "arrangement of signs" we call fiction is the "identification of modes of fictional construction with means of deciphering the signs inscribed in a general aspect of a place, a group, a wall."[15] When seen in such terms, the fictional questioning of the modes of reality, or how the real is narrated in fiction, appears in patterns that transgress the discourse of Veronica Tomassini's models of reference, whether autofiction or conventional novel. With her text/love letter to Sławek, and perhaps even exceeding authorial intentions, Tomassini's fiction reads as an instrument of denunciation of the impossibility of controlling both the poetic lyricism a love letter implies and the social outcry elicited by the narrator's empathetic observations of the marginalized who reside in the caves of Ortigia.

Even in our perennial present, current events become historical facts. They are matter that ties the social body to literature and film, as the latter proposes their re-presentation and analysis to readers. Fictionalizing reality neither necessarily amends it nor necessarily distorts it. But the process of fictionalizing reality constantly brings to the fore its ills, which we are called upon to comment on and scrutinize. Whether we read conventional novels or *scritture di confine,* or watch movies that compel us to react against injustice towards women, as in *Benzina,* the act of fictionalizing one's own life (autobiographical traits to create a pact with the reader can be a tricky business) or discussing social practices that artists believe deserve consideration nevertheless proposes alternative and distinct ways of reading reality. Reality changes just as things change, and we can never overlook the thread between the two. An anachronistic rendition of reality fails to provide proof of authenticity – not the authenticity of reality, but rather that of the text in front of us. Westphal discusses the relationship of the real and the fictional worlds. He wonders, paraphrasing Umberto Eco, how compatible such worlds can be with the "encyclopedia of the audience."[16] Audiences deploy their emotions to produce a response to their act of reading/viewing. Passions are known to all audiences and form ties between them and the authors in an empathic and corporeal way. As Keen states, "novelists do not exert complete control over the responses to their fiction,"[17] and hence readers do not always direct their empathy in the way the author envisions. More to the point, the emotional reaction to artists' acts of aesthetic production prompted by indignation and an ethical urge to expose a societal ill will generate motion in the soul of their recipients.

While disgust can produce healthy rhetoric, thus turning an "ugly feeling" into a productive element of intellectual and literary discourse, we often witness its weakening into short-lived forms of protest in pamphlets. Being disgusted is simply not enough. However, sensuous repugnance for something can be a productive element that fuels indignation and actively promotes the rejection of current politics. If it is true, as Sianne Ngai states, that, out of the seven feelings examined in her study, envy and disgust are the ones "imbued with negativity" and that their "trajectories are directed toward the negation of these objects, either by denying them or by subjecting them to epistemological skepticism,"[18] then contemporary expressions of disgust about bad government, bad social laws, and the vulnerability in which private citizens find themselves play an integral role in the intentions and the outcomes of committed artists. When we read, we think *and* feel because of the acts of imagination and projection presented to us. The corporeal in Tiziano Scarpa's operation is so relevant to his work as to make him declare that *he* himself is a culturally political act. His indignation prompts texts that denounce what does not work in his *epoca,* and his writings consider the personal and the collective reasons that prompt healthy anger. Anger is thus motivated not (only) by personal needs but also, as in Pasolini's case, by the author's bodily and sensory involvement as a response to societal practices of his time as well. Any society needs agents of dissent to demonstrate its ills, to liberate counter-discourses. What happens in our society, Scarpa seems to say, must compel us to a constant re-evaluation of ourselves and of what fundamental things really are. The posture of Scarpa's fictional writer of *Kamikaze d'Occidente,* as a powerful orator in an ancient polis, speaks volumes about his civic commitment as a writer who is literally forced to prostitute himself to support his art but is always generous with his own time, feelings, and words. Happiness, as such, is not about virtuosity. Scarpa prefers an experimentalism that is redolent with emotions and feelings, with the passion he detects in the "nocturnal dimension" of his *maestri,* Pasolini, Busi, and Tondelli.[19] The very concrete case of Mario's true paternity and his new understanding of fatherhood in *Le cose fondamentali* tell us many things about how Scarpa reflects on his role as artist in his society. While disgust can produce healthy rhetoric, thus turning an "ugly feeling" into a productive element of intellectual and literary discourse, we often witness its weakening into short-lived forms of protest. Repugnance can be a productive element that, by creating disgust, also fuels indignation and inspires Italian artists to reject current politics. Contemporary expressions of disgust about bad government abound, of course, but Scarpa also pays attention to (and shows compassion for) the vulnerability in which citizens find themselves in very private and intimate situations. Their everyday decisions about fundamental things play an integral role and a leit-motif in Scarpa's oeuvre.

In the women's literature of the new millennium, negative connotations often attributed to feminist critiques of the family as being too programmatic have been replaced by a feminization of the familial space in a form that is neither myopic nor reductive but focused on new analyses of relational dynamics. Family plots in women's novels are not necessarily humourless, clichéd, home-bound, or programmatically feminist at this conjuncture. The relationships with the mother, husband, or children; the relationships that women entertain through their own sexuality, often exploited, while searching for the vantage point that best represents *them* (work, forms of socialization, even notions of free time as separated from the family nucleus), constitute an all-encompassing social paradigm of issues that demands recognition of its attempt to deconstruct values considered fixed and handed down to readers as such. Mazzucco's compelling enquiry into femicide, domestic crime, and socially constructed gender roles defends the legacy of second-wave feminism as it fails to be heard by women of younger generations. Through her use of a conventional realist mode, Mazzucco builds narratives of individual and societal vulnerability that are informed by her rethinking of the notion of the victim as the manifestation of sexual politics regarding Italian women and familism. She takes into consideration how societal, hence collective, vulnerability results in the exasperating phenomenon of femicide as opposing the right to life,[20] a devastating consequence of Italian society's unsuccessful transformation and weak commitment to women's rights. Mazzucco argues that Roman society, or Italy in general, has neglected even the most basic of women's concerns and rights, just like those presented through the case of the migrants in "Loro." Women's right to bodily integrity and freedom from physical violence is regularly subject to discussion.

In *Un giorno perfetto* Mazzucco promotes a critical reading of a literal, rather than metaphorical, violence against women. She intentionally rescues non-voyeuristic images of physical violence against women from the abstract and literary metaphors that have traditionally framed such topics in patriarchal discourse. By investigating the dynamics that foster domestic abuse and murder in works of fiction, she also depicts the all-too-real exercise of violence against women by exposing media and patriarchal discursive practices in all their revealing verbal clichés, that of the *victim* being the most consequential.[21] When René Girard writes that "the victim, in reality passive, becomes the only effective and omnipotent cause in the face of a group that believes itself to be entirely passive,"[22] he seems to justify the very presence of victims in society ("unanimously despised")[23] to "facilitate the return to normal."[24] Judith Butler's rereading of the verbal cliché regarding victim mythology dismantles such statements regarding the role of the victim. Butler shows that there is always the option for women "to repudiate the notion of vulnerability. Nothing about being socially constituted as women restrains us from simply becoming violent ourselves."[25] The term "domestic" added to the word "violence" hinders understanding of the everyday practice of violence. Violence is "domestic" because it takes place within the woman's residential space, but the term "domestic" should not be considered synonymous with "familiar." Violence is also domestic because it has been part of family life for centuries, *domus* meaning house. Finally, it is also domestic because there is a fiction pertaining to women's physical and verbal abuse as something private and not political. But the victims of domestic violence are made victims. While Butler invokes "the possibility of repudiating vulnerability itself"[26] as the possibility of repudiating a long-lasting mythology of passiveness tied to the figure of the victim, Mazzucco's indignation exposes Italian society's reluctance to give women even the slightest opportunity to repudiate vulnerability.

However, social passion quite often triggers the fiction of the autobiographical, in itself a marker of the historical presence of the individual in a given society. The author's own presence as a character within the story facilitates the exercise of empathy, especially in the case of first-person narratives. Literature locates in an author's personal experience an important contribution in the reconstruction of a real event that is visited by an indignant narrator. Here indignation stems from society's attacks on individuals who are deprived of the opportunity to live unfettered by social conventions. Without empathy, though, it would be difficult to appreciate fully the narrator's excruciating feelings. One could argue with Suzanne Keen, that "for a novel reader who experiences either empathy or personal distress, there can be no expectancy of reciprocation involved in the aesthetic response. The very nature of fictionality renders social contracts between people and person-like characters null and void."[27] Yet, we are compelled to provide an emotional response to what we see and read because, as in the case of *Sangue di cane*, Tomassini elaborates a narrative that, though centred on a tragic love, also investigates the political space and the exclusionary stance of the community within which such love lives. It illustrates the dynamics of a community, its xenophobia, its inability to cope with hospitality, and how such a society rejects everyone outside the narrow confines of social norms. A relational view of the self, as in the case of Tomassini's autofictional approach to her novel, accounts for the partners' ethical responsiveness and dialogical ways of being a member, or being an outcast, of a community.

Simona Vinci the author and Simona Vinci the protagonist of *Stanza 411* co-exist and work towards a critique not only of the institution of love as the perilous locus of relationships but also of her disavowal of society's willingness to let women continue to endure what her mother had to endure in her life. Her personal anger, which led her to write *Stanza 411*, develops into a form of constructive indignation as she denounces women's abuse in many parts of society. The centrifugal and centripetal forces of Rome discussed by Pasolini have much to do with her strategy of beginning her analysis with the observation of her own lived experience and expanding it through a ripple effect to her mother's experience, and to an examination of another couple's violence and of sexual trafficking. The sense of confinement in actual practice, and also in literary criticism, denounced by Adrienne Rich in her famous 1971 speech "When We Dead Awaken,"[28] appears to be a quasi-surmounted obstacle. At the time, Rich rejected the false dichotomy of an all-forgiving and unselfish love as female and a creative love as male, affirming that the term "love" itself required a rethinking. Vinci's own tone "is [that] of a woman almost in touch with her anger, who is determined not to appear angry, who is willing herself to be calm, detached and even charming ..."[29] The protagonist of *Stanza 411* is in touch with her anger and aware that she owns the weapon of writing: from the ashes of a destructive passion she creates a constructive form of indignation that centres her perlocutionary force on herself. The tone is that of a woman and artist who, as Rich writes, wants "to remain calm, detached, and even charming" when she is actually very angry. Consequently, Vinci's autobiographism in composing *Stanza 411* does not allow for immanence, because that would amount to jeopardizing the ability to live not like a woman but rather like an individual, independently, autonomously, and yet in the service of her society. When her writing investigates experiential facts, Vinci explores them not for the sake of the plot but to vivify the action itself, extending it beyond measure, *ex*-orbiting its sphere, just as the details of a nude by Lucian Freud *ex*-orbit the details of a conventional nude. In the same way, Vinci's hyper-realistic self-portrait relates to the novel as the constant possibility to expand and ex-orbit its limits. While her commitment does not take on the hues of a moral crusade, Vinci still exposes the social construction of sex and the economic transactions that take place on different levels. In short, in a time now dilated but close to the present, the elements constructing a personal experiential fact become a verbal weapon to expose the precariousness of (female) individuals affected by economic subjection. What we take away from this novel is the awareness of Vinci and her unmatched ability to wield linguistic tools and to build the differential movement between an object and its simulacrum. The stone tossed into water creates ripples in the liquid mass that constitutes the matter of which mistreated and abused women, from Phaedra onward, are made. Corporeality and materiality compete in the protagonist's cognitive process – a process that departs from life experience and gains a public utility for Vinci's work, opening up the ethical intricacies of her narrative about gender relations and power dynamics.

To conclude, by interrogating traditional conceptions of traumatic irrepresentability and witnessing to their time and the community of which they are members, artists explore the potential of performance for altering perceptions of space, time, and causality, particularly through the materiality of the encounter between audience and artwork. In addition, victimhood (that of Sławek, Emma, Titta, and many other characters) is perceived as an actively constructed identity whose re-enactments of suffering incite unsustainable identifications in the reader/viewer. This possibility notwithstanding, we need to be aware that artists constantly consider the aesthetic possibilities for revising socio-political practices of vulnerability and even legal frailty in their discourse. Vulnerability and the law, discourses of protection, care and control, compassion and support, understanding, as Tiziano Scarpa claims, the "fundamental things" in life, are at the core of these narratives. In the case of Marco Mantello's 2011 novel, *La rabbia*, anger stems from the frustration following the Genoa G8 of 2001, also one of the key political moments for Scarpa's *Kamikaze d'Occidente*. A writer of a younger generation than Scarpa's, Mantello delivers yet another perspective on the father-son relationship, a theme often analysed by Scarpa. Leandro Van Sandt and his son, Filippo, form one of the most original couples in contemporary Italian narrative. While the father is a famous writer, the son refuses to assume any responsibility with respect to his own future. The son is paralysed with fear, irritation, and anger, which he chose as his preferred feeling at an early age.[30] As Leo (Leonardo) claims, "Men of power know how useful anger is, and the contemporary world is in the hands of those who know how to handle it, how to take it towards goals, aspirations, expectations or obviously, illusions."[31] Unresolved anger, rather than conquering serenity, triggers more unhappiness than anything else in this father-son tale of post-Berlusconi Italy.[32] Identity and identity construction manifest the conundrum behind this odd father-son couple, who seem only to embrace power relations and frustrated ambitions rather than address feelings and emotions. Destructive anger, divorced from reason and common sense, devastates their relationship. Anger propels the story forward. The transgression of spaces belongs to passions as well as to politics.

A powerful and beautiful lesson is the realization that the emotional component of what artists produce should never be underestimated. As Keen observes, "novelists themselves often vouch for the centrality of empathy to novel reading and writing and express belief in narrative empathy's power to change the minds and lives of readers."[33] The same kind of hope has generated this book, one that believes that emotions can always be functional in social change when put to work in the distribution of the sensible. We don't know what is really sensible until we prove what is not and what we believe could be changed for a more reasonable and just existence. Returning to Adorno and Rancière, if it's true that art has never promised to offer practical remedies to the ills of society, it can certainly incite us to be better. We can't remain impassive, for when we are moved by something that only art can give us, we can become indignant, as Stéphane Hessel incites us to be. And it is our indignation that compels us to act.

Notes

All translations are mine, unless otherwise indicated

Introduction

1 Rancière, *The Politics of Aesthetics*, 33.
2 Hessel, *Indignatevi*, 6.
3 "I call the distribution of the sensible the system of self-evident facts of sense perception that simultaneously discloses the existence of something in common and the delimitations that define the respective parts and positions within it." Rancière, *The Politics of Aesthetics*, 12.
4 Ngai, *Ugly Feelings*.
5 Ahmed, *The Cultural Politics of Emotion*.
6 Hultquist, "New Directions in History of Emotion."
7 Ibid., 762.
8 Ibid., 764.
9 Ibid., 763.
10 Ibid., 764, emphasis in original.
11 Ibid., 763.
12 Ibid.
13 Ibid.
14 Van Doorn and Zeelenberg, "Anger and Prosocial Behavior."
15 Nussbaum, *Upheavals of Thought*, 2–3. For the judging narrator, see Booth, *The Rhetoric of Fiction*, 20.
16 Nussbaum, *Upheavals of Thought*, 1.
17 James, "What Is an Emotion?"
18 Nussbaum, *Upheavals of Thought*, 2.
19 Ibid., 3.
20 Ibid.
21 "Empathy that leads to sympathy is by definition other-directed, whereas an over-aroused empathic response that creates personal distress (self-oriented and aversive) causes a turning-away from the provocative condition of the other." Keen, "A Theory of Narrative Empathy," 208.

22 Nussbaum, *Upheavals of Thought*, 13.

23 In article 195 of *The Passions of the Soul*, Descartes states the interpersonal nature of indignation:

> Indignation is a species of Hatred or aversion which one naturally has for those who do some evil, whatever its nature. And it is often mingled with envy or pity, but it has nevertheless an altogether different object. For one is indignant only with those who do good or evil to people who do not deserve it, but one bears envy against those who receive the good, and takes Pity upon those who receive the evil. It is true that it is, in a way, doing evil to possess a good one does not deserve. This may be the reason why Aristotle and his followers, supposing that Envy is always a vice, called that which is not unvirtuous by the name of Indignation. (Descartes, *The Passions of the Soul*, 124)

24 Trollope, *The Way We Live Now*.

25 Descartes, *Passions*, 124.

26 "Moto di reazione violenta, spesso rabbiosa, e generalmente non riconducibile a una giustificazione sul piano umano e razionale." Devoto and Oli, *Vocabolario illustrato della lingua italiana*, vol. 2, 1379. Unless otherwise noted, all translations are mine.

27 Nussbaum, *Anger and Forgiveness*, 1–7.

28 Giner-Sorolla, *Judging Passions*, 1.

29 Nussbaum, *Anger and Forgiveness*, 8.

30 Mishra, *The Age of Anger*, 9.

31 Ibid.

32 Ibid., 10.

33 Sollors, ed., "Introduction," *The Return of Thematic Criticism*, xix.

34 Ibid., xx.

35 Keen, "A Theory of Empathy," 217.

36 See Vegetti Finzi, ed., *Storia delle passioni*. Achilles's ire is the first example by which Mario Vegetti opens his essay "Passioni antiche: L'io collerico" in the same volume (39–74).

37 See Kohut, *The Analysis of the Self*. See also Bowlby, *Attachment and Loss*.

38 The "regulation of self-esteem and to maintain it at normal levels" controls rage and ire and at young age such control proves to be difficult in narcissistic individuals. See Kohut, *The Analysis of the Self*, 20.

39 Fisher, *The Vehement Passions*, 172, emphasis added.

40 Ibid.

41 Ibid., 172–3.

42 Hume, *Treatise of Human Nature*, vol. 1, 246; emphasis in original.

43 Fisher, *The Vehement Passions*, 171, emphasis added.

44 Said, *Representations of the Intellectual*, 6.

45 One of the instances Nussbaum allows in her *Anger and Forgiveness*, 8.

46 Grosz, *Time Travels*, 190.
47 Bauman, *The Art of Life*, 50; emphasis in original.
48 Ibid.
49 Ibid., 63; emphasis added.
50 Ngai, *Ugly Feelings*, 7.
51 Auerbach, *Mimesis*, 554.
52 Coetzee, *Elizabeth Costello*, 19.
53 Scarpa, *Le cose fondamentali*. Henceforth CF.
54 Aldo Nove, an artist very close to Tiziano Scarpa, indicates the "spectacle" with the verses of Nanni Balestrini chosen to seal the end of "Il mondo dell'amore": "Nel paesaggio verbale / dietro la pagina un vuoto incolmabile / non mima niente / l'arte dell'impazienza / sovrappone un'altra immagine / mentre passiamo bruciando" (In the verbal landscape / behind the page an unassailable void / it doesn't mime anything / the art of impatience / juxtaposes another image / while we pass by burning). "Il mondo dell'amore," 62.
55 Adorno, "Reconciliation under Duress," 153.
56 Butler, Gambetti, and Sabsay, eds, "Introduction," *Vulnerability in Resistance*, 3.
57 Trollope, *The Way We Live Now*, 2.
58 Sorrentino, *Le conseguenze dell'amore* (*The Consequences of Love)*, and *L'amico di famiglia* (*The Family Friend*).
59 Vinci, *Stanza 411*.
60 Sorrentino, *Hanno tutti ragione*, 314.
61 Tomassini, *Sangue di cane*.

Part One – Anger and Commitment in Scarpa

1 "Ogni opera d'arte, in quanto tale, anche se piccola, è opera di contestazione, non di rivoluzione." Pasolini, "Incontro con Pasolini," 2963.
2 Ricciardi, *After* La Dolce Vita, 9.
3 Perniola, *Berlusconi o il '68 realizzato*, 8.
4 Ibid.
5 Ibid., 11.
6 Ibid., 14.
7 Ibid., 54–5.
8 Bauman, *The Art of Life*, 52–3.
9 Ibid., 53.
10 Rancière, *Aesthetics and Its Discontents*, 21.
11 Ibid.
12 Antonello and Mussnug, "Introduction" to *Postmodern* Impegno, 8.
13 Ibid., 10.
14 Rancière, *The Politics of Aesthetics*, 85.

15 Antonello and Mussnug, "Introduction," 3.
16 Antonio Moresco embodies this type of artist: his reaction to the Italian *status quo* utters his rejection of public participation in any events. See "La restaurazione."
17 Bauman, *Liquid Life*, 1–15.
18 Nussbaum, *Upheavals of Thought*, 4.
19 Bromwich, "Comment: Without Admonition," 323.
20 See Dragosei, *Letteratura e merci.*
21 Hessel, *Indignatevi!*, 30.
22 Ngai, *Ugly Feelings*, 3.
23 Bauman, *The Art of Life*, 72.
24 Butler, *Precarious Life*, xviii.
25 Rancière, *Aesthetics and Its Discontents*, 6; italics added.
26 Pasolini, *La rabbia di Pasolini.*
27 In Antonello and Mussnug, "Introduction," 21.
28 Butler, *Antigone's Claim*, 12.
29 Ibid.
30 Ibid.

1 Pasolini's *La rabbia* and the Spectacularization of Scarpa

1 "These eternally indignant poets, these champions of intellectual anger and philosophical rage" (Pasolini, *La rabbia "Il trattamento," Per il cinema*, vol. 1, 407).
2 Born in Venice in 1963, he received a degree in literature with Alfonso Berardinelli with a thesis titled "Lack: Writings of Inspiration and Inspiration of Writing." Particularly in *Cos'è questo fracasso?*, inspiration is one of Scarpa's leitmotifs. Scarpa writes for various webzines like nazioneindiana.com and ilprimoamore.com, and his interest in theatre, literary narrative, poetry, and the visual arts makes him one of the most eclectic artists today. His first novel, *Occhi sulla graticola*, was published by Einaudi in 1996. Scarpa won the Strega prize with *Stabat Mater* (Turin: Einaudi, 2009). Recently, he penned captions for the Brera Museum in Milan for the Caravaggio exhibition (*Supper at Emmaus*): https://pinacotecabrera.org/en/dialogo/third-dialogue-caravaggio-readings-and-re-readings/.
3 See Nicoletta Marini-Maio for an overview of the theme's treatments in her *A Very Seductive Body Politic.*
4 "[The nation] is *imagined* because the members of even the smallest nation will never know most of their fellow members, meet them, or even hear of them, yet in the minds of each lives the image of their communion." Anderson, *Imagined Communities*, 6.
5 Scarpa, *Il brevetto del geco.*
6 Scarpa, *Il cipiglio del gufo.*

7 Iovino, “Death(s) in Venice,” 3.
8 Scarpa, *Il cipiglio del gufo*, 212–13.
9 Williams, *Resources of Hope*, 4; emphasis added.
10 Lago, “Una satira menippea a Venezia.”
11 Sloterdijk, *Critique of Cynical Reason*, 177.
12 Rancière, *Aesthetics and Its Discontents*, 22.
13 Scarpa, *Cos'è questo fracasso?* Henceforth CQF.
14 Pasolini, “Confessioni tecniche,” 2775–6.
15 Walter Siti in Antonello, *Dimenticare Pasolini*, 105.
16 Ahmed, *The Cultural Politics of Emotion*, 84.
17 Antonello, *Dimenticare Pasolini*, 100.
18 Ibid.
19 Tricomi, “Pasolini, un reazionario di sinistra,” 19.
20 Ibid., 21.
21 Ibid., 22–3.
22 Rancière, *Aesthetics and Its Discontents*, 23.
23 Ibid., 60.
24 Antonello and Mussnug, “Introduction,” 11.
25 Pasolini, “What Is This Coup? I Know,” 228.
26 Ibid., 225–32.
27 Ibid., 227.
28 Ibid.
29 Kayser, *The Grotesque in Art and Literature*, 53.
30 Rancière, *Aesthetics and Its Discontents*, 61.
31 Ahmed writes:

> Being disgusted is not simply about “gut feelings.” Or if disgust is about gut feelings, then our relation to our guts is not direct, but is mediated by ideas that are already implicated in the very impressions we make of others and the way those impressions surface as bodies ... The inter-corporeal encounter of incorporation or ingestion hence involves the perception of “badness” as a quality of something only in the event that the badness fills up, as it were, the mouth of the one who tastes. So disgust, even defined simply as bad taste, shows us how the boundaries that allow the distinction between subjects and objects are undone in the moment of their making. (*The Cultural Politics of Emotion*, 83)

32 Ibid., 93.
33 Ibid.
34 See Tiziano Scarpa's powerful rebuttal of some tenets expressed by Wu Ming in their *New Italian Epic*, “L'epica *popular*, gli anni Novanta, la parresìa.” See also Benedetti, *Il tradimento dei critici*, 113–14, and Benedetti, *Pasolini contro Calvino*, 9–23.

35 Foucault, "The Meaning and Evolution of the Word 'Parrhesia.'"
36 "Ragionamenti in versi" (Discourses in Verses). Raboni, "Poeta senza poesia," 25.
37 Bakhtin, *Rabelais and His World*, 26.
38 Ibid.
39 Scarpa, *Il brevetto del geco*, 114. Henceforth BG.
40 Baumann, *The Art of Life*, 50.
41 Ibid.
42 Ibid.
43 Pasolini, "What Is This Coup? I Know," 228.
44 Ibid.
45 Didi-Huberman, "Film, essai, poem: *La rabbia* de Pier Paolo Pasolini," 20.
46 Pasolini, *La rabbia di Pasolini.*
47 In "Il 'corpo' tormentato de *La rabbia*," Roberto Chiesi claims that the film is "underappreciated also because never studied in its original form and nature" (13).
48 Ibid., 26.
49 Ibid., 16.
50 Ibid., 20.
51 Ibid., 13.
52 See Gabrielli, *Anni di novità e di grandi cose.*
53 Pasolini was certainly not the only one to be accused of this. Francesco Rosi with his *cinema-inchiesta*, Luchino Visconti, and other artists disturbed Italians' enjoyment of the economic boom by showing the fallacies, the collusion of powers, and the misery still present in many parts of the country.
54 According to Zryd's definition, found footage uses non-institutional materials whose cultural discourses are in turn commented. Archival RAI footage is re-used in the case of *La rabbia*, hence the term "found footage" can hardly be applied to this compilation. Zryd, "Found Footage as Discursive Metahistory."
55 "The work of the writer consists of taking words from his dictionary, where they are kept as if in a shrine, in order to use them in a specific manner: specific in respect to the historical moment of the word and of the writer ... The writer's expressive process, that is, his invention, therefore adds to the historicity, that is, to the reality of the language; therefore, he works on the language both as an instrumental linguistic system [and] as a cultural tradition. His act, if one were to describe it toponimically, is one alone: the reworking of the meaning of the sign. The sign was there, in the dictionary, pigeonholed, ready to be used" (Pasolini, "Cinema of Poetry," 169).
56 Rancière, *The Politics of Aesthetics*, 13.
57 Pasolini, "Una visione del mondo epico-religiosa."
58 Pasolini, ibid., *Per il cinema*, vol. 2, 2854, emphasis added.

59 Roberto Chiesi reports a similar response the director gave to Carlo Di Carlo ("Il 'corpo,'" 16 n1).
60 Cadel, "Scorciatoie anticanoniche nell'Italia del dopoguerra," 257.
61 See Benedetti, "La rabbia di Pasolini."
62 In Chiesi, "Il 'corpo,'" 16.
63 Didi-Huberman, "Film, essai, poem," 20.
64 It seems superfluous to bring up Emil Durkheim's 1897 study on suicide and his idea that social periods of disruption brought about greater anomie and higher rates of crime, suicide, and deviance. See Montanari, "Il suicidio nell'opera di Durkheim e di Freud." Suicide is the last tool of agency left to an individual, yet one wonders how independent of the rest of the community that very act can be.
65 *Tu sorellina più piccola, / quella bellezza l'avevi addosso umilmente, / e la tua anima di figlia di piccola gente, / non ha mai saputo di averla, / perché altrimenti non sarebbe stata bellezza. / Il mondo te l'ha insegnata. / Così la tua bellezza divenne sua ... Dello stupido mondo antico / e del feroce mondo futuro / era rimasta una bellezza che non si vergognava / di alludere ai piccoli seni di sorellina, / al piccolo ventre così facilmente nudo. / E per questo era bellezza, la stessa / che hanno le dolci ragazze del tuo mondo, / le figlie degli immigrati di colore, / le figlie dell'Europa povera, / le figlie dei commercianti / vincitrici ai concorsi a Miami o a Roma. / Sparì, come una colombella d'oro*

(You little sister, / that beauty you had it on you humbly, / and your soul of humble people's daughter, / never knew of having it, / because otherwise it would not be beauty. / The world taught it to you. / So your beauty became the world's / Of the stupid ancient world / and the fierce future world / Remained a beauty that was not ashamed / Of alluding to the little sister's small breasts / to the little belly so easily naked. / And it's because of this that it was beauty, the same / that have the gentle girls of your world / the daughters of immigrants of colour, / the daughters of poor Europe, / the daughters of the merchants / winners of contests in Miami or in London. / Beauty disappeared like a golden dove). As in Pasolini, *La rabbia* (55:40–56:20). See with slight variations in Pasolini, *La rabbia «Il trattamento»*, 397–8.

66 Morante, "Pro o contro la bomba atomica," 98–9.
67 See Braidotti "Becoming-World."
68 Didi-Huberman, "Film, essai, poem," 21.
69 Pasolini, "La rabbia," 8.
70 Pasolini, "Una visione del mondo epico-religiosa," 2854.
71 "Documentare la presenza di un mondo che, al contrario del mondo borghese, possiede profondamente la realtà. La realtà, ossia un vero amore per la tradizione che solo la rivoluzione può dare," Pasolini, in Chiesi, "Il 'corpo,'" 16 n1.

72 Descartes, *Passions*, 125–6.
73 Pasolini, "La rabbia," 8.
74 Didi-Huberman, "Film, Essai, Poem," 22.
75 Rancière, *Aesthetics and Its Discontents*, 4.
76 "In a crowd subject to a scam, the presence of even one individual who does not let himself be cheated, can already provide a first point of advantage. But that point, then multiplies itself by a thousand and a hundred thousand if that one happens to be a writer (meaning a poet). Even without realizing it, out of instinct, the poet is intended to expose the cheating. And a poem, once started, it will not stop; but it will run and multiply itself, coming from all sides, as far as not even the poet himself would have expected" (Morante, "Pro o contro," 105; emphasis added). I suggest a reading of this passage in Lucamante, *Forging Shoah Memories*, 173–5.
77 Rancière, *Aesthetics and Its Discontents*, 5.
78 Benjamin, "Theses on the Philosophy of History," 258.
79 Rancière, *The Politics of Aesthetics*, 14.
80 Ibid., 40.
81 Giuseppe Bertolucci, "Interview," 2009.
82 Pasolini, "Una visione del mondo epico-religiosa," 2871.
83 Chiesi, "Il 'corpo,'" 26–7.
84 Editing forces one to create. As Sergei Ejzenštein claims, "editing holds a realistic meaning when it can produce the image that can materialize the theme ... The strength of editing lies in its ability to engage the spectators' emotions and intelligence in the creative process." Sergei Ejzenštein, *Il montaggio*, 104, 105.
85 Rascaroli, "The Essai Film," 34.
86 Giuseppe Bertolucci, "Interview," 2009.
87 Chiesi, "Il 'corpo,'" 24.
88 Butler, *Precarious Life*, xii.
89 Ibid.
90 Pasolini, "Una visione del mondo epico-religiosa," 2871.
91 Pasolini, "Confessioni tecniche e altro," *Per il cinema*, vol. 2, 2776.
92 "La musica nel film può anche essere pensata prima che il film venga girato ... ma è solo nel momento in cui viene materialmente applicata alla pellicola, che essa nasce in quanto musica del film. Perché? Perché l'incontro, e l'eventuale amalgama tra musica e immagine, ha caratteri essenzialmente poetici, cioè empirici ... Ciò che essa aggiunge alle immagini, o meglio, la trasformazione che essa opera sulle immagini, resta un fatto misterioso, e difficilmente definibile" (Pasolini, "Confessioni tecniche e altro," 2796).
93 Pasolini, *La rabbia «Il trattamento»*, *Per il cinema*, vol. 1, 367.

94 Pasolini, "The Cinema of Poetry," 168. See also Francesca Matteoni's article "Cinema strumento di poesia."
95 Pasolini, "The Cinema of Poetry," 171.
96 "Perché la nostra vita è dominata dalla scontentezza, dall'angoscia, dalla paura della guerra, dalla guerra? Per rispondere a questa domanda ho scritto questo film senza seguire un filo cronologico ma forse neanche logico, ma soltanto le mie ragioni politiche e il mio sentimento poetico" (Pasolini, *La rabbia*, DVD Minerva Rarovideo, 15:25–16:00).
97 "The cinematic essai creates an enunciator who is very close to the real, extra-textual author [and] he voices personal opinions that can be related to the extra-textual author." Rascaroli, "The Essai Film," 35.
98 I am paraphrasing Rancière here. See *The Politics of Aesthetics*, 37.
99 Pasolini, "Appendice a *La rabbia*," *Per il cinema*, vol. 1, 408.
100 Ibid.
101 Ibid.
102 Ibid.
103 Ibid.
104 Ibid.
105 Giuseppe Bertolucci, "Interview."
106 Pasolini, "Il cinema secondo Pasolini," *Per il cinema*, vol. 2, 2894.
107 See extras in *La rabbia di Pasolini* DVD.
108 See Anna Tonelli's *Per indegnità morale*, and Wu Ming 1's brilliant excursus on Pasolini's relationship with the police as dealt with by critics during his life and after his death: "La polizia contro Pasolini, Pasolini contro la polizia."
109 "The filmmaker never collects abstract terms [as] ... images are always concrete." Pasolini, "The Cinema of Poetry," 171.
110 In Antonello's and Mussnug's "Introduction," they see postmodern *impegno* as a cultural and ideological site that "embraces multiplicity and the open, process-driven character of personal identity, political and cultural discourse, and the social field at large" (3–4). Instead, Raffaele Donnarumma seems to focalize his analysis of our period in literature more on the conceptualization of genres and ideology. Donnarumma, *Ipermodernità.*
111 Brolli, ed., *Gioventú cannibale: La prima antologia dell'orrore estremo.*
112 Felski, "Introduction," 610.
113 *Buonismo* and *cattivismo* were the two categories in which writers were divided in the mid-1990s. See *La Bestia* 1 (1997).
114 In their pamphlet *Guy Debord Is Really Dead*, the former Luther Blissett group (now Wu Ming) underscore Debord's "emphasis on contemplation of the spectacle," which has for some, in turn, managed to make of the term "Situationist" a "potent elixir promoted as a justification for anything

from half-baked dadaism to easy-minded technological millenarianism" (7).

115 See Stefania Lucamante's "Introduction," to *Italian Pulp Fiction*, 13–37.

116 Scarpa, *Occhi sulla graticola.* Its full title is: *Occhi sulla graticola: Breve saggio sulla penultima storia d'amore vissuta dalla donna alla quale desidererei unirmi in duraturo vincolo affettivo* (Brief essay on the penultimate love story lived by the woman to whom I would like to "be tied" in a lasting sentimental union).

117 See Antonello's "Cannibalizing the Avant-Garde," in Lucamante, *Italian Pulp Fiction*, 38–56.

118 See Gian Paolo Renello's discussion of virtual reality and the posthuman in "The Mediatic Body of the Cannibale Literature," Lucamante, *Italian Pulp Fiction*, 135–60.

119 Foster, *The Return of the Real*, 144.

120 Ibid., 145.

121 Discussions on realism are at the core of Di Martino and Verdicchio, ed., *Encounters with the Real in Contemporary Italian Literature and Cinema.* The editors' introduction is a salient overview of the theoretical and critical studies of the past ten years, ranging from Maurizio Ferraris's *Manifesto del nuovo realismo* to Raffaello Palumbo Mosca's concept of a realism that also means a return to ethics in *L'invenzione del vero.*

122 Especially in Scarpa's *Batticuore fuorilegge*, echoes of Pasolini's poetry appear as a vehicle of satire for high poetry. The incipit of Scarpa's "Il capitalismo straniero" begins with Pasolini's verses only to reverse the sense of them and move to an everyday situation of economic disarray: "Solo l'essere amati, solo l'essere / voluti conta: non l'amare, non / il volere. Mio zio si è suicidato / perché aveva investito tutti i suoi / risparmi (trent'anni da elettricista / dentro una fabbrica di alimentari, la Chiari & Forti di Silea, TV) / in un'operazione finanziaria / che acquisiva terreni in Romania." "Il capitalismo straniero," in *Batticuore fuorilegge*, 151. Henceforth BF.

123 Antonello and Mussnug, "Introduction," 13.

124 Butler, *Bodies That Matter*, 20.

125 Lefebvre, *The Production of Space*, 85.

126 Ibid.

127 Adorno, "Reconciliation under Duress," 152.

128 Ibid., 153.

129 Ibid.

130 Ibid., 159–60; emphasis added.

131 Ibid., 155.

132 Ibid.

133 Ibid., 156.

134 Ibid.

135 Ibid.
136 This process, of course, does not come without problems. The "relation of appropriation art to the image-screen is not so simple" Foster claims, because appropriation art "can be critical of the screen, even hostile to it, and fascinated by it, almost enamored of it." Foster, *The Return of the Real,* 146.
137 Auerbach, *Mimesis,* 554.
138 Baudelaire, *"The Painter of Modern Life" and Other Essays,* 18–20.
139 Adorno, "Reconciliation," 158; emphasis added.
140 Ibid.; emphasis added.
141 We also know that abstract art, perceived in those years as the most telling way to describe the antithesis of artistic commitment, and charged with political intentions, crystallized into a set of artistic rules as well. Carlo Levi amply wrote about and against abstract art, contending that, unlike other forms of naturalism, realism "creates reality for the first time in the act of expression." Levi, *Prima e dopo le parole,* 31.
142 Felski, "Introduction," 607.
143 Ibid.
144 Rancière, *Aesthetics and Its Discontents,* 4.
145 Ibid., 218.
146 Comolli in Brooks, *Realist Vision,* 217.
147 Scarpa, *Corpo,* 33.
148 Adorno, *Aesthetic Theory,* 330, 344.

2 An Apocalyptic Kamikaze

1 Scarpa, "Italy, country of figures and heartthrobs, where is the poet of your law?" (BF 105).
2 "Il peso specifico della parola letteraria è determinato dalla presenza della scrittura nella *carne del mondo* o dall'*assenza di carne,* invece, per alcuni." Saviano, "Se lo scrittore morde"; emphasis added.
3 Refuting the concept of genre, Scarpa creates links between the various forms of narrative, essays, and the autobiographical. Partly justified by the structure of his texts and by Scarpa's statements that all writing can be traced back to the artist's thought without breaks that literary genres conventionally create, I quote then somewhat indiscriminately various pieces of the mosaic composing *Batticuore fuorilegge* in particular, and Scarpa's opus in general.
4 See *Il cipiglio del gufo* for a satire of this obsessive trend that turns amateurs into writers, as the humble teacher Adriano Cazzavillan turns into a successful thriller writer (148–55).
5 Berardinelli, "Lo scrittore, il critico e l'ossessione della performance."

6 For the role of the intellectual and forms of intellectualism, I fully subscribe to Andrea Inglese's ideas in "Residue energie dissidenti (in forma di diario)."

7 Scarpa, *Kamikaze d'Occidente,* 228. Henceforth KO.

8 These political figures predate Berlusconi's era and stand in Scarpa's text as examples of the consummate ability of money and politics (Gelli and Andreotti, respectively) to always maintain a fruitful collaboration at the expense of citizens in the name of an even more important element: power.

9 Marx's words are Pasolini's epigraph: "Il nostro motto dev'essere dunque: riforma della coscienza non per mezzo di dogmi, ma mediante *l'analisi della coscienza non chiara a sé stessa,* o si presenti sotto forma religiosa o politica. Apparirà allora che il mondo ha da tempo *il sogno di una cosa* ..." Pasolini, *Il sogno di una cosa,* 2; emphasis added.

10 Genette, *Seuils,* 153.

11 Antonio Moresco in Scarpa, BF 7. The epigraph prompts two (classical) functions: the commentary on the title and that on the text. According to Genette, through the epigraph, two orders of effects and suggestions are activated, tied to the identity of the *epigraphed* ones and to the very presence of the epigraph (Genette, *Seuils,* 153–5).

12 The entire passage from Moresco's "Piccola nota" reads:

> It seems from many of the comments of the last weeks, that, if one thing exists and it is dominant and takes on the features of the status quo, if not good, it has to be acceptable. The only reasonable, mature, and social attitude is to comply with it, or at least confront it in a constructive dialogue. We can, instead, do otherwise. We can decide not to enter a constructive dialogue, we can say no, even if what is in front of us is infinitely more powerful than us. One can dissent, disobey, think differently, behave differently. One can also be non-organic, "anti-social," outmoded, if the "society" in which we live horrifies us, we can keep our wound open, keep the fire on, continue to think, to dream that even inside this very society and this horror and even of the individuals who belong to this society there is in a remote point of their person the same wound and the same fire, that we can hope or dream to reach if not by showing our same wound and the same dream. ("Piccola nota," https://www.nazioneindiana.com/2005/02/13/. Acc. 10 Mar. 2009)

13 Discussing three quotations encapsulating Masao Maruyama's political thought on the occasion of two lectures by Kenzaburō Ōe on the Japanese thinker, Andrew E. Barshay observes how "politics is a kind of creative institution-making which, in order to prevent the wholesale expropriation or destruction of individuals and groups, has to be rule-bound. In other words, political life is lived as a set of real, vital fictions: 'Selection in the modern

world is not between a "fictitious" environment and a "real" one; it is our fate to live in a world where there are only various fictions and various designs. Unless we realize that fact, we are bound to lose the ability to select the better from among those fictions' ("Politics and Man in the Contemporary World")." Barshay, "Introduction," in Ōe, *On Politics and Literature*, 2.

14 See Gianni Vattimo's reflections, "Pasolini. Fu vera gloria?"

15 Scarpa, *Groppi d'amore nella scuraglia* . Henceforth GS. The word "groppi" reminds us of the name of the protagonist of *Occhi sulla graticola*, Carolina Groppo. Once again, the lexicon is instrumental to stress the knot between the flesh, bodily fluids, and the writing that they elicit.

16 Pierpaolo Antonello enucleates very convincingly the desire for storytellers like Marco Paolini and Ascanio to come to terms with stories that bring together Italian society, in "New Commitment in Italian 'Theatrical Storytelling.'"

17 Not even the collective Wu Ming escape from this prejudice in their *New Italian Epic*. Scarpa is very careful about attesting to the cases of writers who, even in the 1990s, continued to propound commitment. See Scarpa, "L'epica *popular*, gli anni Novanta, la parresia."

18 See Benedetti's discussion of Pasolini's refusal to be a "bestia da stile" (a beast for style) and the importance of the poet's gesture: *Pasolini contro Calvino*, 153.

19 Debord, *Comments on the Society of the Spectacle*, 2.

20 Ibid., 4.

21 Butler, *Precarious Life*, 94–7.

22 Debord, *Comments*, 7.

23 Ibid., 8.

24 Ibid., 9.

25 Ibid.

26 Ibid., 10.

27 Benjamin, "The Work of Art in the Age of Mechanical Reproduction." The subjection of the work of art to the place and time where "it happens to be" (220) defines its uniqueness and its history.

28 Debord, *Comments*, 11–12.

29 "Each moment it has lived becomes a citation *à l'ordre du jour* – and that day is Judgment Day." Benjamin, "Theses on the Philosophy of History," 254.

30 Debord, *Comments*, 13; emphasis added.

31 Ibid., emphasis added.

32 Scarpa in Lucamante, "Intervista con Tiziano Scarpa," 698–9. For my discussion of parody and the novel, please read *A Multitude of Women*, 162–80.

33 "The goal of the story is its disorientation ... the story is in a non-space, in a point of the literary topography, along a road, is always in the making, is escaping from itself towards itself, but it does not escape nor it arrives to

itself. It is its own the joy of the structural imperfection ... a perfect imperfection ...)" (Manganelli, "Che cosa non è un racconto," 35).

34 Sloterdijk, *Critique of Cynical Reason,* 8.

35 In Scarpa's work there are many instances of television as a corrupting medium. Television is not corrupting because it distributes wrong information but because it has slowly been devoid of any possible educational and instructive function. As Mario Perniola states, it is the age of Berlusconi that perfected the process already begun in Pasolini's times of television ("transformed into an entertainment that turns spectators into idiots ... [without] pretending any mental and psychic effort from him" (*Berlusconi,* 16).

36 "When Guy Debord spoke of the 'society of the spectacle,' he omitted to mention that this scenarization of life was organized around sexuality and violence; a sexuality which the 1960s claimed to liberate, whereas what was actually happening was a progressive abolition of societal inhibitions, regarded by the Situationists as so many unbearable straitjackets ... Television – a 'museum of horrors' or a 'tunnel of death' – has, then, gradually transformed itself into a kind of *altar of human sacrifice,* using and abusing the terrorist scene and serial massacres; it now plays more on repulsion than on seduction" (Paul Virilio, in Redhead, ed., *The Paul Virilio Reader,* 259).

37 "When I write something, anything, am I writing an action or a reaction? To whom, to what am I responding?" Scarpa, BF 66.

38 Luperini, "Il tradimento dei chierici e lavoratori della conoscenza."

39 Adorno, *Aesthetic Theory,* 330.

40 Some of his critic friends caution him against his type of participation. For instance, Daniele Giglioli, in "Esercizi di affetti irreparabili," affirms that Scarpa conceives "an idea of literature that takes up and transforms anti-mimetic imperatives of modernism, changing them in a rejection of representing even more than representation." Scarpa's individual ends up, in Giglioli's words, "contributing to the victory of the enemy who believes in fighting."

41 Bauman, *The Art of Life,* 62.

42 Antonelli, "Finzioni e funzioni," 18–19; emphasis original.

43 Bauman, *The Art of Life,* 25.

44 Wu Ming, "Wu Ming / Tiziano Scarpa: Face Off." Acc. 1 Nov. 2016.

45 Scarpa, "Manifesto per una letteratura dell'impegno," 40. Each language in fact lives in a symbiotic relationship with the natural world that, in being natural, pre-exists the individual. The individual "inscribes himself since birth – and progressively integrates himself through learning – in a signifying world made of 'nature' and 'culture' at once. Nature is then not a neutral referent, but it is strongly culturalized." Greimas and Courtés, *Sémiotique,* 218.

46 Indeed, in the being of Scarpa in relation to the other equal to the Self, there exists a tension towards the synthesis of the two characters of Houellebecq's *The Elementary Particles*, the aseptic rationality of Michel and the nearly pathological sexuality of Bruno. Houellebecq, *The Elementary Particles.*
47 Virilio, *Politics of the Very Worst*, 17.
48 Pedullà exposes this phenomenon and speaks of the dictatorship of publishing houses that turns "newspapers into their megaphones": "Aiuto, aiuto, l'editoria del consenso," 10. Saviano speaks of the power of the word in writings that are not testimonies or reportages: "Se lo scrittore morde," 57.
49 Scarpa in Lucamante, "Intervista con Tiziano Scarpa," 736. Massimo Fusillo identifies the time in which the novel moves from its previous status of polyphony – open, that is (as in Scarpa's idea) to become a "hegemonic and canonical genre of all modern nation states." In "Fra epica e romanzo," 21.
50 Berardinelli, "Lo scrittore," 92–4.
51 Private conversation with the writer (26 June 2007).
52 Bauman, *The Art of Life*, 86.
53 (BF 11; Literature is the word of those who only possess the word.)
54 Bauman, *Liquid Life*, 57.
55 Ibid., 4, emphasis original.
56 The list of publications defaming the originality and the creativity of our artists is very long. I limit myself to citing once again Alfonso Berardinelli for his *Non incoraggiate il romanzo*. Aside from the reprint of his letter to Tiziano Scarpa (252–62), Berardinelli, following Yehoshua's idea that the growth of the novel was directly comparable to the growth of democracy, theorizes the end of the novel as we know it (36–7).
57 For an analysis of possible causes for the decline of Italian literary criticism, see Emanuele Zinato's *Le idee e le forme*, and Niccolò Scaffai's recent and illuminating piece, "Non trasformiamo una idiosincrasia in teoria." For a more accurate idea of Scarpa's opinion, please read "Critica letteraria" (in CQF 14–22).
58 Butler, *Antigone's Claim*, 82.
59 Antonelli, "Finzioni e funzioni," 24.

3 The Fundamental Things in Life

1 Tricomi, "Pasolini, un reazionario di sinistra," 20.
2 As Stéphane Hessel writes, when people are indignant, they are willing to "embrace a historical evolution[,] and the great course of history continues on thanks to [them]. Rather than the uncontrolled freedom of the

fox in the henhouse poultry pen, this is a course oriented towards a bigger justice and a bigger freedom." *Indignatevi!*, 10.

3 For an analysis of their premeditated double murder, see Ellen Nerenberg's *Murder Made in Italy*, 127–38. For a more detailed analysis of media coverage of Erika De Nardo "the witch of Novi Ligure," see Monica Baroni's *Streghe, madonne e sante postmoderne*, 91–105.

4 Nussbaum, *Upheavals of Thought*, 203.

5 Ngai, *Ugly Feelings*, 340.

6 Among the novels of disgust for Berlusconism, I'd like to recall at least Franco Cordelli's *Il Duca di Mantova* and Giorgio Vasta's *Spaesamento*. They present instances of the social and political disgust that grew out of the complete disconnect between Italian intellectuals and the political class and the social unrest that the Berlusconi Second Republic created in sixteen years of "disgusting" government.

7 Rancière, *The Politics of Aesthetics*, 39; emphasis original.

8 Perniola, *Berlusconi*, 49–50.

9 Calvino, "Visibility," 91.

10 Nove, "Il mondo dell'amore."

11 Benedetti in Antonello and Mussnug, "Introduction."

12 Antonello and Mussnug, "Introduction," 7.

13 Virilio, *War and Cinema*, 29.

14 Sontag, *Regarding the Pain of Others*, 40–1.

15 Butler, *Precarious Life*, 26.

16 Scarpa's take reveals clear differences from, for instance, the representation of the event Don DeLillo gives us in *Falling Man*. Don DeLillo renders with essential words a powerful description of this human apocalypse. Clearly not engaging with the mystifying power of words, DeLillo speaks as a witness and survivor of the attack. *After*, all that remains, at the end of the novel, is the "light that comes after, carried in the residue of smashed matter, in the ash ruins of what was various and human, hovering in the air above." DeLillo, *Falling Man*, 246.

17 Virilio, in Redhead, ed., *The Paul Virilio Reader*, 259, emphasis in original.

18 Butler, *Precarious Life*, 7.

19 Hume, *Treatise of Human Nature*, 149.

20 Pasolini, *Petrolio*.

21 Benedetti, *Pasolini contro Calvino*, 164.

22 Pasolini, "What Is This Coup? I Know," 230.

23 Hessel, *Indignatevi!*, 23.

24 "Wu Ming / Tiziano Scarpa: Face Off."

25 Scarpa, "L'epica *popular*, gli anni Novanta, la parresìa," 9.

26 Ibid.

27 Ibid.
28 Ibid.
29 See Baudrillard, *The System of Objects*, 205; emphasis in original.
30 See Bataille, *The Accursed Share.*
31 Scarpa, *Occhi sulla graticola*, 5. Henceforth OG.
32 Scarpa, *Cosa voglio da te*, 86.
33 The same concepts are shown in *Cos'è questo fracasso?*:

> Other than expressing themselves, being true to inspiration, give to a style your own imprint: these are the mediocre objectives of those who have never been surprised enough by the originality of the words. It is the language that is original, not us, therefore do not be afraid to plagiarize: steal, copy, write down, because every time you open your mouth you are plagiarizing language. Only silence is original. Everything else is library, exploded and fallen down again at every street corner, thousands of newsstands rained from the sky. (CQF 9)

A variation of this concept returns in *Kamikaze d'Occidente* in the *scheda* dedicated to the *Mostra delle immagini* (KO 111–13).
34 In *scheda* #9, the writer expresses his wish not to be judgmental: "Per una volta, io vorrei affrontare il racconto del mondo senza rappresentarlo come uno scandalo. Non intendo fare comunella con il mio lettore per metterlo d'accordo con me su quanto sono scandalosi tutti gli altri (me compreso)" (KO 49; For once, I would like to approach the telling of the world without representing it as a scandal. I do not want to establish an easy common cause with the reader to make him agree with me on how scandalous everybody is [me included]).
35 According to Roberto Caracci, "the reader feels hence hears [*sic*] behind the narrating voice that of Scarpa and while reading thinks of him, of Scarpa as a man, and not only as a writer: the reader friend-accomplice finds his friend again. This is borderline literary, we are in the post-modern of the anti-literary, in a *borderline* or almost *off-limit* zone in which one is so free to move that in the end we can hug each other – me narrator you reader – outside of the same pages of the book." Caracci, "I due cuori di Tiziano Scarpa."http://www.italialibri.net/dossier/scarpa/scarpa.html.
36 This theme is prefigured in the poem "Eccomi mamma" (Here I am, mother; BF 80–3): "Mamma, puoi star sicura, / non sarò io a renderti nonna. Hai perso, / Ti ho tirato una bella fregatura" (BF 83; Mom, you can be sure / I won't make you a grandma. You lost / I pulled you a nice rip-off).
37 Bodei, *La vita delle cose*, 22.
38 Ibid.
39 Savater, *Etica per un figlio*, 10.

40 Scarpa, "L'epica *popular*, gli anni Novanta, la parresìa."
41 Cordelli, "I ragazzi del Pulp senza una bussola," 6.

Part Two – Anger and Spaces of Vulnerability in Mazzucco and Stambrini

1 Mazzucco, "Loro," 109.
2 Butler, *Antigone's Claim*, 2.
3 Cunniff Gilson, "Vulnerability and Victimization," 72, 87.
4 Ahmed, *The Cultural Politics of Emotion*, 70.
5 Ibid.
6 Pasolini, "The City's True Face," 165.
7 See Michael Herzfeld's informative work on the gentrification of the Monti neighbourhood, *Evicted from Eternity*.
8 Mazzucco, *Un giorno perfetto*.
9 Braidotti, *Transpositions*, 69.
10 For an updated overview of the current debate on gender violence, see Bettaglio, Mandolini, and Ross, eds, *Rappresentare la violenza di genere*.
11 Westphal, *Geocriticism*, 76, 80.
12 Ibid., 86.
13 Ibid.
14 Pasolini, "Quant'eri bella Roma," 1704.
15 Ibid.
16 Ibid., 1703. See also Pasolini's "The City's True Face."
17 Venitucci, "Gentrificazione, cultura 'indipendente' e mercato (prima parte)." For an organic depiction of forced gentrification Michael Herzfeld proposes the Monti neighbourhood as a (negative) model in his *Evicted from Eternity*. While it is not a phenomenon limited to Monti, Herzfeld defines it as "profoundly and surprisingly stratified" (69).
18 Ibid.
19 Ponzanesi, "Imaginary Cities," 156.
20 See Lucamante, "Un difficile consenso."
21 See Foot and Lumley, "Signposts," in *Italian Cityscapes*, 1–11.
22 "Those who assert that Rome is an undeniable presence in Moravia's *oeuvre* fail to recognize that the Capital in his works is practically invisible as a physical and architectural embodiment of space. Moravia inserts Rome into his literature primarily as a referential toponym." Tillson, "A Nearly Invisible City," 254.
23 Moravia, *Boredom*, 67.
24 Ibid., 142.
25 Mazzantini, *Non ti muovere*.
26 Mazzantini, *Fortunata*.

27 Pavolini, *Accanto alla tigre.*
28 Melandri, *Sangue giusto.*
29 The notion of movement is inadequate for a qualitative transformation. See Massumi, *Parables for the Virtual,* 3–4.
30 Ibid., 6.
31 See Benjamin, "The Storyteller."
32 de Certeau, *The Practice of Everyday Life.*
33 Pavolini, *Accanto alla tigre,* 53.
34 Mazzucco, *Un giorno perfetto,* 11. Henceforth GP.
35 Simonetti, *La letteratura circostante,* 364.
36 Ibid.

4 Melania Mazzucco's *Un giorno perfetto*

1 See Facchini, "A Journey from Death of Life."
2 Letizia Modena, "'Senza raccontarli i luoghi non esistono,'" 200.
3 Ammaniti and Brancaccio, "Seratina" (Evening Jaunt).
4 Mazzucco, "Loro."
5 For Cesare Zavattini, everyday events were never "banal." When seen on the screen, these events would make people reflect on their condition. In his view, "the cinema's overwhelming desire to see, to analyze, its hunger for reality, is an act of concrete homage towards other people, towards what is happening and existing in the world." Zavattini, "Some Ideas on Cinema," 218.
6 Mazzucco, *Vita. Vita* constructs a story that incorporates narratives of, and about, a painful migration. *Vita* embodies Mazzucco's aesthetic project, the reworking of life for Italian-Americans by weaving it into a web of complex snapshots, authorial annotations, and reflections characteristic of an Italian contemporary intellectual who abstains from considering Italian migration as an undignified or distant theme and embraces it in full. She translates the oral tradition of her own family into a postmodern epic in which she is one of the characters as the focalization shifts from hers to that of her characters. She narrates the Italian diaspora to the United States to challenge the silence of Italian novelists who traditionally considered the topic of migration as a "non-place."
7 Witzke, "Violence against Women in Ancient Rome," 248.
8 Said, *Representations,* 20.
9 Monica Cristina Storini traces an interesting reading of the novel based on the use of the realistic versus the fantastic in "'*Antonio c'est moi?*'"
10 Verhoeven, *Elle.*

11 See Nugara, "Dicotomie e costruzione dei ruoli di genere nella narrazione di violenza domestica."
12 "Writing with truth the unknown philology of everyday life." Mazzucco in Marietti, "Melania Mazzucco e Sandro Veronesi."
13 Maraini, *Voci*. For an interesting study of this novel see Bellesia, "Variations on a Theme: Violence against Women in the Writings of Dacia Maraini," and Cannon, "*Voci* and the Conventions of the *Giallo*."
14 A destiny shared by Dacia Maraini's Angela Bari in *Voci* and Margaret Mazzantini's Italia in *Non ti muovere*.
15 For this emblematic case, see "Il delitto di via Poma" (The Crime of Via Poma). One of the suspects was Pietro Vanacore, who committed suicide in 2010 and whose surname resembles Antonio Buonocore's, Emma's husband in *Un giorno perfetto*.
16 Felski, "Introduction," 608.
17 Discussing the myth of happiness today, Bauman underscores the importance of Max Scheler's consideration of the vulnerability of humankind:

> vulnerability is unavoidable ... in a kind of society in which relative equality of political and other rights and formally acknowledged social equality go hand in hand with enormous differentiation of genuine power, possessions and education; a society in which everyone "has the right" to consider himself equal to everybody else, while in fact being unable to equal them. (*The Art of Life*, 25)

18 Felski, "Introduction," 608.
19 Mazzucco in Marietti, "Melania Mazzucco e Sandro Veronesi."
20 Ibid.
21 Far richer than the detective novel in psychological complexities, the *noir* relies for its plot on the causes of the characters' immorality. The entire construction of the novel thus needs characters that are more developed and intricate than those of a detective novel; Tzvetan Todorov contends, in his *Poetics of Prose*, that the *noir* fuses the two stories of the detective novel: that of the crime, which in the detective novel has already been committed at the outset of the *fabula*; and that of the investigation that instead composes the actual *noir*. In the *noir*, Todorov states, there is no story to guess, there is "no mystery," as the plot provides each step of the story. The presence of the crime in the story of the investigation creates the suspense (cause-effect) tied with curiosity (effect-cause) (47).
22 Braidotti, "A Critical Cartography of Feminist Post-postmodernism," 170.
23 Ibid., emphasis in original.
24 Touraine, *Le monde des femmes*, 22. While women have massively entered the workplace, their jobs are consistently paid less. "Men keep talking often of women in terms of an object of longing" (*Le monde* 24), thus making it obvious that French society (like Italian society) remains powerfully anchored

to men's system of values despite the entry of women into the work force and laws regulating social entities such as the family. Neo-standard Italian defines *mobbing* as a stagnating work environment in which workers are ultimately forced into inactivity or into leaving their current job. Feminist thinker Lea Melandri shares Touraine's views particularly in "Gli anelli che mancano."

25 De Beauvoir, *The Second Sex*, 435–55. De Beauvoir's comments on marriage as the most evident marker of division in gender roles (and lives) still rings true:

> The male is called upon for action, his vocation is to produce, fight, create, progress, to transcend himself towards the totality of the universe and the infinity of the future; but traditional marriage does not invite woman to transcend herself with him; it confines her in immanence, shuts her up within the circle of herself. (448)

26 See Gillespie, Richards, Givens, and Smith, "Framing Deadly Domestic Violence."

27 Butler, *Precarious Life*, 42.

28 A definition of "post-feminist" is somewhat appropriate because Mazzucco incorporates some of the rights granted to second-wave Italian feminists and moves on to a notion of "woman" more attuned to recent theorizations.

29 The contemporary misogynistic imagination characterizes women through a gender role almost symbiotically connected with the hearth, in a figure of mother/nurturer that overlooks notions of sexual appeal. See Johnson, *Strong Mothers, Weak Wives*; Sceats, *Food, Consumption and the Body in Contemporary Women's Fiction*; and Skubal, *Word of Mouth. Food and Fiction after Freud.*

30 Melandri, *Amore e violenza*, 98.

31 Ibid.

32 See ISTAT, "La violenza e i maltrattamenti contro le donne dentro e fuori la famiglia" (Violence against and mistreatment of women inside and outside the family).

33 School violence is depicted when Emma and Antonio Buonocore's son, Kevin, is bullied by his peers in the restroom (GP 147).

34 Marsden, "Deleuzian Bodies, Feminist Tactics," 308.

35 In "Femminile/Maschile" Silvia Contarini discusses several publications dealing with the supposed disappearance or permanence of feminism in Italian society. In line with Beatrice Busi's reflections (in Contarini, 11), Contarini argues that the experiences women live in different generations and geographic spaces constitute the elements that differentiate feminisms. Rather than declaring the disappearance of feminism, as Marina Terragni theorizes in *La scomparsa delle donne,* Contarini advances the healthy notion of a "rielaborazione" (re-elaboration) of old feminist

practices (12). Bonomi Romagnoli maps, instead, diverse forms of feminism in her reportage *Irriverenti e libere.*

36 Dominijanni, *Il trucco,* 173.

37 Ibid., 172.

38 Ibid.

39 Kahn, "*Lucrece.*"

40 Kazimierz Dabrowski and Michael M. Piechowski draw multi-levels of anger based on its development, integration, and disintegration. In level one, primary integration of anger, the individual has no consideration for others. In fact, he or she does not reflect on behaviour or responsibility for consequences. Anger is combined with aggression aroused by obstacles in the realization of such needs as self-preservation. See Dabrowski and Piechowski, *Theory of Levels of Emotional Development,* 133.

41 Ahmed, *The Cultural Politics of Emotion,* 43.

42 Higgins and Silver, *Rape and Representation,* 4–5.

43 Ibid., 5.

44 Ibid.

45 Ibid.

46 Moretti, *Atlas of the European Novel, 1800–1900,* 5.

47 Ibid., 5; emphasis in original.

48 Braidotti, "A Critical Cartography," 171.

49 Ibid., 79.

50 Ibid.

51 Felski, "Introduction," 607.

52 Ibid., 608.

53 Nussbaum, drawing on Martin Seligman's studies on animal behaviour, discusses depression and helplessness as motives leading to violence, often determined by contingence and (unmet) expectations for oneself. (*Upheaval of Thoughts,* 102–9).

54 In Stockton, *The Economics of Fantasy,* 183.

55 Melandri, *Amore e violenza,* 103.

56 Quoted in Marietti, "Melania Mazzucco e Sandro Veronesi." Mazzucco also taps into this topic, albeit in a melodramatic way, in *Il bacio della Medusa* (*The Medusa's Kiss*). Count Felice Argentero's behavioural code was that of the turn of the century; hence, he safely places his wife Norma in an insane asylum.

57 Deleuze and Parnet, *Dialogues,* 60.

58 Stewart, *Ordinary Affects,* 2.

59 Bordo, "Gentleman or Beast?"

60 Cunniff Gilson, "Vulnerability and Victimization," 75.

61 "Nei suoi pensieri, primo veniva sempre Kevin. Quando fantasticava, sognava di infliggere a Emma la ferita inguaribile, e quella ferita era il

bambino" (GP, 365; in his thoughts, Kevin was always first. When he daydreamed, he thought of inflicting an incurable wound on Emma, and that wound was the child).

62 In his *Critique of Everyday Life*, Lefebvre observes,

> Men have no knowledge of their own lives ... They see them and act them out via ideological themes and ethical values. In particular, they have an inadequate knowledge of their needs and their own fundamental attitudes; they express them badly; they delude themselves about their needs and aspirations except for the most general and basic ones. (quoted in Felski, "Introduction," 609)

63 As Touraine has observed,

> In trying to demonstrate that they affirm themselves as such, women choose the construction as free subjects as their goal ... they reverse the exclusive domination of the heterosexual model of male domination and reject the place traditionally accorded to the couple man/woman by substituting a plurality of changing and partial forms of sexuality. (*Le monde*, 27)

64 Joplin, "The Voice of the Shuttle Is Ours," 42.
65 Cunniff Gilson, "Vulnerability and Victimization," 80.
66 Braidotti, *Transpositions*, 129.
67 Bauman, *The Art of Life*, 25.
68 Perniola, *Berlusconi o il '68 realizzato*, 14.
69 de Beauvoir, *The Second Sex*, 448.
70 The speech continues:

> And they are instilled in us by fundamental institutions, such as families and schools and religious congregations. These institutions, these unseen pillars of civilization, must remain strong in America, and we will defend them. We must stand with our families to help them raise healthy, responsible children. When it comes to helping children make right choices, there is work for all of us to do. (George W. Bush's 2004 *State of the Union Address*)

71 Tolstoy, *Anna Karenina*, 1.
72 Young and McGuire, "Talking about Sexual Violence," 50.
73 Dogliotti and Rosiello, eds, *Il nuovo Zingarelli*, 1551.
74 Young and McGuire, "Talking about Sexual Violence," 50.
75 Masotto, "Violenza."
76 Ibid.
77 Butler, "Rethinking Vulnerability and Resistance," 12.
78 Stockton, *The Economics of Fantasy*, 182.
79 In Cunniff Gilson, "Vulnerability and Victimization," 80.
80 Butler, "Rethinking Vulnerability and Resistance," 25.

81 As Stockton observes, "the metamorphosis of the twentieth-century rape narrative" – one form of violence – "registers a desperate attempt to preserve traditional patterns of robust, entrepreneurial masculinity in the face of economic forms that increasingly disallow illusions of individual authority" (3). Coupled with a progressive loss of self-confidence of (white) men, the feminine becomes the metaphor for the Other, the different one. Postmodern narratives of violence, however, devise a white man subject to "the techno-economy of late capitalism" that, ultimately, "nullifies him as a subject" (Ibid., 21).
82 Gilson, "Vulnerability," 81.
83 Indeed, as Joplin writes, "If women have served as scapegoats for male violence, ... the woman writer and the feminist critic seek to remember the embodied, resisting woman. Each time we do, we resist our status as privileged victim; we interrupt the structure of reciprocal violence" ("The Voice of the Shuttle Is Ours," 55).
84 Butler, "Rethinking Vulnerability and Resistance," 25.

5 Monica Stambrini's *Benzina*

1 *Benzina* also enjoyed a theatrical staging in 2001. Saverio Aversa wrote a review of the play, which was directed by Daniele Falleri and presented at the *Teatro del Garofano* in Rome. Aversa's review was originally found at http://www.gayroma.it/culture/cinemateatro/ci-18giugno2001.htm but is no longer available.
2 See Ross, "Queering the *Habitus*"; Sambuco, "Women, Relationships and Space in Stancanelli's *Benzina* (1998)"; and Karagoz, "Gazing Women."
3 Nove, *Superwoobinda.*
4 Santacroce, *Luminal.*
5 Lucamante, "Introduction."
6 Butler, *Bodies That Matter*, xv; emphasis in original. In "Oltre il genere," Rosi Braidotti made a succinct assessment of gender theory and the range of separation between sex and gender: the body is a "situated self," an embodied positioning of the self; as such, it demands a revision and redefinition of contemporary subjectivity, because "thinking of the body in this way implies sexuality as a process." As early as twenty years ago, then, Braidotti proposed a comparative study of the sex-sexuality paradigm, one that would de-essentialize the body without reducing it to pure nature opposed to social construction as it was being established in the by-now-classic sex-gender paradigm and revindicating the subjectivity of an individual, first and foremost (6–7).
7 Stancanelli, *Benzina*; Stambrini, *Benzina.*
8 Butler, Gambetti, and Sabsay, "Introduction," 2.

9 Butler, *Undoing Gender*, 7.

10 "The abject confronts us ... with our earliest attempts to release the hold of *maternal* entity even before existing outside of her, thanks to the autonomy of language. It is a violent, clumsy breaking away, with the constant risk of falling back under the sway of a power as securing as it is stifling. The difficulty a mother has in acknowledging (or being acknowledged by) the symbolic realm – in other words, the problem she has with the phallus that her father or her husband stands for – is not such as to help the future subject leave the natural mansion. The child can serve its mother as token of her own authentication; there is, however, hardly any reason for her to serve as go-between for it to become autonomous and authentic in its turn. In such close combat, the symbolic light that a third party, eventually the father, can contribute helps the future subject, the more so if it happens to be endowed with a robust supply of drive energy, in pursuing a reluctant struggle against what, having been the mother, will turn into an abject. Repelling, rejecting; repelling itself, rejecting itself Ab-jecting" (Kristeva, *Powers of Horror*, 13).

11 Alice Sebold is another writer who seems fascinated by topics and techniques that strikingly resemble Stambrini's. Both *The* and the recent *The Almost Moon* openly deal with the impossibility of being heard for dead female characters who speak only through their posthumous narration of the events that caused their death.

12 In his 1983 novel, *Benzina*, postmodern writer Quim Monzó depicts a world where all the above-mentioned elements construct a world that, again as in the *Giovani Cannibali* fiction, deals with capitalist alienation and consumeristic nausea.

13 For Braidotti, the role of feminist practice today is (among others) to express

> the need to overthrow the pejorative, oppressive connotations that are built not only into the notion of difference, but also into the dialectics of Self and Other ... [as now.] She, in fact, might no longer be a She, but ... a subject-in-progress, a mutant, the other of the Other, a post-Woman embodied subject cast in female morphology who has already undergone an essential metamorphosis. (*Metamorphoses*, 11–12)

14 Butler, *Undoing Gender*, 7.

15 Unknown, or veiled, is in fact, what we think of women's space in many instances. In theorizing the representation of a non-"universal" corporeal, Elizabeth Grosz sees any of its previous definitions as a "veiled representation and projection of a masculine which takes itself as the unquestioned norm." *Volatile Bodies*, 188. In Grosz's view, a universal corporeal would often imply an "ideal representative" that is perforce male and heterosexual;

someone who, in his representational positioning, would innocently "bring violence to its others ... who are reduced to the role of modifications or variations of the ... human body" (188).

16 Comencini, *La bestia nel cuore.*

17 Tognazzi, *Io e lei.*

18 Grosz, *Time Travels,* 6.

19 Butler, "Rethinking Vulnerability and Resistance," 12.

20 I have taken this expression from Vivian Gornik's 1987 *Fierce Attachments.*

21 For a specific treatment of the maternal in Stancanelli's eponymous novel, see Karagoz, "Gazing Women."

22 *Benzina,* Digital film (2001).

23 Jung, *Aspects of the Feminine, The Collected Works of C.G. Jung.* Vol. 6.

24 Ibid., 6:110.

25 Grosz discusses Kristeva's reflections on the term in her *Volatile Bodies,* 194.

26 Ahmed, *The Cultural Politics of Emotion,* 89.

27 Irigaray in Grosz, *Volatile Bodies,* 195.

28 Grosz, *Volatile Bodies,* 194.

29 Ibid., 195.

30 Sambuco, "Women, Relationships and Space in Stancanelli's *Benzina* (1998)," 135.

31 Butler, *Undoing Gender,* 8.

32 Laderman, *Driving Visions.*

33 Rogoff, "Studying Visual Culture," 2.

34 "That lack of identity extends to her tasteful visuals, her view of lesbians as lipstick, and a last-minute, smiley-faced gesture for which critics, if this were a Hollywood picture, would blame test-screening audiences. Ah, who are we kidding? This *is* a Hollywood picture."

35 Stambrini in Tola, "Libera da Thelma e Louise."

36 Dargis, "'Thelma and Louise' and the Tradition of the Male Road Movie," 89.

37 Ibid, 87.

38 Massumi, *Parables for the Virtual,* 3–4.

39 "The stations measure the road, giving it a sense of scale without actually depicting the space. *Twentysix Gasoline Stations* is a landscape – a 1,400-mile landscape." Brougher, "Words as Landscape," 163.

40 Ibid., 163.

41 This genre sprang from Ruscha's generation, that of his great friend, actor Dennis Hopper, director of *Easy Rider* (1966), which, in turn, owes much to Jack Kerouac's 1957 *On the Road.*

42 Bernardo Bertolucci, *The Dreamers.*

43 Bernardo Bertolucci's *Besieged* is drawn from James Lasdun's *The Siege,* a romantic tale of obsession of a wealthy man for a young and secretive

political refugee. Like *Benzina*, this represents yet another story of marginalized corporeality and societal siege.

44 In the novel, they are going to Greece, where they had spent their previous summer vacation.

45 Stancanelli, *Benzina*, 151. Henceforth BE.

46 Stella and Lenni only seem to retreat into patriarchy when Uncle Ottavio compares Lenni's mother's hair to "petrolio" for its blackness (BE 119). As Giovanna's previous life was deeply dictated by patriarchy, it is only fitting that her hair should be compared to petrol by her brother.

47 Sambuco believes that the gas station offers "a different dimension of the sense of the community, as its boundaries are not really exclusive of the outer world ... it offers interaction with its customers" ("Women, Relationships and Space," 133).

48 Butler, *Undoing Gender*, 8.

49 This choice is criticized by Antonello Schioppa (review of *Benzina*), as it represents a linguistic solution that holds no efficacy and is not really personal, derived, but not reinterpreted, from David Lynch, while Francioni and De Candido interpret such choice in a more positive manner.

50 "This is what the psychotic aura attests to when a feeling of catastrophe about the end of the world ... is associated with an overwhelming feeling of imminent redemption of every possibility or, in other words, the alarming oscillation between a proliferating complexity of sense and total vacuity, a hopeless dereliction of existential chaosmosis" (Guattari, *Chaosmosis*, 81).

51 Grosz, *Volatile Bodies*, 195, 204–6.

52 Baudrillard, *The Vital Illusion*, 11.

53 Touraine, *Le monde des femmes*, 26–7. Also Melandri, *Amore e violenza*, 103.

54 Touraine, *Le monde des femmes*, 31.

55 Ibid., 41.

56 Ibid., 58.

57 Ibid., 60.

58 Butler, *Precarious Life*, 43.

59 Ibid.

60 Rancière, *The Politics of Aesthetics*, 38.

Part Three – Anger and Love in Spaces of Otherness in Sorrentino, Vinci, and Tomassini

1 Ferraris, *Manifesto del nuovo realismo*, 41.

2 Amanda Anderson's book *The Way We Argue Now* tackles the relevance of realist anthropological practices in the age defined by

post-modernism. Though this is the overriding theme, more detail appears in the chapter titled "Realism, Universalism and the Science of the Human," 94–114.

3 Campe and Weber, "Introduction" to *Rethinking Emotion*, 3.

4 "Relational aesthetics ... reaffirms an essential idea: that art consists in constructing spaces and relations to reconfigure materially and symbolically the territory of the common." Rancière, *Aesthetics and Its Discontents*, 22.

5 Foucault, "Of Other Spaces," 27.

6 Ibid., 24.

7 Augé, *Non-places.*

8 Ibid., 26.

9 Rancière, *Aesthetics and Its Discontents*, 110.

10 Palumbo Mosca, *L'invenzione del vero*, 15.

11 Ibid., 13. See also Wayne C. Booth's discussion in his *The Rhetoric of Fiction*, 113–15.

12 Westphal, *Geocriticism*, 105.

13 Palumbo Mosca, *L'invenzione del vero*, 15.

14 Dominijanni, "Wounds of the Common,"140.

15 Vinci, *Stanza 411*, 36. Henceforth S411.

6 Paolo Sorrentino's *The Consequences of Love*

1 "Cinema represents reality. But if reality were that nice there would be no cinema." Godard, *Il cinema è cinema*, 23.

2 "All Sorrentino's films reflect his political commitment dealing with topical social problems such as drugs, usury, political corruption, and the Mafia. *Le conseguenze dell'amore*, however, is not only a commentary on contemporary Italian society. The film is a complex text that crosses genre boundaries: at once a thriller, an action movie, a dark comedy, a stylish film that draws from auteurs' films to depict the existential quest of its protagonist. Some critics have seen the film as an example of a new tendency towards genre hybridity, a mode which characterizes contemporary Italian cinema" (Leotta, "Do Not Underestimate the Consequences of Love," 287).

3 Small, "No Way Out,"113.

4 Hume, *Treatise of Human Nature*, 246.

5 Menarini, "Generi nascosti ed espliciti nel recente cinema italiano," 44.

6 Leotta, "Do Not Underestimate the Consequences of Love," 292.

7 Bonsaver, "Dall'uomo al divo: Un'intervista a Paolo Sorrentino," 327.

8 Crowdus, "Exposing the Dark Secrets of Italian Political History," 35. Sorrentino is also a writer in his own right with *Hanno tutti ragione* (*Everybody's Right*); and *Tony Pagoda e I suoi amici.*

9 Wollen, "The Auteur Theory," 601.
10 Ahmed, "Willful Parts," 231.
11 Piazzesi, "Le (terribili) conseguenze dell'amore," 94; emphasis in original.
12 De Gaetano, *Il corpo e la maschera,* 27; emphasis in original.
13 Ibid., 29.
14 Carocci, "L'immaginazione e il potere," 93.
15 Godard, *Il cinema è cinema,* 41.
16 Pinto Leites and Rocha Da Silva, "Roberto De Gaetano: impulse-images and the cinema between the forms and the forces," 8.
17 Bonsaver, "Dall'uomo al divo," 325.
18 Ibid. In Sorrentino's films, without mocking his sense of the tragic, Luisa Ceretto and Roberto Chiesi see how "Pier Paolo Pasolini's reflections on homologation reveal their prophetic quality and a dramatic confirmation in the berlusconianesimo of right and left." Ceretto and Chiesi, "Isole, alberghi e distanze," 6.
19 Bonsaver, "Dall'uomo al divo," 326.
20 Ibid.
21 Wollen, "The Auteur Theory," 593.
22 Rogers, *Troublesome Helpmate.* Though I use this book as it specifically addresses the issue of misogyny in literature from antiquity onward, the list of publications on misogyny is quite long, from Marilyn French's *The War against Women,* which offers many examples of woman-hatred culture, to Naomi Wolf's *The Beauty Myth.*
23 In speaking of her female students' reception of the movie *Top Gun,* Modleski acknowledges the power of female positive images on screen such as the female astrophysicist. She reflects on the importance of "recognition of one's 'screen surrogate' (an educated woman, in this case), which has been the norm for men in classic cinema, as Laura Mulvey noted." Modleski, "Misogynist Films," 104–5, emphasis added.
24 Chambers, "Il sud, il subalterno, e la sfida critica," 13.
25 Bodei, *Geometria delle passioni,* 7–8.
26 Ibid., 8.
27 Hume, *Treatise of Human Nature,* 266.
28 Ibid., 267.
29 Bodei, *Geometria delle passioni,* 9.
30 Ibid.
31 Harris, "Hume's Four Essays on Happiness and Their Place in the Move from Morals to Politics," 230–1.
32 Bodei, *Geometria delle passioni,* 9.
33 Sesti, extra material in the DVD *L'amico di famiglia.*
34 "All his characters share a disturbed relationship (blocked, chronicised, fossilized), made up with nausea and an ancient anger, diffidence and

impotence, against the totality of the people surrounding them." Sesti, "Prefazione," 10.

35 For Pauline Small,

> the (in)action of the protagonist's existence is primarily spent in lengthy periods of stasis in the main lounge, but these are punctuated by journeys through the other interconnecting spaces essential to the hotel life – corridors, lifts, and stairs – used intermittently to move from one sub-set to another. (Small, "No Way Out," 116)

36 It is difficult to say under which category we should place Sorrentino's auteurship in the conventional split in author theory between the *auteur* or the *metteur en scène.*

37 Mary Wood as in Dana Renga's *Unfinished Business*, 66.

38 Sorrentino's (and Garrone's to some extent) films exhibit a form of patriarchal narcissism that requires subtle, intricate representations of man-to-man experiences, pleasures, and relationships: intense homosociality that stops just short of homoeroticism. One destiny of patriarchal cinema resides in the buddy film, which merely makes explicit the exclusion of the woman who was never fully present in the first place.

39 Renga, *Unfinished Business*, 67.

40 "The capacity for correct anger is, like each of Aristotle's virtues, positioned between two equally negative extremes, one as excess, the other as defect. The excess of anger is obviously the bad-tempered or irascible man, the constantly or excessively angry man, the man enraged by trifles. But it is the defective extreme of anger, for which we have no word, but which Aristotle calls the 'in-irascible' man, that excites Aristotle's close attention" (Fisher, *The Vehement Passions*, 173).

41 Nussbaum, *Upheavals of Thought*, 460.

42 Ibid., 458.

43 Céline, *Journey to the End of the Nigh*t, 407–8.

44 Fisher, *The Vehement Passions*, 22.

45 Ibid.

46 "Love is the main agent of this subversion, having revolutionary consequences over Titta's life. When he surrenders to the temptation of the romance, Titta starts breaking all his self-imposed rules. The protagonist initially perceives love from an accountant's point of view as he is ... When Sofia refuses his expensive present and asks him to express his love Titta protests 'but I'm only an accountant ...' At the end of the film, however, the irrationality of Titta's love will upset his ordered, but alienating life based on materialist calculations" (Leotta, "Do Not Underestimate the Consequences of Love," 293–4).

47 See Schweitzer, "Making Equals."

48 It is not by chance that the first scene of *L'amico di famiglia* picks up the visual discourse from where Titta's story ended. A minimal temporal ellipsis, and here is the head of a nun who, engaged in sunbathing in a direct allusion to Pietro Germi's *Divorce Italian Style*, does not pay attention to poor Geremia. Geremia remains perfectly alone on the beach as the nun gazes admiringly at the sunset over the sea. This situation offers visual and thematic links with the previous film. As in Jacques Pinoteau's eponymous movie (1957), Sorrentino's protagonist in *L'amico di famiglia* is everything but a friend. In Sorrentino's film, Geremia, a grotesque troll whose physical appearance shows Sorrentino's irony of representation and a reified sense of the grotesque, suffers from the abandonment of a handsome father living in a mythical Rome, and is a usurer in a Mussolini town (likely Sabaudia). His claim is that he lends money to help the community, and he has a bizarre refrain that he tells his victims: "Il mio ultimo pensiero sarà per voi" (My last thought will be for you). This existence – accompanied by a devouring relationship with a bed-stricken mother in what Pierpaolo De Sanctis calls "casa-utero" (home-womb) ("'Forme della sensualità.' Il cinema di Paolo Sorrentino," 28) – will go undisturbed until he meets the beautiful Rosalba, Miss Agro Pontino. Geremia enters Miss Agro Pontino's family circle (her father is a poor waiter) and takes advantage of the weaknesses that the family nucleus reveals in the contingency of the "Beauty's" imminent wedding. The only thing this family can sell is, literally, their incredibly beautiful daughter. Geremia, like the dirty scumbag he is, thinks to take advantage of and benefit from the family's economic issues. The "benefit" is the opportunity to have sex with someone he would never, in his entire life, have dreamt of as being attainable. Beauty and the Beast have met. However, sex, is not enough, nor is ruining the bride on her wedding day. An impossible dream, being loved for what he really is, will ruin Geremia. The biggest fraud of his life, the one that proves his downfall, happens because of his sentimental weakness and (now) demonstrated naiveté. Friendship and love at once will ruin him. Again, and from a different perspective, the ruin for men derives from feelings, women, and love.

49 Mulvey, "Visual Pleasures and Narrative Cinema," 7.

50 Ibid., 9.

51 Keen, "A Theory of Narrative Empathy," 215.

52 Ibid., 209.

53 As Giovanna Taviani writes,

> to be on top of reality, to open the eye of the camera on things, means also to live again that reality – and those spaces – through one's own, visceral subjectivity and transfigure it epically, metaphysically or surreally. It means exploring the

real, but also its cracks, its interruptions; means investigating reality below its surface and revealing the absurdity, in the sudden flashes of the removed. Think of the empty metaphysics of Sorrentino … : apologues that transcend daily life to become epiphanies. ("Inventare il vero," 90)

54 "The way a film looks and moves should have some relationship to the way a director thinks and feels," Sarris, "Notes on the Auteur Theory," 586. What amounts to "interior meaning" for Sarris is something "… ambiguous, in any literary sense, because part of it is embedded in the stuff of the cinema and cannot be rendered in noncinematic terms" (587).
55 Piazzesi, "Le (terribili) conseguenze dell'amore," 95; emphasis in original.
56 Nussbaum, *Upheavals of Thought*, 477.
57 Bodei, *Geometria delle passioni*, 25.

7 Simona Vinci's *Stanza 411*

1 Hume, *Treatise of Human Nature*, 394.
2 Ibid., 415.
3 Her entire career deals with this topic, from *Dei bambini non si sa niente* (*Of the Children We Know Nothing*) (1997) to *La prima verità* (The First Truth) (2016). For an analysis of love and evil in Vinci's *Come prima delle madri* see Lucamante, *A Multitude of Women* (60–80).
4 This is a novelistic postmodernist mode of increasing importance in Italy. While the works of Walter Siti are often described as belonging to this narrative mode, we should also mention the works of Tiziano Scarpa, Helena Janeczek, Emanuele Trevi, Lorenzo Pavolini, and Francesca Mazzucato. For a theorization of autofiction we recall Serge Doubrovsky's "Autobiographie/verité/psychanalyse," in *Autobiographies: De Corneille à Sartre*, 68–79; Darrieussecq, "*L'Autofiction*"; Lecarme and Lecarme-Tabone, *L'Autobiographie*; Kotin Mortimer, "Mort de l'autobiographie dans *Le Livre brisé*"; and Ricciardi, *Gli artifici della non-fiction*. See also Lucamante, "Le scelte dell'*autofiction*." In *La letteratura circostante*, Simonetti speaks of "vera e propria *autofiction*" (true and actual autofiction) as juxtaposition between author and protagonist (98). Marchese, in *L'io possibile*, discusses the theory of this form of narrative and examines it in the work of Philip Roth, Bret Easton Ellis, and Walter Siti reaffirming the authority of the author and "the primacy of the reasons of literature over those of life" (270).
5 The writer couple functions as a literary theme passed from romanticism via modernism to postmodernism as an apt metaphor for intersubjective dynamics as, in Tobin Siebers's words, "one cannot conceive of postmodernism without giving sexual happiness its due. The postmodern romance

of community concerns the idea of sexual difference. It gives us one of the best visions of equality, one based on difference rather than sameness." Siebers, *Heterotopia*, 9.

6 V.T. are the initials of Vitaliano Trevisan, a writer with whom Vinci had an intense love affair.

7 Plato distinguishes images in iconic copies and phantasm-simulacra (*Sophist*, 236 b; 264 c). The simulacrum is an image without resemblance, actually based on an essential dissimilarity: it implies an essential reversal with respect to the Idea. The simulacrum differs also in its proportions and its effect – similarity is, according to John Muckelbauer, also produced by different mechanisms. The simulacrum, in short, is not concerned with its model or reference and is "extra-faithful" because it comes from perspectives external to the very model. See Muckelbauer, "Sophistic Travel," 3, 239.

8 After all, "the essential pathos" of criticism is, as Karl Marx wrote, "indignation, [and] its essential work is denunciation." Marx, "Introduction to a Contribution to the Critique of Hegel's Philosophy of Right."

9 I translate here parts of the final paragraph of Berardinelli's review: "Dear Vinci, maybe you should have been paid by that man. It was what you both wanted: annihilate each other, to find an insuperable distance, to feel transient and mortal, to fill each other with an abstract pity. *Now he has returned to nothing, as you wanted from the beginning. The nothing gives the chills.* You had them. Now you can start again." Berardinelli, *Non incoraggiate il romanzo*, 231; emphasis added.

10 See Woolf, *Women and Writing*, 49, emphasis added.

11 Vinci, *Come prima delle madri.*

12 More than other Italian contemporary writers, Vinci embraces Bataille's idea of sexuality, one that is always linked with excess and violence and concerns especially the dissolution of the boundaries of the body and self by way of impulses and appropriation. See Bataille, *Visions of Excess*, 94–5.

13 Vinci, *In tutti i sensi come l'amore.*

14 Fisher, *The Vehement Passions*, 2.

15 Ovid, *Heroides.*

16 Ibid., (IV.3–5).

17 Ferraris, *Manifesto*, 3.

18 Nussbaum, *Upheavals of Thought*, 460.

19 Ibid.

20 Fisher, *The Vehement Passions*, 22.

21 Foucault, "Of Other Spaces," 24.

22 Ibid., 24.

23 Hume, *Treatise of Human Nature*, 268.

24 Lindheim, *Epistolary Narrative and Desire in Ovid's Heroides*, 10–25.

25 Brodski, *In the Place of Language*, xv.
26 Bertoni, *Realismo e letteratura: Una storia possibile*, 16.
27 In Nussbaum, *Upheavals of Thought*, 464.
28 Ibid.
29 Ibid.
30 Freud, *Civilization and Its Discontents*, 18.
31 Brodski, *In the Place of Language*, xv.
32 Ibid., 26.
33 Freud, *Civilization and Its Discontents*, 250.
34 Ibid.
35 Ibid.
36 Ibid., 20.
37 Ibid.
38 Muckelbauer, "Sophistic Travel," 239. [*Nonlocatable* as in the text]. Jean Baudrillard observes how pernicious the use of simulacra can be in current times, for its distancing from the object and the subject, its losing all real dimensions pertaining to the object, create, in turn, all interpretations and none at once (*Vital Illusion*, 77).
39 Domenichelli, "L'immaginario reticolare," 36.
40 Winton, "Footprints in Stone: A Psychogeography of Rome."
41 Freud, *Civilization and Its Discontents*, 17.
42 Ibid.
43 Nussbaum, *Upheavals of Thought*, 546.
44 Ibid.
45 Dubreuil, "Punitive Emotions and Norm Violations," 44.
46 Keen, "A Theory of Narrative Empathy," 215.
47 Dubreuil, "Punitive Emotions and Norm Violations," 46.
48 Fisher, *Vehement Passions*, 178. Fisher locates in book 4 of Plato's *Republic*, in the discussion of the parts of the soul, that

> it is by means of anger that the existence of a third part of the soul, the passions, is established, distinct from reason, but also from the appetites and desires. This third part of the soul discloses an intuitive and aroused sense of justice ... Since for Plato in the *The Republic* justice is the highest of the virtues of society as well as the most profound and encompassing virtue within the soul, it is now possible to see why anger is the passion that first makes evident the third part of the soul. (177–8)

49 This is a subject Vinci holds very dear and that is analysed in all her works.
50 Simona Vinci, www.studioprogetto.net/incubatoio16/I/simona.htm. URL no longer valid.
51 Freud, *Civilization and Its Discontents*, 19.
52 Brooks, *Body Work*, 1.

53 Casadei, *Stile e tradizione nel romanzo italiano contemporaneo*, 120.
54 Tabanelli, "Il post-umano (femmineo) in Simona Vinci," 380.
55 Marchais, "Bambine, ragazze e donne nella scrittura di Simona Vinci," 142.
56 For the treatment of fear and the body, see Simona Vinci, *Parla, mia paura.*

8 Veronica Tomassini's *Sangue di Cane*

1 Derrida, "Hostipitality," 3.
2 As Rosi Braidotti states,

> we have all become the subjects of bio-power, but we differ considerably in the degrees and modes of actualization of that very power. To argue simply along the facile cosmopolitan lines that "we" may all be in *this* together, therefore, amounts to taking a shortcut through the complexity of the global condition. ("Becoming-World," 10; emphasis in original)

3 Tomassini, *L'altro addio.* This novel tackles other aspects of Sławek's story and focuses on the female protagonist. Also, the destructive power of vodka on an entire population, misery, and crime – themes already presented in *Sangue di cane* – return more pointedly in this novel.
4 Tomassini, *Sangue di cane*, 90. Henceforth SC.
5 Derrida, "Hostipitality," 4.
6 Ibid., 4.
7 Weir, "Roberto Esposito's Political Philosophy of the Gift," 165.
8 Esposito, *Communitas*, 6.
9 Weir, "Roberto Esposito's Political Philosophy of the Gift," 155.
10 Ibid., 163.
11 Ibid.
12 Rancière, *Aesthetics and Its Discontents*, 8.
13 Hume, *Treatise of Human Nature*, 181–90.
14 Palumbo Mosca, *L'invenzione del vero*, 15.
15 Giglioli, *Senza trauma: Senza trauma*, 53.
16 Ibid.
17 Ibid., 54.
18 Private communication with the author (20 Jan. 2015).
19 Grell, *L'autofiction.* Kindle ed.
20 Braidotti, "Becoming-World," 10.
21 Esposito, *Living Thought*, 12–13.
22 Partly drawing from Werner Sollors's ideas as filtered through Remo Ceserani's "Il punto sulla critica tematica," 30, I argue that thematic criticism, or thematology considered as the diachronic study of literary themes, implies the recognition that a theme can be infinitely interconnected in a web of themes that constitute, as in the case of the love story

between a man and a woman, both the collective and the individual imaginary.

23 Thucydides, *The Complete Writings of Thucydides*, VII, 87.

24 Esposito, *Communitas*, 7.

25 While *Sangue di cane* focuses on Syracuse's world, *L'altro addio* focuses on the the land the Poles left when they went to Sicily.

26 "We cannot explain the development of individuality apart from its social context. But neither can we formulate a social theory to explain the dynamics of oppression without considering its psychic dimension." Oliver, *The Colonization of Psychic Space*, xiv.

27 Derrida, "Hostipitality," 6.

28 http://www.thefreedictionary.com/deregulation.

29 Hlasko's long story "L'ottavo giorno della settimana" is the most evident source of reference for the narrator. On this story depicting the harsh world of postwar Warsaw, Tomassini bases many of her statements about the systemic alienation of the Poles of Syracuse (SC 12).

30 Tomassini understands the constraints community puts on an individual who is not necessarily a stranger, but, like her, was born into the community: "The community isn't a mode of being, much less a 'making' of the individual subject. It isn't the subject's expansion or multiplication but its exposure to what interrupts the closing and turns it inside out: a dizziness, a syncope, a spasm in the continuity of the subject." Esposito, *Communitas*, 7.

31 My reading of Tomassini's *Sangue di cane* is not subject to Umberto Eco's idea of "overinterpretation." My "wonder" as a reader is not an excess (or in excess), because textual analysis proves the clear connection between the two aspects forming the writer's existence and the balance between the two in the construction of the text. As Eco states, we can determine "what the text says by virtue of its textual coherence and of an original underlying signification system, or what the addressees found in it by virtue of their own systems of expectations." Eco, *Interpretation and Overinterpretation*, 64.

32 Derrida, "Hostipitality," 8.

33 When she enters officially in the "ventre marcio" (SC 23; rotten belly) of the "House of the Dead," she realizes that a "tenerezza visionaria" (visionary tenderness) possessed her like a second skin, "sedotta dal fascino rauco e circense della nostra sfiga" (SC 12; seduced by the raucous and circus-like charm of our bad luck).

34 Braidotti, "Becoming-World," 11.

35 Derrida, "Hostipitality," 10.

36 Private communication with the author concerning Malaparte's quote (*The Skin*, 342).

37 Žižek, *In Defense of Lost Causes*, 29.

38 Ibid.
39 Ibid., 18.
40 De Gaetano, *Il corpo e la maschera*, 109–10.
41 Foster, "Object, Abject, Traumatic," 112.
42 Ibid.
43 Oliver, *The Colonization of Psychic Space*, xv.
44 Ibid., xvi.
45 Ibid.
46 Ibid., xvii.
47 Ibid., xiv–xv.
48 Ibid., xviii.
49 Esposito, *Communitas*, 2.

Afterword

1 Fisher, *The Vehement Passions*, 188.
2 Hume, *Treatise of Human Nature*, 252.
3 Wu Ming 1, "Wu Ming/ Tiziano Scarpa: Face Off," 13.
4 Siebers, *Heterotopia*, 6.
5 Can we still accept the definition of postmodernism (which for Donnarumma is by now defunct since "postmodern culture is our past," *Ipermodernità*, 25) that Italo Calvino gave of "the tendency to make ironic use of the stock images of mass media, or to inject the taste for the marvelous inherited from literary tradition into narrative mechanisms that accentuate its alienation"? Calvino, "Visibility," 95.
6 Siebers, *Heterotopia*, 8.
7 Rancière, *Aesthetics and Its Discontents*, 33.
8 Ibid., 23.
9 Ibid., 24.
10 Ibid., 33.
11 Ibid.
12 Bauman, *The Art of Life*, 52.
13 "With some ambiguities and uncertainties, the category of fiction today essentially covers and replaces the space previously occupied by the notion of literature: we could define fiction as that discourse, narrative or non-narrative, that aligns its materials, taken from verifiable historical reality or invented ones, in ways that are recognizable as artificial or as codified genres. Non-fiction would be, instead, what is outside literature: journalism, chronicles, reportage, the essay, political speeches ... Yet even this definition ... shows immediately its inadequacy as it is based on improper assumptions" (Donnarumma, *Ipermodernità*, 169).
14 Rancière, *The Politics of Aesthetics*, 39.

15 Ibid., 34.
16 Westphal, *Geocriticism*, 95.
17 Keen, "A Theory of Empathy," 214.
18 Ibid., 212.
19 In an interview with Claudio Brancaleoni, Nanni Balestrini expressed his opinion on the duty of a writer: "The task of a writer is not to propose visions of the world or ideological addresses. The writer has to give body to the energies, contradictions, even to the negative[s] that move the world. And this through the materiality of writing." Brancaleoni, "Intervista con Nanni Balestrini," 117.
20 The International Day for the Victims of Feminicide was instituted on 25 November 2013.
21 In the same years, we have at least two non-fictional works that best complement Mazzucco's effort to analyse domestic violence in literature: Concita De Gregorio's *Malamore. Esercizi di resistenza al dolore* (2008), and Silvia Ballestra's *Contro le donne nei secoli dei secoli* (2006). We know that feminism has liquefied into several and various forms that not necessarily and not always capitalize on that of the 1970s, but it has transformed into several ways of thinking about feminism, as Barbara Bonomi Romagnoli affirms in her *Irriverenti e libere: Femminismi nel nuovo millennio.*
22 Girard, *The Scapegoat*, 44.
23 Ibid.
24 Ibid.
25 Butler, *Precarious Life*, 42.
26 Ibid.
27 Keen, "A Theory of Empathy," 212.
28 Rich, "When We Dead Awaken," 1: 20.
29 Ibid.
30 "Un giorno, quando ero molto piccolo, mi fu chiesto di ritrarre il mio sentimento preferito. Senza avere la minima idea delle conseguenze presi in mano i pennarelli e disegnai: la Rabbia" (One day, when I was very young, I was asked to draw my favourite feeling. Without a clue of the consequences, I took the crayons and drew: Anger). Mantello, *La rabbia*, 9.
31 "Gli uomini di potere lo sanno, quanto la rabbia possa essere utile, e il mondo contemporaneo è posseduto da chi è in grado di gestirla, di convogliarla verso scopi aspirazioni pretese e ovviamente illusioni." Ibid., 11.
32 Perniola observes how Berlusconi's rise contributed to the current political and social lack of direction because of his uncanny ability to transform the narrative of Italian economy and ethics from one based on work (see the first article of the Italian Constitution) into one based on social relations with people of every sort. (*Berlusconi o il '68 realizzato*, 15).
33 Keen, "A Theory of Empathy," 215.

Works Cited

Adorno, Theodor W. *Aesthetic Theory*. Ed. Gretel Adorno and Rolf Tiedemann. Trans. Robert Hullot-Kentor. London and New York: Continuum, 2004.

– "Reconciliation under Duress." In *Aesthetics and Politics*, ed. Ernst Bloch et al., 151–76. New York: Verso, 1977.

Ahmed, Sara. *The Cultural Politics of Emotion*. New York: Routledge, 2004.

– "Willful Parts: Problem Characters or the Problem of Character." *New Literary History* 42.2 (Spring 2011): 231–53.

Alò, Francesco. Review of *Benzina*. *Il Messaggero*, 31 May 2002. http://it.movies.yahoo.com/7/7/41207.html.

Ammaniti, Niccolò, and Luisa Brancaccio. "Seratina" (Evening Jaunt). In *Pulp Fiction: The New Narrative of the* Giovani Cannibali *Writers*, ed. Stefania Lucamante, 163–96. Madison-Teaneck, NJ: Fairleigh-Dickinson University Press, 2001.

Anderson, Amanda. *The Way We Argue Now: A Study in the Cultures of Theory*. Princeton: University of Princeton Press, 2006.

Anderson, Benedict. *Imagined Communities*. London: Verso, 1991.

Antonelli, Giuseppe. "Finzioni e funzioni. Appunti per una stilistica strategica." *Atelier* 37 (Mar. 2005): 15–27.

Antonello, Pierpaolo. "Cannibalizing the Avant-Garde." In *Italian Pulp Fiction: The New Narrative of the* Giovani Cannibali *Writers*, ed. Lucamante, 38–56.

– *Dimenticare Pasolini: Intellettuali e impegno nell'Italia contemporanea*. Milan-Udine: Mimesis, 2012.

– "New Commitment in Italian 'Theatrical Storytelling': Memory, Testimony and the Evidential Paradigm." In *Postmodern* Impegno*: Ethics and Commitment in Contemporary Italian Culture*, ed. Antonello and Mussnug, 233–58.

Antonello, Pierpaolo, and Florian Mussnug, eds. *Postmodern* Impegno*: Ethics and Commitment in Contemporary Italian Culture*. Bern: Peter Lang, 2012.

"Approvata la legge contro lo stalking." http://www.ilgiornale.it/news/approvata-legge-contro-stalking.html.

Aristotle. *Nichomachean Ethics.* Trans. Terrence Irwin. 2nd ed. Indianapolis: Hackett, 1999.

Auerbach, Erich. *Mimesis: The Representation of Reality in Western Literature.* Trans. Willard R. Trask. 4th ed. Princeton, NJ: Princeton University Press, 1974.

Augé, Marc. *Non-places: Introduction to an Anthropology of Supermodernity.* Trans. John Howe. London: Verso, 1995.

Aversa, Saverio. *Benzina.* Review. http://www.gayroma.it/culture/cinemateatro/ci-18giugno2001.htm. URL no longer valid.

Bakhtin, Mikhail M. *Rabelais and His World.* Trans. Helen Iswolsky. Bloomington: Indiana University Press, 1984.

Ballestra, Silvia. *Contro le donne nei secoli dei secoli.* Milan: Il Saggiatore, 2006.

Baroni, Monica. *Streghe, madonne e sante postmoderne: Eccedenze femminili tra cronaca e fiction.* Roma: Meltemi, 2002.

Barshay, Andrew E. "Introduction." In Kenzaburō Ōe, *On Politics and Literature: Two Lectures by Kenzaburō Ōe.* Berkeley, University of California, Occasional Papers of the Doreen B. Townsend Center for the Humanities, no. 18 (1999): 1–4.

Bataille, Georges. *The Accursed Share: An Essay on General Economy. Vol. 1: Consumption.* Trans. Robert Hurley. New York: Zone Books, 1991.

– *Visions of Excess: Selected Writings, 1927–1939.* Trans. A. Stockl. Minneapolis: University of Minnesota Press, 1985.

Baudelaire, Charles. "*The Painter of Modern Life" and Other Essays.* Trans. Jonathan Mayne. 2nd ed. New York: Phaidon Press, 2012.

Baudrillard, Jean. *The System of Objects.* Trans. James Benedict. London: Verso, 1996.

– *The Vital Illusion.* Ed. Julia Witwer. New York: Columbia University Press, 2001.

Bauman, Zygmunt. *The Art of Life.* Cambridge: Polity Press, 2008.

– *Liquid Life.* Cambridge: Polity Press, 2005.

Bellesia, Giovanna. "Variations on a Theme: Violence against Women in the Writings of Dacia Maraini." In *The Pleasure of Writing: Critical Essays on Dacia Maraini,* ed. Ada Testaferri and Rodica Diaconescu-Blumenfeld, 121–34. West Lafayette, IN: Purdue University Press, 2000.

Benedetti, Carla. *Pasolini contro Calvino: Per una letteratura impura.* Turin: Bollati Boringhieri, 1998.

– "La rabbia di Pasolini: Come da un film sperimentale di montaggio può rinascere l'antica forma tragica." *Arabeschi. Rivista internazionale di studi su letteratura e visualità,* 6 (2015): 40–54.

– *Il tradimento dei critici.* Turin: Bollati Boringhieri, 2002.

Benini, Stefania. *Pasolini: The Sacred Flesh.* Toronto: University of Toronto Press, 2015.

Benjamin, Walter. "The Storyteller." In *Illuminations: Essays and Reflections,* ed. Hannah Arendt, 83–111. Trans. Harry Zohn. New York: Schocken Books, 2007.

– "Theses on the Philosophy of History." In *Illuminations*, ed. Arendt, 253–64.
– "The Work of Art in the Age of Mechanical Reproduction." In *Illuminations*, ed. Arendt, 217–51.
Berardinelli, Alfonso. *Non incoraggiate il romanzo.* Venice: Marsilio, 2011.
– "Lo scrittore, il critico e l'ossessione della performance. Lettera a Tiziano Scarpa." In *Sul banco dei cattivi*, ed. Giulio Ferroni, Massimo Onofri, Filippo La Porta, and Alfonso Berardinelli, 77–94. Rome: Donzelli, 2006.
– "Simona Vinci." *Non incoraggiate il romanzo*, 228–31.
Bertolucci, Bernardo. *Besieged.* Fine Lines Features, 1998.
– *The Dreamers.* Medusa Film, 2003.
Bertolucci, Giuseppe. Interview. *La rabbia di Pasolini.* Minerva Raro-video, 2009.
– "Pressbook per *La rabbia di Pasolini.*" http://www.cinetecadibologna.it/files/stampa/settembre2008/pressbook%20%20La%20Rabbia%20di%20Pasolini%20%20ITALIANO%20definitivox.pdf. Acc. 16 May 2018.
Bettaglio, Marina, Nicoletta Mandolini, and Silvia Ross, eds. *Rappresentare la violenza di genere: Sguardi femministi tra critica, attivismo e scrittura.* Milano: Mimesis, 2018.
Bodei, Remo. *Geometria delle passioni.* Milan: Feltrinelli, 1991.
– *La vita delle cose.* Rome-Bari: Laterza, 2009.
Bonomi Romagnoli, Barbara. *Irriverenti e libere: Femminismi nel nuovo millennio.* Rome: Editori Internazionali Riuniti, 2014.
Bonsaver, Guido. "Dall'uomo al divo: Un'intervista a Paolo Sorrentino." *The Italianist* 2 (2009): 325–37.
Booth, Wayne C. *The Rhetoric of Fiction.* 2nd ed. Chicago: The University of Chicago Press, 1983.
Bordo, Susan. "Gentleman or Beast? The Double Bind of Masculinity." *The Male Body*, 229–64. New York: Farrar, Straus & Giroux, 1999.
Bowlby, John. *Attachment and Loss.* New York: Basic Books, 1982.
Braidotti, Rosi. "Becoming-World." In *After Cosmopolitanism*, ed. Rosi Braidotti, Patrick Hanafin, and Bolette Blaagaard, 8–27. New York: Routledge, 2013.
– "A Critical Cartography of Feminist Post-postmodernism." *Australian Feminist Studies* 20.47 (July 2005): 169–80.
– *Metamorphoses: Toward a Materialist Theory of Becoming.* Cambridge: Polity Press, 2002.
– "Oltre il genere." *Leggendaria* 23 (2000): 5–7.
– *Transpositions: On Nomadic Ethics.* Cambridge: Polity Press, 2006.
Brancaleoni, Claudio. "Intervista con Nanni Balestrini." *Allegoria* 45 (2003): 107–17.
Brodski, Claudia. *In the Place of Language: Literature and the Architecture of the Referent.* New York: Fordham University Press, 2009.
Brolli, Daniele, ed. *Gioventú cannibale: La prima antologia dell'orrore estremo.* Turin: Einaudi Stile Libero, 1996.

Bromwich, David. "Comment: Without Admonition." In *Politics and Poetic Value*, ed. Robert von Hallberg, 320–35. Chicago: University of Chicago Press, 1987.

Brooks, Peter. *Body Work: Objects of Desire in Modern Narrative.* Cambridge, MA: Harvard University Press, 1993.

– *Realist Vision.* New Haven: Yale University Press, 2005.

Brougher, Kenny. "Words as Landscape." In *Ed Ruscha*, ed. Kenny Brougher and Neal Benezra, 157–77. Washington: The Hirshhorn Museum and the Museum of Modern Art, Oxford, 2000.

Buckle, Steven. "Hume on Passions." *Philosophy* 87 (2012): 189–213.

Bush, George. "State of the Union Address 2004." www.americanrhetoric.com /speeches/stateoftheunion2004.htm.

Butler, Judith. *Antigone's Claim: Kinship between Life and Death.* New York: Columbia University Press, 2002.

– *Bodies That Matter: On the Discursive Limits of Sex.* New York: Routledge, 1993.

– *Precarious Life: The Powers of Mourning and Violence.* London: Verso, 2004.

– "Rethinking Vulnerability and Resistance." In *Vulnerability in Resistance*, ed. Butler, Gambetti, and Sabsay, 12–29.

– *Undoing Gender.* New York: Routledge, 2004.

Butler, Judith, Zeynep Gambetti, and Leticia Sabsay, eds. *Vulnerability in Resistance.* Durham and London: Duke University Press, 2016.

Cadel, Francesca. "Scorciatoie anticanoniche nell'Italia del dopoguerra." *Italica* 89.2 (2012): 253–69.

Calvino, Italo. "Visibility." *Six Memos for the Next Millennium: The Charles Eliot Norton Lectures 1985–86*, 81–99. New York: Vintage, 1993.

Campe, Rüdiger, and Julia Weber, eds. *Rethinking Emotion: Interiority and Exteriority in Premodern, Modern, and Contemporary Thought.* Berlin: Walter de Gruyter, 2014.

Cannon, JoAnn. "*Voci* and the Conventions of the *Giallo*." *Italica* 78.2 (2001): 193–202.

Caracci, Roberto. "I due cuori di Tiziano Scarpa." http://www.italialibri.net /dossier/scarpa/scarpa.html. Acc. 11 Jan. 2018.

Carocci, Enrico. "L'immaginazione e il potere." In *Gli indivisibili. Esordi italiani del nuovo millennio*, ed. Vito Zagarrio, 92–7. Rome: Kaplan, 2009.

Casadei, Alberto. *Stile e tradizione nel romanzo italiano contemporaneo.* Bologna: Il Mulino, 2007.

Céline, Louis-Ferdinand. *Journey to the End of the Night.* Trans. Ralph Manheim. New York: New Directions Books, 2006.

Ceretto, Luisa, and Roberto Chiesi. "Isole, alberghi e distanze." In *Una distanza estranea. Il cinema di Emanuele Crialese, Matteo Garrone e Paolo Sorrentino*, ed. Luisa Ceretto and Roberto Chiesi, 6–10. Torre Bordone: Federazione italiana Cineforum, 2006.

Ceserani, Remo. "Il punto sulla critica tematica." *Allegoria* 58 (2008): 25–33.

Chambers, Bill. Review of *Gasoline*. https://www.filmfreakcentral.net/screenreviews/benzina.htm. URL no longer valid.

Chambers, Iain. "Il sud, il subalterno, e la sfida critica." In *Esercizi di Potere: Gramsci, Said, e il postcoloniale*, ed. Iain Chambers, 5–15. Rome: Meltemi, 2006.

Chiesi, Roberto. "Il 'corpo' tormentato de *La rabbia*. La genesi del progetto, la 'normalizzazione' del 1963." *Studi pasoliniani* 3 (2009): 13–26.

Coetzee, J.M. *Elizabeth Costello*. New York: Viking, 2003.

Cohen, William A., and Ryan Johnson, eds. *Filth: Dirt, Disgust, and Modern Life*. Minneapolis: University of Minnesota Press, 2005.

Comencini, Cristina. *La bestia nel cuore*. 01 Distribution, 2005.

Contarini, Silvia. "Femminile/Maschile: Lavori in corso." *Narrativa* 30 (2008): 7–29.

Cordelli, Franco. *Il Duca di Mantova*. Milan: Rizzoli, 2004.

– "I ragazzi del Pulp senza una bussola." *Tuttolibri. La Stampa*, Turin, 27 June 1996: 6.

Crowdus, Gary. "Exposing the Dark Secrets of Italian Political History: An Interview with Paolo Sorrentino." *Cineaste* (2009): 32–7.

Cunniff Gilson, Erinn. "Vulnerability and Victimization: Rethinking Key Concepts in Feminist Discourse on Sexual Violence." *Signs: Journal of Women in Culture and Society* 42.1 (2016): 71–98.

Dabrowski, Kazimierz, and Michael M. Piechowski. *Theory of Levels of Emotional Development: Multilevelness and Positive Integration*. With the assistance of Marlene King and Dexter R. Amend. New York: Dabor Science Publications, 1977.

Dargis, Manhola. "*Thelma & Louise* and the Tradition of the Male Road Movie." In *Women and Film: A Sight and Sound Reader*, ed. Pam Cook, and Philip Dodd, 86–92. Philadelphia: Temple University Press, 1993.

Darrieussecq, Marie. "L'*Autofiction*: Un genre pas sérieux." *Poétique* 107 (1996): 369–80.

de Beauvoir, Simone. (1952). *The Second Sex*. Trans. H.M. Parshley. Harmondsworth: Penguin, 1984.

Debord, Guy. *Comments on the Society of the Spectacle*. Trans. Malcolm Imrie. London: Verso, 1990.

de Certeau, Michel. *The Practice of Everyday Life*. Trans. Steven Rendall. Berkeley: University of California Press, 1988.

De Gaetano, Roberto. *Il corpo e la maschera: Il grottesco nel cinema italiano*. Rome: Bulzoni, 1999.

De Gregorio, Concita. *Malamore. Esercizi di resistenza al dolore*. Milan: Mondadori, 2008.

Deleuze, Gilles, and Claire Parnet. *Dialogues*. Trans. Hugh Tomlinson and Barbara Habberjam. London: Athlone Press, 1987.

DeLillo, Don. *Falling Man*. New York: Scribner, 2007.

Derrida, Jacques. "Hostipitality." Trans. Barry Stoker. *Angelaki* 5.3 (2000): 3–17.
De Sanctis, Pierpaolo. "'Forme della sensualità.' Il cinema di Paolo Sorrentino." In *Divi & antidivi*, ed. De Sanctis, Monetti, and Pallanch, 23–37.
De Sanctis, Pierpaolo, Domenico Monetti, and Luca Pallanch, eds. *Divi & Antidivi: Il cinema di Paolo Sorrentino.* Rome: Laboratorio Gutenberg, 2010.
Descartes, René. *The Passions of the Soul.* Trans. Stephen Voss. Indianapolis/Cambridge: Hackett Publishing Company, 1989.
Devoto, Giacomo, and Gian Carlo Oli. *Vocabolario illustrato della lingua italiana.* Vol. 2. Milan: Readers Digest, 1977.
Didi-Huberman, Georges. "Film, essai, poem: *La rabbia* de Pier Paolo Pasolini." *Les Cahiers du Mnam* 124 (Summer 2013): 18–35.
Di Martino, Loredana, and Pasquale Verdicchio, eds. *Encounters with the Real in Contemporary Italian Literature and Cinema.* Cambridge: Cambridge Scholars Publishing, 2017.
Dogliotti, Miro, and Luigi Rosiello, eds. *Il nuovo Zingarelli. Vocabolario della lingua italiana.* 11th ed. Bologna: Zanichelli, 1986.
Domenichelli, Mario. "L'immaginario reticolare: Memoria personale, memoria culturale e tematologia." *Allegoria* 58 (2008): 34–47.
Dominijanni, Ida. *Il trucco. Sessualità e politica nella fine di Berlusconi.* Rome: Ediesse, 2014.
– "Wounds of the Common." *Diacritics* 39.4 (Winter 2009): 135–45.
Donnarumma, Raffaele. *Ipermodernità. Dove va la narrativa contemporanea.* Bologna: Il Mulino, 2014.
Doubrovsky, Serge. *Autobiographies: De Corneille à Sartre.* Paris: PUF, 1988.
Dragosei, Francesco. *Letteratura e merci: Da Joyce a Cappuccetto Splatter.* Milan: Feltrinelli, 1999.
Dubreuil, Benoît. "Punitive Emotions and Norm Violations." *Philosophical Explorations* 13.1 (Mar. 2010): 35–50.
Eco, Umberto. *Interpretation and Overinterpretation.* Ed. Stefan Collini. Cambridge: Cambridge University Press, 1992.
Ejzenštein, Sergei. *Il montaggio.* Ed. Pietro Montani. Venice: Marsilio, 1986.
Epstein, Mikhail. "Hyper in 20th Century Culture: The Dialectics of Transition from Modernism to Postmodernism." *Postmodern Culture.* muse.jhu.edu/journals/postmodern_culture/v006/6.2epstein.html.
Esposito, Roberto. *Communitas: The Origin and Destiny of Community.* Trans. Timothy Campbell. Stanford, CA: Stanford University Press, 2010.
– *Living Thought: The Origins and Actuality of Italian Philosophy.* Trans. Zakiya Hanafi. Stanford, CA: Stanford University Press, 2012.
Facchini, Monica. "A Journey from Death of Life: Spectacular Realism and the 'Unamendability of Reality' in Paolo Sorrentino's *The Great Beauty.*" In *Encounters with the Real*, ed. Di Martino and Verdicchio, 181–204.
Felski, Rita. "Introduction." *New Literary History* 33.4 (2002): 607–22.

Ferraris, Maurizio. *Manifesto del nuovo realismo.* Rome-Bari: Laterza, 2012.

Fisher, Peter. *The Vehement Passions.* Princeton, NJ, and Oxford: Princeton University Press, 2002.

Foot, John, and David Lumley, eds. *Italian Cityscapes: Culture and Urban Change in Contemporary Italy.* Exeter: University of Exeter Press, 2004.

Foster, Hal. "Object, Abject, Traumatic." *The MIT Press* 78 (Autumn 1996): 106–24.

– *The Return of the Real: The Avant-Garde at the End of the Century.* Cambridge, MA: MIT Press, 1996.

Foucault, Michel. "The Meaning and Evolution of the Word 'Parrhesia': Discourse and Truth, Problematization of Parrhesia." https://foucault.info/parrhesia/foucault.DT1.wordParrhesia.en/. Acc. 31 May 2018.

– "Of Other Spaces." *Diacritics* 16.1 (Spring 1986): 22–7.

Francioni, Gabriel, and De Candido, Andrea. *Benzina.* Review. http://www.kinematrix.net/torino2001/benzinarece.htm.

Frasca-Spada, Marina. "Simple Perceptions in Hume's *Treatise.*" In *New Essays on David Hume,* ed. Mazza and Ronchetti, 37–54.

French, Marilyn. *The War against Women.* New York: Ballantine Books, 1993.

Freud, Sigmund. *Civilization and Its Discontents.* Ed. James Strachey. New York: W.W. Norton, 1961.

Fusillo, Massimo. "Fra epica e romanzo." In *Il romanzo. Part II, "Le forme,"* ed. Franco Moretti, 20–35. Turin: Einaudi, 2002.

Gabrielli, Patrizia. *Anni di novità e di grandi cose. Il boom economico fra tradizione e cambiamento.* Bologna: Il Mulino 2011.

Gadda, Carlo Emilio. *Quer pasticciaccio brutto de via Merulana.* Milan: Garzanti, 1983.

Garrone, Matteo. *L'imbalsamatore.* Fandango, 2002.

– *Primo amore.* Fandango, 2004.

Genette, Gérard. *Seuils.* Paris: Seuil, 1987.

Giglioli, Daniele. "Esercizi di affetti irreparabili." http://www.alternativerivista.it/article.php3?id_article=805.

– *Senza trauma: Scrittura dell'estremo e narrativa del nuovo millennio.* Macerata: Quodlibet, 2011.

Gillespie, Kirkland Lane, Tara N. Richards, Eugena M. Givens, and Dwayne Smith. "Framing Deadly Domestic Violence: Why the Media Spin Matters in Newspaper Coverage of Femicide." *Violence against Women* 19.2 (2013): 222–45.

Giner-Sorolla, Roger. *Judging Passions: Moral Emotions in Persons and Groups.* London: Psychology Press, 2012.

Girard, René. *The Scapegoat.* Trans. Yvonne Freccero. Baltimore, MD: Johns Hopkins University Press, 1986.

Godard, Jean-Luc. *Il cinema è cinema.* Trans. Adriano Aprà. Intro. Pier Paolo Pasolini. Milan: Garzanti, 1971.

Gornik, Vivian. *Fierce Attachments: A Memoir.* New York: Farrar, Straus, Giroux, 1987.

Greimas, Algirdas Julien, and Joseph Courtés. *Sémiotique. Dictionnaire raisonné de la théorie du langage.* Paris: Hachette, 1979.

Grell, Isabelle. *L'autofiction.* Paris: Arman Colin, 2014. Kindle ed.

Grosz, Elizabeth. *Time Travels: Feminism, Nature, Power.* Raleigh, NC: Duke University Press, 2005.

– *Volatile Bodies: Toward a Corporeal Feminism.* Bloomington, IN: Indiana University Press, 1994.

Guattari, Felix. *Chaosmosis: An Ethico-Aesthetic Paradigm.* Trans. Paul Bains and Julian Pefanis. Bloomington and Indianapolis: Indiana University Press, 1995.

Harris, James A. "Hume's Four Essays on Happiness and Their Place in the Move from Morals to Politics." In *New Essays on David Hume,* ed. Mazza and Ronchetti, 223–37.

Herz, Rachel. *That's Disgusting: Unraveling the Mysteries of Repulsion*: New York: W.W. Norton and Company, 2012.

Herzfeld, Michael. *Evicted from Eternity: The Restructuring of Modern Rome.* Chicago: Chicago University Press, 2009.

Hessel, Stéphane. *Indignatevi!* Trans. Maurizia Balmelli. Turin: Add editore, 2010.

Higgins, Lynn A., and Brenda R. Silver, eds. *Rape and Representation.* New York: Columbia University Press, 1991.

Hlasko, Marek. "L'ottavo giorno della settimana." *L'ottavo giorno della settimana.* Trans. F.I. [*sic*]. Milan: Mondadori, 1959. Orig. *Ósmy Dzień Tygodnia.*

Houellebecq, Michel. *The Elementary Particles.* Trans. Frank Wynne. New York: Alfred A. Knopf, 2000.

Hultquist, Aleksondra. "New Directions in History of Emotion and Affect Theory in Eighteenth-Century Studies." *Literature Compass* 13.12 (2016): 762–70.

Hume, David. *A Treatise of Human Nature.* Vol. 1. Ed. David Fate Norton and Mary J. Norton. Oxford: Clarendon Press, 2011.

"Il delitto di via Poma; 29 coltellate per Simonetta Cesaroni." www.misteriditalia.it/altri-misteri/via-poma. Acc. 6 Jan. 2010.

Inglese, Andrea. "Residue energie dissidenti (in forma di diario)." *Atelier* 44 (Dec. 2006): 25–7.

Iovino, Serenella. "Death(s) in Venice: Bodies and the Discourse of Pollution from Thomas Mann to Porto Marghera." In the James K. Binder Lectureship in Literature Series, Department of Literature, University of California San Diego, Vol. 8 (2014): 1–33.

ISTAT. "La violenza e i maltrattamenti contro le donne dentro e fuori la famiglia." www.istat.it/salastampa/comunicati/non_calendario/20070221_00/testointegrale.pdf. Acc. 5 Jan. 2010.

James, William. "What Is an Emotion?" *Mind* 9 (1884): 188–205.

Johnson, Miriam M. *Strong Mothers, Weak Wives: The Search for Gender Equality.* Berkeley: University of California Press, 1988.

Joplin, Patricia Klindienst. "The Voice of the Shuttle Is Ours." In *Rape and Representation,* ed., Higgins and Silver, 35–64.

Jung, Carl Gustav. *Aspects of the Feminine. Collected Works of C.G. Jung,* Vol. 6. Trans. R.F.C. Hull. Princeton, NJ: Princeton University Press, 1982.

Kahn, Coppélia. "Lucrece: The Sexual Politics of Subjectivity." In *Rape and Representation,* ed. Higgins and Silver, 141–59.

Karagoz, Claudia. "Gazing Women: Elena Stancanelli's *Benzina.*" *Italica* 83.3/4 (Fall 2006): 391–407.

Kayser, Wolfgang. *The Grotesque in Art and Literature.* Trans. Ulrich Weisstein. New York: Columbia University Press, 1981.

Keen, Suzanne. "A Theory of Narrative Empathy." *Narrative* 14.3 (2006): 207–36.

Kohut, Heinz. *The Analysis of the Self: A Systematic Approach to the Psychoanalytic Treatment of Narcissistic Personality Disorders.* Chicago: University of Chicago Press, 2002.

Kotin-Mortimer, Armine. "Mort de l'autobiographie dans *Le Livre brisé.*" *Temps modernes* 611–12 (2000–1): 128–66.

Kristeva, Julia. *Powers of Horror: An Essay on Abjection.* Trans. Leon S. Roudiez. New York: Columbia University Press, 1982.

La Bestia 1 (1997).

La Gioia, Nicola. "Intervento." Pub. 12 Mar. 2006. http://www.omero.it/rivista.php?itemid=636&catid=95. URL no longer valid

Laderman, David. *Driving Visions: Exploring the Road Movie.* Austin: University of Texas Press, 2002.

Lago, Paolo. "Una satira menippea a Venezia: Una lettura di *Occhi sulla graticola* di Tiziano Scarpa." *Studi novecenteschi* 2 (2009): 419–30

Lasdun, James. *The Siege.* New York: W.W. Norton, 1995.

Lecarme, Jacques, and Elisabeth Lecarme-Tabone. *L'Autobiographie.* Paris: Armand Colin, 1997.

Lefebvre, Henri. *The Production of Space.* Trans. Donald Nicholson-Smith. Oxford: Blackwell, 1991.

Leotta, Alfio. "Do Not Underestimate the Consequences of Love: The Representation of the New Mafia in Italian Cinema." *Italica* 88.2 (2011): 286–96.

Levi, Carlo. *Christ Stopped at Eboli.* Trans. Frances Frenaye. New York: Farrar, Straus and Giroux, 1947.

– *Prima e dopo le parole. Scritti e discorsi sulla letteratura.* Ed. Gigliola De Donato and Rosalba Galvagno. Rome: Donzelli, 2001.

Lindheim, Sarah H. *Epistolary Narrative and Desire in Ovid's Heroides.* Madison, WI: University of Wisconsin Press, 2003.

Lucamante, Stefania. "Un difficile consenso: Roma al termine della notte? Alcune considerazioni sulla narrativa d'ambiente romano negli anni zero." *Rivista di letteratura italiana* XXXI.1 (2013): 193–210.

– *Forging Shoah Memories: Italian Women Writers, Jewish Identity, and the Holocaust.* New York: Palgrave Macmillan, 2014.

– "Intervista con Tiziano Scarpa." *Italica* 83.3/4 (Fall/Winter 2006): 691–706.

– "Introduction." In *Italian Pulp Fiction: The New Narrative of the* Giovani Cannibali *Writers,* ed. Lucamante, 13–37.

– *Isabella Santacroce.* Fiesole: Cadmo, 2002.

– *A Multitude of Women: The Challenges of the Contemporary Italian Novel.* Toronto: University of Toronto Press, 2008.

– "The Privilege of Memory Goes to the Women: Melania Mazzucco's *Vita* and the Italian Migration." *Modern Language Notes* 124.1 (2009): 293–315.

– "Proposte per una poetica 'liquida' dell'ideologia e dell'estetica contemporanee: Tiziano Scarpa e la parola *altrui* della letteratura." *Poetiche* 9.3 (2007): 491–535.

– "Le scelte dell'*autofiction*: Il romanzo della memoria contro il potere della Storia." *Studi novecenteschi* 56 (1998): 367–81.

Lucamante, Stefania, ed. *Italian Pulp Fiction: The New Narrative of the* Giovani Cannibali *Writers.* Madison, NJ: Fairleigh-Dickinson University Press, 2001.

Luperini, Romano. "Il tradimento dei chierici e lavoratori della conoscenza." *Italian Culture* XXIV–XXV (2006–7): 169–81.

Luther Blissett (group). *Guy Debord Is Really Dead.* London: Sabotage Editions, 1995.

Malaparte, Curzio. *The Skin.* Trans. David Moore. Intro. Rachel Kushner. New York: New York Review Books. 2013. (English edition of *La pelle.* Milan: Adelphi, 2010).

Manganelli, Giorgio. "Che cosa non è un racconto." *Il rumore sottile della prosa,* 31–5. Milan: Adelphi, 1994.

Mantello, Marco. *La rabbia.* Massa: Transeuropa Edizioni, 2011.

Maraini, Dacia. *Voci.* Milan: Rizzoli, 1994.

Marchais, Natalie. "Bambine, ragazze e donne nella scrittura di Simona Vinci." *Narrativa* 30 (2008): 141–50.

Marchese, Lorenzo. *L'io possibile. L'autofiction come forma paradossale del romanzo italiano.* Massa: Transeuropa, 2014.

Marietti, Benedetta. "Melania Mazzucco e Sandro Veronesi. Confronto d'autore tra due romanzi italiani che ci raccontano come siamo." dweb.repubblica. it /dweb/2005/12/17/attualita/attualita/165san480165.html. Acc. 4 Jan. 2010.

Marini-Maio, Nicoletta. *A Very Seductive Body Politic: Silvio Berlusconi in Cinema.* Rome: Mimesis International, 2015.

Marsden, Jill. "Deleuzian Bodies, Feminist Tactics." *Woman: A Cultural Review* 15.3 (2004): 308–19.

Marx, Karl. "Introduction to a Contribution to the Critique of Hegel's *Philosophy of Right*." (1843). https://www.marxists.org/archive/marx/works/1843/critique-hpr/intro.htm. Acc. 18 July 2017.

Masotto, Giordana. "Violenza. Un discorso da mettere sottosopra." http://www.ilcalderonemagico.it/femm_violenza.html. Acc. 4 Jan. 2010.

Massumi, Brian. *Parables for the Virtual: Movement, Affect, Sensation*. Durham, NC: Duke University Press, 2002.

Matteoni, Francesca. "Cinema strumento di poesia." https://www.nazioneindiana.com/2010/01/26/cinema-strumento-di-poesia/. Acc. 26 Sept. 2016.

Mazza, Emilio, and Emanuele Ronchetti, eds. *New Essays on David Hume*. Milan: Franco Angeli, 2007.

Mazzantini, Margaret. *Fortunata*. (Script). Dir. Sergio Castellitto. Universal Pictures, 2017.

– *Non ti muovere*. Milan: Mondadori, 2001.

Mazzucco, Melania. *Il bacio della Medusa*. Milan: Baldini e Castoldi, 1996.

– *Un giorno perfetto*. Milan: Rizzoli, 2005.

– "Loro." In *Patrie impure*, ed. Benedetta Centovalli, 107–19. Milan: Rizzoli, 2003.

– *Vita*. Milan: Rizzoli, 2003.

Melandri, Francesca. *Sangue giusto*. Milan: Rizzoli, 2017.

Melandri, Lea. *Amore e violenza: Il fattore molesto della civiltà*. Turin: Bollati Boringhieri, 2011.

– "Gli anelli che mancano." *Leggendaria* 67 (Feb. 2008): 12.

Menarini, Roy. "Generi nascosti ed espliciti nel recente cinema italiano." In *Lo spazio del reale nel cinema italiano contemporaneo*, ed. Riccardo Guerrini, Giacomo Tagliani, and Francesco Zucconi, 42–54. Genoa: Le Mani, 2009.

Mishra, Pankaj. *The Age of Anger: A History of the Present*. New York: Farrar, Straus, and Giroux, 2017.

Modena, Letizia. "'Senza raccontarli i luoghi non esistono': Il GRA di Roma fra urbanistica e transmedia storytelling." *Forum Italicum* 50.1 (2016): 194–221.

Modleski, Tania. "Misogynist Films: Teaching *Top Gun*." *Cinema Journal* 47.1 (2007): 101–5.

Montanari, Andrea. "Il suicidio nell'opera di Durkheim e di Freud: Da anomia della società a fenomenologia della civiltà." *Il lettore di provincia* XLI.135 (July/Dec. 2010): 75–91.

Monzó, Quim. *Benzina*. Barcelona: Quaders Crema, 1982.

Morante, Elsa. "Pro o contro la bomba atomica." In *Pro o contro la bomba atomica e altri scritti*, ed. Cesare Garboli, 95–117. Milan: Adelphi, 1987.

– *La Storia: Romanzo*. Turin: Einaudi, 1974.

Moravia, Alberto. *Boredom*. Trans. Angus Davidson. New York: New York Review of Books, 2004.

Moresco, Antonio. "Piccola nota." https://www.nazioneindiana.com/2005/02/13/. Acc. 20 Mar. 2009.

– "La restaurazione." https://www.nazioneindiana.com/2005/04/09/la-restaurazione/. Acc. 27 Sept. 2017.

Moretti, Franco. *Atlas of the European Novel, 1800–1900.* London: Verso, 1998.

Muckelbauer, John. "Sophistic Travel: Inheriting the Simulacrum through Plato's 'The Sophist.'" *Philosophy and Rhetoric* 34.3 (2001): 225–44.

Mulvey, Laura. "Visual Pleasures and Narrative Cinema." *Screen* 16.3 (1975): 6–18.

Nerenberg, Ellen. *Murder Made in Italy: Homicide, Media, and Contemporary Italian Culture.* Bloomington, IN: Indiana University Press, 2012.

Ngai, Sianne. *Ugly Feelings.* Cambridge, MA: Harvard University Press, 2005.

Nove, Aldo. "La fine dell'amore." http://www.aldonove.com/poesia.swf. URL no longer valid.

– *Mi chiamo Roberta, ho 40 anni, guadagno 250 euro al mese ...* Turin: Einaudi, 2006.

– "Il mondo dell'amore." In *Gioventù cannibale: La prima antologia dell'orrore estremo,* ed. Daniele Brolli, 56–62. Turin: Einaudi Stile Libero, 1996.

– *Superwoobinda.* Turin: Einaudi Stile Libero, 1998.

Nugara, Silvia. "Dicotomie e costruzione dei ruoli di genere nella narrazione di violenza domestica." In *Negli archivi e per le strade. Il ritorno alla realtà nella narrativa di inizio millennio,* ed. Luca Somigli, 571–87. Rome: Aracne, 2013.

Nussbaum, Martha. *Anger and Forgiveness: Resentment, Generosity, Justice.* Oxford: Oxford University Press, 2016.

– *Upheavals of Thought: The Intelligence of Emotions.* Cambridge: Cambridge University Press, 2001.

Oliver, Kelly. *The Colonization of Psychic Space: A Psychoanalytical Social Theory of Oppression.* Minneapolis: University of Minnesota Press, 2004.

Onofri, Massimo. "La retorica del sublime basso: Salvatore Niffoi, Erri De Luca, Isabella Santacroce." In *Sul banco dei cattivi,* ed. Giulio Ferroni, Massimo Onofri, Filippo La Porta, and Alfonso Berardinelli, 33–54. Rome: Donzelli, 2006.

Ovid. *Heroides.* Ed. Howard Jakobson. Princeton, NJ: Princeton University Press, 1974.

Özpetek, Ferzan. *Un giorno perfetto.* Fandango, 2008.

Palumbo Mosca, Raffaello. *L'invenzione del vero. Romanzi ibridi e discorso etico nell'Italia contemporanea.* Viterbo: Gaffi, 2014.

Pasolini, Pier Paolo. "The Cinema of Poetry." In *Heretical Empiricism,* ed. Louise Barnett, 167–86. Trans. Ben Lawton and Louise Barnett. Bloomington: Indiana University Press, 1988.

– "The City's True Face." *Stories from the City of God: Sketches and Chronicles of Rome, 1950–1968,* 163–70. Trans. Marina Harss. New York: Other Press, 2003.

– "Confessioni tecniche e altro." In *Per il cinema*, ed. Walter Siti and Franco Zabagli, vol. 2, 2768–96. Milan: Meridiani Mondadori, 2001.

– "Incontro con Pasolini." In *Per il cinema*, ed. Walter Siti and Franco Zabagli, vol. 2, 2954–67. Milan: Meridiani Mondadori, 2001.

– *Mamma Roma.* Arco Film, 1962.

– *Petrolio.* Turin: Einaudi, 1992.

– "Quant'eri bella Roma." In *Saggi sulla politica e sulla società*, ed. Walter Siti and Silvia De Laude, 1702–10. Milan: Meridiani Mondadori, 1999.

– "La rabbia." *Nuovi argomenti* (Sept.–Oct.1960): 8

– *La rabbia di Pasolini.* Intro. Tatti Sanguineti. Ed. Roberto Chiesi. Minerva RaroVideo, 2009.

– *La rabbia «Il trattamento».* In *Per il cinema*, ed. Walter Siti and Franco Zabagli, vol. 1, 343–411. Milan: Meridiani Mondadori, 2001.

– *Ragazzi di vita.* Milan: Garzanti, 1955.

– *Il sogno di una cosa.* (1962). Milan: Garzanti, 2000.

– "Una visione del mondo epico-religiosa." In *Per il cinema*, ed. Walter Siti and Franco Zabagli, vol. 2, 2844–79. Milan: Meridiani Mondadori, 2001.

– "What Is This Coup? I Know." In *In Danger: A Pasolini Anthology*, ed. and intro. Jack Hirschman, 225–32. Trans. Pasquale Verdicchio. San Francisco: City Lights Books, 2010.

Pavolini, Lorenzo. *Accanto alla tigre.* Rome: Fandango libri, 2010.

Pedullà, Gabriele. "Aiuto, aiuto, l'editoria del consenso." *Alias* (20 Jan. 2007): 10.

Perniola, Mario. *Berlusconi o il '68 realizzato.* Udine: Mimesis, 2011.

Piazzesi, Chiara, "Le (terribili) conseguenze dell'amore. Declinazioni cinematografiche recenti dei paradossi dell'amore e del desiderio." *Segni e comprensione* XX.57 (Jan.–Apr. 2006): 85–97.

Pinto Leites, Bruno Bueno, and Alexandre Rocha Da Silva. "Roberto De Gaetano: Impulse-Images and the Cinema between the Forms and the Forces." *Intexto* 33 (1 Aug. 2015): 4–14.

Plato. *The Sophist.* Ed. and trans. Nicholas P. White. Indianapolis, IN: Hackett Classics, 1993.

Ponzanesi, Sandra. "Imaginary Cities: Space and Identity in Italian Literature of Immigration." In *Italian Cityscapes: Culture and Urban Change in Contemporary Italy*, ed. Foot and Lumley, 150–68.

Raboni, Giovanni. "Poeta senza poesia." *L'Espresso*, Rome, 22 Oct. 1995: 25.

Rancière, Jacques. *Aesthetics and Its Discontents.* Trans. Steven Corcoran. Cambridge: Polity Press, 2009.

– *The Politics of Aesthetics.* Trans. Gabriel Rockhill. London: Bloomsbury, 2006.

Rascaroli, Laura. "The Essai Film: Problems, Definitions, Textual Commitments." *Framework*, 49.2 (Oct. 2008): 24–47.

Redhead, Steve, ed. *The Paul Virilio Reader.* New York: Columbia University Press, 2004.

Renello, Gian Paolo. "The Mediatic Body of the Cannibale Literature." In *Italian Pulp Fiction: The New Narrative of the* Giovani Cannibali *Writers*, ed. Lucamante, 135–60.

Renga, Dana. *Unfinished Business: Screening the Italian Mafia in the New Millennium.* Toronto: University of Toronto Press, 2013.

Ricciardi, Alessia. *After* La Dolce Vita*: A Cultural History of Italy*. Stanford, CA: Stanford University Press, 2012.

Ricciardi, Stefania. *Gli artifici della non-fiction. La messinscena narrativa in Albinati, Franchini, Veronesi.* Massa: Transeuropa, 2011.

Rich, Adrienne. "When We Dead Awaken." *College English* 34.1 (1972): 18–30.

Rogers, Katherine M. *Troublesome Helpmate: History of Misogyny in Literature.* Seattle: University of Washington Press, 1966.

Rogoff, Irit. "Studying Visual Culture." In *The Visual Culture Reader*, ed. Nicholas Mirzoeff, 14–26. New York: Routledge, 1998.

Ross, Charlotte. "Queering the *Habitus*: Lesbian Identity in Stancanelli's *Benzina*." *Romance Studies* 22.3 (November 2004): 237–50.

Rüdiger, Campe, and Julia Weber. "Introduction." *Rethinking Emotion: Interiority and Exteriority in Premodern, Modern, and Contemporary Thought*, ed. Campe and Weber, 1–20. Berlin: Walter de Gruyter, 2014.

Said, Edward. *Representations of the Intellectual. The 1993 Reith Lectures.* New York: Pantheon Books, 1994.

Sambuco, Patrizia. "Women, Relationships and Space in Stancanelli's *Benzina* (1998)." *Romance Studies* 22.2 (July 2004): 127–37.

Santacroce, Isabella. *Luminal.* Milan: Feltrinelli, 1998.

Sarris, Andrew. "Notes on the Auteur Theory in 1962." In *Film Theory and Criticism: Introductory Readings*, ed. Gerald Mast, Leo Braudy, and Marshall Cohen, 585–8. 2nd ed. Oxford: Oxford University Press, 2004.

Savater, Fernando. *Etica per un figlio.* Rome-Bari: Laterza, 2007.

Saviano, Roberto. "Se lo scrittore morde." *La repubblica* (Rome), 3 May 1997: 1, 57.

Scaffai, Niccolò. "Non trasformiamo una idiosincrasia in teoria." *Alias,* 20 May 2018: 4.

Scarpa, Tiziano. *Amore®*. Turin: Einaudi, 1998.

– *Batticuore fuorilegge.* Rome: Fanucci, 2006.

– *Il brevetto del geco.* Turin: Einaudi, 2015.

– *Il cipiglio del gufo.* Turin: Einaudi, 2018.

– *Corpo.* Turin: Einaudi, 2004.

– *Cosa voglio da te.* Turin: Einaudi, 2003.

– *Le cose fondamentali.* Turin: Einaudi, 2010.

– *Cos'è questo fracasso? Alfabeto e intemperanze.* Turin: Einaudi Stile Libero, 2000.

– "L'epica *popular*, gli anni Novanta, la parresìa." https://www.nazioneindiana.com/2009/03/04/l%E2%80%99epica-popular-gli-anni-novanta-la-parresia/. Acc. 1 Nov. 2016.

– *Groppi d'amore nella scuraglia*. Turin: Einaudi, 2005.
– *Kamikaze d'Occidente*. Milan: Rizzoli, 2003.
– "Manifesto per una letteratura dell'impegno (Tiziano Scarpa remix)." In *Il '68 di chi non c'era ancora*, ed. Raul Montanari, 32–48. Milan: Rizzoli, 1998.
– *Occhi sulla graticola*. Turin: Einaudi, 1996.
– *Stabat Mater*. Turin: Einaudi, 2009.
– *Verbale n. 2847*. Milan: Italian Factory, 2005.
– *La vita, non il mondo*. Rome-Bari: Laterza, 2010.
Scarpa, Tiziano, Aldo Nove, and Raul Montanari. *Nelle galassie oggi come oggi. Covers*. Turin: Einaudi, 2001.
Sceats, Sarah. *Food, Consumption and the Body in Contemporary Women's Fiction*. Cambridge: Cambridge University Press, 2000.
Schioppa, Antonello. *Benzina*. Review. http://www.blackmailmag.com/Benzina.htm. Acc. 21 Oct. 2007.
Schweitzer, Ivy. "Making Equals: Classical *Philia* and Women's Friendship." *Feminist Studies* 42.2 (2016): 337–64.
Sebold, Alice. *The Almost Moon: A Novel*. New York: Little, Brown and Co., 2007.
– *The Lovely Bones: A Novel*. Boston: Little, Brown, 2002.
Seger, Monica. *Landscapes in Between: Environmental Change in Modern Italian Literature and Film*. Toronto: University of Toronto Press, 2015.
Seneca. *Anger, Mercy, Revenge*. Trans. Robert A. Kaster and Martha C. Nussbaum. Chicago, University of Chicago Press, 2010.
Sesti, Mario. Extra-material DVD *L'amico di famiglia*. Fandango, 2006.
– "Prefazione." In *Divi & Antidivi*, ed. De Sanctis, Monetti, and Pallanch, 7–13.
Siebers, Tobin. *Heterotopia: Postmodern Utopia and Body Politics*. Ann Arbor: University of Michigan Press, 1994.
Simonetti, Gianluigi. *La letteratura circostante: Narrativa e poesia nell'Italia contemporanea*. Bologna: Il Mulino, 2018.
Skubal, Susanne. *Word of Mouth. Food and Fiction after Freud*. London: Routledge, 2000.
Sloterdijk, Peter. *Critique of Cynical Reason*. Trans. Michael Eldred. Minneapolis: University of Minneapolis, 1987.
Small, Pauline. "No Way Out: Set Designs in Mafia Films." *Italian Studies* 66.1 (Mar. 2011): 112–27.
Sollors, Werner, ed. "Introduction." *The Return of Thematic Criticism*. Cambridge, MA: Harvard University Press, 1993.
Sontag, Susan. *Regarding the Pain of Others*. New York: Picador Farrar Straus and Giroux, 2003.
Sorrentino, Paolo. *L'amico di famiglia*. Fandango, 2006.
– *Le conseguenze dell'amore*. Fandango, 2004.
– *Everybody's Right*. Trans. Howard Curtis. London: Harvill Secker, 2012.
– *Hanno tutti ragione*. Milan: Feltrinelli, 2010.

– *Il peso di Dio: Il vangelo di Lenny Belardo.* Turin: Einaudi, 2017.
– *Tony Pagoda e i suoi amici.* Milan: Feltrinelli, 2012.
– *L'uomo in più.* Indigo Film, 2001.
– *Youth.* Medusa, 2015.

Southworth, James. "William James' Theory of Emotion." PhD diss., University of Western Ontario, 2014. Electronic Thesis and Dissertation Repository. Paper 2315.

Stambrini, Monica. *Benzina.* Digital Film, 2001.

Stancanelli, Elena. *Benzina.* Turin: Einaudi stile libero, 1998.

Stella, Gian Antonio, and Sergio Rizzo. *La casta. Così i politici italiani sono diventati intoccabili.* Milan: Rizzoli, 2007.

Stewart, Kathleen. *Ordinary Affects.* Durham, NC: Duke University Press, 2007.

Stockton, Sharon. *The Economics of Fantasy: Rape in Twentieth-Century Literature.* Columbus: Ohio State University Press, 2006.

Storini, Cristina Monica. "'*Antonio c'est moi*? Sul realismo di *Un giorno perfetto* di Melania Mazzucco." In *Roma Noir 2008. Hannibal the cannibal c'est moi? Realismo e finzione nel romanzo noir italiano,* ed. Elisabetta Mondello, 107–28. Rome: Robin, 2008.

Tabanelli, Roberta. "Il post-umano (femmineo) in Simona Vinci." *Annali d'Italianistica, Humanisms, Posthumanisms & Neohumanisms* 26 (2008): 379–88.

Tanner, Laura. *Intimate Violence: Reading Rape and Torture in Twentieth-Century Fiction.* Bloomington: Indiana University Press, 1994.

Taviani, Giovanna. "Inventare il vero. Il rischio del reale nel nuovo cinema italiano." *Allegoria* 57 (2008): 82–93.

Terragni, Marina. *La scomparsa delle donne. Maschile, femminile e altre cose del genere.* Milan: Mondadori, 2007.

Testaferri, Ada. "De-tecting *Voci.*" In *The Pleasure of Writing: Critical Essays on Dacia Maraini,* ed. Rodica Diaconescu-Blumenfeld and Ada Testaferri, 41–60. West Lafayette, IN: Purdue University Press, 2000.

Thucydides. *The Complete Writings of Thucydides: The Peloponnesian War. The Unabridged Crawley Translation.* Intro. John H. Finley Jr. New York: Modern Library 1951.

Tillson, Victoria. "A Nearly Invisible City: Rome in Alberto Moravia's 1950s Fiction." *Annali d'Italianistica* 28 (2010): 237–55.

Todorov, Tzvetan. *The Poetics of Prose.* Trans. Richard Howard. Oxford: Basil Blackwell, 1977.

Tognazzi, Maria Sole. *Io e lei.* Lucky Red, 2015.

Tola, Miriam. "Libera da Thelma e Louise." (Interview with Monica Stambrini). http://www.tamtamcinema.it/persona.asp?id=431. Acc. 10 Sept. 2003.

Tolstoy, Lev. *Anna Karenina: A Novel in Eight Parts.* Trans. Richard Peaver and Larissa Volokhonsky. New York: Penguin Classics, 2002.

Tomassini, Veronica. *L'altro addio.* Venice: Marsilio, 2017.

– *Christiane deve morire.* Rome: Gaffi, 2014.
– *Sangue di cane.* Milan: Laurana, 2010.
Tonelli, Anna. *Per indegnità morale. Il caso Pasolini nell'Italia del buoncostume.* Rome-Bari: Laterza, 2015.
Touraine, Alain. *Le monde des femmes.* Paris: Fayard, 2006.
Tricomi, Antonio. "Pasolini, un reazionario di sinistra." In *La nuova gioventù? L'eredità intellettuale di Pasolini,* ed. Emanuela Patti, 15–32. Novi Ligure: Joker, 2009.
Trollope, Anthony. *The Way We Live Now.* [1875]. Oxford: Oxford University Press, 2008.
Van Doorn, Janne, and Marcel Zeelenberg. "Anger and Prosocial Behavior." *Emotion Review* 6.3 (July 2014): 261–8.
Vasta, Giorgio. *Spaesamento.* Rome-Bari: Laterza, 2010.
Vattimo, Gianni. "Pasolini. Fu vera gloria?" *L'Espresso,* 22 Oct. 1995: 22–4. Rep. "Pasolini, Cattivo maestro." In *Fratello selvaggio: Pier Paolo Pasolini tra gioventù e nuova gioventù,"* ed. Gian Maria Annovi, 137–40. Massa: Transeuropa, 2013.
Vegetti, Mario. "Passioni antiche: L'io collerico." In *Storia delle passioni,* ed. Vegetti Finzi, 39–74.
Vegetti Finzi, Silvia, ed. *Storia delle passioni.* Bari: Laterza, 1995.
Venitucci, Luca. "Gentrificazione, cultura 'indipendente' e mercato (prima parte)." 26 Dec. 2009. *Intercapedine.* http://intercapedine.wordpress.com/2009/12/26/gentrificazione-cultura-indipendente-e-mercato-prima-parte/. Acc. 12 Jan. 2018. URL no longer valid.
Verhoeven, Paul. *Elle.* Distr. SBS Productions. France + 2 Cinema, 2016.
Vinci, Simona. *Come prima delle madri.* Turin: Einaudi, 2003.
– *Dei bambini non si sa niente.* Turin: Einaudi stile libero, 1997.
– *Parla, mia paura.* Turin: Einaudi, 2017.
– *La prima verità.* Turin: Einaudi, 2016.
– *Stanza 411.* Turin: Einaudi, 2006.
– *In tutti i sensi come l'amore.* Turin: Einaudi, 1999.
Virilio, Paul. *Politics of the Very Worst.* Trans. Michael Cavalieri. Los Angeles: Semiotext(e), 1999.
– *War and Cinema: The Logistics of Perception.* [1984]. Trans. Patrick Camiller. London: Verso, 1989.
Von Trier, Lars, and Thomas Vinteberg. "Dogma 95 Manifesto." http://www.dogme95.dk/menu/menuset.htm.
Weir, Lorna. "Roberto Esposito's Political Philosophy of the Gift." *Angelaki* 18:3 (2013): 155–67. DOI: 10/1080/0969725x.2013.834672. Acc. 5 Sept. 2017.
Westphal, Bertrand. *Geocriticism: Real and Fictional Spaces.* Trans. Robert T. Tally Jr. New York: Palgrave Macmillan, 2011.
Williams, Raymond. *Resources of Hope: Culture, Democracy, Socialism.* [1958]. London: Verso, 1989.

Winton, Tracey. “Footprints in Stone: A Psychogeography of Rome.” Pdf available at: https://www.academia.edu/2656237/Footprints_in_Stone_A_Psychogeography_of_Rome.

Witzke, Serena. “Violence against Women in Ancient Rome: Ideology versus Reality.” In *Topographies of Ancient Greek and Roman Violence*, ed. Garrett G. Fagan and Werner Riess, 248–74. Ann Arbor: University of Michigan Press, 2015.

Wolf, Naomi. *The Beauty Myth: How Images of Beauty Are Used against Women.* New York: Harper Perennial, 2002.

Wollen, Peter. “The Auteur Theory.” In *Film Theory and Criticism: Introductory Readings*, ed. Gerald Mast, Leo Braudy, and Marshall Cohen, 589–605. 2nd ed. Oxford: Oxford University Press, 2004.

Wood, Robin. “Ideology, Genre, Auteur.” In *Film Theory and Criticism: Introductory Readings*, ed. Gerald Mast, Leo Braudy, and Marshall Cohen, 475–85. 2nd ed. Oxford: Oxford University Press, 2004.

Woolf, Virginia. *Women and Writing.* New York: Harvest, 2003.

Wu Ming 1. *New Italian Epic.* Turin: Einaudi, 2012.

– “La polizia contro Pasolini, Pasolini contro la polizia.” *Internazionale.* http://www.internazionale.it/reportage/wu-ming-1/2015/10/29/pasolini-polizia-anniversario-morte. Acc. 20 Feb. 2017.

– “Wu Ming/Tiziano Scarpa: Face Off. Due modi di gettare il proprio corpo nella lotta. Note su affinità e divergenze, a partire dal dibattito sul NIE.” http://www.ilprimoamore.com/blogNEW/blogDATA/spip.php?article2342. Acc. 1 Nov. 2016.

Young, Stacy L., and Katherine C. McGuire. “Talking about Sexual Violence.” *Women and Language* 26.2 (Fall 2003): 40–52.

Zavattini, Cesare. “Some Ideas on the Cinema.” Trans. Pierluigi Lanza. In *Film: A Montage of Theories*, ed. Richard Dyer MacCann, 216–28. New York: E.P. Dutton, 1966.

Zinato, Emanuele. *Le idee e le forme. La critica letteraria in Italia dal 1900 ai nostri giorni.* Rome: Carocci, 2010.

Žižek, Slavoj. *In Defense of Lost Causes.* London: Verso, 2009.

Zryd, Michael. “Found Footage as Discursive Metahistory: Craig Baldwin’s Tribulation 99.” *The Moving Image* 3.2 (2003): 40–61.

Index

www.ingramcontent.com/pod-product-compliance
Lightning Source LLC
LaVergne TN
LVHW090149080826
844660LV00013B/737/J